A BIRDER'S GUIDE
TO THE
RIO GRANDE VALLEY

MARK W. LOCKWOOD
WILLIAM B. MCKINNEY
JAMES N. PATON
BARRY R. ZIMMER

1999

Original text by James A. Lane (1971–1978),

with revisions by Harold R. Holt (1983–1992)

American Birding Association

Library of Congress Catalog Card Number: 98-73686
ISBN Number: 1-878788-18-3
Third Edition
    2   3   4   5   6   7   8   9
Printed in the United States of America

Publisher
    American Birding Association, Inc.
Editor
    Cindy Lippincott
Layout and Typography
    Cindy Lippincott; using CorelVENTURA, Windows version 8.0
Maps
    Cindy Lippincott; using CorelDRAW version 5.0
Photography
    front cover: *Crested Caracara*; Barry R. Zimmer
    back cover: *Ringed Kingfisher*; Steve Bentsen
    inside: *Sage Sparrow*; Mark W. Lockwood
            Black-throated Sparrow; Barry R. Zimmer
            White-tipped Dove; Brad McKinney
Illustrations
    Narca Moore-Craig

Distributed by
    American Birding Association Sales
    PO Box 6599, Colorado Springs, Colorado 80934-6599 USA
    phone: 800 / 634-7736 or 719 / 578-0607
    fax: 800 / 590-2473 or 719 / 578-9705
    email: abasales@abasales.com
    website: www.americanbirding.org

Dedicated to

Harold R. Holt

1915 – 1998

ACKNOWLEDGEMENTS

In December 1998 the American Birding Association and untold thousands of birders around the world lost a steadfast friend when Harold R. Holt passed away. Harold devoted most of the last twenty years of his life to updating, publishing, and distributing the little series of birdfinding guides begun in 1969 by his friend, Jim Lane. His heartfelt duty, and yet his and his wife LaVona's greatest pleasure, was touring the country in their motorhome to seek out new sites and changed directions to keep the guides current. Harold took great pride in helping birders find birds, and in 1990 ABA took great pride in accepting the role of keeping the series ever useful and always in print. Although we rightfully and happily give full credit to the authors of the masterful new editions of the original Lane Guides, Jim's and Harold's legacy is the guides' inception and their continued unparalleled usefulness to birders living in and visiting these wonderful birding areas.

A very special and talented team of authors created the third edition of *A Birder's Guide to the Rio Grande Valley*. Aside from updating and adding to the birdfinding text in their areas of primary expertise, each author reviewed the Introduction and the entire text to help create a coordinated whole. In addition, each took responsibility for writing one-quarter of the nearly 600 species accounts, which replace the bar-graphs in this edition.

Mark W. Lockwood, conservation biologist, Natural Resource Program of the Texas Parks and Wildlife Department, was responsible for the Del Rio/Amistad area, the central Trans-Pecos (Big Bend National Park, Big Bend Ranch State Park, Alpine, Fort Davis, and Balmorhea), and the Edwards Plateau. Mark acknowledges important contributions by Doug Booher, who reviewed the Edwards Plateau section, Chuck Sexton, who provided details for Balcones Canyonlands NWR, Mark Flippo, who reviewed the Big Bend National Park section, Nick Jackson, who reviewed the Kerrville section and checked several other sites, Kelly Bryan, who provided details and most of the text for Big Bend Ranch State Park and the Devils River State Natural Area segments, and Junie Sorola, who reviewed the Del Rio text and suggested a few new locations from that area.

William B. McKinney, high school science teacher and college instructor at the University of Texas–Brownsville, tackled the popular Lower Rio Grande Valley from the coast upriver to San Ygnacio. Brad wishes to thank the following people for their special help: Janette McKinney reviewed and edited Brad's entire text, her encouragement helping to make this project possible for Brad; Kim Eckert reviewed the Falcon Dam area text; Oscar Carmona reviewed the Harlingen text; Will Carter reviewed the Weslaco area text; Lisa Williams provided much of the information about Chihuahua Woods Preserve. In addition, Brad thanks Laura Moore (McAllen), Mike Quinn, Carol Levine, and Tim Brush (Santa Ana National Wildlife Refuge), and Michael Delesantro (Edinburg area) for their helpful contributions.

James N. Paton, high school science teacher from El Paso, revised and added to the text covering the Pecos Valley, El Paso, El Paso Valley, Guadalupe Mountains, and New Mexico sites in Las Cruces, the Organ Mountains, and Carlsbad Caverns. Jim thanks John Sproul for the Feather Lake account, Nancy Lowery for information about Rio Bosque Park, and JoBeth Holub and John Karges for providing information on an important new site, Chandler Ranch/Independence Creek Preserve.

Barry R. Zimmer, full-time birding tour leader for Victor Emanuel Nature Tours and co-author of the recent *Birds of the Trans-Pecos*, worked with Jim Paton on the Trans-Pecos text. Barry is grateful to John Sproul, Kevin Zimmer, and Jim Peterson for their help with his section of the guide, and to his wife Yvonne for her constant support and encouragement.

Jeffrey S. Pippen, research associate, Department of Botany at Duke University, approached the compilation of an annotated list of butterflies occurring along the Rio Grande in Texas with both enthusiasm and dedication. I his valuable addition to the guide will surely appeal to those birders interested in other winged creatures.

Allan H. Chaney provided updates for his authoritative 2nd-edition list of *Other Vertebrates Exclusive of Fish*. It is gratifying to see that avian taxonomy is not the only such science to stand on ever-shifting sands!

Our thanks to Narca Moore-Craig for providing illustrations in her appealing and unique style. Her artist's insight adds much to our own understanding of the essence of these species.

There are so many Rio Grande specialties of interest to birders that it was both a pleasure and a dilemma to review photos for the covers, but we think you'll agree that Barry Zimmer's Crested Caracara portrait and Steve Bentsen's alert female Ringed Kingfisher are stunning studies of birds specializing in two radically different habitats along the Rio Grande. Mark Lockwood's Sage Sparrow, Brad McKinney's White-tipped Dove, and Barry Zimmer's Black-throated Sparrow were too good to leave behind—you'll find them in the text pages.

The list of contributors and field checkers to the first two editions of *A Birder's Guide to the Rio Grande Valley of Texas* is long and star-studded. In spite of the substantial amount of revision that the text underwent for this third edition, their contributions remain important as the local fount of information unselfishly given to James A. Lane and then Harold R. Holt to help make this guide the single best source for the Rio Grande Valley.

Paul J. Baicich's role in working with Harold on the second edition (i.e., the first ABA-produced edition in 1993) must be acknowledged. Paul's enthusiasm and expertise as ABA/Lane Birdfinding Guide series editor from 1990–1997, when he assumed editorship of *Birding* magazine, helped to establish the series—both new titles and revised Lane/Holt titles—as the most highly acclaimed North American birdfinding guides. His footsteps are large and not so easy to fill.

Mistakes do creep into these guides and on-the-ground situations change rapidly in some of the areas covered. Please let us know if you find something that should be changed in the next printing or the next edition.

Cindy Lippincott, Editor
Colorado Springs, Colorado
January 1, 1999

TABLE OF CONTENTS

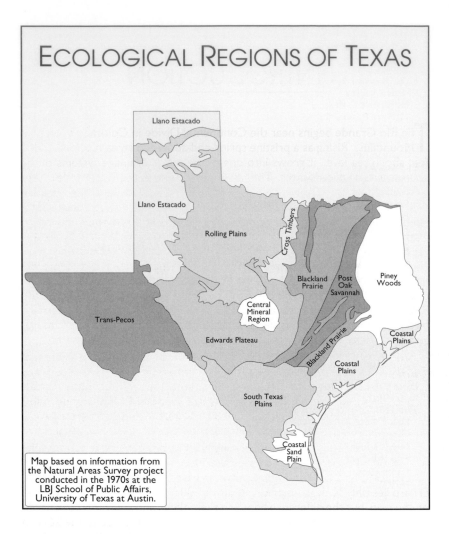

ECOLOGICAL REGIONS OF TEXAS

Llano Estacado

Llano Estacado

Rolling Plains

Cross Timbers

Blackland Prairie

Post Oak Savannah

Piney Woods

Trans-Pecos

Central Mineral Region

Edwards Plateau

Blackland Prairie

Coastal Plains

Coastal Plains

South Texas Plains

Coastal Sand Plain

Map based on information from the Natural Areas Survey project conducted in the 1970s at the LBJ School of Public Affairs, University of Texas at Austin.

INTRODUCTION

The Rio Grande begins near the Continental Divide in Colorado's San Juan Mountains. Rising as a pristine spring-and-snow-fed stream, about 12,000 feet above sea level, it grows into one of the major drainage systems of the southwestern United States. The 1,896-mile course of the Rio Grande makes it the fifth longest river in North America. Once bordered by riparian woodlands through New Mexico and west Texas, and by vast stands of Sabal Palms at its delta, the Rio Grande has suffered greatly at the hands of modern man. Most of the woodlands have long since been removed, and five major reservoirs punctuate its flow. At Presidio the river often dwindles to just a trickle before being replenished by the Río Conchos coming out of Mexico. Here, and at many other locations, the river bottom is choked by dense thickets of introduced Tamarisks (salt cedar). Despite these problems, the Rio Grande corridor is still able to provide a wide diversity of habitats for birds, mammals, amphibians, reptiles, and insects—and the river itself has not lost its capacity to be, in a great many locations, breathtakingly beautiful.

For many North American birders there is a certain mystique in the fact that the Rio Grande forms the boundary between Texas and Mexico. Many tropical bird species reach the northern limit of their ranges in the various habitats found along this international border. The Lower Rio Grande Valley is known as one of the premier places to find Mexican birds during the winter season, with new species routinely added to the Texas state list from this area.

One factor contributing to the incredible diversity of birds found along the Rio Grande is that the river crosses the 100th meridian of longitude, often thought of as a rough dividing line between eastern and western bird species. El Paso lies only 10 degrees of longitude, or 500 air-miles, west of Brownsville on the map, but the difference between their plants and animals is striking. At El Paso the average rainfall is only 8 inches per year compared to the 26-inch annual rainfall of the subtropical Lower Rio Grande Valley. Between these extremes lie the magnificent Chihuahuan Desert with its mountain islands, the Stockton and Edwards Plateaus, and the brush-covered plains of South Texas.

Much of the region along the Rio Grande is arid. As a result, thorny shrubs, forming vast areas of scrub-type habitat, generally dominate the landscape. Similar plant communities, however, often have vastly different avifauna. This is certainly true along the Rio Grande, for there is very little overlap in the avian communities of the brush country of the South Texas Plains and the thorn scrub of the Chihuahuan Desert. Large trees in these arid lands are mostly limited to the riparian corridors that weave through these

1

habitats and tend to accentuate the uniformity rather than the biodiversity of the areas.

REGIONS OF TEXAS

Texas is divided into ten ecological or physiographic regions, each with a wide variety of habitats. The area covered by this guide lies within three of these regions: the South Texas Plains, the Edwards Plateau, and the Trans-Pecos. The extreme southern tip of South Texas is further separated as the Lower Rio Grande Valley. (Many Texans, and we, refer to the four-county area between Falcon Dam to the Gulf simply as "Lower Valley.") The introductory comments prefacing each major section of this guide describe these regions in greater detail.

Texas is a large state and good birding opportunities are found throughout. However, each region has its own specialty birds, and though some adjacent regions are easily visited on the same birding trip, others are widely separated from one another. For example, the spectacular trans-gulf migration action takes place, for the most part, along the Gulf coast. Most of the tropical species that reach Texas are limited to the Lower Valley or to Big Bend. A few Rocky Mountain species can be found in Texas only in the Guadalupe and Davis Mountains. In addition, two of the state specialties are restricted to the Edwards Plateau. Beyond the scope of this guide are other physiographic regions with their local specialties: the Pineywoods, the Coastal Bend, the Llano Estacado (High Plains), Post Oak Savannah, and so on.

Needless to say, most visiting birders will want to make several trips to Texas in order to visit the best birding locations at their most productive times of year. After all, some 613 species have been documented in this huge state, comprising over 75% of all species in the ABA Area (basically, the 49 mainland US states plus Canada). Of those, a surprising 579 species have occurred in the area covered here. This book will help you find as many of these species as possible, while visiting some of the most exciting and beautiful birding locations along the Rio Grande, or indeed, in North America.

WHEN TO COME AND WHERE TO GO

The birdfinding chapters follow the Rio Grande from South Padre Island and Brownsville upriver to El Paso and Las Cruces, New Mexico. Major detours explore the Edwards Plateau, the Devils River drainage, the Pecos Valley, Guadalupe Mountains National Park, New Mexico's Organ Mountains, and Carlsbad Caverns National Park. By the shortest route it is over 800 highway-miles between Brownsville and El Paso. Rather than trying to cover it all in one prolonged trip, most birders will want to make several trips in different seasons to visit all of the areas covered in this guide.

For many people the Lower Valley or Big Bend National Park tops their list of places to visit in Texas. On an extended trip along the Rio Grande, you will probably find that beginning in the Lower Valley and working northward is most productive. Many of the migrants return to the Lower Valley in late March and April, which allows you to start your trip slightly earlier than if you were to begin farther north or west. Migration is much more pronounced in the Lower Valley, so the major objectives for the remainder of the trip would be to track down the summer residents, birds which are not just passing through and will be around later in the spring than the migrants. It is important to consider the general arrival time of any species that you are particularly interested in seeing. For example, the breeding populations of Painted and Varied Buntings usually arrive about the 20th of April (or later). That fact may alter the timing of your trip.

If you have only a limited amount of time to cover the land along the Rio Grande, it is probably best to research the various areas that are of interest to you and choose one. As mentioned before, the distances between the primary birding areas covered in this guide might be considerable.

If you are *really* limited for time, it is possible to cover the Lower Valley in three or four days—visiting places like Laguna Atascosa and Santa Ana National Wildlife Refuges, Bentsen-Rio Grande Valley State Park, and the Falcon Dam area. Another day or two could be spent on the Edwards Plateau. Driving to Big Bend from McAllen takes almost a day. (The closest major airport to Big Bend is at Midland/Odessa—a 230-mile drive from Panther Junction, but less than the 320 miles from El Paso's airport.) You will need at least two to three days to quickly cover a few of the best birding locations in the park. The reservoirs in the Trans-Pecos, particularly Lake Balmorhea, Imperial, and all of those in the El Paso area are well worth a trip by themselves. The El Paso/Las Cruces area offers great birding in a variety of habitats, all close to an airport. The Davis Mountains are well worth a visit and can easily be added to a trip to Big Bend if time allows.

If you visit in April, spend a day along the Gulf Coast looking for migrants, preferably at South Padre Island (morning). This guide discusses several sites along the Lower Coast, but your major birding resource for a coastal trip is *A Birder's Guide to the Texas Coast* (ABA/Lane Birdfinding Guide series). Further notes about when to visit each region covered by this book are found in the introductory comments for each section.

WHERE TO STAY

Hotels, motels, and bed-and-breakfast establishments are found in most of the towns along the Rio Grande. Of course, particularly in the Trans-Pecos, there are very few *towns* in some of the areas covered in this guide!

Reservations are highly recommended in the Lower Valley during the winter, particularly between mid-December and the beginning of March.

Reservations are necessary for Big Bend and Guadalupe Mountains National Parks throughout the year. Near Big Bend, there are small hotels in Lajitas and Study Butte. If those are unavailable, Alpine and Marathon are the next closest towns, 110 and 60 miles from Panther Junction respectively. Whites City, New Mexico, is 30 miles north of Guadalupe Mountain National Park and has the only motels within 55 miles of the park. In contrast, the Edwards Plateau is an area where motels and campgrounds abound.

Two of the parks have lodges, both recommended destinations due to their location in excellent birding areas. Chisos Mountains Lodge at Big Bend (National Parks Concessions, Inc., Big Bend National Park, TX 79834; phone 915/477-2291) has fairly good food and accommodations; nightly rates begin at about $65. Indian Lodge in the Davis Mountains (Davis Mountains State Park, Fort Davis, TX 79734; phone 915/426-3254) is a beautiful spot to spend a vacation. Reservations are required at both facilities.

Campgrounds are available at almost all state parks in Texas as well as at the national parks. Campsites are generally available on a first-come-first-served basis at the national parks, but Texas State Parks has a handy central reservation system in Austin—campground reservations can be made by calling 512/389-8900. At a few of the state parks other facilities, such as the cabins at Garner State Park, may be rented. Campsites at Aguirre Springs National Recreation Area east of Las Cruces, New Mexico, are on a first-come-first-served basis.

Private trailer parks are plentiful in the Lower Valley and on the Edwards Plateau, but there are very few in the Trans-Pecos. The national and state parks in that part of the state are your best bet for trailer sites with hook-ups. Bentsen State Park and Falcon State Park have trailer hook-ups. Camping in isolated spots by the side of the road is not recommended.

Private campgrounds are found at Brownsville, Mission, and Falcon. Brazos Island State Recreation Area (23 miles east on SH-4) offers open beach camping with no facilities.

LISTS, CHECKLISTS, AND MAPS

A list of state parks can be obtained from Texas Parks and Wildlife Department, 4200 Smith School Road, Austin, TX 78744.

Maps and other tourist information are available from the Texas Highway Department, Austin, TX 78763, or from the Tourism Division of the Texas Department of Commerce, Box 12728, Austin, TX 78711.

Detailed county maps can be bought for a small fee from Texas Highway Department, Planning Survey Division, Box 5051, Austin, TX 78763.

The Roads of Texas is a road-atlas-sized book of detailed county maps which is very helpful for birders exploring the back roads of Texas. It can be purchased at 800/458-3808. A similar Shearer Publishing atlas is *The Roads of New Mexico.*

DeLorme publishes a *Texas Atlas & Gazetteer*, available from ABA Sales or at many bookstore locations. This atlas provides a large and well-labeled section of city maps, although the country maps are labeled about as well (or as incompletely) as the Shearer atlases above.

Texas Parks and Wildlife distributes a handy brochure, **Birding Texas** (Riskind and Lockwood), which contains information on local checklists, birding festivals, bird books, birding trails, organizations, and other miscellaneous information. *Birding Texas* is free of charge; request it from the above Texas Parks and Wildlife address. Most Valley wildlife refuges have free checklists; there is a nominal charge for some.

Checklist of Lower Rio Grande Valley Birds (Brad McKinney) is an annotated checklist covering 496 species in all sections of the Valley. It was revised in 2002 to include 7th edition *A.O.U. Check-list* taxonomy. This 58-page booklet can be purchased from ABA Sales (see page ii).

Information on the **Great Texas Birding Classic** can be obtained by contacting the Texas Parks and Wildlife Department at the above address. This birding competition is open to all age groups and runs for one week in late April and early May. Three sections are included in the Classic—the Lower, Central, and Upper Coast, and birders can compete in one or all of the sections. On 27 April 1998, 230 species were tallied in the four-county area of southernmost Texas during this event—just one species short of the all-time Big Day record set in the 1970s (in California by Californians). Proceeds from the Classic are earmarked for the purchase of prime bird habitat along the Texas coast.

TWO SPECIAL PERMITS FOR TEXAS STATE PARKS

State Parklands Passport provides a half-price discount on park fees for those 65 or older, or for veterans with a 60% or greater VA disability. The Passport is available at most state parks; those eligible must apply in person with proper identification or proof of disability.

Conservation Passport is an annual state park entrance permit, which provides holders with a small discount on camping fees and other items in the park. The cost is $50 per person per year, from date of purchase. It is available at most state parks or by mail from: Texas Parks and Wildlife Department, 4200 Smith School Road, Austin, TX 78744 (send $50, driver's license number, date of birth, and vehicle registration number). You can also purchase the Conservation Passport by calling 800/792-1112. Most state parks have a daily entrance fee of $2–3 per day per person, with additional fees for showers and camping.

Rare Bird Alerts and Web Sites

Before your departure, and during your birding trip to the Rio Grande region, you will want to check one or more Rare Bird Alerts or bird-related web sites for up-to-date information on unusual sightings. The RBA numbers do change from time to time, so check *Winging It's* compilation of Rare Bird Alerts for the current listing.

Statewide — 713 / 369-9673
maintained by Houston Audubon Society; includes sightings from the Upper Texas Coast

Lower Rio Grande Valley — 956 / 584-2731; sighting reports 713 / 464-2473
run by World Birding Center

Austin area — 512 / 926-8751
maintained by the Travis Audubon Society

San Antonio area — 210 / 308-6788
run by the San Antonio Audubon Society

West Texas — no RBA

New Mexico — 505 / 323-9323

TexBirds Archive Web Site — http://listserv.uh.edu/archives/texbirds.html
includes a search function to find all of the RBAs, electronic or phone

Other Birding Resources

Texas Ornithological Society

The Texas Ornithological Society has two publications, *The TOS Newsletter* and the *Bulletin of the Texas Ornithological Society*. The *Bulletin* publishes scientific papers dealing with birds in Texas. TOS holds spring and fall meetings at various locations around the state. Attending one of these meetings can put you in touch with birders and ornithologists from all over the state as well as giving you an chance to go on local field trips and take part in other activities. The **Texas Bird Records Committee** maintains the official *Checklist of the Birds of Texas*, last updated in 1995 (3rd edition). TOS membership is $20 per year. To join TOS, contact Texas Ornithological Society, Memberships, PMB #189, 6338 N. New Braunfels Avenue, San Antonio, TX 78209. TBRC website: http://www.texasbirds.org/tbrc.

If you see a bird that is currently on the Master List of Review Species, the Texas Bird Records Committee wants to hear from you. Most helpful would be your photos, videotape, or sound recording of the species along with your written details of the sighting. You may send these materials to Mark Lockwood, Secretary TBRC, 2001 Fort Davis Hwy #15, Alpine, TX 79830 or Dr. Keith Arnold, Department of Wildlife and Fisheries Sciences, Texas A&M University, College Station, TX 77843. Please, also, *quickly* notify local birders and the local RBA of your discovery! (That's what birder-owned GPS receivers and cell phones are for!) See pages 273–274 for further information about the Review List and how to report your sightings.

NEW MEXICO ORNITHOLOGICAL SOCIETY

NMOS publishes the *NMOS Bulletin* on a quarterly basis. The organization is currently updating (3rd edition) *New Mexico Bird Finding Guide*, which covers the entire state. See page 275 for the NMBRC Review List.

New Mexico Ornithological Society, PO Box 3068, Albuquerque, NM 87190

THE GREAT TEXAS COASTAL BIRDING TRAIL

The Great Texas Coastal Birding Trail (The Trail) has been developed to help birders find the great avian resources along the Texas coast, and to insure that the Texas coastal birding experience is rich and varied. Private citizens, landholders, conservation groups, businesses, governmental agencies, and communities are working together to build this natural promenade.

The Texas Parks and Wildlife Department (TPWD) and the Texas Department of Transportation (TxDOT) have jointly sponsored the Trail. Highway enhancement funds allocated to each state through the Intermodal Surface Transportation Efficiency Act of 1991 (STEA) have provided financial support for its development.

The Lower Texas Coast (LTC) section of the Trail (to be completed in September 1999) will consist of over 100 distinct birding sites. Each site will be marked with the Trail logo and with a unique site number. Several sites will be enhanced with boardwalks, kiosks, observation platforms, and/or landscaping. The Trail map will inform visitors about birds that may be found at each site, the best season to visit the locations, and contacts for information about food and lodging in the vicinity.

The LTC Trail will be comprised of several separate loops. Each will encompass an array of associated sites and birds. The color-coded loops on the front and back of the map will provide easy access to related information. Site symbols on the map will be shaped and colored to show access, indicate fees when applicable, and denote the availability of developed overnight facilities at each location.

Sponsoring coastal communities and landholders have generously pledged their backing, and invite the Trail and its visitors into their local communities. Local goods-and-services providers—hotels, motels, B&Bs, campgrounds, restaurants, auto rental agencies, airlines, book stores, gift shops, and gas stations—champion the Trail and are the foundation for its future. They need and deserve your support.

To obtain a copy of the Trail maps (both the upper and central coastal trails are completed), contact the following:

Texas Parks and Wildlife Department
4200 Smith School Road, Austin, TX 78744-3291
Trail Information: 512 / 389-4937
Park Reservations: 512 / 389-8900
Website: http://www.tpwd.state.tx.us

AUDUBON SOCIETIES AND CHAPTERS

Audubon Society chapters and independent Audubon Societies are active in Alpine, Austin, San Antonio, El Paso, and the Lower Valley. You can find their most current contacts and addresses in *A Birder's Resource Guide*, the American Birding Association's membership directory, published annually in August.

OTHER HELPFUL ADDRESSES

Valley Nature Center
Rio Grande Valley Bird Observatory
301 South Border Avenue, PO Box 8125, Weslaco, TX 78596; 956/969-2475

The Great Texas Coastal Birding Trail
c/o Texas Parks and Wildlife Department, Nongame and Urban Program,
4200 Smith School Road, Austin, TX 78744

The Rio Grande Birding Festival
Harlingen Chamber of Commerce
311 E. Tyler, Harlingen, TX 78550; 800/531-7346

Texas Tropics Nature Festival
PO Box 790, McAllen, TX 78505-0790; 800/250-2591

World Birding Center Project Office
900 N. Bryan Road, Mission, TX 78572; 956 / 584-9156

AMERICAN BIRDING ASSOCIATION

Each year ABA members are asked whether they are willing to answer written or telephoned inquiries from birders who are planning trips to their local area. Many of the over 1,000 Texas ABA members have indicated a willingness to help visitors with information, or even to accompany them on local field trips. Codes used in the annual ABA membership directory enable other ABA members to contact these generous people. See pages 279–280 for information about how you can become an ABA member and receive this helpful directory, which also includes a Yellow Pages section wherein you will find listings from several bed-and-breakfast establishments in the Valley.

INSECTS

Mosquitoes can be an annoyance in Texas during spring and summer, although they aren't *too* bad in the winter months. There are two basic strategies against mosquitoes: wear tops with long sleeves and pants with long legs, which seems to do the job most of the time, or use insect repellents for the really bad days (see below).

Chiggers and ticks can add to the misery in summer. Chiggers are tiny red mites that are found in grassy areas throughout the year but are most numerous in spring. Their bites leave raised welts that itch like crazy. The welts usually appear within a few hours and generally last for weeks. Chiggers attack wherever your clothing fits tightly, such as around the waistline and under socks. Soaking the affected areas in a 50/50 mixture of water and chlorine bleach is said to help shorten the period of itching—this is but one of the many home remedies reputed to help stop the itching. Another remedy is tincture of benzyl benzoate. A pharmacist can help you sort out the most effective treatments from the placebos. The best advice is not to get chiggers in the first place. In Texas never lie down in the grass in spring. Try to avoid areas of grass and weeds, or walk rapidly when crossing them. Spray your socks and pant legs with an insect repellent *before* going afield. Tuck your pants legs into your socks, no matter how dorky you may think it looks.

Ticks prefer brushy places and are fairly common in South Texas and on the Edwards Plateau, though they are generally not much of a problem in the Trans-Pecos. There are primarily three species of ticks found in the area covered in this guide. The incidence of Lyme and other diseases in Texas is very low, but it is always best to take precautions to discourage bites. Ticks stand out against light-colored clothing. Check yourself often. Applying insect repellent to your pants and socks can help dissuade chiggers and ticks. Applying sulfur dust to these areas is also effective.

All of these arthropods are more common in wet years. Insect repellents are effective and are sold widely. Liquid types, such as DEET, are very effective against mosquitoes, biting flies, and gnats. A major advance to repel mosquitoes, chiggers, ticks, and biting flies is Permanone. It is available in most states as Permakill, Permanone, or Permethrin Arthropod Repellent. Before a trip it is sprayed on clothing and binds with the fabric, remaining effective through five launderings. Non-toxic to humans and other mammals, Permanone has tested as high as 99.9 percent effective in repelling insects when combined with DEET used on exposed skin.

Africanized bees arrived in South Texas in 1990. The following year over 200 swarms were found in the Lower Rio Grande Valley, as far north as the Edwards Plateau and Corpus Christi, and as far west as Laredo. Since then they have spread to El Paso and Las Cruces. Although attacks are very rare, they have occurred. The sting of an Africanized bee is no different from the sting of a European honey bee, which is also an introduced species. The concern about the Africanized bee is that they tend to attack in larger numbers and pursue for longer distances when they feel threatened. Their defensive behavior is most often triggered by lawn-mowers and other machinery used near their swarms. The only known protection, when you are being attacked, is to out-run the bees, or as Mike Quinn, a ranger at Santa Ana NWR states, "duck into your vehicle and use this book to swat the bees that follow you in."

Fire ants are probably the most feared insect in our region. Originally from the state of Mato Grosso in Brazil, the red fire ant, *Solenopsis invicta*, has spread throughout the southeastern United States from Texas to North

Carolina. It entered the US sometime between 1933 and 1945 on a boat shipment to Mobile, Alabama, perhaps in the dirt carried in the ship's ballast.

There are five species of fire ants in the United States. Most of the publicity, however, has been given to the two imported species, the red fire ant and the black (*S. richteri*) fire ant (although the latter is confined to Mississippi and Alabama). In Texas the red fire ant is found in the eastern half of the state; in our region it is most likely to be encountered in the Lower Valley, yet it may also be found sporadically west to about Del Rio and north along parts of the Edwards Plateau.

Fire ants are similar to the ordinary house and garden ant, one-eighth- to one-quarter-inch long and reddish-brown in color. They usually construct their nests in open grassy areas such as pastures, lawns, and unused cropland. The nests are readily identified by their crusty texture and conical shape, which ranges from one to two feet in diameter and one to one and one-half feet high. Once you've been bitten, you won't forget what the nests look like!

The bites of these aggressive ants produce painful blisters that may become infected. The ants sting repeatedly and, as they sting, produce a chemical that incites other ants to sting as well. Each bite results in a pustule which itches for a few days and may leave a scar. Try not to scratch the bites. For relief a simple application of 50/50 chlorine bleach and water, if used immediately, can reduce pain and itching. A paste of meat tenderizer and water may also be effective. Also, products containing cortisone may help.

On a brighter note, 298 species of **butterflies** have been recorded for the Lower Rio Grande Valley, many of which are spectacularly patterned and colored. Look for Gulf Fritillary, Zebra, Mexican Bluewing, Malachite, and Red-bordered Pixie, among others. American Snouts and Lyside Sulphurs occur in huge numbers, especially in the fall.

BIRDING BEHAVIOR

With the increased popularity of birding, it is important to reduce human impacts whenever possible. This is especially true in the heavily birded areas of the Lower Rio Grande Valley and Big Bend. On pages 276–277 of this guide is the American Birding Association's *Code of Birding Ethics*. We encourage all who use this book to take the spirit and letter of the *Code* to heart. Generally, the code indicates that birders must: always act in ways that do not endanger the welfare of birds or other wildlife; always act in ways that do not harm the natural environment; always respect the rights of others; and assume special responsibilities when birding in groups.

For the region covered in this book, we wish to emphasize two aspects of birding ethics. First, birders should always, but especially in Texas, respect the private property of others. Trespassing in Texas is a *major* offense and birders must be especially sensitive to this fact. Many landowners perceive birders and naturalists to be a threat because they might report rare or endangered species from private lands. The sites described in the book are usually public ones. For those that are not, the text usually indicates how to obtain permission to bird.

Second, the use of tapes on public property is generally against regulations; tapes are illegal at Santa Ana and Laguna Atascosa National Wildlife Refuges. Using tapes to agitate owls, secretive species, and, especially, endangered and threatened species is *always* inappropriate and, in some cases, illegal.

HOW TO USE THIS BOOK

The main purpose of this guide is to help you find the special birds of the region. If a specific location is considered to be an outstanding birding spot, it is shown in **bold-faced type**. Most of the specialties can be found by stopping only at these good sites.

Mileages between points in the chapters are typically included in parentheses (6.7 miles). *Mileage presented in this format is invariably the distance from the last point so mentioned.* You may choose to re-set your trip-odometer at each measured site to make the next point easier to find, or not, depending on your own approach to following directions.

Note: The Otabind (or lay-flat) binding used for this reprint will become standard for the ABA's birdfinding guide series. It is more durable, more widely accepted by bookstores and book distributors, and less expensive than the wire-O binding previously used for the series.

NOMENCLATURE

As long-time birders know, bird taxonomy is by no means a static science. The American Ornithologists' Union—the ultimate authority on North American birds—recently published the 7th edition of *The A.O.U. Check-list of North American Birds* (June 1998). Authors, publishers of field guides, compilers of checklists, and many thousands of birders are scrambling to assimilate newly-split species into their lists and are rearranging those lists to be in sync with the new taxonomic sequence of the *A.O.U. Check-list*.

The new AOU nomenclature and sequence are used throughout this guide. Following are some bird names which differ from those used in the older field guides and in previous editions of this book. Where the species' name has bounced back and forth like a yo-yo, e.g., White-tailed/Black-shouldered Kite, only the most recent date is provided.

Further "field-identifiable forms" are listed in the *Birds of the Region* section. Learning to identify these forms will prepare you for future taxonomic splits.

Names Used in this Book . . . . *Former Name or Derivation*

Pacific Loon . . . . *split from* Arctic Loon (1985)
Clark's Grebe. . . . . *split from* Western Grebe (1985)
Band-rumped Storm-Petrel . . . . *formerly* Harcourt's Storm-Petrel (1983)
Masked Booby . . . . *formerly* Blue-faced Booby (1983)
Neotropic Cormorant . . . . *formerly* Olivaceous Cormorant (1991)
Tricolored Heron . . . . *formerly* Louisiana Heron (1983)
Green Heron. . . . . *formerly* Green-backed Heron (1993)
Black-bellied Whistling-Duck. . . formerly Black-bellied Tree-Duck (1976)
Fulvous Whistling-Duck . . . . formerly Fulvous Tree-Duck (1976)
"Mexican Duck" Mallard. . . . . Mexican Duck *lumped with* Mallard (1983)
White-cheeked Pintail . . . . *formerly* Bahama Pintail (1983)
White-tailed Kite . . . . *formerly* Black-shouldered Kite (1993)
Montezuma Quail . . . . *formerly* Harlequin Quail (1973)
Common Moorhen . . . . *formerly* Common Gallinule (1983)
American Golden-Plover . . . . . . *split from* Lesser Golden-Plover (1993)
Red-necked Stint. . . . . *formerly* Rufous-necked Stint (1995)
Wilson's Snipe . . . . *split from* Common Snipe (2002)
Red-necked Phalarope. . . . . *formerly* Northern Phalarope (1983)
White-tipped Dove . . . . *formerly* White-fronted Dove (1983)
Magnificent Hummingbird . . . . . . *formerly* Rivoli's Hummingbird (1983)
Elegant Trogon . . . . *formerly* Coppery-tailed Trogon (1983)
Red-naped Sapsucker . . . . . . *split from* Yellow-bellied Sapsucker (1985)
Greater Pewee. . . . . *formerly* Coues' Flycatcher (1983)
Pacific-slope Flycatcher . . . . *split from* Western Flycatcher (1989)

Cordilleran Flycatcher . . . . *split from* Western Flycatcher (1989)
Dusky-capped Flycatcher . . . . . . *formerly* Olivaceous Flycatcher (1983)
Brown-crested Flycatcher . . . *formerly* Wied's Crested Flycatcher (1983)
Couch's Kingbird . . . . *split from* Tropical Kingbird (1983)
Plumbeous Vireo . . . . *split from* Solitary Vireo (1997)
Cassin's Vireo. . . . . *split from* Solitary Vireo (1997)
Blue-headed Vireo. . . . . *split from* Solitary Vireo (1997)
Yellow-green Vireo . . . . *split from* Red-eyed Vireo (1987)
Western Scrub-Jay. . . . . *split from* Scrub Jay (1995)
Mexican Jay. . . . . *formerly* Gray-breasted Jay (1995)
Tamaulipas Crow . . . . *formerly* Mexican Crow (1997)
Chihuahuan Raven . . . . *formerly* White-necked Raven (1983)
Juniper Titmouse. . . . . *split from* Plain Titmouse (1997)
Tufted (Black-crested) Titmouse . . . *lumped with* Tufted Titmouse (1976)
Sedge Wren . . . . *formerly* Short-billed Marsh Wren (1983)
Marsh Wren. . . . . *formerly* Long-billed Marsh Wren (1983)
American Pipit . . . . *formerly* Water Pipit (1989)
Tropical Parula . . . . *formerly* Olive-backed Warbler (1973)
Gray-crowned Yellowthroat . . . . *formerly* Ground-Chat (1983)
Spotted Towhee . . . . *split from* Rufous-sided Towhee (1995)
Eastern Towhee . . . . *split from* Rufous-sided Towhee (1995)
Canyon Towhee . . . . *split from* Brown Towhee (1989)
Nelson's Sharp-tailed Sparrow. . . . *split from* Sharp-tailed Sparrow (1995)
Dark-eyed Junco . . . . *lumped from* Oregon, White-winged,
. . . . Slate-colored, and Gray-headed Juncos (1973)
Yellow-eyed Junco. . . . . *formerly* Mexican Junco (1973)
Altamira Oriole. . . . . *formerly* Lichtenstein's Oriole (1983)
Audubon's Oriole. . . . . *formerly* Black-headed Oriole (1983)
Baltimore Oriole. . . . . *resplit from* Northern Oriole (1995)
Bullock's Oriole . . . . *resplit from* Northern Oriole (1995)

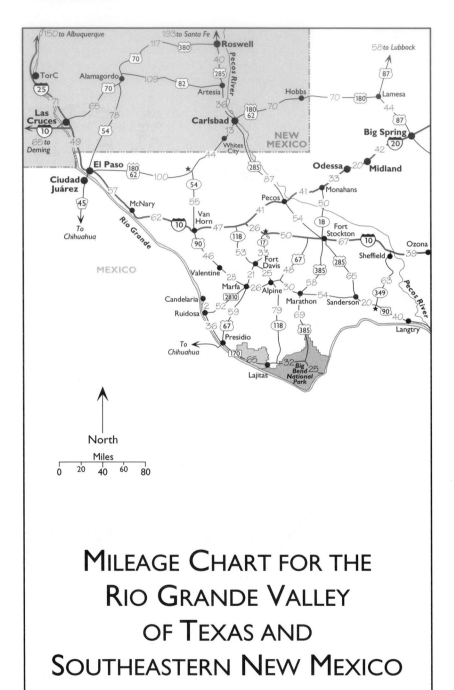

MILEAGE CHART FOR THE
RIO GRANDE VALLEY
OF TEXAS AND
SOUTHEASTERN NEW MEXICO

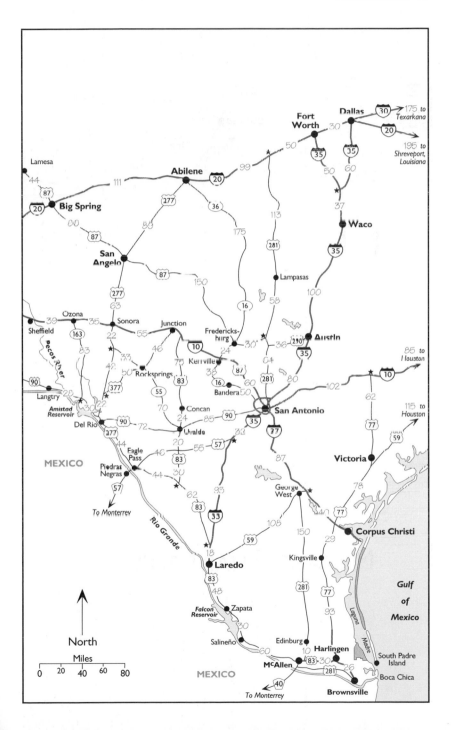

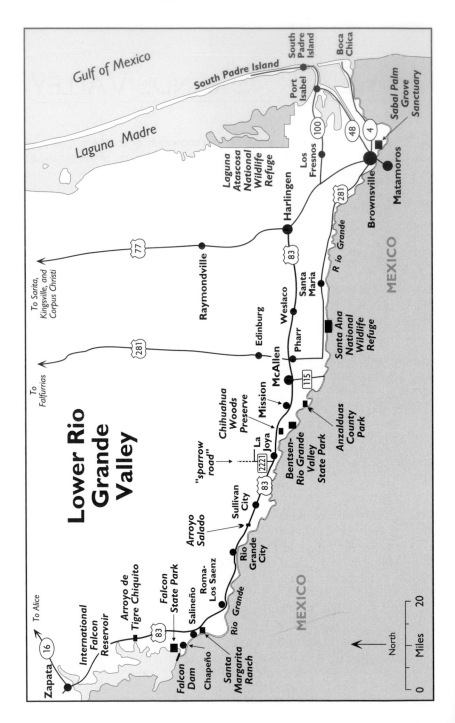

LOWER RIO GRANDE VALLEY

Weaving and etching its way from the snowmelt of southern Colorado, the Rio Grande winds through mountains and deserts of the Southwest bringing life to an arid land before reaching the Gulf of Mexico. From its headwaters in the San Juan Mountains, the river flows through New Mexico and into Texas, forming an international boundary between the United States and Mexico. Coursing through the delta flood plain, the Rio Grande makes its final stretch to the sea and carries a life blood that is shared by all who depend on it.

In the year 1519, after months of sailing the coastal waters searching for a direct route to the Orient, Spanish explorers finally made landfall at a rain-swollen river mouth known today as Boca Chica. Alonso Alvarez de Piñeda, the first European to set eyes on this river, was so impressed that he named it Río de las Palmas, after the towering Sabal Palms lining its banks. Various names have been given to the river in the years since: those from the south called it Río del Norte, the Indians referred to it as Río Bravo (wild river), and others labeled it Río Turbio, a reference to its muddy color. There is something fitting about the final choice—the Rio Grande—for the name Great River begins to do justice to its power and importance in the natural history of the Southwest.

The palm forests that so impressed Alvarez de Piñeda once flourished in the Rio Grande delta, covering nearly 40,000 acres on both sides of the river. In this semitropical arid climate, thorn scrub forests thrived on rich alluvial deposits from the Rio Grande whose banks once flooded seasonally. From the river's edge towered Montezuma Bald Cypresses, their massive trunks and spreading roots offering a sense of permanence amidst the moving water. This was the realm of the Gray Hawk, and sounds of tropical birds echoed through every bend in the river.

Land clearing of the area for crops and cattle by European settlers in the latter part of the 18th century began the large-scale destruction of this highly diverse and delicate habitat. By the time Dr. James C. Merrill explored this region in the 1876, there were few Jaguars roaming north of the border. Still, the diversity of birds was amazing, as detailed in Dr. Merrill's "Notes on the ornithology of southern Texas," in which 252 species were documented from the Brownsville area between February 1876–June 1878.

Today, with over 95 percent of its lands converted to agriculture and other developments, the delta's diverse assemblage of birds is largely confined to private ranches and a few wildlife sanctuaries left along the river, like Santa Ana National Wildlife Refuge, Bentsen-Rio Grande Valley State Park, and

17

Sabal Palm Grove Sanctuary. The situation has been worsened by the recent wholesale clearing of Mexico's northeastern forests.

To make more habitat for Long-billed Thrashers and Ferruginous Pygmy-Owls, not to mention endangered Ocelots and Jaguarundis, additional forest tracts were needed to connect the existing wilderness areas along the Rio Grande. Because most of the land in Texas is privately owned, the landowner would play a critical role in restoring to health this biological oasis.

Collaborating closely with Texas Parks and Wildlife, the U.S. Fish & Wildlife Service really got the ball rolling with the initiation of the Wildlife Corridor project in 1979. Through the joint effort of groups both public and private, 77,000 acres have now been acquired along the river, which is a sizable chunk toward the project's goal of 132,500 acres. The 1998 acquisition of the Boca Chica Tract, which added 12,000 acres to the Lower Rio Grande Valley National Wildlife Refuge, was one of the most significant land preservation actions in recent memory. Containing a variety of habitat types, including coastal tidal flats and brushy *lomas* (low hills), the Boca Chica Tract supports a wide variety of species, including endangered Texas Tortoises, Peregrine Falcons, and Brown Pelicans. This coastal expanse is also a haven for waterfowl as well as a critical stopover for many migratory shorebirds and songbirds.

Another new addition to the wildlife corridor is Chihuahua Woods, a 243-acre preserve within earshot of Bentsen-Rio Grande Valley State Park near Mission. Purchased by the Texas Nature Conservancy, Chihuahua Woods is representative of the Tamaulipan thorn scrub vegetation so typical of the Lower Rio Grande Valley. Already two of the region's most-sought-after birds—Hook-billed Kite and Clay-colored Robin—have been found there.

Although the once mighty Rio Grande has long since been tamed by dams, there is still an abundance and diversity of birds that has to be seen to be believed. In the four-county area of southernmost Texas alone, 484 species have been recorded, and the list is growing each year. During 1996 and 1997, birders added four new birds to the local checklist, three of which were new for the state: Ruddy Quail-Dove (Bentsen-Rio Grande Valley State Park, March 1996), Orange-billed Nightingale-Thrush (Laguna Atascosa National Wildlife Refuge, April 1996), and Stygian Owl (Bentsen-Rio Grande Valley State Park, December 1996). The most recent addition came in May 1997 when a White-collared Swift was spotted in a flock of Cliff Swallows near Fort Brown at Brownsville. What may show up next is anyone's guess!

CLIMATE

Key elements in the region's rich natural history are the subtropical climate and the deep, fertile deltaic soils deposited by the Rio Grande. Rainfall is only moderate in the Valley, yet the evaporation rate is very high. The annual precipitation is about 26 inches, becoming slightly less in the western end near Falcon Dam.

The rainfall is highly erratic and significant droughts have occurred. Often there is no rainfall at all during March and April, and only a limited amount of moisture comes from the 15 or so cold fronts that occur each year. The strong year-round winds also contribute to the moisture deficit of the area. Except for a narrow corridor along the river or along resacas, the plants and animals are adapted to the arid and semi-arid conditions.

Most rainfall occurs in the months of August, September, and October. Farmers and Valley residents alike welcome these life-giving rains of the tropical cyclone season. At this vital time, crops are quenched, reservoirs are filled, and the parched desert chaparral is given new life.

Due to its southern location and the moderating influences of the Gulf of Mexico, Valley temperatures rarely drop below freezing during the winter months. However, strong arctic fronts occasionally reach the Valley so traveling birders should bring clothes for all seasons. After a cold front pushes through, it's not long before the gulf-blown cumulus clouds return to the skies, once again wrapping a warm and humid blanket over the Valley.

WHEN TO COME

The first or second week of November is a great time to visit—most of the winter birds have arrived and the Rio Grande Valley Birding Festival, one of the country's premier birding extravaganzas, takes place during this time in Harlingen. This is also the greenest time of the year, and the butterflies can be spectacular. Your chances of locating normally hard-to-find birds, like Red-billed Pigeons, Muscovy Duck, and Hook-billed Kite are slightly better in November than during the other winter months.

Many birders like to come a little later in winter when the birds are numerous and the mosquitoes have dwindled somewhat. At places like Bentsen State Park, where trailer sites are filled with feeders, it is an "Altamira Oriole and Green Jay show" from sunup to sundown. December is also a good time to participate in one of the Christmas Bird Counts in the Valley.

January and February are usually the coldest months, yet this can be the best time for Mexican vagrants to show up. Bentsen State Park, Santa Ana NWR, and Falcon Dam seem to get the most rarities, but they also get the most birder coverage. Rare birds can be found anywhere along the river (in residential areas as well), as long as there is suitable habitat. The cold weather also increases the possibility of spotting a rare gull, especially along Boca Chica Beach and at the Brownsville Dump. With wintering birds in peak numbers and most of the Rio Grande specialties present, this is really a fine time to visit South Texas.

If your goal is to see as many species as possible, then spring would be the time to come. Depending on local weather conditions, the coastal migrant traps of South Padre Island and Boca Chica can have large numbers of colorful buntings, warblers, tanagers, and orioles. This is also the season when Northern Beardless-Tyrannulets, Red-billed Pigeons, and Elf Owls are most vocal, and Muscovy Ducks are often seen along the river. Even Hook-billed Kites are more likely to be seen in April and May as they circle overhead within their breeding territories.

When a local birder mentions the "dog days of summer," it is more a reference to the heat than to the lack of birds. If you can bear the heat and mosquitoes, then summer can be an exciting time along the Rio Grande. However, it's always best to get started before sunup. Members of the dawn chorus include Buff-bellied Hummingbird, Great Kiskadee, Couch's Kingbird, Hooded and Altamira Orioles, and other Rio Grande specialties. In June, Botteri's Sparrows are on territory and can usually be located in their specialized coastal habitats (zacahuiste grassland); Green Parakeets and Red-crowned Parrots can be found nesting in palm trees in Brownsville and several other Valley cities. Summer is the best time to find Groove-billed Anis.

Summer is generally thought of as the off-season for Mexican rarities but this is simply not the case. Gray-crowned Yellowthroat, Green-breasted Mango, Green Violet-ear, and Yellow-green Vireo are just some of the recent finds during this season.

Fall migration starts with shorebirds in mid-July and reaches its peak in late September. Large concentrations of migrant passerines are not so common as in spring, but your chances of finding rare or out-of-place species are greater. During mid-October, hawk migration is in full swing at places like Santa Ana NWR and Bentsen SP. By early November, the honking of geese overhead announces the coming of winter as several hundred thousand ducks splash down in the numerous freshwater ponds and vast saltwater expanses of Laguna Atascosa NWR. Strategically situated on the Laguna Madre, this 45,000 acre refuge has also produced its share of rare birds during fall, some of the most recent being Collared Forest-Falcon (August 1996), Jabiru (August 1997), and Northern Wheatear (November 1994).

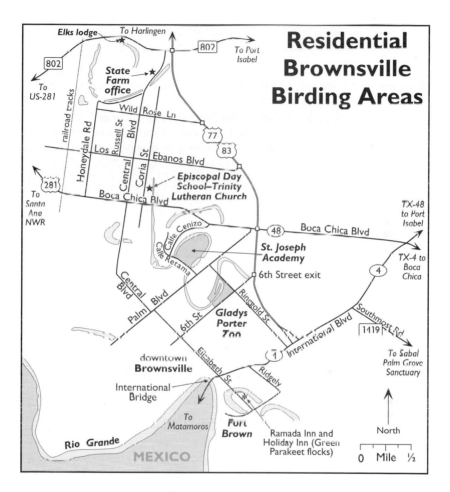

Residential Brownsville Birding Areas

BROWNSVILLE

Located 25 miles inland from the Gulf of Mexico, Brownsville has a rich history dating back over 300 years. To this once remote place came men and women under five national banners—Spain, Republic of Mexico, Confederate States of America, Republic of Texas, and the United States of America. Here lived hundreds of Indian groups that were collectively known as the Coahuiltecan Groups, including the fierce Karankawa tribes, now extinct.

Texas' southernmost city was named after Major Jacob Brown, who died in defense of Fort Texas during the Mexican War in 1846. Old Fort Brown was located near the foot of today's International Bridge leading across to Matamoros, Mexico. During the Civil War the Brownsville/Matamoros connection became the "backdoor to the Confederacy," the main exporter of cotton to Europe and a major import-site of materials and supplies for the

South. Brownsville, now with over 100,000 inhabitants, has outgrown its frontier character, yet is still connected economically and culturally with Matamoros, its sister city across the border.

The intersection of expressway US-77 and FM-802 in Brownsville is the starting point for birding instructions in the Brownsville area. From this point you are only 5 minutes from Red-crowned Parrot roosts off Central Boulevard, 10 minutes from Green Parakeet roosts at Fort Brown, 15 minutes from the Brownsville Sanitary Landfill and its Tamaulipas Crows, and 20 minutes from Sabal Palm Grove Sanctuary with resident Buff-bellied Hummingbirds and other regional specialties. The Brownsville birding areas from *Residential Brownsville* through *Fort Brown* can all be done in one day; the remainder are dependent on your interests and itinerary.

RESIDENTIAL BROWNSVILLE

Brownsville is famous for its *resacas* (the Spanish name for oxbow lake). These crescent-shaped former river channels were pinched off long ago when the Rio Grande changed its course. Most of the city's resacas are kept at a constant level, although a few of them are seasonal and may dry up completely during the hot summer months. The most productive birding is found at resacas that are lined extensively with native trees. This section of the book describes several of these prime birding sites—each has the potential for Green Parakeets and Red-crowned Parrots, and two of the sites might produce Tropical Kingbirds.

Birding the sites in residential Brownsville, as outlined below, can take anywhere from two to three hours; however, if you are stopping by just to find Red-crowned Parrots, you can be on your way again in thirty minutes.

Residential Brownsville can produce such species as White-winged Dove, Green Parakeet, Red-crowned Parrot, Vermilion and Brown-crested Flycatchers, Couch's Kingbird, Scissor-tailed Flycatcher, Tropical Parula (rare), Black-throated Gray (rare) and Yellow-throated Warblers, Hooded Oriole, and migrant passerines. You might also find many of the region's residents/ specialties—Plain Chachalaca, White-tipped Dove, Buff-bellied Hummingbird, Great Kiskadee, Green Jay, Long-billed Thrasher, Olive Sparrow, Bronzed Cowbird, and Altamira Oriole. Rarities that have turned up over the years are Tropical Kingbird, Black-whiskered Vireo, Clay-colored Robin, and Golden-crowned Warbler.

RED-CROWNED PARROT WINTER ROOST AND TROPICAL KINGBIRDS

The best spot for Red-crowned Parrots is near the intersection of Honeydale Road and Los Ebanos Boulevard. Large flocks of over 100 birds occur in this general area during the winter months. Green Parakeets also occur in the area, but are best seen at Fort Brown (see *Fort Brown* section). It is best to get to the neighborhood before dawn, because the parrots can be high in the sky by sunrise. Another strategy is to catch the birds in late afternoon. This works well for birders who want to bird elsewhere during the early morning hours.

With the onset of the nesting season in early April, Red-crowned Parrots begin to disperse from their winter roosts. Although the birds are more difficult to find during this season, there are usually small numbers of non-breeding birds still hanging around the area. In past years, breeding pairs have been seen on nearby streets (Honey Drive and Fairfax), both off Honeydale Road.

To reach the Honeydale Road/Los Ebanos Boulevard area from southbound US-77, exit at Business US-77/FM-802 and get into the right lane as you approach the traffic light at FM-802 (street sign says Ruben M. Torres). Turn right at the light; you immediately come to another traffic light at Central Boulevard/Old US-77 (also marked as Business 77/83). Get into either of the two left-turn lanes, turning left onto Central Boulevard. For the next half mile, watch for parrots on both sides of the street. The resaca (0.2 mile) on the left usually holds good numbers of Black-bellied Whistling-Ducks and, on rare occasions, a Fulvous Whistling-Duck.

Continuing on Central Boulevard, you come to a **Felipe Benavides State Farm Agent sign** (0.3 mile) on the right side of the street. If you want to check for Tropical Kingbirds, turn right at Old US-77 (which goes past the State Farm Agent office) and park in the rear of the State Farm parking lot. *Caution:* watch for fast-moving traffic on Old US-77.

In 1991, the second state record of Tropical Kingbird was found within 20 yards of this parking lot. Since then, the kingbirds have nested in the vicinity and are now well-established, year-round residents. Both Tropical and Couch's Kingbirds are often seen on utility wires and other high perches. Look for them using lower perches on windy days. (Prior to 1991, there was a single record of Tropical Kingbird for Texas. Since that year there have been nine Tropical Kingbird records in the Lower Valley, with breeding documented in Port Isabel, Harlingen, Old Cannon Pond [south of Harlingen], Rancho Viejo, and Brownsville. Several of these pairs have become permanent residents. In winter there have been flocks as large as seven individuals found in the Brownsville area. The kingbirds have ranged as far west as Santa Ana National Wildlife Refuge [February 1996].)

Also, look for Least Bittern, Green Heron, Fulvous Whistling-Duck (summer), Vermilion (winter), Brown-crested (summer), and Scissor-tailed (summer) Flycatchers, and Ringed and Green Kingfishers along the

A fairly reliable area for Green Parakeets and Red-crowned Parrots has been near the Elks Lodge on FM-802. For the past few summers a pair of Red-crowneds and two pairs of Green Parakeets have nested there. The Elks Lodge is located on the south side of FM-802 just 0.6 mile west of the intersection of US-77/FM-802. The parrots can often be seen leaving the Washingtonian Palm cavities in early morning and returning in late afternoon. If you find parrots nesting here, please don't approach too closely. Use a spotting scope.

nearby resaca. On 25 May 1991 a Black-whiskered Vireo was found behind the State Farm office, providing a sixth Texas record. A Green Violet-ear was discovered in June 1989 feeding at bottlebrush flowers within a block of the insurance office. Another Mexican hummingbird, Green-breasted Mango, made its North American debut in Brownsville in September 1988 only a few miles away. (In addition to potential vagrant hummingbirds from south of the border, residential Brownsville is a pretty good spot for finding other species—Buff-bellied (year round), Ruby-throated and Black-chinned (rare) in migration, and Blue-throated (very rare), Broad-tailed (rare), and Rufous Hummingbirds (winter).

Continue south on Central Boulevard to a traffic light at Wild Rose Lane (0.3 mile) and turn right. A serious search for parrots can now begin as you drive along Wild Rose Lane. The road makes a dog-leg left turn (0.4 mile) and becomes Honeydale Road, a good street for finding both Green Parakeets and Red-crowned Parrots. Red-crowns have even been seen sitting on the telephone lines at sunup. At the 4-way stop **Honeydale Road intersects Los Ebanos Boulevard** (0.5 mile)— you have three choices:

1. Go straight and pull over to either side of the street. This is the easiest (and maybe the most productive) option. Here, you can comb the area for flying parrots. The loud and raucous parrots will usually announce their presence before you see them. From November to March there can be flocks of over 100 birds between 6:45 AM–7:10 AM, and again in the late afternoon before dusk. Be aware that mixed in with the Red-crowned Parrots are the occasional White-fronted, Lilac-crowned, Red-lored, and Yellow-headed Parrots. These parrots are all presumed escapes.

2. A right turn onto Los Ebanos Boulevard takes you to railroad tracks (0.2 mile), which can also be a good vantage point for seeing the parrot flocks. Walk along the wooded areas near the tracks to look for many of the Valley specialties, spring and fall migrants, and mixed-species flocks (winter).

3. A left turn onto Los Ebanos Boulevard can also be good for parrots as well as many of the Valley specialties. Drive slowly to Russell Street (0.3 mile), turn left, and park on the right. You can walk back along Los Ebanos toward Honeydale to listen for parrots overhead. In the wooded areas along Los Ebanos, look for Plain Chachalaca, White-tipped and White-winged Doves, Brown-crested Flycatcher (summer), Great Kiskadee, Green Jay, Long-billed and Curve-billed Thrashers, Olive Sparrow, Hooded Oriole (summer), and neotropical migrants (in spring). Western species—Western Tanager, Black-headed Grosbeak, Lazuli Bunting, and Scott's Oriole—are rare, but have been recorded in this general area, primarily between February to May.

To check nearby for Green Parakeets and Red-crowned Parrots, continue driving east on Los Ebanos Boulevard to the traffic light at Central Boulevard (0.1 mile). Go straight through the intersection to another traffic light at Coria Street (0.1 mile). Before reaching Coria Street notice the tall, dead Washingtonian Palms on the right side of Los Ebanos. These palms are riddled with nesting holes, some of which might be occupied by Green Parakeets during the nesting season (April–July). Both parakeets and parrots are often seen in this area during the winter. Turn right onto Coria Street.

EPISCOPAL DAY SCHOOL / TRINITY LUTHERAN CHURCH

Continue south on Coria Street to the **Episcopal Day School/Trinity Lutheran Church** (0.3 mile) on the left. The wooded area near the resaca in the back of the church can produce Anhinga (winter), White-winged Dove, Brown-crested Flycatcher (summer), Great Kiskadee, Hermit Thrush (winter), Long-billed Thrasher, and Olive Sparrow. There is usually ample parking at the rear of the church parking lot (next to the school).

In two recent winters a Tropical Parula has been found in the back woodlot moving with a mixed-species flock, but this is a rare find indeed. More often one sees Blue-headed Vireo, Tufted (Black-crested) Titmouse, Ruby-crowned Kinglet, Blue-gray Gnatcatcher, Orange-crowned and Yellow-rumped Warblers, and sometimes a Nashville, Yellow-throated, Black-and-white, or Wilson's Warbler. The first modern ABA-Area record of Golden-crowned Warbler (December 1979) occurred not far from here. Since then, two more Golden-crowned Warblers have been discovered in the Brownsville area. In winter Clay-colored Robin is also a possibility here.

RIO VIEJO / SAINT JOSEPH ACADEMY

Once back on Coria Street you immediately come to Boca Chica Boulevard, one of the city's busiest streets. Turn left here to Calle Cenizo (0.6 mile) and turn right to drive through Rio Viejo, one of Brownsville's oldest and most beautiful neighborhoods. Continue on Calle Cenizo, bearing left at the fork (0.3 mile) to a stop sign at Calle Retama (0.3 mile).

In winter this entire neighborhood can offer good birding. It is best to park at the Saint Joseph Academy student parking lot (see below) and walk back through the neighborhood. Look for Green Parakeet, Red-crowned Parrot, White-winged Dove, Buff-bellied Hummingbird, Vermilion Flycatcher, Tropical and Couch's Kingbirds, and Yellow-throated Warbler. Occasionally, Nashville, Black-throated Green, Pine, and Wilson's Warblers can be spotted in mixed-species flocks. Although not to be expected, Red-naped Sapsucker, Tropical Parula, Black-throated Gray Warbler, and Bullock's Oriole have been found here.

To get to **Saint Joseph Academy**, turn left onto Calle Retama to Calle San Jose, an unmarked street (0.1–0.2 mile) on the left. Turn left onto Calle San Jose; the school is straight ahead and off to the left is a student parking lot, a good place to park.

The area around the football field has been a good spot for Tropical and Couch's Kingbirds. Look for them perched on utility wires, fences, or any of the surrounding vegetation. Also, look for Scissor-tailed Flycatchers in summer. The wooded area down by the resaca harbors many of the region's specialties, including Neotropic Cormorant, Anhinga, Green Heron,

Black-bellied Whistling-Duck, White-tipped Dove, Green Parakeet, Red-crowned Parrot, Ringed and Green Kingfishers, Brown-crested Flycatcher, Great Kiskadee, Long-billed Thrasher, Olive Sparrow, and Bullock's Oriole (rare in winter). In winter White-winged Dove, Vermilion Flycatcher, and the occasional Eastern Bluebird can be seen on the utility wires. At this season you may get to compare the smaller Neotropic Cormorant with the more numerous and much larger Double-crested Cormorants. *During school hours, it is advisable to ask permission to bird the school grounds.*

To get back to the expressway (US-77) after birding Saint Joseph Academy, turn left at Calle Retama and go to the traffic light at Palm Boulevard (0.2 mile). Turn left onto Palm Boulevard, drive to Boca Chica Boulevard (0.7 mile), and turn right. The expressway is one-half block ahead.

GLADYS PORTER ZOO

If you have extra time in Brownsville, a visit to Gladys Porter Zoo can be rewarding. A variety of native birds is on display in the Audubon Aviary and Walk-through Aviary. On the grounds you might see wild birds—Neotropic Cormorant, Green Heron, Common Moorhen, and Great Kiskadee. Buff-bellied Hummingbirds are found on the grounds at any time of year, though they are more likely in spring, summer, or early fall. To reach the zoo, located at 500 Ringgold Street, just follow the signs from the 6th Street exit off US-77. (See *Residential Brownsville Birding Areas* map, page 21, to figure out how to reach the zoo from St. Joseph Academy.)

FORT BROWN

Fort Brown is an area near the Brownsville/Matamoros International Bridge now occupied by several large hotels. The primary reason for going here is to see the impressive Green Parakeet roost. In late afternoon, you can have great looks at the parakeets and be on your way in less than fifteen minutes. Of course, you are within walking distance of several Mexico bars which could delay you for several hours.

Fort Brown is best visited during the afternoon. The Green Parakeets begin squawking and circling overhead about 1½ hours before sundown, which would still allow you plenty of time for a late afternoon shot at the Red-crowned Parrots (in residential Brownsville). From FM-802, take US-77 south through Brownsville to International Boulevard (3.4 miles). Exit right onto International Boulevard (toward the University of Texas at Brownsville). Get into left lane, because sometimes the large trucks destined for Mexico will be in the slow-moving right lane. After about ½ mile, exit left onto Ridgely Street. This is also called the Fort Brown Alternate Route because it keeps you away from the congestion of the international bridge. Proceed down Ridgely Street and you will see the college on your right. There could be Green Parakeets anywhere along this road. You will come to a sharp right turn (0.5 mile), then a baseball field on your left. Turn right at Elizabeth Street

(0.3 mile)—the Ramada Inn and Holiday Inn are on your right (0.2 mile). Pull into the parking lot at Holiday Inn and begin searching the tops of the Washingtonian Palms for parakeets. There can be up to 300 birds flying overhead at any one time, providing quite a spectacle. Although the numbers are greater in winter, Green Parakeets can be found year round at Fort Brown. On 18 May 1997 a visiting birder found and photographed a White-collared Swift soaring with Cliff Swallows at Fort Brown. This sighting was a Valley first and provided only the second photographically documented record for Texas. This large tropical swift could be expected in the Valley at any season, so have your video camera ready!

For those wanting to walk across to Matamoros, Mexico, there is good parking along Elizabeth Street. To get back to US-77 from here, just turn right onto Elizabeth Street and proceed to International Boulevard (0.4 mile) Turn right and continue for about a mile until you see the sign for Expressway 77/83 North (Harlingen).

Black-bellied Whistling-Ducks
Narca Moore-Craig

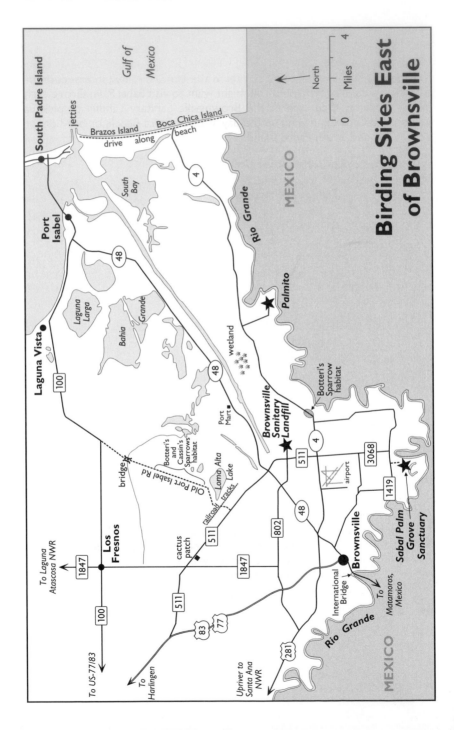

Birding Sites East of Brownsville

BIRDING EAST OF BROWNSVILLE

Several longer birding trips take you east toward or to the Gulf of Mexico. The starting point for all of these trips is the US-77/FM-802 intersection on the north side of Brownsville. You might want to visit Sabal Palm Grove early in the morning, then stop at the Brownsville Sanitary Landfill to pick up Tamaulipas Crow, and wind up the day at Boca Chica Beach, or head out to Port Isabel and South Padre Island.

SABAL PALM GROVE AUDUBON CENTER

Surrounded by agricultural lands, **Sabal Palm Grove Sanctuary** lies cradled in a bend of the Rio Grande just 6 miles southeast of Brownsville. With its majestic palms and dense jungle-like habitat, this 527-acre refuge is the most unique of the Lower Rio Grande Valley's wilderness areas. After the September rains, watch for tropical butterflies such as Blue Metalmark amidst the many blooms. Other striking butterflies found in the palm forest are Zebra and Gulf Fritillary, both passion-flower specialists. The sanctuary is also one of the last places to encounter endangered amphibians and reptiles, such as Speckled Racer.

The sanctuary bird list stands at 275 species, boasting many of the Valley specialties and several Mexican rarities. You are likely to find Least Grebe, Plain Chachalaca, White-tipped Dove, Groove-billed Ani, Common Pauraque, Buff-bellied Hummingbird, Great Kiskadee, Green Jay, Tropical Parula (rare), Black-throated Gray (rare) and Yellow-throated Warblers, Long-billed Thrasher, Olive Sparrow, Hooded Oriole, Lesser Goldfinch, winter warblers, and migrant passerines. Rarities have included Clay-colored Robin, Gray-crowned Yellowthroat, Golden-crowned Warbler, Crimson-collared Grosbeak, and Blue Bunting.

Sabal Palm Grove Audubon Center (phone 956/541-8034; PO Box 5052, Brownsville, TX 78523) is open 9:00 AM–5:00 PM Tuesday–Sunday between 1 October–30 May, with the exception of the Thanksgiving, Christmas, and New Year's Day holidays. Between 1 June and 30 September the Center is open only on Saturdays and Sundays. The daily entrance fee is $4/adults, $3/Audubon members, $2/children, $1/age 6 and under. Website: www.audubon.org/local/sanctuary/sabal. Even if the visitors center is closed, you still may walk the trails year round between sunrise and sunset or visit the recently improved bird-feeding station.

Allow at least two to three hours to walk the forest trail, scan the oxbow lake, and observe the feeders near the visitors center. If you explore the trails that lead to the river and out across the oxbow lake, you could easily spend more time here. Although mosquitoes are seasonal, you may find insect repellent to be indispensable. Carry water—there is no drinking water source beyond the visitors center.

To reach Sabal Palm Grove Sanctuary from the US-77/FM-802 junction (see map on page 28), drive east on FM-802 to FM-511 (6.4 miles). (The entrance to the Brownsville Sanitary Landfill is straight ahead.) Turn right (south) onto FM-511, staying on this road as it becomes FM-3068 (3.5 miles). FM-3068 ends at FM-1419 (1.5 miles). Turn right; the entrance road to Sabal Palm Grove Sanctuary is on the left (0.6 mile). Follow this dirt road a little over a mile to the visitors center parking lot.

If you are driving this road before sunup or after sundown, look for the red eyeshine of Common Pauraques, which may be sitting in the middle of the road. During the day White-tailed Kites, Red-tailed Hawks (winter), American Kestrels (winter), and other raptors might be working the fields or perched on utility poles. In spring and summer check the wires for Couch's Kingbird and Scissor-tailed Flycatcher. In the sunflower fields during spring migration look for Blue Grosbeak, Indigo Bunting, Dickcissel, and Bobolink (rare). As you near the parking lot, you will see historic Casa de Colores Museum, built in 1876. This grand old house was once part of the Rabb Plantation, which originally occupied 20,000 acres.

A little farther along on the left is the Native Trail–People and the Land which crosses successional forest on its way to the Rio Grande. This is a good trail for spotting raptors, such Swallow-tailed (rare in spring) and White-tailed Kites and Red-tailed Hawk. Also found here are Ladder-backed Woodpecker, Couch's Kingbird (summer), and neotropical migrants in both spring and fall. From the weedy margins along the Rio Grande, a Gray-crowned Yellowthroat delighted hundreds of birders from February–April 1988. In May 1989 another Gray-crowned Yellowthroat (or possibly the same bird) was found in similar habitat not far from the original location. Although Gray-crowned Yellowthroats were locally common in the Brownsville area before the turn of the century, they are extremely rare today. Until the Sabal Palm bird in 1988, this species—then known as Ground-Chat—had not been documented north of the border since 1894.

Before stepping onto the forest trail, check the feeders at the visitors center for Buff-bellied Hummingbirds. Although virtually absent throughout most of the Valley in winter, these hummingbirds are reliable at Sabal Palm Grove. Hooded Orioles begin showing up by April and will remain through October. While sitting at the feeders, you will be surrounded by the pleasant sounds of rustling palm fronds and the cooing of White-tipped Doves. The nearby seed-feeders and recirculating water pools attract Plain Chachalacas, White-tipped Doves, and Green Jays from the dense undergrowth.

The heart and soul of the refuge is the *boscaje de la palma*, a 32-acre relic forest of old-growth Sabal Palms. The lush vegetation along the forest trail that is so beautiful can also make the birding quite difficult—there are plenty of good hiding places for Carolina and House (winter) Wrens, Long-billed Thrasher, Olive Sparrow, and Lincoln's Sparrow (winter). In some winters, temperate species such as American Woodcock, Carolina Chickadee, and Winter Wren show up at the sanctuary, but this is rare.

At the resaca look for Least Grebe, White-faced Ibis, Mottled Duck, Cinnamon Teal (rare, winter), Purple Gallinule (rare, summer), Swallow-tailed Kite (rare, spring), Spotted and Solitary Sandpipers, Groove-billed Ani (spring), Eastern Phoebe (winter), and Great Kiskadee. The composition of birds can change rapidly at the resaca, depending on water level and season. Although somewhat cumbersome on the narrow forest trail, a spotting scope comes in handy for viewing waterbirds that are feeding or resting on the far side of the lake.

In winter Yellow-throated Warblers often can be located by their loud, rich chips high in the palm tree crowns. In the canopy of Texas Ebony, look for mixed-species flocks, including Blue-headed Vireo, Tufted (Black-crested) Titmouse, Ruby-crowned Kinglet, Blue-gray Gnatcatcher, Orange-crowned and Yellow-rumped (Myrtle) Warblers, and sometimes a Nashville or Black-throated Green Warbler. Tropical Parula and Black-throated Gray Warblers are rare but regular most winters. The open-deck platform near forest trail marker #12 is a good spot for winter warblers and Lesser Goldfinch. In spring check the trailhead fork for migrant passerines, especially after the passage of cold fronts. Some of the more typical migrants include Ruby-throated Hummingbird, Warbling Vireo, Swainson's Thrush, Summer and Scarlet Tanagers, Indigo and Painted Buntings, and Baltimore Oriole.

Although South Texas specialties and neotropical migrants are wonderful in their own right, it is the lure of a Mexican rarity that brings many birders back to the grove. Clay-colored Robin, Golden-crowned Warbler, Crimson-collared Grosbeak, and Blue Bunting have all been recorded in winter along the forest trail. A Yellow-green Vireo was seen here on 21 April 1998, providing a first refuge record. Both Ruddy Ground-Dove (winter) and Yellow-green Vireo (summer) have been found in recent years within a few miles of the grove.

When the winds die down in late afternoon, the forest trail turns quiet, but it's not long before Great Horned Owls and Common Pauraques signal the coming of nightfall. In this waning light of day is your best chance of seeing an Ocelot or Jaguarundi, two of South Texas' rare and endangered cats.

BROWNSVILLE SANITARY LANDFILL

Birding the landfill may take between one to two hours (depending on how difficult those Tamaulipas Crows are). Many birders like to add on a trip to the city landfill after visiting Sabal Palm Grove Sanctuary because the two spots are relatively close to each other. Just don't wait too long, because the landfill is officially closed after 3:30 PM (and begging doesn't help). The landfill hours are from 9 AM–3:30 PM (closed Sundays).

Birds you will be looking for at this appealing locale include Zone-tailed Hawk (rare), banded, released Aplomado Falcon, Tamaulipas Crow, Chihuahuan Raven, and Horned Lark. Such rarities as California, Thayer's, Lesser Black-backed, Slaty-backed, and Glaucous Gulls have been recorded.

To reach the **Brownsville Sanitary Landfill** from Sabal Palm Grove Sanctuary, simply use directions to Sabal Palm Grove *in reverse*: after driving north on the entrance road from the sanctuary, turn right onto FM-1419 (Southmost Road) and proceed until you reach FM-3068 (0.6 mile). Turn left (north) at FM-3068 (Indiana Road) and go straight until you reach FM-802 (5.0 miles). Turn right at FM-802, which is the entrance road to the landfill. At the stop sign (0.8 mile) turn right to the landfill office. Drive around the left side (not up on the scales) of the office building and show your binoculars to the landfill staff. You can then drive to the birding area around site #43 (inquire; this site could be subject to change).

When Tamaulipas Crows, formerly known as Mexican Crows, were first discovered at Brownsville's landfill in 1968, they quickly became North America's premier "trash birds." The local crow population, which numbered about 200 birds (Christmas Bird Count data) in the late 1980s, has declined to just four birds in 1998. Although their numbers fluctuate from year to year, Tamaulipas Crows (at least presently) can no longer be thought of as the most numerous crow-like bird at the dump.

Tamaulipas Crows are very rare in summer. When they are reported, it is usually in the vicinity of the landfill or at a nearby nesting site (see box to the right). The crows have nested in recent years at both the NOAA Weather Station (20 South Vermillion Avenue and Boca Chica Boulevard) and at the Port of Brownsville (TX-48 and FM-511).

Tamaulipas Crows often sit quietly amidst the ravens and grackles, while occasionally flying off to forage near the moving trash. (The trash moves ahead of bulldozers, not of its own volition; it probably is not alive.) With patience, the crows can be located by their soft, frog-like *ahrrrr, ahwr, ahwr, ahrrrr* calls. These low, guttural calls are unlike the loud croaking of the ravens. Tamaulipas Crows are distinguished from Chihuahuan Ravens by their smaller size, slimmer bill, and rounder head. In flight, the crow's deeper, flapping

For the past two summers a pair of Tamaulipas Crows has nested under the large soccer-ball-shaped radar dish at the **NOAA Weather Station** near the Brownsville International Airport. To look for them, pull into the parking lot from Boca Chica Boulevard (TX-4) and ask permission from the office staff. During migration you might want to check the surrounding fields for Upland Sandpipers and American Golden-Plovers. If the gate to the parking lot is locked, it is still possible to observe the radar dish from a distance with a spotting scope.

Another place to look for nesting crows is at the Port of Brownsville, which is adjacent to the landfill. In past years the crows built nests on cranes, platforms, or other large structures. In April 1997 a pair of crows was seen flying around the area together, perhaps scouting for potential nest sites. Check in with the security agents at the guard station and tell them you are looking for Tamaulipas Crows. You will be given a guest pass. The Port of Brownsville is open 8 AM–5 PM (closed Sundays).

wingbeats and square tail are distinctive. They are similar in size to Great-tailed Grackles. While sorting through the grackles, the easiest field mark to look for is the crow's dark eye color (grackles have pale eyes). Also, note the crow's shorter tail and shaggier neck.

Like dumps everywhere, this one attracts numerous gulls. On any given winter day there can be thousands of gulls around the moving trash. Most common are Laughing, Ring-billed, and Herring Gulls (in that order). Franklin's Gulls may be abundant overhead during April migration, but usually don't hang around too long at the landfill. Vagrants that have showed up over the years include California, Thayer's, Lesser Black-backed (almost annual), Glaucous, and Great Black-backed Gulls. The most amazing discovery came in February 1992, when a Slaty-backed Gull provided a first record for Texas.

Many raptors hang around the landfill to feed on resident rodents. During winter check for Sharp-shinned, Cooper's, White-tailed, and Red-tailed Hawks and Peregrine Falcon. In migration, Broad-winged and Swainson's Hawks swing by. Possible rarities include Zone-tailed Hawk and Aplomado Falcon. Always check for bands on the falcons; so far all Aplomados seen at the dump are thought to come from the release program at nearby Laguna Atascosa National Wildlife Refuge.

To return to US-77, simply head back out the entrance road to FM-511 (0.8 mile from landfill office). Go straight (onto FM-802) and stay on this road until you intersect US 77 (6.4 miles).

BOCA CHICA BEACH

Allow at least three hours for the 18-mile drive to Boca Chica Beach from the FM-511/TX-4 intersection in east Brownsville. On the way you encounter a variety of habitat types, including thorn scrub forest edge, wetlands, coastal prairie, bayshore tidal flats, and sandy beach. Specialty birds for these habitats are Northern Gannet, Brown Pelican, Magnificent Frigatebird, Roseate Spoonbill, Fulvous Whistling-Duck, Mottled Duck, Peregrine Falcon, Snowy, Wilson's, and Piping Plovers, Groove-billed Ani, Couch's Kingbird, Scissor-tailed Flycatcher, and Botteri's Sparrow. You would be lucky to encounter one of the recorded rarities, such as Sooty Shearwater, Purple Sandpiper, Lesser Black-backed, Western, and Glaucous Gulls, Bridled Tern, and "Mangrove" Yellow Warbler.

To get to **Boca Chica Beach** from US-77, get on eastbound FM-802; continue east to FM-511 (6.4 miles) (the entrance to the Brownsville Sanitary Landfill straight ahead). Turn right onto FM-511 and continue to TX-4 (1.5 miles). Turn left.

Note the zacahuiste (bunch grass) on both sides of the road (2.0 miles) which is the nesting habitat of Botteri's Sparrows. Birds should be on territory by late April. A search for this shy and local songster should begin in the early hours when it is most vocal. Its song is a varied series of hesitant chips which breaks into a bouncing-ball trill. Most Botteri's Sparrows withdraw into Mexico by early September.

Well off the highway on the left is a wetland (2.2 miles) which holds water most of the year, making it attractive to many species of waterbirds. A spotting scope is a must here. Check for Eared Grebe, White and White-faced Ibises, Fulvous Whistling-Duck (summer), lots of waterfowl, Solitary Sandpiper, Wilson's Phalarope, and other shorebirds. Take time to check a small dirt road bordered by native trees leading to the right. Many of the resident specialties can be found here. In spring look for Groove-billed Ani, Brown-crested Flycatcher, Couch's Kingbird, and Scissor-tailed Flycatcher.

TX-4 is usually good for Chihuahuan Ravens and several species of raptors. You can't miss seeing the large raven nests built on the cross-beams of some of the utility poles. As you head toward the coast you might see White-tailed Kite, Harris's Hawk, and, in winter, Osprey, Northern Harrier, White-tailed and Red-tailed Hawks, American Kestrel, and Peregrine Falcon. During spring look for kettles of migrating Mississippi Kites and Broad-winged and Swainson's Hawks streaming northbound. On rare occasions, a Ferruginous Hawk (winter) or a banded Aplomado Falcon is spotted somewhere in the area.

You will notice that much of TX-4 has posted U.S. Fish & Wildlife signs. The USF&WS recently purchased12,000 acres of this critical coastal habitat. According to wildlife experts, the Boca Chica Tract has been one of the most important land acquisitions in the entire Wildlife Corridor project.

Look for Palmito Hill Road on your right (3.3 miles), which winds for 2.5 miles through a variety of habitats. The vegetation here is somewhat fragmented, but there are still good hedgerows that can attract warblers and other migrant passerines. If you are in the exploring mood, this rarely birded area is worth checking out. Being so close to the Rio Grande, you just never know what Mexican rarity may be lurking nearby. You will likely need to turn around at a locked gate and backtrack to TX-4.

Continuing east on TX-4, you come to an historical marker on the right (0.2 mile). The Battle of Palmito Ranch, which took place at this site, was the last engagement of the Civil War. The Confederates forces won this battle 24 days after Robert E. Lee surrendered at Appomattox.

You will also notice clay dune *lomas* (low hills) which are vegetated by stunted mesquites, ebonies, and other native trees. During April these islands of brush are magnets for neotropical migrants. There are also numerous seasonal (dry in summer) mudflats along the way, which might hold shorebirds. In early May it is possible to see White-rumped, Baird's, and Pectoral Sandpipers together with other peep on these mudflats. You may see Gull-billed and Black (late April through September) Terns feeding for insects over the grassy fields before you get to the open gulf. Although rare in winter, check for Burrowing Owl sitting atop the concrete rubble (on the north side of the highway) in the last mile or so before reaching the Gulf (10.3 miles).

You can drive the sandy beach for miles; two-wheel drive is usually all that is necessary. However, in rare instances spring tides or high surf can make the beach road virtually impassable (with or without four-wheel drive). Probably the worst spot is the soft sand at the end of TX-4, so proceed here with great caution. Along the open beach, look for Snowy, Wilson's, and Piping Plovers (summer) amongst the numerous Sanderlings. Also fairly common are Black-bellied Plover, Willet, and Ruddy Turnstone. Large flocks of Red Knots may be present along the beach during migration, but this species can be tough to find in winter. Most of the year, you will see Caspian, Royal, Sandwich, and Forster's Terns feeding along the surf line. Common, Least, and Black Terns do not arrive until spring. Resident Laughing Gulls share the beach with Ring-billed, Herring, and the occasional Bonaparte's during winter. Vagrant gulls, such as Lesser Black-backed and Glaucous, show up some winters. In April 1995 an extremely rare Western Gull was found here.

Going right (south) takes you to the mouth of the Rio Grande (2.5 miles). There is usually is a large concentration of birds in the shallow river delta on both sides of the river. This is a great place to add many species to your Mexico list. Look for American White and Brown Pelicans, Roseate Spoonbill, American Avocet, American Oystercatcher, Black Skimmer, and a variety of gulls, terns, and other waterbirds. While looking for Clapper Rail and Seaside Sparrow in the Black Mangrove trees, you may flush nearly 100 Black-crowned (and occasionally Yellow-crowned) Night-Herons from their daytime roost. With the passage of cool fronts in spring, the mangroves can be very good for migrant warblers. On 20 March 1990, a "Mangrove" Yellow Warbler was found in this stand of Black Mangroves, providing the second record of this distinct subspecies for Texas and the United States.

Going left (north) on the beach from TX-4 takes you to the jetties (5 miles). Occasionally a Peregrine Falcon will be seen soaring or perched atop the high dunes. At the jetties look for many of the same birds previously mentioned for the beach and the river mouth, as well as Common Loon, Eared Grebe, and Northern Gannet in winter, and Magnificent Frigatebird in summer. In February 1991 a Purple Sandpiper was found in a flock of Ruddy Turnstones on the jetties, providing the southernmost record for this species in the United States. On the Lower Coast, pelagic species are rarely seen from land, but could turn up at any time of year. Cory's Shearwater, Masked Booby, and Pomarine Jaeger have been seen just offshore from the jetties; a Sooty Shearwater was found along the beach in January 1992. Bridled and Sooty Terns are most likely to show up following tropical storm activity in the Gulf.

If you should encounter a beached dolphin or whale while driving on Boca Chica Beach, please call the Coastal Study Lab (University of Texas at Brownsville) at South Padre Island (956/761-2644) during normal business hours or the Texas Marine Mammal Stranding Network at 800/962-6625 (day or night).

OLD PORT ISABEL ROAD / LOMA ALTA LAKE

In this low-lying region of impermeable clay soils, Old Port Isabel Road can be a real adventure if it's wet. After a rain it is four-wheel drive only. Fortunately, it is dry most of the time. All birding on this 7-mile stretch is done from the car. This is wide-open country that is exposed to wind, so it's advisable to get out early in the morning.

Old Port Isabel Road is best in spring when Cassin's and Botteri's Sparrows are on territory. As a bonus, banded Aplomado Falcons are occasionally seen in the area. In 1995, an Aplomado Falcon pair nested in the vicinity, representing the first nesting of the species in Texas in over 50 years.

Your target birds on this trip are Fulvous Whistling-Duck, White-tailed Kite, Osprey, Harris's and White-tailed Hawks, Aplomado Falcon (banded), Peregrine Falcon, Whimbrel, Brown-crested and Scissor-tailed Flycatchers, Verdin, Cactus Wren, Curve-billed Thrasher, Sprague's Pipit, Green-tailed Towhee, Cassin's and Botteri's Sparrows, and Pyrrhuloxia.

To reach **Old Port Isabel Road** from US-77/FM-511, go east on FM-511 as though you were heading to the Port of Brownsville. Keep an eye out for several species of raptors, including White-tailed Kite, White-tailed Hawk, and Harris's Hawk. At the intersection with FM-1847 is Palo Alto Battlefield National Historic Site (3.4 miles), marking the first battle of the Mexican-American War. The large tracts of native brush are off-limits to the general public, yet birding can still be done along the fence line.

Another roadside birding spot that is worth a quick look is just down the highway on the right (0.5 mile). The cactus patch can be good for "western" species, like Verdin, Cactus Wren, and Pyrrhuloxia. In winter, look for Green-tailed Towhee (rare) and Vesper, Savannah, and Grasshopper Sparrows. Don't spend too much time at either spot as the birding is better on Old Port Isabel Road.

As you approach Old Port Isabel Road (2.8 miles), turn left onto a dirt road at the Loma Alta Skeet and Trap sign. Loma Alta Lake can be scanned with a spotting scope for waterbirds from the railroad tracks (0.6 mile), but you will get only distant views. A little farther down the road a seasonal wetland provides much closer viewing (1.6 miles). Birds found here include White and White-faced Ibises, Fulvous Whistling-Duck (summer), Mottled Duck, Whimbrel (spring), Long-billed Curlew, Gull-billed Tern, Chihuahuan Raven, Eastern Meadowlark, and many other wetland species.

In spring and summer check for Cassin's and Botteri's Sparrows singing on territory (0.3 mile, for about the next 2.5 miles). Although both occupy the same general area, they prefer different habitats: Botteri's is found near the zacahuiste (bunch grass) while Cassin's prefers scrubby areas and can sometimes be spotted skylarking from prickly pear or mesquite. Sprague's Pipits are sometimes seen in winter as they walk in the open grassy fields on the east side of the road (0.8 mile). Also in the area, look for Say's Phoebe (rare, winter), Brown-crested (summer) and Scissor-tailed Flycatchers,

Bewick's Wren, Sage (rare, winter) and Curve-billed Thrashers, and Pyrrhuloxia. It is even possible to see a Peregrine or Aplomado Falcon zip by. Old Port Isabel Road reaches a small bridge (2.7 miles) that is often closed. If the bridge is open, you can drive through until the road intersects TX-100 (1.4 miles). Going right (east) on TX-100 takes you to Port Isabel/South Padre Island. Going left takes you to Los Fresnos and then to US-77. If the bridge is closed, just turn around and go back to FM-511. Turning right onto FM-511 will get you back to Brownsville. Turning left will take you to Port of Brownsville. Off to the right (0.4 mile from rejoining FM-511) is a tree-lined resaca that might have Least Grebes and a varied assortment of waders, shorebirds, and waterfowl depending on water level and season. You can park at the Coastal Mart (0.1 mile) and walk back to the edge of the resaca. Farther along are several grain elevators on the left (1.3 mile) where occasionally a Yellow-headed Blackbird can be picked out from the hundreds of other blackbirds (mostly Red-wings). Look also for Common Ground-Doves in the area.

Just ahead at the junction of TX-48 is the Port of Brownsville (0.2 mile). Because of its close proximity to the Brownsville Municipal Landfill, the Port is a good spot to check for Tamaulipas Crow in late spring or early summer when most of the crows have returned to Mexico (see box on page 32). Turning left onto TX-48 takes you to Port Isabel / South Padre Island. On the way to the island, look for Aplomado Falcons (banded) near the Port Mart (3.6 miles) on the left side of TX-48 across from the Amfels shipyard.

PORT ISABEL / SOUTH PADRE ISLAND

Only a thirty-minute drive from Brownsville is the resort town of South Padre Island. South Padre Island occupies the southern end of Padre Island, which at 113 miles in length is the world's longest barrier island. South Padre has good shorebird habitat (Black Mangrove bayshore) and several wooded areas which provide critical stopovers for neotropical migrants. In summer, pelagic birding trips venture to offshore waters in search of shearwaters, storm-petrels, and other pelagic species. From Port Isabel, the deep water off the continental shelf occurs at only 45–50 miles offshore, the closest point along the entire Texas coast.

Expected species on South Padre Island include Brown Pelican, Reddish Egret, Roseate Spoonbill, Peregrine Falcon, Clapper and Virginia Rails, Sora, Snowy, Wilson's, and Piping Plovers, Whimbrel and other shorebirds, and neotropical migrants (spring and fall). Occasionally you might find Northern Gannet, Magnificent Frigatebird, Black Rail, and Pomarine Jaeger. Recorded rarities have been Pacific Loon, Yellow-nosed Albatross, Blue-footed and Brown Boobies, Harlequin Duck, Ruff, Iceland, Lesser Black-backed, Glaucous, and Great Black-backed Gulls, Bridled Tern, and Brown Noddy. The best season for visiting is spring (April–first week of May), although fall (September–October) and winter may also be productive.

To get to South Padre Island from Brownsville, drive east on FM-802 (from US-77) to TX-48 (5.0 miles). Turn left onto TX-48 which takes you all the way to Port Isabel. For the next ten miles, watch for the occasional Horned Lark flying low across the highway or Gull-billed Terns swooping down for insects.

In winter, Ospreys are often found in the vicinity of the shrimp basin (6.0 miles), while Northern Harriers and Chihuahuan Ravens can usually be seen soaring over the flat floodplain. The Brownsville Ship Channel boat ramp (3.1 miles) usually has a variety of herons, shorebirds, gulls, and terns nearby. Look here in spring for Whimbrel and Long-billed Curlew. For the next several miles, the road traverses Bahía Grande—or the Great Tidal Flat—named after the vast tidal flats seen on this stretch of road. Depending on the season, rainfall, and tides, this area can have numerous ducks and shorebirds.

Once you pass a sharp left curve (3.6 miles), watch for Harris's Hawks, which are sometimes seen in small family groups along the highway. Harris's Hawks and other raptors are often seen searching for prey near mesquite-covered *lomas*. As you approach the intersection of TX-100 (2.6 miles), it is possible to see Reddish Egret, Roseate Spoonbill, American Avocet, Long-billed Curlew, and a variety of waterbirds feeding in the shallow tidal flats on both sides of the highway. These tidal flats can be good for a variety of shorebirds in spring and fall.

Turn right at the intersection of TX-100 (0.7 mile) and travel through Port Isabel. During spring and fall, migrant passerines can be found in the native vegetation around town. In May 1994, a pair of Tropical Kingbirds nested in the tall lights of Tarpon Stadium off to the right (0.7 mile).

The old Port Isabel Lighthouse (0.7 mile) still stands as a monument to 19th century coastal trade and commerce. The lighthouse was erected by the U.S. government in 1852. The light was extinguished during the Civil War (becoming permanently so in 1905), but is now maintained as a Texas State Historical Structure by the Texas Parks and Wildlife Department.

A new tourist attraction is the Port Isabel Historical Museum located on 314 E. Railroad Street. The museum displays many artifacts, including those from a 1554 Spanish galleon that once sailed along the Texas coast, the Mexican-American War, the last battle of the Civil War, and other events that shaped the Laguna Madre area. You can get to the museum by turning right onto Tarnava Street (opposite the lighthouse). One block later you will turn right at E. Railroad Street and less than a block away you will see the restored home of Charles Champion (founder of the town) on the right. Entrance fees are $3/adults, $2/seniors, $1/children, and $0.50 for kids five and under.

The causeway between Port Isabel and South Padre Island passes over the shallow yet expansive Laguna Madre, providing a high vantage point to see cormorants, gulls, terns, and an occasional Brown Pelican. It takes a sharp eye to spot a high-soaring Magnificent Frigatebird, an occasional visitor from late spring through early fall. Just as the causeway ends at South Padre Island, you can pull over to scan the Black Mangrove tidal flat to the right (south) that frequently has Reddish Egret, Yellow-crowned Night-Heron, Clapper Rail, American Oystercatcher, Black Skimmer, and a variety of terns and shorebirds. During spring Snowy, Wilson's, and Piping Plovers, Whimbrel, and Hudsonian Godwit (rare) have turned up along this stretch of bayshore.

Similarly productive mudflats, best at low tide, are scattered all along the bayshore. Driving north on Padre Boulevard, look for a tidal flat (behind the miniature golf course [0.9 mile]) which sometimes has Snowy and Piping Plovers as well as a variety of terns, shorebirds, and waders. Another good spot is at Bahía Grande (about 3 miles north of the miniature golf course), just south of the South Padre Island Convention Center.

The small woodlots on the island are magnets for migrants in spring and fall. Many of the small patches of trees and landscaped yards are found off Laguna Boulevard—streets such as Campeche, Retama, Oleander, and Morningside are a few that can be loaded with warblers and other colorful migrants. Migrants often seen in spring and fall include Ruby-throated Hummingbird, Eastern Wood-Pewee, Great Crested Flycatcher, Western and Eastern Kingbirds, Scissor-tailed Flycatcher, Warbling Vireo, Swainson's Thrush, Summer and Scarlet Tanagers, Rose-breasted and Blue Grosbeaks, Indigo and Painted Buntings, and Baltimore Oriole. After a north wind shift in April, you may run into dozens of birders combing the area.

During migration, 38 warbler species have been recorded from these woodlots, though a good day yields only 18–22 species. Although the composition of migrant flocks is dominated by eastern species, western species show up from time to time—Yellow-headed Blackbirds and Bullock's Orioles can be found each spring, while Townsend's Warbler, Western Tanager, Black-headed Grosbeak, and Lazuli and Varied Buntings make appearances about every other year. Groove-billed Anis can also be found on island woodlots during migration, but seem to be more numerous in fall.

White-tipped Dove
Brad McKinney

Another must stop is the **Laguna Madre Nature Trail**, located at South Padre Island Convention Center boardwalk. Local birders simply refer to it as "the boardwalk." The boardwalk is located about 4 miles north of the causeway on Padre Boulevard—just follow the signs to the brightly colored convention center (on the left) as you reach the end of development. This spot is fast becoming one of the premier wetlands in the Valley. Actually, there are several different habitats found here, including freshwater marsh, salt marsh, shallow bayshore, landscaping, and low dunes. A newly vegetated Warbler Rest Stop, complete with circulating water baths, is now located under the whale wall at the entrance to the boardwalk. Attracted by the freshwater pond, lots of warblers and other migrants can be found in the area each spring.

In winter, the boardwalk is *the spot* for seeing rails in South Texas—all six species have been recorded here! Most common are Clapper Rail and Sora, followed by King and Virginia Rails. One of the best places to look for Black Rail has been near the Endangered Species sign (near the end of the right fork). In the cattails, look for Least Bittern (year round), Black-crowned and Yellow-crowned Night-Herons, Common Yellowthroat, Savannah, Seaside (rare), Lincoln's, and Swamp Sparrows as well as Sedge and Marsh Wrens (uncommon). Purple Gallinule is best seen here during April and May. Throughout much of the winter, a Peregrine Falcon sits atop the water tower railing watching over the wetland below.

Behind the Convention Center is a tidal mudflat that is a good spot for Reddish Egret and a variety of shorebirds, including Snowy, Wilson's, Semipalmated, and Piping Plovers, Pectoral Sandpiper, Dunlin, and Stilt Sandpiper. In the shallow bay waters just beyond the mudflat, the Valley's first Pacific Loon was discovered in April 1998 during an ABA Convention field trip. During winter look for Common Loon, Eared Grebe, Red-breasted Merganser, and a variety of waterfowl in these waters. Texas' first Harlequin Duck was found in the nearby waters of Laguna Madre in late January 1990.

To drive along the open coast, you can enter Andy Bowie Park, located across the street from the Convention Center ($4/day fee). (You can also drive several miles north along Padre Boulevard until you see a passable road leading toward the beach. Four-wheel drive is highly recommended here.) In winter you will see Ring-billed, Herring, and occasionally Bonaparte's amongst the numerous Laughing Gulls and shorebirds. Vagrant gulls occasionally are spotted on the beach, and although Lesser Black-backed and Glaucous Gulls are the most likely possibilities, Great Black-backed (February 1990) and Iceland Gulls (January 1977) have also been found here. Although the only record for Ruff on South Padre Island dates back to December 1902, there is no telling what could show up along the beach at South Padre Island.

In spring you will likely see Black-bellied Plover, Ruddy Turnstone, Sanderling, Red Knot, and Caspian, Royal, Sandwich, Forster's, and Least Terns. Also look for Snowy and Piping Plovers and Black Tern (more common in May). During a spring fallout, neotropical migrants often seek sand dune vegetation to forage and for shelter. In fall, this island is a major staging area for the Peregrine Falcon migration.

Occasionally, Common Loon and Northern Gannet can be spotted offshore in winter and Magnificent Frigatebird in summer. The best spot seems to be at the rock jetties on the south tip of the island. Birding the jetties at Isla Blanca Park will also cost you $4/day. During spring fallouts Isla Blanca Park can be good for migrants, especially along the dunes. On rare occasions in spring, Sooty Terns have been seen in late afternoon flying from their spoil island nest sites toward the open Gulf. Occasionally, pelagic species have been recorded along the coast, especially after the passage of tropical storms. At South Padre Island there are fall records for Brown Booby, Blue-footed Booby (first state record, 5 October 1976), Sabine's Gull, Bridled Tern, and Brown Noddy. Port Isabel is the site of the first state record of Yellow-nosed Albatross (14 May 1972) and two recent June sightings of Long-tailed Jaeger.

From June through September, offshore Texas waters have been good for many pelagic species. Although individual numbers are low (compared to the east and west coasts), the diversity is fairly high. Pelagic trips depart about once a month (May–September) from Freeport and (recently) South Padre Island. Expected species include Cory's and Audubon's Shearwaters, Leach's and Band-rumped Storm-Petrels, Masked Booby, and Bridled and Sooty Terns, as well as a variety of fish and dolphins, and occasionally Sperm Whales. Trips to date have resulted in fifteen species of pelagic birds, including Black-capped Petrel, Greater and Sooty Shearwaters, and Red-billed Tropicbird. For further information on Texas deep-water pelagic trips, write to Dwight Peake, 30 LeBrun Court, Galveston, TX 77551; dpeake@mail.phoenix.net. Lower Laguna Madre birding tours, on a large catamaran, that visit the shallower parts of the bay (virtually inaccessible by any other means) depart Sea Ranch Marina on South Padre Island. Departures are scheduled at your convenience. Frequently encountered wildlife includes many colonial waterbirds, such as Reddish Egret, as well as Roseate Spoonbill, oystercatchers, skimmers, Bottlenose Dolphins, and so on. Contact George Colley or Scarlet at 956/739-2473.

Birding North and West of Brownsville

Just north of the area covered by this guide is Laguna Atascosa National Wildlife Refuge, a must visit for birders at any season. Fortunately, another *ABA/Lane Birdfinding Guide*, **A Birder's Guide to the Texas Coast**, examines the birding possibilities at this exciting refuge in great detail. Several other sites are close to Brownsville and can be covered in a few hours as short excursions or along the way to another site. Harlingen is a major destination in its own right.

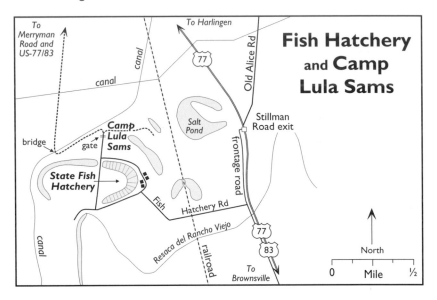

Fish Hatchery Road / Camp Lula Sams

The Fish Hatchery (Texas Parks and Wildlife Department, Coastal Fisheries Division) is a series of ponds in north Brownsville that attracts a variety of waterbirds. The numerous hedgerows on Fish Hatchery Road can be good for Couch's Kingbirds and other resident specialties.

You can expect to see Least Grebe, White-faced Ibis, Mottled Duck, Ringed Kingfisher, Couch's Kingbird, Scissor-tailed Flycatcher, and resident specialties mentioned below. Tropical Kingbird once put in an appearance.

To find **Fish Hatchery Road** from Brownsville at the US-77/FM-802 intersection, drive north on US-77 to the Stillman Road exit (3.0 miles). Exit right and then turn left (west) at the stop (Stillman Road). Turn left (south) again, now on the south frontage road, and continue until you see Fish Hatchery Road on the right (0.4 mile). Turn right to the ponds (0.7 mile). You can see the office straight ahead but you want to go right on the caliche road to view the many ponds. Scan the ponds for Least Grebe, Anhinga (winter),

Least Bittern (summer), White-faced Ibis, Mottled Duck, and Ringed Kingfisher. Also, check the forest edges for Couch's and Tropical Kingbirds and Scissor-tailed Flycatcher as you continue toward the Camp Lula Sams gate (0.4 mile).

Surrounded by native brushlands just minutes from US-77, Camp Lula Sams (280 North Fish Hatchery Road) offers birders an alternative to standard area motels. This 87-acre private wildlife refuge has many of the regional specialties including Plain Chachalaca, Buff-bellied Hummingbird, Brown-crested Flycatcher, Great Kiskadee, Green Jay, and Long-billed Thrasher.

It also has a 5-acre resaca that attracts many wetland species. Camp Lula Sams has overnight accommodations; home-style meals are available by special arrangement only. For reservations, call 956/350-9093 for a recorded message. They will return your call.

If you continue on past the gate, you will come to a bridge that is often not passable. This is usually the turn-around point. If you are able to cross the bridge, the road winds around pasture land, eventually coming to Merryman Road which is very near US-77. If you choose not to cross the bridge, you can backtrack toward the Texas Parks and Wildlife office to scan the other ponds.

U.S. FISH & WILDLIFE WETLAND ON US-281

Bordered by large stands of Black Willow and other native trees, this seasonal wetland is probably the most productive in Brownsville. It is located about 2 miles west of the US-77 / Boca Chica Boulevard intersection. The wetland has no official parking or observation area, yet it is still accessible for birders seeking a little adventure.

To get to the USF&W wetland drive west on Boca Chica Boulevard (US-281) for 2.1 miles to the large willow trees on the left (south) side of the highway. Parking is not an easy thing here, but you can try pulling into the parking lot at F-G Commercial A/C adjacent to the wetland or at Villarreal's Fruit Stand across the street. Viewing the wetland requires walking along the narrow grassy strip at the curbside until you find an opening in the cattails. There is just enough room to set up a spotting scope to scan sections of the resaca.

Depending on the season and water level, there may be quite an assemblage of birds present. Look for Least Grebe, Anhinga, Green Heron, Fulvous Whistling-Duck (summer), Mottled Duck, Ringed Kingfisher, and Great Kiskadee, and in winter, Red-shouldered Hawk, Yellow-bellied Sapsucker, Eastern Phoebe, and Wilson's Warbler. Although not yet recorded here, seemingly ideal habitat exists for Masked Duck.

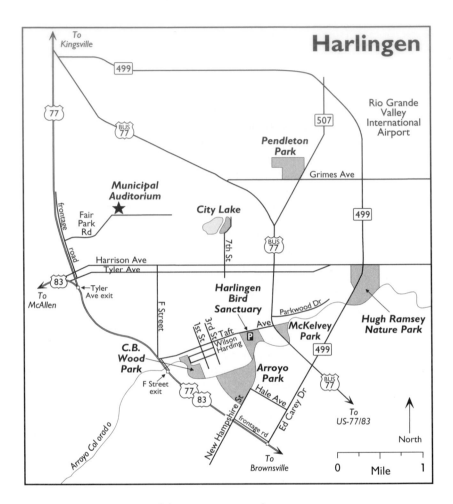

HARLINGEN AREA

Harlingen is more than just the home of the Rio Grande Valley Birding Festival. There is a variety of city parks along the Arroyo Colorado River where the birding can be quite good. If you are staying in Harlingen or you have extra time in the Valley, you may want to check out these sites. Many of the Rio Grande specialties can be found here, including Buff-bellied Hummingbird, Green Kingfisher, and Northern Beardless-Tyrannulet (rare). You can also find Red-crowned Parrots flying around various residential areas at dusk and dawn. Although rare, look for Tropical Parula in winter in patches of tall trees where you might encounter mixed-species flocks.

Recently, Tropical Kingbirds have been found in the vicinity of the Municipal Auditorium at 1204 Fair Park Road. This is also the headquarters of the annual Rio Grande Valley Birding Festival. To get to the auditorium from northbound US-77, take the Tyler exit (right) and drive north on the frontage road. You will go through two traffic lights before coming to Fair Park Road. Turn right on Fair Park Road and follow it to the auditorium.

HARLINGEN CITY PARKS ALONG THE ARROYO COLORADO

Hugh Ramsey Nature Park

To get to Hugh Ramsey Nature Park from northbound US-77, exit at Ed Carey Drive. Head east on Ed Carey Drive to the traffic light at Business US-77 (1.0 mile). Continue straight at the traffic light (you are now on 499 North) and look for the entrance to the park on your right (1.0 mile). The main trail winds around the wooded areas and another trail overlooks the river. The trails have no markers and are not being maintained, but access is easy. At all of the parks along the Arroyo Colorado River, there is a diverse assemblage of native vegetation.

Many of the Rio Grande specialties can be found here, including Plain Chachalaca, Common Ground-Dove, White-tipped Dove, Common Pauraque, Buff-bellied Hummingbird, Great Kiskadee, Couch's Kingbird (summer), Scissor-tailed Flycatcher (summer), Green Jay, Verdin, Long-billed and Curve-billed Thrashers, Olive Sparrow, and Hooded (summer) and Altamira Orioles. Northern Beardless-Tyrannulet, very rare outside Hidalgo County, has occurred here. In winter, look for all three kingfishers and Yellow-crowned Night-Herons down along the river. Green Kingfisher is occasionally spotted flying low over the water.

Arroyo Park

To get to Arroyo Park from US-77, exit at Ed Carey Drive. Continue north on the frontage road to New Hampshire Street (0.5 mile). Turn right at New Hampshire and continue until you see the Arroyo Park parking lot on your left (0.5 mile). Walk along the main sidewalk out in the direction of the native vegetation. The sidewalk trail allows an overlook of the river. The best birding is to the left (south). You can get off the sidewalk to explore on the walking trails, but the walking trails are not marked or maintained so caution is advised. The birds here are similar to those at Hugh Ramsey Nature Park. Black-chinned Hummingbird and Verdin have occasionally been found nesting in the scrubby vegetation. Northern Beardless-Tyrannulet has also been spotted in these woods.

C.B. Wood Park

Exit US-77 at F Street and continue north. Reset your odometer at the first traffic light (you will continue straight through the light). Proceed to Taft Avenue (0.2 mile) and turn right. At First Street (0.5 mile), turn right. At Harding Street (0.2 mile), again turn right. Continue to C.B. Wood Park (0.1 mile) where you will see the parking lot off to your right. The best birding is to the east (or left, if you are approaching the Arroyo Colorado). Follow a primitive walking trail toward the thick vegetation. There are some good vantage points from which you can view the river.

Most of the Rio Grande specialties can be found here. Plain Chachalaca, White-tipped Dove, Great Kiskadee, Green Jay, Long-billed Thrasher, and Olive Sparrow are in these woods. Also look for Verdin, Bewick's Wren, Curve-billed Thrasher, and Pyrrhuloxia. In spring listen for the *perr-wheeer* calls of Common Pauraque at sundown or before dawn.

Harlingen Bird Sanctuary

The unofficial name of this Arroyo tract is the Harlingen Bird Sanctuary. This may be the most extensive birding habitat within the city but it currently has only a makeshift parking lot. The birds found here are similar to those at the other city parks. However, this is the best spot in Harlingen to find Verdin, Cactus and Bewick's Wrens, and Pyrrhuloxia.

To get to this site from C.B. Wood Park, just continue on around the parking lot (street becomes Wilson Street) to First Street (0.2 mile). Turn left at First Street and proceed to Taft Street (less than 0.1 mile). Turn right at Taft Street and continue to the makeshift parking lot on the right (0.5 mile). Trails lead down to the Arroyo Colorado.

McKelvey Park

McKelvey Park is located on the east side of Business US-77 (77 Sunshine Strip) less than one mile north of Ed Carey. You can also get there from the Harlingen Bird Sanctuary by crossing Commerce and Business US-77 (the two parks are just a few blocks away from each other). The vegetation at McKelvey Park is not as extensive as the above parks, but there is a nice hedgerow of tall native trees in the back.

Many of the Rio Grande specialties can be found here. A pair of Great Horned Owls can sometimes be heard in the trees. It is also a good spot for mixed-species flocks in winter and passerines in migration. Red-crowned Parrots are seen occasionally on the edge of the park at dawn and dusk.

Red-crowned Parrot Roosts

Parrots wander around many areas of Harlingen, including McKelvey Park, Parkwood Street (off Business US-77), and City Lake (76 Drive). Recently, the best spot for parrots has been near Pendleton Park and the K-Mart near the intersection of Morgan Street and Grimes Avenue. Both Green Parakeets and Red-crowned Parrots have been found nesting in the palms at the back of the Wal-Mart in nearby San Benito.

City Lake

To get to City Lake from northbound US-77, exit at Tyler Avenue. Turn right (east) and drive to 7th Street, where you turn left. 7th Street turns into 76 Drive and it won't be far until you see the City Library and Cultural Arts Center. Park on the street nearby and walk across the street to the lake.

In spring you may see Purple Martins in the martin houses and Black-bellied Whistling-Ducks in the duck boxes around the lake. You are likely to see Green Heron, a resident flock of Laughing Gulls, and Gull-billed (uncommon), Caspian, and Forster's Terns. Occasionally, Bonaparte's Gull and Tropical Kingbird can be found at the lake. Migrating raptors tend to soar across this area in spring and fall.

On the opposite side of the lake are some large trees, known locally as Boggus Woods. These trees can be good for Great Kiskadee, Green Jay, and other Rio Grande specialties, mixed species flocks in winter, and migrant passerines in spring and fall. Occasionally both Red-crowned and Yellow-headed Parrots can be seen here. Both Spotted Towhee and Tropical Parula have been found here in winter.

UPRIVER ON OLD MILITARY HIGHWAY (US 281)

From Brownsville west to Rio Grande City, the fertile flood plain of the Rio Grande was once covered by dense thickets and subtropical woodlands. Most of this habitat has been replaced by cities, farms, and citrus groves, restricting many of the native species to the remaining patches of natural vegetation. Several wildlife refuges are located on Old Military Highway (US-281), the most notable being Santa Ana National Wildlife Refuge, located about 45 miles west of Brownsville.

To get to Santa Ana NWR from the junction of US-77/FM-802 in Brownsville, go west on FM-802 to US-281 (2.2 miles). Turn right (west) onto US-281 and start watching for an irrigation canal that crosses the highway (1.7 miles). If it has not recently rained, you can turn right onto the dirt road on the west bank. This road takes you to La Paloma Reservoir (0.7 mile), which can be good for ducks in winter, shorebirds in migration, and Neotropic Cormorants during most of the year.

Continue west on US-281 to River Bend Country Club (0.3 mile), where you might find Wood Storks in late summer/early fall and Fulvous Whistling-Ducks in summer. Actually, Wood Storks could show up anywhere on this road between Brownsville and Santa Ana NWR from late June through September.

As you drive west on Old Military Highway, look for the occasional Couch's Kingbird, Scissor-tailed Flycatcher (summer), or Ringed Kingfisher perched on utility wires above canals or other wet areas. It is easy to stop along the highway, so pull over to investigate some of the little ponds along the both sides of the road.

The abundance of Least Grebes in the Valley is highly unpredictable—some years they are fairly common, but normally they are hard to find. In those scarce years, they can sometimes be seen on **Old Cannon Pond**. Continue up the highway, watching on the right for a roadside rest area with a cannon (19.0 miles). Just beyond the cannon a dirt road leads to the pond (1.4 miles), which is located on the Resaca del Rancho Viejo tract of the Lower Rio Grande Valley National Wildlife Refuge. The tract is not open to the public; *do not leave the road to cross the fence here.* Because of the thick vegetation, you might need to wait a while for the grebes to paddle into view. This area also attracts Neotropic Cormorant, Black-bellied Whistling-Duck, White-tailed Kite, a variety of resident shorebirds, raptors, and land birds. Continue up the dirt road to the electrical station (0.5 mile). It is here that Tropical Kingbirds have nested for the past several years. Also nesting in the area are Couch's and Western Kingbirds.

Return to US-281 and continue west. To visit the La Feria Sod Farm, turn right at FM-506 (2.5 miles). Turn right again at FM-3067 (2.9 miles). The sod farm is on the left side of the highway (1.3 miles). During migration, check the wet fields in the area for American Golden-Plover, Upland and Buff-breasted Sandpipers, Horned Lark, and Sprague's Pipit.

Continue west on US-281 to a sign reading El Zacatal. The resacas on both sides of the highway here can be good for grebes, waders, ducks, and shorebirds. In spring look for Wilson's Phalaropes and a variety of sandpipers. You might even find a Least Grebe or a Ringed Kingfisher here.

WESLACO

One of the best wetlands in the area is **Llano Grande Lake** south of Weslaco. (See map on opposite page.) To reach it, continue west on US-281 to FM-1015 (4.9 miles) in the small community of Progreso. Turn right (north) to a dirt road leading right (2.3 miles). By driving along the levee, you have a great vantage point for studying ducks, waders, and shorebirds. In winter look for Least and Pied-billed Grebes, American White Pelican, Yellow-crowned Night-Heron, and lots of ducks, including Blue-winged, possibly Cinnamon, and Green-winged Teals. In migration look for Black-necked Stilt, American Avocet, Greater and Lesser Yellowlegs, Solitary, Semipalmated, Western, Least, White-rumped, Pectoral, and Stilt Sandpipers, Long-billed Dowitcher, and Wilson's Phalarope.

Just a little farther north on FM-1015 is the **Methodist Camp Thicket** (0.4 mile). With tall specimens of ash, cedar, Black Willow, and hackberry, this area is prime bird habitat. Many of the Valley specialties can be found in the woods year round. Just stop by at the office to ask permission to bird, or call in advance at 956/565-6006.

In addition to Llano Grande Lake and the Methodist Camp Thicket, there are several other spots worth checking in the Weslaco area. Audubon House, also called **Chapman Woods**, is a good place to look for Green Parakeet and Red-crowned Parrot flocks, mixed-species flocks (including Tropical Parula) in winter, migrant passerines in spring and fall, and resident specialties year round. Recently the trails, water source, and observation blind have been refurbished. Audubon House is located at 1019 South Texas Boulevard (FM-88). Request permission to bird the property from the Frontera Audubon Society office at 956/968-3275.

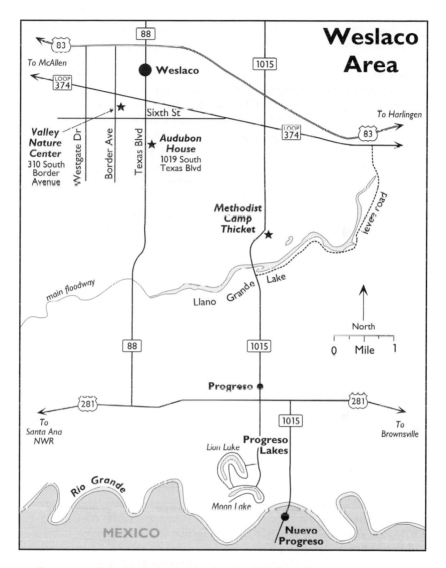

Parrots and parakeets are seen almost daily from October through April flying over Weslaco neighborhoods in the vicinity of Sixth Street and Border Avenue. They roost in big trees near Sixth Street between Westgate Drive and Border Avenue. The main flock roosts at the Audubon House thicket. For the latest on Weslaco parrot sightings, contact Valley Nature Center, 310 South Border Avenue, at 956/969-2475 or Frontera Audubon Society at 956/968-3275.

If you want to try another spot for Tropical Kingbirds stop at Progreso Lakes, a small community south of Weslaco on FM-1015. The birds have been found recently in the vicinity of the two resacas. To reach Progreso Lakes, travel south on FM-1015 past the town of Progreso. At the intersection with US-281 continue south to Progreso Lakes. The resaca is straight ahead about 1.5 miles. The birds have been found perched on tall trees and wires.

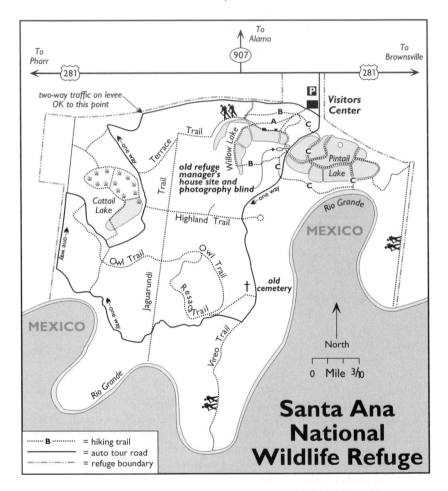

SANTA ANA NATIONAL WILDLIFE REFUGE

Santa Ana National Wildlife Refuge offers some of the best birding in South Texas. Virtually all of the Rio Grande specialties can be found here, including Hook-billed Kite, Northern Beardless-Tyrannulet (summer), and Tropical Parula. There is a good assortment of wintering waterfowl and other waterbirds on Willow, Pintail, and Cattail Lakes, and migrant raptors funnel over the refuge in large numbers during spring and fall. Mixed-species flocks are present in winter, and you'll find an assortment of passerines in migration. A number of Mexican rarities have been recorded here over the years.

At Santa Ana you will be looking for Least Grebe, Least Bittern, Hook-billed Kite, Plain Chachalaca, Purple Gallinule, Common Ground-Dove, White-tipped Dove, Groove-billed Ani, Common Pauraque, Buff-bellied Hummingbird, Northern Beardless-Tyrannulet, Great Kiskadee, Couch's Kingbird, Scissor-tailed Flycatcher, Green Jay, Long-billed Thrasher, Tropical Parula (rare), Black-throated Gray Warbler (rare), Olive Sparrow, and Altamira Oriole.

Recorded rarities include Crane Hawk, Short-tailed Hawk, Northern Jacana, Curlew Sandpiper, Ruddy Ground-Dove, Mangrove Cuckoo, Green-breasted Mango, Tropical Kingbird, Rose-throated Becard, Clay-colored Robin, White-throated Robin, Golden-crowned Warbler, Yellow-faced Grassquit, Crimson-collared Grosbeak, and Blue Bunting.

The refuge was originally part of a 15-square-mile land grant awarded by Mexico to Benigno Leal in 1834. This ranch was combined with adjacent lands to form the Alamo Tract which, between 1910–1930, was converted mostly to farmland. The southern section though retained its natural riverine forest environment and in 1943 was acquired by the U.S. government to form Santa Ana National Wildlife Refuge.

To reach the refuge from the previous stop, continue west on US-281 (from its intersection with FM-1015) to FM-493 (6.9 miles). Start watching for the sign for Santa Ana National Wildlife Refuge, turning left onto the entrance road (4.6 miles). Stop in at the visitors center (usually open 9 AM–4:30 PM, but hours change seasonally and it is closed some holidays) for maps of the refuge's trail system, checklists of birds, vertebrates, and butterflies, and to take a look at the recent sightings in the log book. User fees will be implemented in early 1999 ($3/car/visit or $10/annual pass). Access is free the first Sunday of each month. Scheduled slide shows about Santa Ana NWR and the Wildlife Corridor are shown in the auditorium. The refuge offers guided nature tours periodically throughout the fall and winter seasons. These tours are free, but reservations are required; call 956/787-3079 for details. *Private vehicle traffic is allowed on the refuge drive throughout the year on Tuesdays and Wednesdays only.* When the drive is closed, you must either walk in (dawn to dusk daily) or take the tram, which is operated by Valley Nature Center (Weslaco), 956/969-2475. The tram runs five times a day; cost is $3/adults and $1/children 12 and under.

Some birders ride their bicycles on the refuge drive when it is closed to automobiles—the drive is currently open to bicycles any time of year from sunrise to sunset. Keep bicycles off the walking trails, park them off the refuge drive, and do not travel the wrong way on the one-way refuge drive. Hiking off the trails is not permitted; there are no picnic facilities; pets *are* allowed, but must be on a leash. For more information: Santa Ana National Wildlife Refuge, Route 2, Box 202A, Alamo, TX 78516; phone 956/787-3079.

To reach Santa Ana National Wildlife Refuge from McAllen, drive east on US-83 for about 10 miles to the FM-907 exit in Alamo. Go south on FM-907 for about 8 miles to where the road intersects US-281, jogging left for 0.3 mile to the Santa Ana NWR entrance road.

Santa Ana NWR consists of 2,088 acres of undisturbed riparian forest, the largest block of such habitat on the Rio Grande between Falcon Dam and Boca Chica. The refuge is covered by a tangle of brush and subtropical trees similar to those found in northeastern Mexico. This native vegetation harbors many unusual plants, mammals, reptiles, birds, and insects. A few of the plants around the visitors center are labeled, but the rest of the flora and fauna offers a real challenge in identification.

Nearly 400 species of birds have been recorded at Santa Ana NWR, a list second only to nearby Laguna Atascosa NWR (407 species). Most of the diversity comes during spring and fall migration, although winter is probably the best birding season here. Soon after you step from your car, you will realize that this is a birder's paradise.

Some of the best birding is along the walking trails not far from the parking lot and headquarters building. Most of the trails offer short walks that can be completed in less than 45 minutes. Just south of the visitors center entrance a trail crosses a bridge over an irrigation canal, passes two ponds (good for Least Grebes and Least Bitterns in spring), and ends at a trailhead. Here you can choose which trail to take. If time is short, choose *Trail A*, which passes through beautiful patches of moss-draped forest of Sugar Hackberry and Cedar Elm on the way to **Willow Lake**. Least Grebe, Neotropic Cormorant, White-faced Ibis, Ringed and Green Kingfishers, and other birds are found at the lake. In winter this is usually a good spot for Anhinga and a sprinkling of ducks, including Cinnamon Teal.

In summer the nest-boxes can be filled with Black-bellied Whistling-Ducks and the cattails usually harbor Least Bitterns. There might be Fulvous Whistling-Ducks straight out on the water or in the impoundment off to the right. Wood Storks usually arrive at Santa Ana NWR by late June and are occasionally seen soaring overhead.

Although Masked Ducks have occurred on Willow Lake in all seasons, your best chance of spotting one is in summer. Masked Duck is an erratic Mexican vagrant, often absent for many years from South Texas before finally reappearing (sometimes in small flocks of three to five individuals). Their presence in the Valley often coincides with wet years. There are perhaps a half dozen refuge records in the past twenty years.

In spring, scan the overhanging brush around the lake for flycatchers and warblers. Santa Ana is one of the Valley's best spots for finding MacGillivray's Warbler during migration. Listen for the "bouncing-ball" call of Olive Sparrow or the melodic song of Long-billed Thrashers along the forest trail.

Both species can be found in the leaf litter or in the thick tangle. Also listen for White-tipped Doves—their soft resonant cooing resembles the sound made by blowing across a bottle mouth. All three species are much more easily heard than seen.

As you walk along the lakeshore, you come to three observation points (two decks and a blind). Birds you might have seen along Trail A up to this point include Plain Chachalaca, Common Ground-Dove, Golden-fronted and Ladder-backed Woodpeckers, Brown-crested Flycatcher (summer), Couch's Kingbird (summer), Green Jay, Carolina and House (winter) Wrens, and Hooded (summer) and Altamira Orioles. In winter the tall trees periodically come alive with sounds of mixed-species flocks consisting mostly of Blue-headed Vireos, Tufted (Black-crested) Titmice, Ruby-crowned Kinglets, Blue-gray Gnatcatchers, and Orange-crowned Warblers. You might also find Eastern Phoebe working the forest edge. Occasionally, Golden-crowned Kinglet, Tropical Parula, and Black-throated Gray Warbler can be found as well. In the early 1990s a Virginia's Warbler spent most of the winter in the vicinity of the trailhead, providing the only winter record of this species for Texas.

Each of the three lake-observation points provides excellent views of the water and shoreline. Just past the third observation point (deck), Trail A turns away from the lake and returns to the trailhead, but you will notice an unimproved trail to the right (notice the small gap in the concrete curb). This connects with Trails B and C, past "two reedy sections" of Willow Lake with variable water levels. (Be sure to go right at the fork where you see the B/C Trail marker). As you come to a small pond on the left, you will be approaching the old manager's residence. The small pond is good for Green Kingfisher. Groove-billed Ani and Altamira Oriole can usually be found somewhere nearby during summer. In winter keep a eye open for Rose-throated Becard—there have been at least two recent sightings in the area. Most sightings of this species in Texas have been of females. Becards formerly nested at the refuge but have not done so for many years.

The **old manager's residence** has been torn down, together with related buildings but the gravel parking lot will probably remain. When walking along the narrow concrete path through the flowering shrubs you may notice a plaque commemorating the former site as a registered natural landmark. The red-flowering shrimp plants near the plaque often draw Buff-bellied Hummingbirds year round, Ruby-throated Hummingbirds in migration, and Rufous Hummingbirds in winter. Long-billed Thrashers and Olive Sparrows can often be heard scratching about the leaf litter in the surrounding area.

Some years Groove-billed Anis and Altamira Orioles have nested in trees surrounding the parking lot. This area of tall trees is good for mixed-species flocks in winter, warblers and other passerines in migration, and occasionally a Clay-colored Robin. Tropical Parulas have nested in the moss-draped Texas Ebony and Cedar Elms; they are most easily located when singing during the breeding season. The best spots to find them in spring and summer seem to be on Resaca Trail and the north end of Vireo Trail. Tropical Parulas can show up at any season, especially in winter, when they quietly move with mixed-species flocks. Some winters, temperate species like Cassin's Vireo, Carolina Chickadee, and Red-breasted Nuthatch have made rare appearances. Also, look for Winter Wren along nearby walking trails during the winter months.

The area around the old manager's residence can be good for birds of prey. Hook-billed Kites and Gray Hawks are occasionally seen soaring overhead. In winter, several raptor species may be in the area, including Sharp-shinned, Cooper's, Harris's (year round), Red-shouldered, and Red-tailed Hawks and Merlin. During hawk migration, which peaks in late March and mid-October, look for kettles of Broad-winged and Swainson's Hawks as well as Mississippi Kites. Occasionally a Zone-tailed Hawk is spotted among the migrating Turkey Vultures.

This route to the old manager's residence will have led you through a selection of fine birding areas. From this site, you have several options: The shortest way back to the visitors center is along the main road which returns to the levee. Many of the woodland species seen previously on the walking trail can be found along the way. Also check the wires for Couch's Kingbird and Scissor-tailed Flycatcher, especially from March through September.

The levee road is the best vantage point for viewing migrating hawks and it is here that spring and fall hawk-watches take place. This is a good spot to see Harris's Hawks or look for resident specialties such as Hook-billed Kite and Gray Hawk. In winter you might see Sharp-shinned, Cooper's, Red-shouldered, and Red-tailed Hawks and Northern Harrier. Undoubtedly, the rarest raptor seen from the levee was the Crane Hawk. This first ABA-Area record delighted (and occasionally frustrated) hundreds of birders from 20 December 1987 through 9 April 1988.

The big hawk show comes from late March through mid-April when the Broad-winged Hawks migrate. They often come by the thousands to rest and roost in the trees. From the levee in the morning or evening, you can see huge kettles forming. On 27 March 1976 an estimated 100,000 Broad-winged Hawks passed over the refuge.

Amidst the soaring Turkey Vultures, Mississippi Kites, and Broad-winged and Swainson's Hawks, are Ospreys, Swallow-tailed Kites (rare), dark-phase Broad-winged Hawks, and the occasional Merlin or Peregrine Falcon.

After returning to the visitors center, it is pleasant to relax at the benches overlooking the feeding stations. Here you can get close-up views of Plain Chachalacas, White-tipped Doves, Buff-bellied Hummingbirds (summer), and Green Jays. Keep alert to the possibility of vagrant hummingbirds—Green Violet-ear (summer), Green-breasted Mango (fall), and Broad-billed Hummingbird (winter) have been recorded in the area.

White-tipped Doves are also found out on the trails where they prefer to walk rather than fly. When these chunky birds do take to the air, they usually fly low through the forest. On the other hand, a Red-billed Pigeon flashes across at tree-top level, resembling a dark falcon. Red-billed Pigeons are rarely seen at Santa Ana NWR except in late spring and summer. The best place to look for them is along Vireo Trail toward the river.

From the old manager's residence, you can reach the photography blind by taking the trail south of the parking lot. The refuge is no longer putting bird seed out, so there is nothing attracting birds to this site. Many birders choose to walk out to nearby **Pintail Lake**, where the birding is usually good.

Pintail Lake is found directly across the road on *Trail C*. While walking the trail, you may hear the raucous cries of Great Kiskadees or the quiet rattle of a low-perching Green Kingfisher. Green Kingfishers can be seen in several areas around the lake, especially at the eastern end of the complex. Also look for Eastern Phoebe (winter), Vermilion Flycatcher (winter), and Couch's Kingbird (summer) on exposed perches bordering the lake. There is at least one winter record of Tropical Kingbird at Santa Ana NWR (March 1995, Pintail Lake). This species may be expanding westward in the Valley from its Cameron County stronghold, so keep your eyes peeled.

Spring is the best time to look for breeding-plumaged Glossy Ibis amidst the many White-faced Ibises at Pintail Lake. There is only a brief period from April through June when their distinctive facial pattern becomes visible. The surrounding vegetation is also a likely spot to find Groove-billed Anis during the breeding season. Several rarities have been discovered here in recent years, including Northern Jacanas (both immature and adult) and Curlew Sandpiper (two spring records).

Least Grebes can usually be located on the main impoundment at Pintail Lake, however, in some years they can be hard to come by. Look for King and Virginia Rails, Sora, Purple Gallinule (summer), Sedge (rare) and Marsh Wrens (winter), and Common Yellowthroat in the cattails. Depending on season and water level, you can find a variety of ducks, waders, and shorebirds.

The open area around the lake provides a good vantage for viewing soaring Hook-billed Kites or Gray Hawks. If you happen to chance upon either of these raptors, consider yourself very fortunate for these birds are notoriously difficult to find—unless, of course, you are not looking for them. One is more likely to see a White-tailed Kite or a Harris's Hawk. Check the log book in the visitors center for recent sightings.

While birding in the old manager's residence/Pintail Lake area, keep an eye out for Short-tailed Hawk, a rare Mexican visitor to South Texas. This species was first documented in Texas in July 1989 (Santa Margarita Ranch), yet has been found almost every other year since in the Valley. All seven Texas records have occurred between March and October. Of the three Santa Ana records, two were found near Pintail Lake.

If time allows, you should attempt walking all of *Trails A and B*. One of the best spots for Clay-colored Robin in recent years has been on *Trail B*, between the two small bridges overlooking a narrow water channel. Almost unbelievably, two Clay-colored Robins were joined by two White-throated Robins here in March 1998. (There was also a pair of White-throated Robins at Bentsen-Rio Grande Valley State Park during the same period.) White-throated Robin is a Mexican species that is extremely rare in the United States. Before the boon of 1998, this species had been documented only once in the United States (Laguna Vista, Cameron County, in February 1990).

Green Kingfishers often fish along this canal. Before reaching the bridges, *Trail B* passes through large stands of prickly pear cactus. In this arid scrub, look for Cactus Wren, an occasional Pyrrhuloxia, and Altamira Oriole. There have been at least four winter records for Golden-crowned Warbler at Santa Ana NWR since 1984 and most, if not all, have come from along *Trail B*. A first U.S. record for Yellow-faced Grassquit also occurred in this general area in late January 1990. Other Mexican rarities to show up at Santa Ana are Ruddy Ground-Dove (two winter records), Mangrove Cuckoo (August 1982), Varied Thrush, Gray-crowned Yellowthroat (March 1989), and Blue Bunting (four fall/winter records).

Trail B joins the Terrace Trail, which leads to Cattail Lake. It is a nice hike—but a fairly long one. Many choose to drive there (when the main road is open to vehicles). Least Grebes and, on rare occasions, Masked Ducks have shown up at the lake. In summer look for Purple Gallinule and Least Bittern along the banks. Common Pauraques sometimes flush from the shaded thickets on the south corner of the pond, where you might also encounter a Giant Toad. Hook-billed Kites and Gray Hawks are occasionally spotted in the area, especially in summer. A Short-tailed Hawk was recently found (summer) on the Terrace Trail near Cattail Lake.

Keep a look out for wild Muscovy Ducks at Cattail, Willow, or Pintail Lakes during late spring and summer. Although very rare in the mid-Valley, this bird is turning up with higher frequency in recent years. The ducks may be expanding their range downriver from their Falcon Dam-area stronghold.

After spring and summer rains, frogs and toads are abundant about the lakes. Most will be Rio Grande Leopard Frogs, Giant Toads, and Gulf Coast Toads; however, you could find Great Plains Narrowmouth Toad, Sheep Frogs, and Mexican Tree Frogs as well.

The most common turtle at the refuge is the Red-eared Slider Turtle of mud-bottomed ponds and sluggish streams. It can be identified by a bright red stripe behind the eye, which is easily seen because these large turtles often crawl out on rocks and logs to bask. However, the red stripe fades in older individuals. There are two other turtles here. Yellow Mud Turtle is uncommon in ponds, canals, and streams with mud bottoms, but it may be missed because it is mainly nocturnal and it does not crawl out of the water to bask. It is a small (5"), dull, unmarked turtle with a strong musky odor. If its head is sticking out of the water, you may note that it has a yellow throat but no stripes. The large pancake-like Spiny Softshell may be found in refuge lakes and along the Rio Grande.

You may also find an endangered Texas Tortoise, which was once fairly common throughout the dry, brushy areas of South Texas. It has clubfeet and a high rounded shell. Young tortoises have a yellow square in the center of each large scute.

There are no rattlesnakes at Santa Ana NWR. The only venomous snake is the non-aggressive Texas Coral Snake. One of the most commonly seen snakes is the endangered Texas Indigo Snake, often referred to as a Black Snake. This is the longest snake in North America, occasionally exceeding eight feet. Other commonly encountered snakes include Great Plains Rat Snake, Diamondback Water Snake, Bull Snake, Eastern Checkered Garter Snake, and Gulf Coast Ribbon Snake.

To explore the refuge you should drive the one-way, 7-mile road (when it is open for vehicles). Bicycles are allowed year round and are a good way to cover the entire road. In late spring and early summer, look for Hook-billed Kite, Gray Hawk, Northern Beardless-Tyrannulet, and Tropical Parula.

There are many places to stop along the road, nearly all of them worthwhile. The cactus patch behind the Old Spanish Cemetery hides a pair of Cactus Wrens and sometimes a Greater Roadrunner. Many years ago, Rose-throated Becards tried to nest near the big tree across the road. You may not find the becards, but you will see the remains of what was once the largest Texas Ebony Tree in the United States.

Much of the area is covered by jungle-like thickets, which can be difficult to bird by car. To get a feel for the refuge, try hiking some of the trails, such as Vireo Trail. From the head of Vireo Trail it is a one-mile hike to the Rio Grande. *Caution:* This trail is no longer being regularly maintained by refuge staff. Unless you plan to do a lot of walking, it is advisable to attempt this hike on Tuesday or Wednesday (when the refuge drive is open to vehicles). The closest parking lot is at the Old Spanish Cemetery (0.2 mile). Be sure to take along a trail map, and bring plenty of water.

One of the hardest-to-find of the permanent residents is Northern Beardless-Tyrannulet. This bird definitely follows the rule that *the longer the name, the smaller the bird.* And what a nondescript little bird it is! The best field marks on this tiny pale-gray flycatcher are its faint eye line, tiny bill, and erectile crest. It is best located by voice, a plaintive *dee-dee-dee.* The bird forages at all tree levels and is usually seen in an upright posture. Summer is the best season to find tyrannulets, though males may begin singing on territory as early as March. This bird has been found in thickets all over the refuge—along the Vireo Trail, the Owl Trail, the Highland Trail, and near the old manager's residence.

With an exciting mix of Rio Grande specialties, migrants, and potential rarities from Mexico, Santa Ana NWR is a must stop on any birder's visit to the Valley.

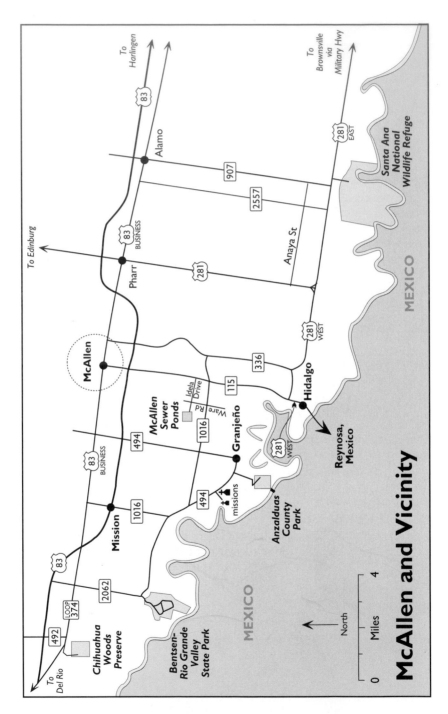

McAllen and Vicinity

MCALLEN

Many birders use McAllen as their trip headquarters. The city of 80,000 is named after John McAllen, a Scot who arrived in the Valley in the early 1850s. The town itself was not founded until 1909, a few years after the arrival of the Missouri-Pacific Railroad. At that time, commerce began to grow around citrus and vegetable crops.

Today, McAllen has an airport, plenty of motels and restaurants, and is a quick drive from either Santa Ana NWR or Bentsen-Rio Grande Valley State Park. There is good birding in town at the McAllen Sewer Ponds and in the residential areas. McAllen is home to the Texas Tropics Nature Festival, held each spring at the Holiday Inn Civic Center off US-83.

Your target birds in the vicinity include Least Grebe, White-faced Ibis, Black-bellied and Fulvous Whistling-Ducks, Cinnamon Teal, White-rumped and Baird's Sandpipers, Green Parakeets, Red-crowned Parrots, Burrowing Owl, Buff-bellied Hummingbird, Scissor-tailed Flycatcher, Couch's Kingbird, Sprague's Pipit, Hooded Oriole, and Lesser Goldfinch. Rarities such as Glossy Ibis, Clay-colored Robin, and Crimson-collared Grosbeak have been found locally.

MCALLEN SEWER PONDS

When you drive out the entrance road at Santa Ana NWR, turn left (west) onto US-281 to its junction with FM-2557 (1.8 miles). A Burrowing Owl has been seen nearby in recent winters; to look for Burrowing Owl, turn right onto FM-2557 to dirt Anaya Street (1.0 mile). Turn left and begin scanning the crop fields and dirt mounds for the owl. You should check these fields for Sprague's Pipits during winter. Burrowing Owls are very hard to find in South Texas, though they are occasionally chanced upon along the back roads. Another recent spot for Burrowing Owl is near the intersection of FM-88 and FM-1422 north of Edcouch-Elsa; see map on page 69. For the latest on Burrowing Owls, check with refuge staff at Santa Ana NWR or the park host at Bentsen State Park. Directions to Burrowing Owl sites might be posted in the log book at Bentsen.

Back on US-281, you will soon see where the highway heads north (right) to Pharr (2.1 miles). Instead of turning right to Pharr, however, go straight ahead on US-281-West toward Hidalgo and Reynosa. Go past FM-336 (3.2 miles) to the end of the road (1.1 mile) in Hidalgo. Turn right onto Spur 115. (If you turn left, you wind up in Reynosa, Mexico). To get to the **McAllen Sewer Ponds**, pass FM-1016 (2.8 miles) and turn left at the first signal (1.0 mile) onto Idela Drive. The McAllen Sewer Ponds begin at South 37th (1.3 miles), where you will find water-filled impoundments off the dikes on the left. Drive up onto the levee that encircles the ponds on your left where the sign welcoming birders is located. (Avoid driving the levee after heavy rains.)

The ponds can be productive at times for ducks, waders, and shorebirds. Least Grebes are sometimes found here, especially in winter and spring. If water levels are high enough, there will usually be a few Black-bellied Whistling-Ducks around. The ponds are best in spring and fall when shorebirds are moving through. This is a good spot to find American Golden-Plover, Hudsonian Godwit (rare), Semipalmated, Western, Least, White-rumped, Baird's, Pectoral, and Stilt Sandpipers, and Wilson's Phalarope. Occasionally Fulvous Whistling-Duck (spring) and Cinnamon Teal (winter) are found somewhere on the ponds; there are also at least two spring sightings of Glossy Ibis (April and May). Water levels and season are important in the abundance and diversity of birds here.

RESIDENTIAL MCALLEN

Like Brownsville and Harlingen, McAllen is another city with parrot roost sites. Every winter Green Parakeets and Red-crowned Parrots roost somewhere in McAllen. Some recent sites have been on the east end of **Dallas Avenue** (in the vicinity of Mockingbird Street) and on the north side of town on **Wisteria Avenue** just west of 10th Street. Other birds found in this latter residential area include Black-bellied Whistling-Duck, Plain Chachalaca, White-tipped Dove, Buff-bellied Hummingbird (summer), Great Kiskadee, Couch's Kingbird (summer), Scissor-tailed Flycatcher, Green Jay, Long-billed and Curve-billed Thrashers, Bronzed Cowbird, Hooded Oriole (summer), and Lesser Goldfinch (uncommon).

Some birders drive up and down North Main Street, north of LaVista, with their car windows open for one hour after sunrise or one hour before sunset to listen for flocks of roosting parrots. However, sites do change from year to year, and it is usually less time-consuming to check the Lower Rio Grande Rare Bird Alert (956/969-2731) for current locations.

During winter you can usually find mixed-species flocks and winter warblers, including Orange-crowned, Nashville (uncommon), Black-and-white (uncommon), Yellow-rumped, and Wilson's. In migration a fair number neotropical migrants and migrating Mississippi Kites and Broad-winged Hawks fly directly over this neighborhood. Some years, Clay-colored Robins show up in this area as well as at the intersection of Fresno and 1st Streets. Although Clay-colored Robins are more likely to occur in winter, they have appeared in spring and summer as well. Also in residential McAllen a pair of Crimson-collared Grosbeaks showed up in the winter of 1985–1986.

ANZALDUAS COUNTY PARK

As you exit the McAllen Sewer Ponds, you will be at the west end of Idela Drive. Head back (east) on Idela Drive to Ware Road (0.5 mile). Turn right (south) and proceed to West Military Highway (FM-1016). Turn right (west) and continue to FM-494 (1.5 miles). Turn left onto FM-494 and drive through Granjeño. As the road turns right (1.4 miles), continue past the cemetery, turning left at the **Anzalduas County Park** and Dam sign (1.5 miles). Proceed to the entrance of the park (0.6 mile). (This entrance road has some sharp, winding curves before it reaches the office). The daily fee is $4/car on Saturday and Sunday; no fee is charged on weekdays.

The best time to visit Anzalduas is on weekdays, when there is no entrance fee and it is less crowded. In winter, check the short, grassy field between the office and the Rio Grande for Sprague's Pipits and Eastern and Western Meadowlarks. The vast majority of meadowlarks found in large winter flocks (especially in shortgrass habitats) are believed to be Westerns. Of course, call note is the best means of separating these very similar species in winter.

Tall trees around the picnic grounds and restrooms can hold Inca Dove, Common Ground-Dove, Golden-fronted and Ladder-backed Woodpeckers, Scissor-tailed Flycatcher, Tufted (Black-crested) Titmouse, and Altamira Oriole. In winter look for Vermilion Flycatcher and mixed-species flocks, including Black-throated Gray Warbler and Tropical Parula. Zone-tailed Hawk, Red-naped Sapsucker, and Clay-colored Robin have made rare winter appearances. In spring look for Summer Tanager and other migrants. Brown-crested Flycatcher, Couch's Kingbird, and Hooded Oriole are a few of the summer residents found at Anzalduas.

Northern Beardless-Tyrannulet and Tropical Parula are very local nesters in the park. During spring, when males are singing, they are more conspicuous than at any other time of year. Breeding records of Clay-colored Robin are extremely rare in the Valley, but recent summer sightings (of paired birds) suggest that nesting may be taking place.

Anzalduas has had its share of Mexican rarities. There is one winter record for Ruddy Ground-Dove from November 1986. Because Ruddy Ground-Doves are frequently found associating with Inca Doves near towns in Mexico, it seems that your chance of spotting one may be as good in a disturbed area as it would be in a wildlife refuge. Two Rose-throated Becards were found at Anzalduas in June 1972, returning the following two summers. Another Rose-throated Becard showed up in January 1990. All recent becard sightings in the Valley have been during the winter season. A Social Flycatcher, which resembles a "little Kiskadee," was seen from mid-March through early April 1990 at the park. Until this sighting Social Flycatcher had not been recorded north of Mexico.

Ringed and Green Kingfishers can be found at several sites along the river, from the boat ramp (near the restrooms) to the clear waters below the dam. In winter sort through waterfowl on the Rio Grande for vagrants, such as Eurasian Wigeon. In the last decade, there have been several records of Eurasian Wigeon in South Texas, mostly in large flocks of American Wigeons.

You can get to the dam from the office by turning left at the stop sign (0.2 mile) and crossing over the levee to the area below the dam (0.7 mile).

Northern Beardless-Tyrannulet has turned up in this section of the park. The wooded area along the fence is the Gabrielson Tract of the Lower Rio Grande Valley National Wildlife Refuge, currently not open to the public. The airspace over the Gabrielson Tract is a good spot to look for soaring Hook-billed Kites at any time of day. Look for their distinctive silhouette—paddle-shaped wings, long banded tail, and large bill.

Hook-billed Kites and other raptors occur anywhere in the park. Like Santa Ana NWR (to the east) and Bentsen State Park (to the west), Anzalduas County Park gets good numbers of migrating raptors in spring and fall. In migration, look for kettles of Mississippi Kites and Broad-winged and Swainson's Hawks along with a sprinkling of other buteos, accipiters, and falcons. Occasionally, Zone-tailed Hawks will turn up in winter or in migration, frequently in the company of Turkey Vultures.

If you go back to the park entrance and walk left (west) down the levee, you will soon come to another section of the refuge, the Madero Tract. This area is not open either, but you can scan it from the road.

Return to FM-494 and turn left. As soon as you pass the big Oblate Monastery (0.8 mile), cross the tracks and turn left onto the first road over the levee (0.2 mile) to tiny La Lomita Mission, founded in 1865 and rebuilt in 1899. It abuts the west end of the refuge tract and has a pleasant little picnic ground.

BENTSEN–RIO GRANDE VALLEY STATE PARK

This park provides the best winter birding in the Lower Valley. Head straight for the famous trailer loop where you should encounter many birds and birders. Plain Chachalacas, White-tipped Doves, Green Jays, Altamira Orioles, and other native birds are attracted to the numerous feeders and water drips set up by the campers. Mexican rarities, including Clay-colored Robin and Blue Bunting, are seen here almost every year. You can bird several different areas at Bentsen, including the trailer loop, two nature trails (one of which overlooks the Rio Grande), and resaca woodlands.

Specialty birds to look for here include Least Grebe, Hook-billed Kite, Plain Chachalaca, White-tipped Dove, Common Pauraque, Buff-bellied Hummingbird, Northern Beardless-Tyrannulet, Great Kiskadee, Green Jay, Long-billed Thrasher, Tropical Parula (rare), Black-throated Gray Warbler (rare), Olive Sparrow, and Altamira Oriole.

Recorded rarities have been Jabiru, Roadside and Short-tailed Hawks, Collared Forest-Falcon, Northern Jacana, Ruddy Ground-Dove, Mottled and Stygian Owls, Broad-billed Hummingbird, Elegant Trogon, Rose-throated Becard, Masked Tityra, Clay-colored and White-throated Robins, Varied Thrush, Crimson-collared Grosbeak, and Blue Bunting.

To reach Bentsen from the previous stop—La Lomita Mission—continue west on FM-494 and FM-1016 (also signed as Military Road) to the curve (0.8 mile). Instead of going right with FM-1016, take the unmarked road straight

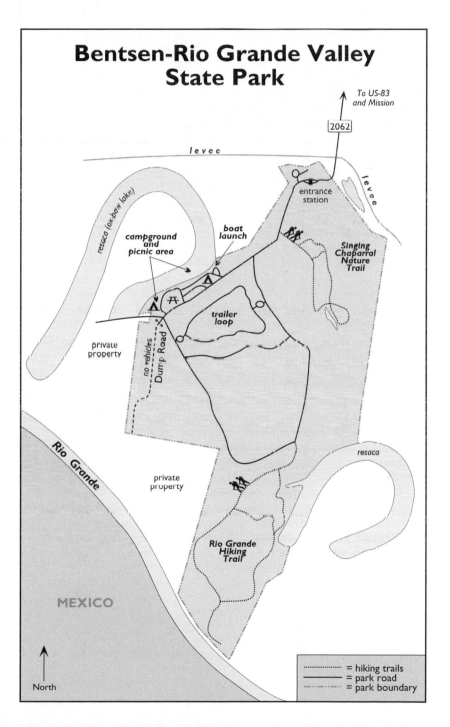

Bentsen-Rio Grande Valley State Park

To US-83
and Mission

2062

levee

levee

resaca (ox-bow lake)

entrance
station

campground
and
picnic area

boat
launch

Singing
Chaparral
Nature
Trail

trailer
loop

private
property

no vehicles
Dump Road

Rio Grande

private
property

resaca

MEXICO

Rio Grande
Hiking
Trail

North

.... = hiking trails
———— = park road
— ·· — ·· — = park boundary

ahead as you cross the railroad tracks. You might check the little pond (1.7 miles) on the left at the stop sign for Least Grebes. Look for soaring Hook-billed Kites on this stretch of road. Continue on to the next stop sign (1.6 miles) at FM-2062 (Bentsen-Palm Drive). Turn left and drive directly into **Bentsen-Rio Grande Valley State Park** (0.2 mile). Given its long, hyphenated name, most birders just call the park "Bentsen."

You can also reach Bentsen State Park from US-83 just west of Mission. When you enter the small of town of Palmview, look for the sign to Bentsen-Rio Grande Valley State Park (at FM-2062). Turn left (south) onto FM-2062 and proceed straight to the park entrance (3.5 miles).

The fee is $2/person/day, plus fees for camping and hot showers. For further information, contact Bentsen-Rio Grande Valley State Park, PO Box 988, Mission, TX 78572; for rates and reservations, call 512/389-8900; for information only, call 800/792-1112; to reach the park staff call 956/585-1107; web site: http://www.tpwd.state.tx.us.

Before entering the park you can turn right and drive along the levee if you wish. This is a fine area for hawkwatching, and the first half-mile has sometimes been a good spot for Hook-billed Kites and Red-billed Pigeons (in summer). During winter, the adjacent farm fields should be scanned for Sprague's Pipits. At dusk, the levee road can produce Common Pauraques.

The 587-acre park is one of the finest in the state park system. It is on land donated in 1944 to the state by Senator Lloyd Bentsen's parents. Much of the original subtropical vegetation has been preserved, and it abounds with birds. This is a nice spot to camp, although it is crowded on weekends, particularly in winter. It is also packed during the Easter holidays.

The birds here are about the same as at Santa Ana (over 290 species have been recorded in the park), but are generally easier to see. Around the campground, picnic area, and trailer loop, the well-fed birds are fairly tame. The inner road loop consists of trailer sites and picnic tables where many "winter Texans" feed the birds. There you can get close looks at Plain Chachalaca, White-tipped Dove, Golden-fronted and Ladder-backed Woodpeckers, Green Jay, Tufted (Black-crested) Titmouse, and Altamira Oriole. Other birds you might see on the loop include Harris's Hawk, Red-billed Pigeon (rare, summer), Groove-billed Ani (summer), Eastern Screech-Owl (daytime roost), Northern Beardless-Tyrannulet (rare), Ash-throated Flycatcher (spring/fall), Great Crested Flycatcher (spring/fall), Brown-crested Flycatcher (summer), Couch's Kingbird (summer), Scissor-tailed Flycatcher, White-eyed Vireo, Golden-crowned Kinglet (rare, winter), Long-billed Thrasher, Yellow-rumped Warbler (winter), Bronzed Cowbird, Pine Siskin (irregular, fall/winter/spring), and American Goldfinch (winter). Some notable winter birds found along the trailer loop in recent winters include Western Tanager, Black-headed Grosbeak, Dickcissel, Common Grackle, and Audubon's Oriole. Although Audubon's Oriole is locally common on the river around Falcon Dam, it is rarely encountered east of Bentsen.

The inner loop is also a good spot for mixed-species flocks in winter, including Blue-headed Vireo, Tufted (Black-crested) Titmouse, Ruby-crowned Kinglet, Blue-gray Gnatcatcher, and Orange-crowned and Yellow-rumped Warblers. Sometimes Nashville, Black-throated Gray, Black-throated Green, Black-and-white, and Wilson's Warblers move with the flock as well. Few things get a birder's heart racing like sighting a Tropical Parula, which stands out as the rarest and most colorful member of the mixed-species flock. Tropical Parulas are often seen in the tops of tall native trees draped with Spanish moss.

Across from trailer site #22 is a sign to Eagle Pond, a small concrete bird bath at the end of a short (100 yard) nature trail. On the way to Eagle Pond, a small side-trail to the right leads to a photo blind. In winter the feeders and water drip at the photo blind attract Plain Chachalaca, White-tipped Dove, Golden-fronted Woodpecker, Green Jay, Tufted (Black-crested) Titmouse, Northern Cardinal, Orange-crowned Warbler, Olive and Lincoln's Sparrows, and Indigo Bunting. A pair of Blue Buntings has been seen periodically at the photo blind as well as at the nearby trailer sites. In March 1996 Texas' first Ruddy Quail-Dove showed up at the photo blind, delighting hundreds of birders during its five-day stay.

With large numbers of birders concentrated along the trailer loop, it's no wonder that so many rarities have been found here. In addition to the regular rarities, such as Clay-colored Robin and Blue Bunting, the trailer loop has produced some outstanding birds: Roadside Hawk (October 1982–February 1983), Short-tailed Hawk (8 March 1994), Broad-billed Hummingbird (23 June 1962), Elegant Trogon (14 September 1977), Rose-throated Becard (winter), Masked Tityra (first U.S. record, February/March 1990), White-throated Robin (second ABA-Area record, February/March 1998), Varied Thrush (December 1990), and Crimson-collared Grosbeak (November 1987).

Two other good birding spots are within walking distance of the trailer loop—the "dump road" and the campground/picnic area along the resaca. The entrance to the dump road is just across the street at campsite #142 at the open gate. This road offers another place to search for parulas, tyrannulets and other specialties. The primitive campsites along the resaca hold mixed-species flocks in winter and also occasionally attract a Northern Beardless-Tyrannulet or Tropical Parula. The tall trees along the resaca can also be good for migrants. At the boat ramp, you may see Great Kiskadee, one or more of the three kingfishers, Osprey, or even Peregrine Falcon. It was from this boat ramp that many fortunate birders saw North America's first Collared Forest-Falcon (22 January–24 February 1994).

If time allows, the nature trails are worth walking. The Singing Chaparral Nature Trail (1-mile loop) traverses thorn scrub woodlands (chaparral or *matorral*). Although the birds are shyer and less numerous when compared to those frequenting the trailer loop, you might see Hook-billed Kite (rare), Harris's Hawk, Red-billed Pigeon (summer), Common Ground-Dove, Groove-billed Ani (summer), Northern Beardless-Tyrannulet, Ash-throated (spring) and Brown-crested (summer) Flycatchers, White-eyed Vireo, Black-tailed Gnatcatcher (rare), Hermit Thrush (winter), Long-billed Thrasher, Yellow-rumped Warbler (winter), and mixed-species flocks (winter).

Rio Grande Hiking Trail, located on the outer loop of Park Road 43, is a 2-mile loop to the Rio Grande. The trail passes through a variety of habitats—from slightly elevated areas of dry, sandy soil where you will see prickly-pear cactus and mesquite to the low marshy areas along the resaca and river where willows and cattails grow. The vegetation and birds found here are similar to those on the Singing Chaparral Nature Trail. Notable birds found on this trail include Hook-billed Kite, Gray Hawk (especially in the vicinity of the resaca), Elf Owl, and Northern Beardless-Tyrannulet. Although very rarely seen, both Lazuli and Varied Buntings occurred in recent years along this trail.

By midday, when the birding has quieted down throughout the park, check the outer loop (Park Road 43) for soaring raptors. One may see Hook-billed and White-tailed Kites, Gray, Harris's, and White-tailed Hawks year round, Northern Harrier, Sharp-shinned, Cooper's, Red-shouldered, and Red-tailed Hawks in winter, and Mississippi Kite and Broad-winged and Swainson's Hawks in migration. Although most Red-tailed Hawks seen in winter are of the eastern race, you might find Harlan's and western forms as well. A rare Short-tailed Hawk was discovered near the Rio Grande Hiking Trail entrance on 27 April 1998. Other likely spots for soaring birds of prey are the field at the end of the dump road and the agricultural field outside the park on FM-2062. The latter can be especially good during harvesting or burning.

Another chief attraction at Bentsen is the night birds. Barn Owl, Eastern Screech-Owl, Great Horned and Elf Owls (summer), Common Nighthawk (summer), and Common Pauraque can be found. During migration, you might see Lesser Nighthawk, Common Poorwill, Chuck-will's-widow, and Whip-poor-will. The best spot for Elf Owls of late has been along the park road near the entrance to the Rio

UNUSUAL OWLS AT BENTSEN

While driving on a road outside Bentsen State Park in February 1983, an astute observer noticed a road-killed owl that he did not recognize. After placing a coin next to the owl for scale, he photographed it and sent the slides to the Texas Bird Records Committee. The pictures represent the first ABA-Area record for Mottled Owl, a Mexican species found commonly about 200 miles south of the border.

An even more amazing sighting was that of a live, cooperative Stygian Owl found on 26 December 1996 near the entrance to the Rio Grande Hiking Trail. This dark, stocky version of Long-eared Owl had not even been considered as a potential vagrant to South Texas; it nearest range is several hundred miles south in central Verzcruz, Mexico. Incredibly, another record of Stygian Owl has recently surfaced—this a December 1994 photograph incorrectly identified until news of the 1996 discovery prompted

Grande Hiking Trail. The best strategy for finding this owl is to ask around for directions to any known nest cavities and wait there until dusk, when the tiny owls usually begin to vocalize.

Common Pauraques come out to sit on the roadways as soon as darkness falls. The glow of their bright orange eye shine is easy to pick out as you drive the park road slowly. On very dark nights they may quit feeding after a very short time, but they start again just before dawn, a good time to see them.

Owls may frequent the roadways, but most often stick to the trees. Eastern Screech Owls often sit around the lights outside the restrooms to catch insects. Check the log book or the park host for the latest on daytime screech-owl roosts. They prefer cracks and cavities in mesquite trees. Great Horned Owls like the open areas along the river or at the edge of the farmlands. Barn Owls can sometimes be found perching on the tall white irrigation pipes on FM-2062 or on the levee road heading east towards Anzalduas. In some winters, a Long-eared Owl is discovered at the park.

Also near Bentsen State Park a Jabiru was found in August 1985. This majestic long-legged wader is the New World's largest flying bird, reaching a height of five feet. It is so tall that it would shrink a nearby White Ibis to the size of a sandpiper. This species is a post-breeding vagrant, having turned up five times in the state between July and September.

CHIHUAHUA WOODS PRESERVE

The Nature Conservancy of Texas' new 243-acre wildlife preserve, located just 2.5 miles from Bentsen State Park, allows birders a unique Valley wilderness experience. The preserve is open only during daylight hours and access is walk-in only. You are welcome to explore, but please stay on obvious roads or trails. A 1-mile self-guided nature trail leads through Tamaulipan thorn scrub vegetation that is so typical of the Valley. Be aware that cactus and thorns are abundant; sturdy leather shoes or boots are advised. No restroom facilities are available, but Bentsen State Park is just a few minutes away.

To get to **Chihuahua Woods Preserve** from Bentsen-Rio Grande Valley State Park, drive north on FM-2062 to Business US-83 (2.7 miles). Turn left (west) and proceed to where the highway curves right (2.0 miles). At the curve, go straight onto the blacktop road that parallels the railroad tracks for approximately 0.1 mile. Where the blacktop crosses the tracks, the preserve entrance is on your left.

Directions to Chihuahua Woods from McAllen: Take US-83 west of Mission to FM-492 (at stop light). Turn left (south) onto FM-492 and go about 1 mile to to Business US-83 (at blinking light). Turn right (west) and go to the point where Business US-83 curves right (0.8 mile). Follow above directions.

The birds found at Chihuahua Woods are similar to those found at Bentsen-Rio Grande Valley State Park. On an early morning walk in the preserve you should easily tally Plain Chachalaca, Common Ground-Dove, White-tipped Dove, Great Kiskadee, Green Jay, Olive Sparrow, and Altamira Oriole. Notable sightings include Hook-billed Kite, White-tailed Hawk, Peregrine Falcon (winter), Red-billed Pigeon (summer), Groove-billed Ani, Northern Beardless-Tyrannulet, Clay-colored Robin, and Tropical Parula.

This park contains a desert component (like Falcon Dam), which is reflected by western species such as Ash-throated Flycatcher, Black-tailed Gnatcatcher, Sage Thrasher (winter), and Black-throated Sparrow. Chihuahua Woods Preserve is still developing wildlife lists, so details of any sightings that you make would be appreciated. If you take photographs on the preserve, The Nature Conservancy would appreciate donation of any culled slides for use in their brochures and slide programs.

Walk-in access (parties are limited to six adults) is permitted during daylight hours only. Any other access must be requested from TNC's South Texas Land Steward at 956/580-4241. No camping or overnighting is allowed. *Do not use taped calls to attract wildlife.*

For more information, contact The Nature Conservancy, South Texas Office, PO Box 6281, McAllen, TX 78502-6281; phone/fax: 956/580-4241.

NORTH OF EDINBURG

For those with extra time to spend, a trip to the farmlands north and east of Edinburg might produce a list of different birds. In winter there may be Sandhill Crane, Ross's Goose, wintering waterfowl, White-tailed Hawk, Crested Caracara, Green Kingfisher, Vermilion Flycatcher, Couch's Kingbird, Scissor-tailed Flycatcher, Curve-billed Thrasher, Pyrrhuloxia, and a variety of winter sparrows.

From TX-107 in Edinburg, go north on US-281. (See map on following page.) Opposite FM-2812 (6.3 miles) you can reach Edinburg Lake (Retama Reservoir) by turning left onto a road which soon (0.3 mile) turns to gravel and leads to a T-intersection (1.0 mile). Turn left and go up the bank on the right (0.3 mile). This lake is at its best in winter, when you may find ducks and shorebirds. Despite the signs, birders can walk the dikes during daylight hours. Alternately, you can continue on the road as it swings right to a parking lot at the road's end (0.2 mile). From here you can walk up onto the dike.

A Northern Jacana lingered along the road to the right (north) at the T from mid-November to late December 1981. The cattail-lined slough here is spring-fed. Masked Ducks have been found here occasionally. Check these areas for Green Kingfishers.

Continuing up US-281 to FM-490 (4.3 miles) turn right toward Hargill. The patches of mesquite can offer Vermilion (winter) and Ash-throated (spring) Flycatchers, Curve-billed Thrasher, Pyrrhuloxia, and Painted Bunting (summer). A few little ponds in the area are good for shorebirds and have even produced Masked Duck.

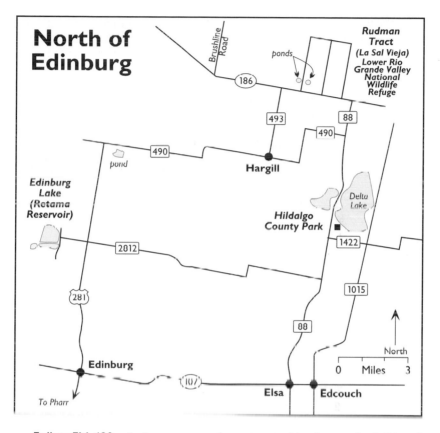

North of Edinburg

Follow FM-490 as it zigzags across the area, watching for ponds. At Hargill (8.0 miles) turn left onto FM-493 until it reaches TX-186. Turn right here to a dirt road on the left (1.0 mile) where you turn. Bird the pasture on the left to the small pond (0.5 mile); another pond is just across the road. Both are good for ducks and Vermilion Flycatchers in winter; Crested Caracaras frequent the fields nearby. Continue a total of three miles, then turn right and continue a mile. You are now birding the Rudman Tract of the Lower Rio Grande Valley National Wildlife Refuge.

There are three county roads here, each three miles long and a mile apart, with a county road along the north, and TX-186 along the south. The **Rudman Tract** is excellent for hawks and winter sparrows. Among the raptors, look for White-tailed Kite, Harris's and White-tailed Hawks, and Crested Caracara. The easternmost road in this complex is just one-half mile west of FM-88.

Another nearby area worth checking is the La Sal del Rey and La Sal Vieja salt lakes. This is a LRGVNWR plot viewable from TX-186 and perimeter roads. Continuing west on TX-186, you will pass the Tres Corrales Ranch ponds. These and other nearby ponds can have a Ross's Goose hidden among the numerous Snow Geese. Soon after you pass these ponds, you come to a rest area on your left. Immediately past that is a small gravel road on the right. This is known as Brushline Road and it bisects the 5,000-acre La Sal del Rey Tract. Although this tract is closed (except during Christmas Bird Counts), this road and other open roads that connect to it are fair game for birders. This area is good for raptors and winter sparrows. In migration the weedy fields can hold Blue Grosbeaks, Indigo Buntings, Dickcissels, and a variety of other birds. *Do not enter any gated roads even if the gates are open.*

To reach Delta Lake, backtrack on TX-186 (heading east) to FM-88. Turn right and proceed to Delta Lake (4.5 miles). The lake can be good for ducks and shorebirds. Continue 0.4 mile and turn left into Hidalgo County Park, open dawn to dusk, for more ducks and migrant passerines. An Elegant Trogon was observed here for a week in January 1990.

At FM-2812 (3.7 miles) turn right (west) to check more fields and ponds. At US-281 (11.5 miles), turn left and return to Edinburg (6.0 miles). Within the city of Edinburg you can find some of the resident specialties in wooded or brushy areas. In summer you might see Chimney Swifts (uncommon nesters) and Couch's and Western Kingbirds. Blue Jay, which is accidental in the Valley, has also been found in town. Edinburg was the site of the 2nd state record of Fork-tailed Flycatcher, discovered 4 February 1961. Amazingly, three Band-rumped Storm-Petrels, strictly an offshore species, made landfall in Edinburg on June 1954, surely the result of storm activity in the Gulf of Mexico.

Red-billed Pigeon
Narca Moore-Craig

UPRIVER TO THE PECOS

LA JOYA

After leaving the citrus groves of the coastal plain at Mission, you may hardly notice the rise in elevation except for the increasingly scrubby vegetation and the ridge-forming Goliad sandstone. The hard, pebbly, gray sandstone and pinkish claystones continue to Falcon Dam, where the ridges and mesas become quite prominent, especially on the side of the highway away from the river.

In this more arid land you'll be looking for a new suite of birds: Crested Caracara, Scaled Quail, Mountain Plover, Cave Swallow, Verdin, Cactus Wren, Cassin's, Brewer's, Black-throated, and White-crowned Sparrows, and Pyrrhuloxia. With great luck you'll spot a Ruddy Ground-Dove.

Depart McAllen on westbound US-83. By the time you reach La Joya (11 miles from Mission, and an infamous speed-trap), you will have entered the arid, hilly brushlands—or chaparral country—which covers much of the coastal plains below the Edwards Plateau. For over 200 miles to the north and west the land is poor, alkaline, and marginal in productivity. Previously overgrazed, the region recently has been converted to pastures and irrigated fields.

For birders who do not plan to travel farther west than the McAllen/Mission area, it is still possible to see some of the desert birds fairly close at hand. As you leave La Joya, the road curves to the left and goes down a slight grade. In the middle of the curve, FM-2221 heads north. At a stop sign, this road turns right (6.0 miles from US-83). Instead of turning right, continue straight down a caliche (and very dusty) road, which goes on for another two miles before you need to turn around. Check the field to your right for Mountain Plovers, which have overwintered here in recent years. This road—dubbed "sparrow road" by Valley birders—can be really jumping in winter. Cassin's, Chipping, Clay-colored, Brewer's (rare), Vesper, Lark (usually abundant), Black-throated (rare), Savannah, Grasshopper, Le Conte's (rare), Lincoln's, and White-crowned Sparrows all have been seen along the barbed-wire fence or in the trees along the road. In the thickets of mesquite, acacia, and cactus look for Scaled Quail, Northern Bobwhite, Common Ground-Dove, Greater Roadrunner, Verdin, Cactus Wren, Black-tailed Gnatcatcher (rare), Curve-billed Thrasher, occasionally Lark Bunting, and Pyrrhuloxia (common). Birding is best in the early morning. In warm seasons you might encounter a rattlesnake if you decide to wander into the brush.

Farther west on US-83 is the small town of Sullivan City. Watch for a roadside sign for a wash called Arroyo Salado (9.6 miles from FM-2221). Cave Swallows nest under the culvert here, and can be seen in the area at almost any time of year. (A severe winter freeze might push the swallows out, however).

Many of the towns along the highway west of Mission date back to the 1750s, when Spanish General José de Escandon established settlements along the Rio Grande, such as Carnestolendas, located on the north bank of the river near present-day Rio Grande City. Later on, both Rio Grande City and Roma-Los Saenz were busy steamboat ports. For much of the last half of the nineteenth century this area (and much of the Rio Grande Valley as well) was the scene of cattle raids and land disputes comparable to the classic days of the Wild West. Modern-day civilization has slowly crept into the region, yet much of this frontier character remains to this day.

As you continue west into Starr County, you will notice an increase in the number of ravens and hawks. American Crows do not occur in this area, so any crow-sized bird is likely to be a Chihuahuan Raven—although you may need to look at a lot of them before the wind ruffles their neck feathers enough to expose the white below. Harris's Hawk is the most common buteo for much of the year, but you may also see lots of Red-tails in winter. Also, keep an eye out along the highway for Northern Harrier, Sharp-shinned, Cooper's, and White-tailed Hawks, Crested Caracara, and American Kestrel. Although rarely seen in the area, Ferruginous Hawk should be watched for—some winters they move into South Texas in higher numbers. During spring and fall, you can expect anything.

This region is on the main migration route for Mississippi Kites and Broad-winged and Swainson's Hawks. Broad-wings roost in trees or thickets, while Swainson's roost on the ground, preferring newly plowed fields before the lumps have been broken by the disc. If your timing is just right, and you arrive in a favorable area in the morning before the thermals rise, you could possibly find hundreds or even thousands of Swainson's Hawks standing around in the fields.

Ringed, Belted, and Green Kingfishers are found at various places along the river. They become more numerous when there is extensive riparian vegetation lining the river together with clear water for fishing. About the only areas where clear water can be found is below the dams, which slow the water and allow the suspended particles to settle. One of the clearest places is the 15-mile stretch below Falcon Dam, and kingfishers are common here.

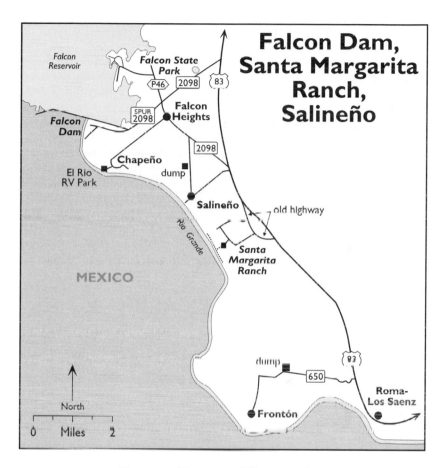

ROMA BLUFFS / FRONTÓN

There are several places where you can gain access to the river below Falcon Dam. One is just below Roma-Los Saenz (46 miles west of Mission). Go west on US-83 and turn left onto FM-650 (1.0 mile west of town) toward Frontón. The Roma-Los Saenz city dump (2.5 miles) on the right attracts Chihuahuan Ravens, and the adjacent fields are good for Sage (rare, winter) and Curve-billed Thrashers and winter sparrows. Frontón is 2.5 miles farther down the road. Take the first left as you enter the residential area at Frontón, and drive one-half mile to the river. There is not much birding in the area, but you might find something. Altamira and Audubon's Orioles are resident here. If you are lucky you will see a Muscovy Duck on the river. There has been a recent sighting of Clay-colored Robin along the river. Here the Rio Grande follows a much more southerly direction on its way from Del Rio.

SANTA MARGARITA RANCH

The caliche road into **Santa Margarita Ranch** crosses through desert chaparral on its way to a nice stretch of riparian woodland along the river. This is a good spot for desert and water birds as well as many Rio Grande specialties.

This private ranch can be reached by driving west on US-83 from the Frontón Road (FM-650). After 5.7 miles, the highway curves right, but you should bear left onto the old highway. After crossing a little bridge (where you can pause to look for Cave Swallows), turn left onto an unmarked dirt road (0.7 mile), following it as it bends right and tops a hill overlooking the ranch buildings. Turn left at the entrance road (1.1 miles) and proceed to the first house on the left. If no one comes, go to the second house on the right. *Because of the loose, unpredictable dogs stay in your car and beep your horn.* Someone will come out.

Santa Margarita Ranch was deeded to the Gonzalez family in an old Spanish Land Grant. It is not public property. A charge of $ 2/person is made for the privilege of birding here, and it is two bucks well spent. The residents, however, want to make sure that they will not be held liable for an injury or accident—snakebites included—on the property, and that visitors understand that they bird at their own risk.

The road to the river is gated and often locked, so you will likely need to walk rather than drive down to the river. Park along the main road near the gate, but do not block the road.

In June 1974 a flock of Brown Jays, and later a nest, was discovered on the ranch. This brought a rush of birders and set in motion the "Patagonia Picnic Table Effect." (This is the phenomenon—named after the famous roadside rest area in Southeastern Arizona—wherein the news of one good bird brings in many observers. They in turn discover more rarities, which in turn attract more observers, ad infinitum.) Some rarities seen over the years include Eurasian Wigeon (December 1989–January 1990), Roadside Hawk (2nd ABA-Area record, 7 January 1979), Short-tailed Hawk (1st state record, 22–28 July 1989), Zone-tailed Hawk, a pair of Sulphur-bellied Flycatchers (May–August 1975, returning the following two summers), and Clay-colored Robin.

You will also find Santa Margarita Ranch good for Muscovy Duck (best in spring and summer), Hook-billed Kite (rare), Gray Hawk (rare), Plain Chachalaca, Red-billed Pigeon (summer), White-winged and White-tipped Doves, Greater Roadrunner, Groove-billed Ani (summer), Common Pauraque, Ringed and Green Kingfishers, Golden-fronted and Ladder-backed Woodpeckers, Northern Beardless-Tyrannulet (rare, summer), Great Kiskadee, Ash-throated (spring) and Brown-crested Flycatchers, Couch's Kingbird (summer), Scissor-tailed Flycatcher, Green Jay, Cactus Wren, Long-billed and Curve-billed Thrashers, Olive, Rufous-crowned (rare), and

Black-throated Sparrows, Blue Grosbeak (summer), Indigo, Varied (rare), and Painted Buntings, Pyrrhuloxia, and Altamira and Audubon's Orioles. Rarely seen but possible along the river are Surf Scoter, Oldsquaw, Common Black-Hawk, and Zone-tailed Hawk.

The easiest way to find Ringed and Green Kingfishers is to walk straight down the half-mile trail from the parking area to the river and watch for them to fly across the water. Be sure that they are on the American side before you count them on your ABA list. The large, massive-billed Ringed Kingfisher is often seen flying high above the river with strong sweeping wingbeats. It can be located by its loud, deep kak-kak-kak calls. You may find a Green Kingfisher out in the open near the middle of the river, but it is more likely to be hidden among the willows along the shore. The way to find this secretive little bird is to walk quietly downriver along the trail, checking every branch overhanging the water. Those with sharp ears may hear the kingfisher's dry rattle (while perched) or a rough zchurrk as it takes flight low over the water. This small bird needs shallow water for fishing, preferring isolated pools that remain when the river is low. The depth of the river fluctuates greatly depending upon release of water from the dam; however the lowest water levels usually occur early in the morning.

Brown Jays have been found feeding in the mesquite thickets up and down the river but are very local and are even absent some years. The best season to find Brown Jays is winter, when they travel in small noisy flocks. When not vocalizing, these large birds are shy and difficult to see, so it's best to get out early. Listen for their harsh, screaming kyeeaah! kyaah!, which is similar to the call of Red-shouldered Hawk.

If you do not find the kingfishers or the jay at the ranch, try some of the other places farther upriver such as Salineño (Sah-lee-NAYN-yo), Chapeño (Chah-PAYN-yo), or below Falcon (FAAL-kun) Dam. As you leave the ranch, turn left (west) onto the gravel road. Follow it around until it returns to the old highway (1.6 miles). Here you can turn left to reach US-83 (0.4 mile). Along the way check the arid brushlands for Scaled Quail, Greater Roadrunner, Vermilion (winter) and Ash-throated (summer) Flycatchers, Cactus Wren, Black-tailed Gnatcatcher, Cassin's and Black-throated Sparrows, Pyrrhuloxia, and Bullock's Oriole (summer).

SALINEÑO

For many years now, **Salineño** has been *the* birding hot spot of the Falcon Dam area. In addition to a good view of the river, numerous bird feeders at a nearby property are maintained by a dedicated core of "Winter Texan" birders from November through March. Several other habitats in the area are worth checking, including riparian woodland, arid thorn scrub forest, a water treatment pond, and the dump road.

Go west on US-83 to the sign for Salineño (1.2 miles). Turn left—this road can be good for a variety of birds in winter and spring. Some winters, Say's Phoebe is discovered here, but that is rare. One spot to check for phoebes is the open fence on the right side next to some concrete picnic tables (0.4 mile). The brushy areas a little farther down can produce Cassin's, Chipping, Clay-colored, Vesper, Lark, Black-throated, Grasshopper, and White-crowned Sparrows and Lark Bunting. Watch for Scaled Quail, Greater Roadrunner, Bell's Vireo (summer), Verdin, Bewick's Wren, and winter warblers.

One thing you are sure to notice are the brightly-colored wreaths at the town cemetery. In the adjacent fields in winter you are likely to see both Eastern and Western Meadowlarks (but good luck trying to sort them out!). As the road forks, bear right and watch for three speed bumps before the town square. Continue straight through to the Rio Grande. When the river is low, or normal, the lookout provides good views for many birds, both on the water and in the trees lining the bank. A spotting scope is very useful.

Birds seen from the lookout include Least (rare) and Pied-billed Grebes, American White Pelican, Neotropic and Double-crested Cormorants, Anhinga (rare), several herons and egrets, Greater White-fronted and Snow Geese (flying high overhead), many species of waterfowl, and often all three kingfishers. On rare occasions a Black Phoebe can be found along the river in winter.

Salineño is one of the best spots in the area for Muscovy Ducks but they are generally difficult to find. Although Muscovies can be seen flying up and down the river in all seasons, your chances are better in spring and fall. Common winter waterfowl include American Wigeon (abundant), Gadwall, Mottled Duck, Blue-winged Teal, Northern Shoveler, Northern Pintail, Green-winged Teal, Ring-necked Duck, Lesser Scaup, Bufflehead, and Ruddy Duck. Occasionally, Wood Duck, "Mexican Duck" Mallard, Cinnamon Teal, Canvasback, and Redhead are seen as well.

On the shore (if there is any), look for Greater and Lesser Yellowlegs, Spotted, Western, and Least Sandpipers, and American Pipit. In the morning the tall trees along the bank can come alive with bird song. Usually seen in the nearby woodlands or flying back and forth across the river are Golden-fronted and Ladder-backed Woodpeckers, Great Kiskadee, Couch's Kingbird, Green and Brown (rare) Jays, and Altamira and Audubon's Orioles. Also look for Osprey and Gray (rare), Harris's, and Red-shouldered Hawks perched on snags on both sides of the river. Although Red-billed Pigeons can be seen flying across the river throughout the year, they are more likely in spring and summer. Though rarely seen, Hook-billed Kite, Common Black-Hawk, Zone-tailed Hawk, Rose-throated Becard, and Blue Bunting have visited the area.

One of the biggest attractions at Salineño are the bird feeders just up the road from the river lookout. About 60 yards back from the river's edge is a fenced-in area of mobile homes with a long rolling-gate, the entrance to the

Salineño Birder Colony. Birders are welcome inside—just roll the gate back to the closed position after entering. The residents are avid, accomplished birders themselves, and enjoy helping visitors look for specialties. They are happy to pass along information about the birds and other birding areas in the vicinity. If no one is around, or if you find a No Tresspassing sign at this location, please do not enter the property.

Many birds are attracted to the numerous feeders and plants around the colony, such as Inca and White-tipped Doves, Black-chinned and Anna's (rare, fall) Hummingbirds, Golden-fronted and Ladder-backed Woodpeckers, Great Kiskadee, Green and Brown (rare) Jays, Bewick's Wren, Tufted (Black-crested) Titmouse, Long-billed and Curve-billed Thrashers, Orange-crowned and Yellow-rumped Warblers, Olive and Lincoln's Sparrows, Northern Cardinal, Altamira and Audubon's Orioles, Lesser (rare) and American Goldfinches, and others. Brown Jays have been absent from the feeders for the past several years, but occasionally one or two jays are sighted in the vicinity or along the river.

On the way to the water treatment pond (just up the road), check the thorn scrub for Bell's Vireo (rare, summer), Verdin, Cactus Wren, Black-tailed Gnatcatcher (rare), Chipping Sparrow, and others. At the water treatment pond you can usually find Sora, Common Moorhen, Common Yellowthroat, Red-winged Blackbird, and occasionally a Green Kingfisher, Groove-billed Ani, or Altamira Oriole. Every now and then some lucky birder will spot a Gray Hawk, Clay-colored Robin or White-collared Seedeater in the area.

As you leave the Salineño Birder Colony, you can return straight to US-83 or try the **Salineño dump road**. To get to the dump road turn left at the first street (0.2 mile). This road is hard-topped for 0.4 mile but turns to dirt, which can be very slick and impassable after a rain. Slow *way* down for the new speed-bumps. Where the road begins to bear right, you should be able to spot the Bank Swallow burrows in the exposed bank off to the left. The road passes the Salineño dump and continues on to FM-2098. It can be good for sparrows and other birds in winter. Here you might find Scaled Quail, Greater Roadrunner, Chihuahuan Raven, Verdin, Cactus Wren, Curve-billed Thrasher, Cassin's, Black-throated, and White-crowned Sparrows, and Pyrrhuloxia. Seldom seen but possible are Black-chinned Hummingbird (summer), Rock Wren (winter), Green-tailed Towhee (winter), and Lesser Goldfinch.

CHAPEÑO

This is another spot along the river worth checking for Muscovy Duck, Hook-billed Kite, Gray Hawk, Red-billed Pigeon, Brown Jay, and Audubon's Oriole. Lately, **Chapeño** has been the best site in the area for Brown Jays, which have been scarce or absent elsewhere.

To reach the former settlement of Chapeño go one-quarter mile beyond (west of) the Salineño Road on US-83 and turn left onto FM-2098, which leads to Falcon Dam. As you enter the town of Falcon Heights, watch on the left for Chapeño Road (2.8 miles) opposite the Catholic church. (If you took the Salineño-dump-road detour through to FM-2098, that intersection would leave you about 1.5 miles from the turn-off by the church.) Turn left onto Chapeño Road and continue until the road bends left (2.5 miles). Just after the bend, a sign for El Rio RV Park points off to the right. Follow the narrow road to the manager's house (on the right) and park. The manager maintains bird feeders which have attracted up to eight Brown Jays in recent winters. Just down from this house, the road parallels the river for a few hundred yards and then curves down to the river. If the gate to the little picnic ground is open, go on through; if not, it's easy to find a way around it. There is a daily fee (around $2) to bird on the property.

All three kingfishers can be found along this broad sweep of the river. As with other nearby spots, Muscovy Ducks are difficult to find but may be seen perching in trees overhanging the water, swimming in the river, or flying across the water. Also found in the riparian areas are Hook-billed Kite, Gray Hawk, Red-billed Pigeon, and Audubon's Oriole. A dirt road nearby leads to a boat ramp with cattails on both sides of the small clearing. In these cattails, White-collared Seedeaters have been reported sporadically.

After backtracking on Chapeño Road to FM-2098, turn left (west). At the western edge of Falcon Heights, there is a major intersection (0.5 mile). From this point, FM-2098 goes northeast for 2.5 miles to rejoin US-83. Drive east on FM-2098 and you will find a lake on the left (north) side (1.7 miles) which in winter may have Least Grebe, Greater White-fronted Goose, Hooded Merganser, and Ruddy Duck.

Back at the intersection, Park Road 46 goes north 1.0 mile into Falcon State Park, and Spur Road 2098 goes west for 2.0 miles to the dam. On both sides of this latter road is Starr County Park, offering limited facilities on the north side of the road. This park is good for Cactus Wren, Northern Mockingbird, Curve-billed Thrasher, wintering sparrows, and Pyrrhuloxia. Sometimes Red-billed Pigeon (summer), Groove-billed Ani (spring), and Black-tailed Gnatcatcher are seen in the county park.

FALCON STATE PARK

Falcon State Park (573 acres) is located at the south end of 98,960-acre International Falcon Reservoir. Like much of the surrounding area, the park's gently rolling hills are covered with patches of thorny brushland, consisting mostly of mesquite, huisache, Mexican Olive, Texas Ebony, and a variety of cacti and native grasses. Although the vegetation looks sparse, there is a good collection of birds and reptiles here, especially desert species. If you are camping, this is a good spot from which to work. The entrance fee is $2/person (children under 12 free), plus a fee for camping, hot showers,

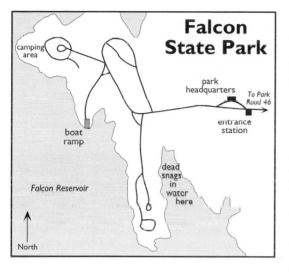

hook-ups, or screened shelters. For more information, contact Falcon State Park, PO Box 2, Falcon Heights, TX 78545; telephone 956/848-5327.

In the brushy thorn scrub along the road and around the campgrounds, you should see Harris's Hawk, Common Ground-Dove, Greater Roadrunner, Golden-fronted and Ladder-backed Woodpeckers, Cactus and Bewick's Wrens, Northern Mockingbird, Curve-billed Thrasher, Cassin's, Lark, and Black-throated Sparrows, Northern Cardinal, Pyrrhuloxia, and Bronzed and Brown-headed Cowbirds. Also look for Northern Bobwhites running around the campgrounds or park roads during the day. You may hear Great Horned Owl at night or, if you are lucky, see one on an afternoon perch.

In spring and summer, expect Ash-throated Flycatcher, Blue Grosbeak, Painted Bunting, Dickcissel, and Bullock's Oriole. In winter look for American Kestrel, Say's Phoebe (rare), Vermilion Flycatcher, Loggerhead Shrike, Eastern Bluebird (Mountain Bluebird is accidental), Sage Thrasher (rare most years), Lark Bunting, Cassin's, Chipping, Clay-colored, Brewer's (rare), Field, Vesper, Lark, Black-throated, Savannah, Grasshopper, and White-crowned Sparrows, Brewer's Blackbird, and Lesser Goldfinch.

Hooded Orioles can usually be found in summer around the office. One year they nested in the light standard right next to the bulb. Hooded and Altamira Orioles occasionally visit the camping areas if someone has put out sugar-water feeders.

The best area for active feeders is in the trailer section. This is a good spot for Northern Bobwhite, Greater Roadrunner, and sparrows. If you have not seen Black-throated Sparrow by now, try searching down the hill (toward the lake) in the scrubby vegetation. You could also find Bell's Vireo (summer) and Verdin in the taller mesquites along the bottom of the wash.

As a rule the lakeshore is not very productive, but you can scope for Common Loon (rare), Neotropic and Double-crested (winter) Cormorants, American White Pelican, ducks, a few coots, and Gull-billed Tern (uncommon nester). Scan the lake for vagrant gulls in winter—Thayer's and Glaucous Gulls and Black-legged Kittiwake have been recorded in the Falcon Dam area.

A small sheltered bay full of dead snags can yield Spotted Sandpiper, Green Kingfisher, and American Pipit. To reach it go to the far end of the loop in the area of screened shelters. Here you will find a path leading to the beach, where you should turn left and follow the shore until you come to the bay.

Since the lake has been established, the number of frogs and toads has increased considerably. They may be abundant after heavy rains in spring and summer. Rio Grande Leopard Frog and Gulf Coast Toad are usually most common, but you may find others such as Blanchard's Cricket Frog, Mexican Burrowing Toad, and Sheep Frog.

With the abundance of food, the snake population has increased also. By driving the back roads at night, you may find Eastern Checkered Garter Snake, Western Ribbon Snake, Mexican Hognose Snake, Western Coachwhip, Schott's Whipsnake, Western Rough Green Snake, Texas Indigo Snake, Texas Patchnose Snake, Great Plains Rat Snake, Texas Glossy Snake, Bull Snake, Desert Kingsnake, Texas Longnose Snake, Ground Snake, Western Hooknose Snake, Texas Night Snake, Northern Cat-eyed Snake, Flathead Snake, Texas Blackhead Snake, Massasauga, and Western Diamondback Rattlesnake. Despite the potential, on most nights you will not be lucky enough to find a single snake.

FALCON DAM

Falcon Dam was dedicated in October 1953 by Mexican President Adolfo Ruiz Cortines and U.S. President Dwight D. Eisenhower. This dam, built for conservation, irrigation, power, flood control, and recreation purposes, trapped the waters of the Rio Grande to form a 60-mile-long lake. From the spillway, scan the river for cormorants, ducks, kingfishers, and other birds before heading to the riparian woodland below the dam.

From a viewpoint near the middle of the dam, you can survey the lake for ducks, gulls, and terns. Once in a great while, a vagrant gull will turn up here in winter, such as Thayer's and Glaucous Gulls or Black-legged Kittiwake. However, you must pass through U.S. Customs on the way back, and that can be a real inconvenience if your car is packed with gear. It's easiest to just ask if you can park at customs and walk out on the dam road.

The area below the dam is much better. To reach it, go west (toward Falcon Dam) on Spur Road 2098 for 1.0 mile and veer left onto a small, paved road. (This road is reached well before you come abreast the customs station.) Drive to the spillway parking area (1.8 miles). Check the utility poles for Great Horned Owls while driving this road at dawn. (There is a gate near customs that is locked from 6 PM to 6 AM, and all day on holidays.)

From the top of the wall you can scan the concrete spillway below where Neotropic and Double-crested Cormorants can be compared. When there is a trickle of water, shorebirds may be common, particularly during migration. Most of them will be Least Sandpipers, but this is a good spot for finding Baird's.

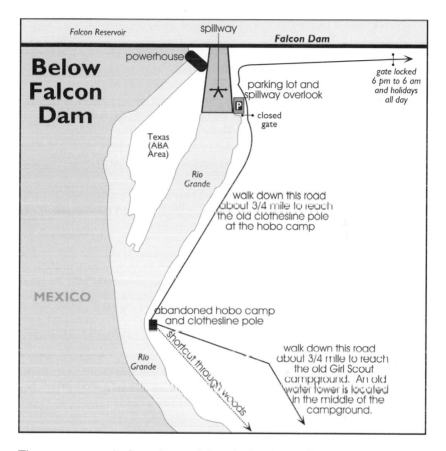

Below
Falcon
Dam

Falcon Reservoir   spillway   ***Falcon Dam***

powerhouse

*gate locked
6 pm to 6 am
and holidays
all day*

parking lot and
spillway overlook

closed
gate

Texas
(ABA
Area)

*Rio
Grande*

walk down this road
about 3/4 mile to reach
the old clothesline pole
at the hobo camp

MEXICO

abandoned hobo camp
and clothesline pole

*Rio
Grande*

shortcut through woods

walk down this road
about 3/4 mile to reach
the old Girl Scout
campground. An old
water tower is located
in the middle of the
campground.

There are records from here of Purple Sandpiper (December 1975) and Northern Jacana (November 1992–April 1993). With luck Cave Swallows will be soaring overhead, Ringed and Green Kingfishers will be fishing at water's edge, and, in summer, Red-billed Pigeons will be perched in the tall trees along the bank. In summer, some Cliff Swallows nest on the dam face.

Although Zone-tailed Hawks are rare in the Valley, they seem to turn up most often at the Falcon Dam spillway, almost always with Turkey Vultures. A number of dabbling ducks winter in the river below the spillway, including Mottled Duck and "Mexican Duck" Mallard. Also in winter, look for Black Phoebe on a variety of low perches at the base of the spillway or Rock Wren in the rock mound below. Also in the rocks, look for Blue Spiny Lizards sunning themselves in late morning. These large lizards (5–14 inches) with black collars are endemic to south Texas and northeastern Mexico.

Walk past the gate on the dirt road leading downriver. In about three-quarters of a mile you reach the **old "hobo camp"** and clothesline pole in a grove of Texas Ebony trees. (Alternately, you may choose to follow a rough trail, which starts just beyond the rock mound and follows the river bank.) The grove attracts about the same species as are found at Santa Margarita Ranch or Salineño, but some lucky people have seen such things as Gray Hawk, Ferruginous Pygmy-Owl, Brown Jay, Varied Bunting, and White-collared Seedeater.

At the west end of the abandoned campsite, by the old clothesline pole, there is access to the riverbank. This is an excellent vantage point for spotting Ospreys, Red-billed Pigeons, and Ringed Kingfishers as they fly up and down the river. In summer look for Hook-billed Kites soaring over their breeding territories. Of course, you can just sit here and watch the river go by.

You may explore the area further by one of two routes which wind up at the same place, an **old Girl Scout campground** farther downriver. If you take the road to the left, the distance is approximately three-quarters of a mile to where it meets the river. Sometimes Red-billed Pigeons are seen in the area, especially in spring and summer. Before you actually reach the river, a trail goes off the right to the old Girl Scout campground (an old water tower sits in the middle of the campground). In past years, Ferruginous Pygmy-Owls were found in this area, but there have been very few recent reports. A rough trail through the woods, paralleling the river, is shorter by one-quarter mile and might yield Ferruginous Pygmy-Owl, Brown Jay, or Audubon's Oriole.

Small flocks of Brown Jays could be seen anywhere beginning about midway between the spillway parking lot and the hobo camp to the Girl Scout camp. Audubon's Orioles are most often found in vicinity of the river and the Girl Scout camp. Other rarities recorded in the area are Tropical Kingbird (June 1991), Rufous-backed Robin (1st Texas record, 29 December 1975), and Rufous-capped Warbler (1st Texas record, 10 February 1973).

It is advisable not to bird remote areas around here alone because of the proximity of known routes used by drug runners in the vicinity of Falcon Fam and other parts of Starr County.

ZAPATA / SAN YGNACIO

Zapata and San Ygnacio are two towns along the Rio Grande where you have a reasonable chance of seeing White-collared Seedeaters in winter. You might also find Red-billed Pigeons in summer along the river.

Between Falcon Dam and Big Bend, the land is arid, thinly vegetated, and relatively unproductive. There are still a few places to stop, however. About 7.3 miles from the intersection of US-83 and Spur Road 2098 at Falcon Dam check a culvert at a creek called Tigre Chiquito for Cave Swallows, especially if you missed them at Arroyo Salado or other culverts on US-83. If a lot of water is backed up from Falcon Dam, look for waterbirds and ducks here. Also be alert for Crested Caracaras along this stretch of highway.

For a few years now, a small flock of White-collared Seedeaters has frequented **City Park** in Zapata upriver from Falcon Dam (27.0 miles from

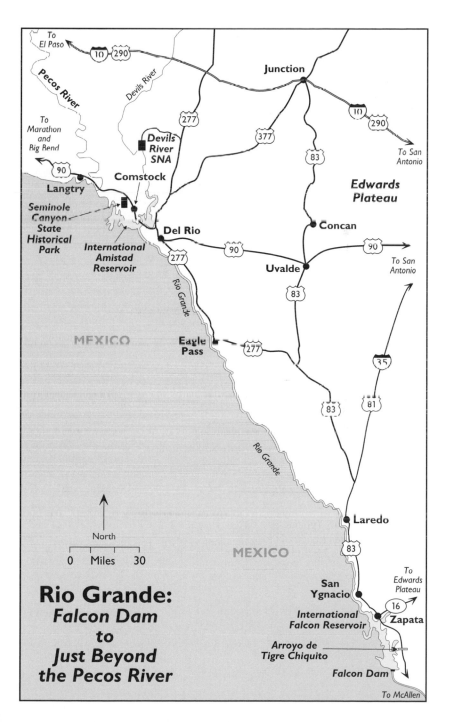

Rio Grande:
Falcon Dam to Just Beyond the Pecos River

US-83 and Spur Road 2098). The park is two blocks west on 9th Avenue from US-83. Search the cattail pond and surrounding area (including the grassy fence-line behind the library) for the seedeaters. These tiny birds are most often found in winter, but have also been seen in summer when they appear to be very local nesters. Be aware that much of the wooded area around the pond was bulldozed in the spring of 1998, which may affect the local seedeater population.

Also at City Park, you can expect some of the Rio Grande specialties such as Green Jay or Altamira Oriole year round, Say's Phoebe, Vermilion Flycatcher, or Song Sparrow in winter, neotropical passerines in migration, and Couch's Kingbird in summer. House Finch, rare in the Valley, has shown up at Zapata City Park during spring and early summer. Hopelessly lost, a Red-billed Tropicbird, a pelagic species rarely encountered in the Gulf of Mexico, was found along the river at Zapata on 29 April 1989.

Continue upriver on US-83 toward San Ygnacio. Some 2 miles west of Zapata turn right at the sign for the hamlet of Las Palmas. This road winds through open desert scrub, which can be good for Black-throated Sparrows and, occasionally, Scaled Quail. Check the largest trees on the western horizon in the afternoon for Red-billed Pigeons. Return to US-83.

Continue upriver on US-83 to **San Ygnacio** (12.0 miles). White-collared Seedeaters have occured here in winter fairly regularly for a number of years. They have been found behind the post office and elsewhere, such as the cemetery, which can be reached by following Hidalgo Street to where it becomes a dirt road out of town. (The bank of the river nearby is an excellent vantage point for observing Red-billed Pigeons from mid-March through August.)

Currently the best area for the seedeaters is down along the river at the end of Washington, Grant, or Trevino Streets. Recent "improvements" have reduced the amount of cane along the river and some other weedy seedeater-attractive areas around town. From the end of Trevino Street, walk north or upriver on the path between town and the river as far as the boat ramp area. This is about one-half mile north of the end of Trevino Street. White-collared Seedeaters are possible anywhere along this path. On this hike you pass by a dry resaca bed that has had no water for years—just weedy seedeater habitat! On occasion, Red-billed Pigeons, Brown Jays, and Altamira and Audubon's Orioles have been found in the general area. Once again, *when walking down by the river never travel alone and always respect the rights of local landowners.*

Rarities that have turned up in San Ygnacio include Lesser Black-backed Gull (April 1989) and Clay-colored Robin (February 1988).

If you have no luck with the seedeaters at the traditional spots in Zapata or San Ygnacio, stop at the rest area on US-83 about 3 miles north of San Ygnacio. Look for the seedeaters in the long grass behind the rest stop.

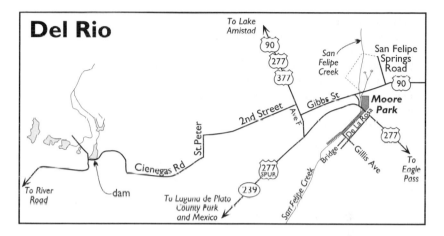

DEL RIO

Del Rio is located on the Rio Grande at the northwesternmost point of the South Texas Plains. This area is not birded as regularly as other areas in this guide, but it does have great potential. The Serranias del Burros are only 50 miles to the west and, as with the southwestern Edwards Plateau, the avifaunas of three of Texas' physiographic regions come together. Unfortunately, there is very little public land away from the shores of nearby Lake Amistad and the riparian zones along the Rio Grande are accessible in only a few locations. From Del Rio you may travel eastward onto the Edwards Plateau or westward toward Big Bend, the Davis Mountains, and El Paso.

One of the places in Del Rio worth checking is the area around San Felipe Springs. The springs are the third-largest in Texas with a outflow of about 90 million gallons of water per day into San Felipe Creek. The creek winds its way through the municipal golf course as well as several city parks. The springs are located at the end of San Felipe Springs Road which is 1.6 miles east of the intersection of US-90 and US-277. Upon reaching San Felipe Springs Road turn left and drive to the end. At the end of the road you pass through a gate (open 7 AM–5:30 PM) and continue on to the spring pumphouse. Park and bird around the spring. Back at the fork, walk across the bridge to bird along the west side of the creek, especially in the wooded area north of the maintenance shed. Before going up the creek behind the shed *be sure to get permission* at the clubhouse on US-90. The property belongs to the San Felipe Country Club and they are happy to allow public access to this area for birdwatching. Birds found here year round include Ringed and Green Kingfishers, Black Phoebe, Vermilion Flycatcher, Great Kiskadee, Olive Sparrow, and Lesser Goldfinch. In summer watch for Couch's and Western Kingbirds.

Return to US-90 and turn right. Almost immediately you will see the beginning of Moore Park on your left. Green Kingfishers are often found near the railroad bridge or on down near the park's swimming pool. Because of its small size and secretive habits, this bird is easy to overlook. This park can be very crowded on weekends and during summer.

To check the rest of the park system along the creek on the south side of US-277, continue west on US-90, turning left (south) onto US-277 (0.25 mile) to De La Rosa (0.3 mile); turn right (southwest) in two blocks and park at the Amphitheater Center. A paved trail follows the creek through the park for another half mile. Or continue to drive southwest on De La Rosa for three blocks, turning right after one block onto Gillis Avenue, then left onto Bridge Street to the creek, pond, and picnic area. The whole park is also good for spring and fall migrants such as Spotted Sandpiper, Hermit Thrush, Nashville, Orange-crowned, Yellow, Yellow-rumped, and Wilson's Warblers, and Spotted Towhee. Snowy Egrets are here throughout the year; be sure to look carefully into the trees on the other side of the creek for Yellow-crowned Night-Herons.

Laguna de Plata is a new county park being developed as a birding area. The park consists of a 10-acre wetland and about 60 acres of fallow fields with some woodland habitat. The site offers excellent habitat for waterfowl during the winter and can be great for shorebirds during migration when water levels are favorable. Black-bellied Whistling-Duck, Wood Duck, Groove-billed Ani, Vermilion Flycatcher, Great Kiskadee, Verdin, Long-billed Thrasher, and Olive Sparrow are summer residents. White-tailed Kites are occasionally seen feeding over the open fields.

To reach Laguna de Plata, take Spur 239 west from the intersection with US-90 (Gibbs Street) and US-377 (Avenue F) in the center of Del Rio. Follow Spur 239 (Sergio Gonzales Jr. and Alfredo Gutierrez Jr., M.D. Loop) for 3 miles to the International Bridge. Turn right at the bridge onto Garza Lane and proceed for another 2 miles to the Val Verde County Sports Complex. Park in the sports complex, and Laguna de Plata is directly across the street. The park is open from dawn to dusk.

Another good area is the roadside thickets between the Rio Grande and the railroad just west of the city. Here you should find Scaled Quail, Northern Bobwhite, Black, Eastern, and Say's Phoebe's, Ash-throated and Brown-crested Flycatchers, Cactus, Canyon, and Carolina Wrens, Rufous-crowned Sparrow, Northern Cardinal, Pyrrhuloxia, and Orchard, Hooded, and Bullock's Orioles. Golden-fronted and Ladder-backed Woodpeckers are common. Bronzed and Brown-headed Cowbirds are common in summer. Olive Sparrows, although difficult to find, are actually present in good numbers—being familiar with their call notes makes finding them much easier. White-tailed Kites hunt over the tree-lined fields.

To reach this area of thickets and other habitats from the downtown starting point of US-90 (Gibbs Street) and US-277/377 (Avenue F), go two blocks north and turn left (west) onto 2nd Street. Drive to the end (1.2 miles) at the cemetery, turning left onto St. Peter and right onto Cienegas Road (0.2 mile) to a farm pond and dam (1.7 miles). Look over the ducks (some are domestic) and the cormorants. Neotropic Cormorants can be common here, especially in summer. Occasionally, Least Terns are found feeding over these ponds. At the corner turn left under the railroad to check the ponds and thickets along the way to River Road, where you turn right (2.0 miles). Summer residents include Black-bellied Whistling-Duck and Groove-billed Ani, along with many of the above species. The road follows along the river north to a locked gate (5.0 miles). You can park here and walk farther up the road along the railroad tracks. Additional birds such as Black Phoebe, Vermilion Flycatcher, Great Kiskadee, and Couch's Kingbird may be found.

AMISTAD NATIONAL RECREATION AREA

The creation of Lake Amistad just northwest of Del Rio with the building of Amistad Dam in 1969 has attracted many species that were either absent from this area of the state or were previously rare. The reservoir, administered by both Mexico and the United States, covers 64,860 acres at conservation pool level of 1,117 feet above mean sea level, storing 3,505,439 acre-feet of water. The United States' shoreline is 851 miles long, while Mexico has 304 miles. The recreation area provides boating, fishing, swimming, hunting, and camping. (There are five small primitive camping areas (free) with picnic tables under shelters and chemical toilets.) Birding opportunities are numerous on the water and along the shore and also in the dry scrub of higher ground, composed of Blackbrush, guajillo, cenizo, yucca, Sotol, mesquite, Creosote Bush, leatherplant, and various cacti.

To reach the recreation area, drive north from Del Rio on combined US-90/277/377 to the National Park Service headquarters on the right in about 1 miles. Here you can pick up information, brochures, and books. One-quarter mile beyond, US-90 swings westward (see below) and US-277/377 continues north. There are two areas to visit along the lakeshore by taking US-277/377, the first of which is found after crossing over the east arm of the reservoir (6.0 miles). Here a small campground offers a place to scan that part of the lake. In winter look for and Neotropic and Double-crested Cormorants, waterfowl, including Cinnamon Teal, Franklin's, Bonaparte's, and Ring-billed Gulls, and Forster's Tern. Search the moist, open grassy areas along the shoreline for Le Conte's Sparrows. This area may produce several desert species including Verdin, Cactus Wren, Curve-billed Thrasher, Canyon Towhee, Black-throated Sparrow, and Pyrrhuloxia. Vesper, Savannah, Song, and Lincoln's Sparrows and Lark Bunting can be found during winter. Vermilion and Scissor-tailed Flycatchers and Blue Grosbeak are common in spring and summer. Continue north on US-277/377 to the Rough Canyon Recreation Area turn-off (7.2 miles). Follow Recreation Road 2 (7.2 miles) to the marina. Rough Canyon is on the Devils River arm of Lake Amistad. Many of the same species mentioned above can be found here.

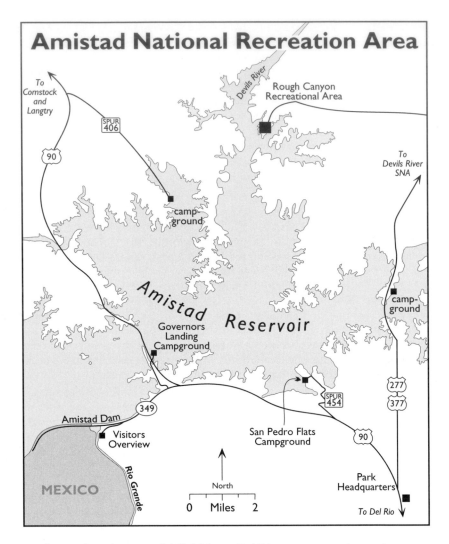

Amistad National Recreation Area

As you travel west with US-90 from Del Rio you may explore other areas of Lake Amistad. One of the best places to see waterbirds on the lake is at San Pedro Flats Campground. To reach the campground take Spur Road 454 (2.4 miles) and follows the signs. Resident species include Harris's Hawk, Scaled Quail, Green Kingfisher, Chihuahuan Raven, Verdin, Cactus, Rock, and Canyon Wrens, Blue-gray Gnatcatcher, and Pyrrhuloxia. In summer look for Pied-billed Grebe, Snowy Egret (rare), Black-necked Stilt, Least Tern, Lesser and Common Nighthawks, and Hooded Oriole. Interior Least Tern and Snowy Plover nest at Amistad. There have even been nesting Laughing Gulls at this lake. In winter watch for Horned Grebe, numerous dabbling ducks,

Red-breasted Merganser, Say's Phoebe, Sage Thrasher, and Green-tailed and Canyon Towhees. Mountain Bluebirds can sometimes be seen in search of insects in the grasslands. There is a record of Eurasian Wigeon from this area. In migration look for American White Pelican, White-faced Ibis, Mississippi Kite, Snowy Plover (very rare), Long-billed Curlew, Solitary, Spotted, Upland, Western, Least, and Pectoral Sandpipers, and Forster's Tern. Bald and Golden Eagles may occasionally be seen. Osprey is a regular winter resident and Peregrine Falcons are regularly seen during migration. At least 17 species of sparrows have been found here during migration and winter.

Continue west on US-90 to TX-349 (5.2 miles) and turn left (south) to the visitors center on the dam (2.5 miles). Turn around and go back to the road (0.4 miles) that leads to the Visitors Overview, a short trail giving a good view of the river below the dam, and the downriver face of the dam. Ringed and Green Kingfishers like the clear, shallow water below dams. This is also a good locations for observing White-throated Swifts and a variety of swallows during migration.

Return north on TX-349 to just north of the railroad, turning left to Governors Landing Campground (1.2 miles). Check for passerines along this road, and look in the small ponds for Least and Pied-billed Grebes and ducks. It is not too unusual to find Canyon Wrens nesting in the roof supports of the picnic-table shelters.

Continue on US-90 west over the long bridge crossing the Devils River arm of Amistad Reservoir to Spur Road 406 (10.1 miles) and turn right to the campground at the end (4.7 miles). This good birding area has most of the same species as San Pedro Flats, but it has many more larger bushes and trees.

This area of the state has a tremendous diversity of reptiles. The common lizards in this rocky, thorny area of limestone between Del Rio and Big Bend are Texas Banded Gecko (nocturnal), Collared Lizard, Texas Earless Lizard, Crevice Spiny and Texas Spiny Lizards, Canyon, Big Bend Tree, Desert Side-blotched, Texas Horned, and Round-tailed Horned Lizards, and Texas Spotted Whiptail. The common snakes are Mexican Hognose Snake, Western Coachwhip, Central Texas and Schott's Whipsnakes, Mountain Patchnose Snake, Great Plains and Trans-Pecos Rat Snakes, Bull Snake, Gray-banded and Desert Kingsnakes, Texas Longnose Snake, Western Hooknose Snake (rare), Texas Night Snake, and Blacktail and Western Diamondback Rattlesnakes. Along the river and in other moist areas, look for Plains and Trans-Pecos Blind Snakes, Blotched Water Snake, Texas Checkered and Blackneck Garter Snakes, Western Ribbon Snake, Flathead Snake, Southwestern Blackhead Snake, Copperhead, and even the very rare Devils River Blackhead Snake.

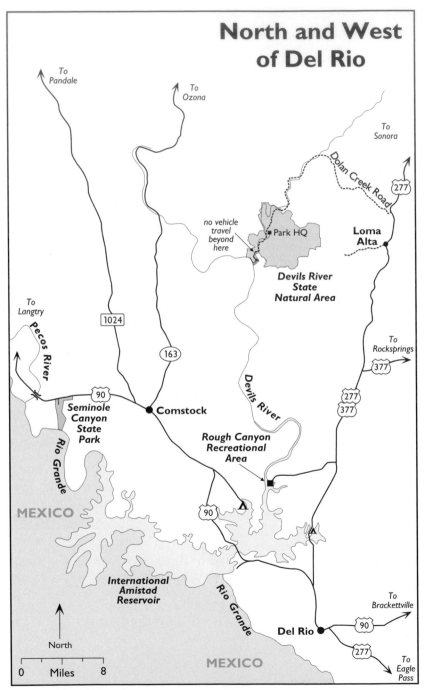

North and West of Del Rio

To Pandale

To Ozona

To Sonora

Dolan Creek Road

277

no vehicle travel beyond here

Park HQ

Loma Alta

Devils River State Natural Area

To Langtry

Pecos River

1024

163

To Rocksprings

377

Devils River

277
377

90

Seminole Canyon State Park

Comstock

Rough Canyon Recreational Area

Rio Grande

MEXICO

90

International Amistad Reservoir

Rio Grande

Del Rio

To Brackettville

90

North

277

To Eagle Pass

0   Miles   8

MEXICO

DEVILS RIVER STATE NATURAL AREA

Another option is to continue northward on US-277 to Devils River State Natural Area ($3/person entrance fee). From the Rough Canyon turn-off, travel north for 32 miles to Dolan Creek Road. This gravel road is found just opposite a covered picnic site located 3.5 miles north of Loma Alta (a store with basic supplies and gas, the last opportunity for such). Once on Dolan Creek Road proceed west for 18.6 miles to the park entrance. Dolan Creek Road is well-maintained, but includes numerous low-water crossings; extreme caution is advised in rainy weather.

Park headquarters is located just off (east of) the main road 3.5 miles into the park from the entrance. Shower facilities are available here, and a lodge and bunkhouse located nearby are available for public use (fee). Otherwise, primitive camping is the only other accommodation available for overnight use. The park is somewhat remote; the nearest medical facilities and major supplies are located in Del Rio, 1½ hours away.

The Natural Area is open seven days/week, but advance reservations are required (830/395-2133). There is a staff of only two at the Natural Area currently. As a result, it is sometimes difficult to reach them, but they do have an answering machine (if a fax machine answers, try calling back later). It is recommended that you make reservations at least two weeks in advance. The primitive areas do not have picnic areas, and there are none of the amenities found in traditional state parks. You must bring in your own supply of drinking water; you much pack out all of your trash; ground fires and pets are not allowed in the park.

Black-throated Sparrow
Barry R. Zimmer

Devils River State Natural Area is wonderfully diverse with a variety of upland and aquatic habitats and abundant birdlife. As with other areas in this region, eastern, western, and subtropical birds can all be found here. The best birding is from the headquarters complex down to Dolan Creek Canyon to Dolan Springs and along the Devils River. Typical upland birds include both Scaled Quail and Northern Bobwhite, Greater Roadrunner, Ladder-backed Woodpecker, Say's Phoebe, Verdin, Cassin's, Rufous-crowned, and Black-throated Sparrows, Cactus, Rock, and Bewick's Wrens, Curve-billed Thrasher, Canyon Towhee, Northern Cardinal, Pyrrhuloxia, and House

Finch. In summer look for Vermilion Flycatcher (also common near water habitats), Ash-throated Flycatcher, Yellow-breasted Chat, Summer Tanager, Varied and Painted Buntings, Blue Grosbeak, and Hooded and Scott's Orioles.

Vertical cliffs in the limestone hills along Dolan Creek create habitat for such birds as Cliff Swallow and Canyon Wren. Occasionally White-throated Swifts are encountered along these bluffs. Turkey Vulture, Golden Eagle, American Kestrel, and Common Raven use shelves and crevices in the cliffs for nesting and roosting areas. In the larger live oaks at the base of these cliffs and elsewhere in the park look for nesting Cooper's, Red-shouldered, and Zone-tailed Hawks.

Vireo diversity at the park is high with six species represented as breeders and an additional four species as migrants. Migrants include Cassin's, Blue-headed, Warbling, and Philadelphia (rare). Black-capped Vireo is common from late March through early September, occupying shrub thickets and oak mottes in the riparian corridors of the park. On mesa slopes and drier habitats with scattered trees and shrubs Gray Vireo can usually be found without much difficulty. Look for Bell's Vireo in the drier riparian thickets and thorn scrub habitats, especially in Huisache along the river. White-eyed Vireo prefers understory thickets, particularly those associated with the more mature riparian woodlands such as Plateau Live Oak and Pecan. This species overwinters in similar habitat, and males can be in full song by late January. Finally, both Yellow-throated and Red-eyed Vireos occupy the mid-story and canopy of mature woodlands. At some locations within the park all six nesting species can be found in close proximity to each other.

Approximately four miles down the canyon on the main road public access by vehicle ends. Park at the parking lot provided and continue your birding adventure on foot (or by bicycle), using the main road as a trail. It is about a fifteen-minute walk to Dolan Springs and another five minutes to reach the river. Explore the old private campground at Dolan Springs. In the live-oak woodlands located there, summer birds can include Golden-fronted Woodpecker, Eastern Wood-Pewee, Brown-crested Flycatcher, White-eyed, Black-capped, and Yellow-throated, Vireos, Carolina Wren, Blue-gray Gnatcatcher, Northern Parula, Yellow-throated and Black-and-white Warblers, and Summer Tanager. Cooper's Hawks have nested annually near the north end of the woodland. At night this is a good place to find both Eastern and Western Screech-Owls and Elf Owl, but make sure you are able to get back to your car in the dark.

Just below the old campground is Dolan Springs, a wonderful aquatic system which eventually joins the Devils River. *Be careful not to trespass on private property at the south end of the drainage.* This is a good place to observe Green Kingfisher. Also, in the marsh-like vegetation surrounding the open water, Common Yellowthroat is resident. In winter Marsh Wren and Song, Lincoln's, and Swamp Sparrows are usually common. An occasional Green Heron, Virginia Rail, Sora, Common Moorhen, or American Coot can be observed. This aquatic system, coupled with the live-oak woodland on the terrace just above, make the Dolan Springs area an excellent place to look for migrants in both spring and fall.

Finally, you cannot fully appreciate the diversity of habitats at the park unless you include the Devils River frontage as a place to look for birds. Again, the final leg of the trip to the river will be on foot or bicycle, unless you contract with the park staff to provide shuttle service to the river and back. The portion of the park that lies along the river includes just the eastern bank from where the main road joins the riparian zone, north approximately 1.5 miles to the old fish camp. At the camp one of the few remaining terrace woodlands can be found. At times Eastern Wood-Pewee, Acadian Flycatcher, Great Crested Flycatcher, Yellow-throated Warbler, and Indigo Bunting are present.

The property to the south, north, and west is all privately owned and, therefore, off limits to park visitors without permission. A road leads north along the river inside the steep bluff and is available for use as a trail. If you desire to walk this stretch to bird, be prepared to walk through standing water and numerous springs. Be careful not to unduly damage the sensitive aquatic systems. The initial stretch of the river is a large section of standing water which appears to be lake-like. At the north end of this section is a series of rapids, islands, and marshy thickets. At times good numbers of waterfowl, shorebirds, gulls, terns, and other aquatic birds can be observed here. Look for Ringed Kingfisher flying up and down the river. In fact, all three kingfishers are often present.

Devils River State Natural Area is situated in a strategic location in the southwestern Edwards Plateau and is an excellent location for birding. The diversity of habitats and associated birdlife make the park a excellent destination for anyone looking for an out-of-the-way spot that has tremendous potential, but is extremely underbirded. Rarities that have been recorded at the park include Flammulated Owl, Broad-billed Hummingbird, Acorn Woodpecker, Hammond's Flycatcher, Great Kiskadee, Tropical Parula, Golden-cheeked Warbler, and Rufous-capped Warbler.

SEMINOLE CANYON STATE HISTORICAL PARK

Seminole Canyon State Historical Park (PO Box 820, Comstock TX 78837; phone 915/292-4464) on US-90, 9 miles west of Comstock, west of Amistad Reservoir. The primary function of this 2,173-acre park (entrance fee $3) is to protect the Indian rock art (pictographs) found within Seminole Canyon. Along the walls of the canyon are several deep overhangs that provided shelter for the pre-Columbian cultures that inhabited the area. Seminole Canyon contains some of the most spectacular examples of this pre-Columbian artwork. These pictographs are believed to be North America's oldest and are thought to have been painted as long as 8,000 years ago. The pictographs are accessible only by guided tours provided by the park staff. The visitors center contains exhibits depicting the lifestyle of early man based upon artifacts and rock art. While at the visitors center, pick up brochures and a preliminary bird checklist.

Windmill Trail starts from the visitors center and leads one-half mile to Seminole Spring in a draw near Main Canyon. This is a fairly easy hike. Birds to look for here and along the way are Zone-tailed Hawk, Green Kingfisher, Black Phoebe, Varied Bunting, and Hooded Oriole.

The Rio Grande Trail (6-mile round-trip) leads from near the campground to a scenic overlook on the Rio Grande shores of Amistad Reservoir. About halfway is a cut-off trail to the Pressa Canyon overlook. On this upland area watch for Scaled Quail, Verdin, Black-throated Sparrow, and Pyrrhuloxia. In winter Lark Buntings are rather common along with other wintering sparrows. During spring and fall migrations watch for waterfowl and shorebirds at the river, and flycatchers and warblers along the trail. White-throated Swifts nest on the canyon walls along with Black and Turkey Vultures, Chihuahuan and Common Ravens, and Canyon Wrens.

On leaving the park, continue west on US-90 to the first road on the left (1.5 miles) and turn left (south) to the National Park Service's Pecos River District Headquarters (1.3 miles). The scenic view of the mouth of the Pecos River at the Rio Grande is great. What you see today has looked much the same for thousands of years. The water level, however, is now 50 feet deeper because of backwater from Amistad Dam. From the self-guiding, quarter-mile Nature Trail and overlook you also can see the US-90 bridge built in 1959.

LANGTRY

The Texas Department of Transportation maintains a travel information center at Langtry (17.0 miles). It is open during regular business hours seven days a week. The Judge Roy Bean Museum is located within this facility. When Roy Bean was made the justice of the peace in 1882, he changed the name of Eagle's Nest Spring to Langtry. He performed his official duties in the Jersey Lillie Saloon. Both the saloon and town were named after the English actress Emilie Charlotte (Lillie) Langtry, whom Bean greatly admired. Bean's colorful manner and unorthodox justice earned him great notoriety. He became known as "The Law West of the Pecos". The Jersey Lillie is maintained within the grounds of the information center.

In the fall of 1976, a Rufous-backed Robin spent a week in the cactus garden at the information center. The beautiful garden has a large variety of plants, all labeled, including 34 cacti, yuccas, and agaves, 19 species of trees, and 44 species of shrubs and others. Resident birds include Scaled Quail, Cactus and Rock Wrens, Curve-billed Thrasher, Black-throated Sparrow, Pyrrhuloxia, Hooded Oriole, House Finch, and others.

From Langtry travel westward on US-90 toward the Big Bend country of West Texas. In the small town of Dryden (40.0 miles) you can either turn north on TX-349 to investigate the Pecos Valley or continue on US-90 to Marathon and Big Bend National Park.

If you continue westward toward Big Bend, the next town is Sanderson (20.5 miles). If time permits, be sure to check the courthouse grounds and adjoining city park. Turn right (north) on 2nd Street and go two blocks to Hackberry Street where the courthouse is located. There are many cottonwoods and Pecans on the grounds. This area is rarely birded, so who knows what might turn up at this migrant trap.

THE PECOS VALLEY

The Pecos is a name synonymous with the Old West. The Pecos River makes a 926-mile journey from the snowy Sangre de Cristo Mountains of northern New Mexico to the Rio Grande northwest of Del Rio. It cuts a thin and muddy path through a section of west Texas that, to the birder traveling on Interstates 10 or 20, must look terribly bleak and unpromising. There is, however, a handful of good birding spots. Several of these offer a productive break on the long trek between the Edwards Plateau and Big Bend.

CHANDLER RANCH /
INDEPENDENCE CREEK PRESERVE

The most varied birding in the Pecos Valley is around the small town of Sheffield, and the single best birding spot is Chandler Ranch/Independence Creek Preserve. To reach Chandler Ranch, exit Interstate 10 at exit 325 (TX-290/TX-349—Iraan/Sheffield) and go south on TX-290 to the junction with TX-349 in Sheffield (4.9 miles). Turn right onto TX-349 (notice the sign for the Chandler Guest Ranch and Independence Creek Preserve), and proceed to Independence Creek Road (22.3 miles). If you are traveling US-90 between Del Rio and Big Bend, turn north onto TX-349 in Dryden and go about 38 miles to this intersection. Take Independence Creek Road (dirt) east to the Chandler Ranch (5.4 miles). The road crosses Independence Creek in another 1.3 miles. Some of the best habitat is to the right and left immediately after the creek crossing.

Chandler Ranch is a guest ranch offering hunting and fishing in addition to birding. Indeed, it is open only to hunters from the beginning of October through December. The enclosed Independence Creek Preserve is a 702-acre conservation easement of The Nature Conservancy. The preserve was established primarily to protect breeding Black-capped Vireos, as well as rare fish of the Pecos watershed. The clear waters of Independence Creek flow past majestic oak groves to meet the Pecos River, banked on the east by impressive cliffs. The rocky hills are cloaked with junipers, and mesquite brushland dominates the intervening areas.

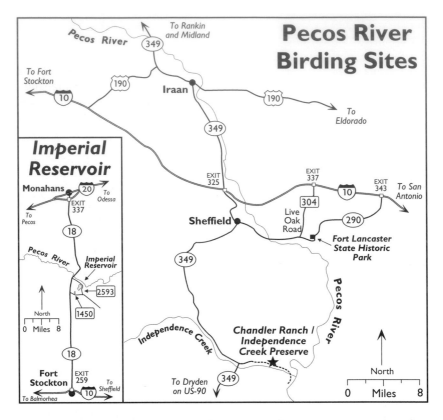

Prior arrangements are needed for any visit. For a day-visit contact either Chandler Ranch (PO Box 10, Dryden, TX 78851; phone 915/753-2345) or the Trans-Pecos office of The Nature Conservancy (PO Box 1619, Alpine, TX 79831; phone 915/837-1778). Contact the TNC office at least two weeks in advance. It can send you a bird checklist, as well as maps of the easement and preserve instructions, and in return would appreciate a list of any birds you find. The excellent birding is best experienced through an overnight stay. (The ranch would make for a perfect overnight stop on the road between the eastern Edwards Plateau and Big Bend.) A cabin is available for $75 per night for one or two people, with a $25 charge for each additional person. You will need to bring food, but the cabin has all other amenities including a refrigerator and some kitchen supplies. A bunkhouse may be available for a lower rate. This sleeps up to thirty and you would need to provide bedding as well as food. Camping on the easement is done only for researchers or TNC functions. It is not necessary to be a TNC member to visit the preserve.

The bird life is a fascinating blend of east and west, with a number of species at the extremity of their ranges, the oak groves acting as an island for a handful of eastern breeders. April–June is perhaps the best time for a visit, and is certainly the time to see Black-capped Vireos. The area around the stream crossing and just to the east is good for this species. As with all Black-capped Vireo sites, *do not use tapes.* Look for breeders such as Zone-tailed Hawk, Scaled Quail, Common Ground-Dove, Eastern and Western Screech-Owls, Common Poorwill, Black-chinned Hummingbird, Green Kingfisher, Golden-fronted Woodpecker, Say's Phoebe, Vermilion, Ash-throated, and Scissor-tailed Flycatchers, White-eyed, Bell's, Black-capped, and Yellow-throated Vireos, Common Raven, Tufted (Black-crested) Titmouse, Verdin, Bewick's Wren, Yellow-breasted Chat, Summer Tanager, Cassin's and Lark Sparrows, Northern Cardinal, Blue Grosbeak, Varied and Painted Buntings, and Orchard and Bullock's Orioles. Some of these species are resident. Gray Vireo may breed on the juniper-clad hillsides. Red-shouldered Hawk, Northern Bobwhite, Eastern Wood-Pewee, Brown-crested Flycatcher, Carolina Wren, and Red-eyed Vireo have been seen and may breed at least sporadically. The ranch lies in the contact zone between Eastern and Western Screech-Owls; the Easterns are of the south Texas *mccallii* race. Ringed Kingfisher has been seen here twice, and you are close enough to south Texas to perhaps expect a stray like Couch's Kingbird, Long-billed Thrasher, or Olive Sparrow. Look in the oaks for Eastern Fox Squirrels at the extreme western edge of their natural range. Nearly anything could drop in during migration.

SHEFFIELD AREA

Several locations closer to Sheffield deserve mention. Go east on US-290 from Sheffield for 4.0 miles to the Pecos River. Look here for Cave Swallows with the Cliffs and Barns. Continue east to Live Oak Road (CR-304) (3.7 miles). A left turn here leads to some roadside oak groves good for Golden-fronted Woodpecker and Tufted (Black-crested) Titmouse. These isolated groves must look inviting to migrants as well. *Please stay on the roads.* It is possible to continue north on CR-304 to Interstate 10 exit 337 (Live Oak Road). Look for a possible Green Kingfisher at any stream crossings with flowing water.

Continuing east on US-290 from the junction with CR-304, notice the entrance to Fort Lancaster State Historical Park (1.0 mile). The fort was established in 1855 to protect settlers traveling the road between San Antonio and El Paso. It was abandoned in 1861. Soon after the fort entrance US-290 climbs a steep canyon to a picnic area (2.2 miles). In the canyon across from the picnic area, look from the roadside for Gray Vireo, a local breeder. Black-capped Vireo has occurred here. Listen for Canyon Wren. The view west is impressive. Interstate 10 exit 343 (TX-290 West) is reached by continuing east across barren flats for 8.8 miles. Detouring along TX-290 is a welcome reprieve for the interstate traveler.

The 400-mile stretch of Interstate 10 between El Paso and the hard-earned trees along the North Llano River west of Junction is dull and monotonous. Bird life is sparse. Smack dab in the middle of this drive is Fort Stockton, on the creosote-covered bedrock of the Stockton Plateau. For the traveler looking for a change of pace, nearby Imperial Reservoir is well worth a visit at any season.

IMPERIAL RESERVOIR

Imperial Reservoir is reached by taking Interstate 10 exit 259 (TX-18/FM-1053) in Fort Stockton. Head north on TX-18 to FM-1450 (23.3 miles). Take FM-1450 east to RR-2593 (3.2 miles), then north to the entrance on the left (2.9 miles). From Interstate 20, take exit 80 in Monahans and head south on TX-18 through Grandfalls. A $5 fee is charged per car for boating, fishing, or picnicking; it is possible that you might be asked to pay for a birding visit. Starting in 2000 the entrance gate has been closed much of the time. You may well be reduced to scoping the reservoir from outside the gate, putting you a considerable distance from the water.

Imperial Reservoir consistently has the best shorebird habitat in the Trans-Pecos. It is possible to drive along the east shore part way around the lake. A scope is necessary. Snowy Plovers breed, and recent observations suggest at least a few may be present all year. Expect to see Least Terns in the summer—they breed at least sporadically. An assortment of shorebirds is likely, and numerous waterfowl winter on the lake. Western and Clark's Grebes have been seen, but are not to be counted on as at Lake Balmorhea or McNary Reservoir to the west. Check for a stray loon between October and March, and look for odd herons and waterbirds in the warmer months.

The potential of this isolated body of water is evidenced by the rare birds reported in recent years: Red-throated and Pacific Loons, Brown Pelican, Reddish Egret, Roseate Spoonbill, Black-bellied Whistling-Duck, American Golden-Plover, Whimbrel, Hudsonian Godwit, Dunlin, Laughing Gull, Sabine's Gull, and Black-legged Kittiwake. Part of the lake is surrounded by Tamarisk which may hold a few migrants; the surrounding desert has little to offer. If you have a few hours to spare and enjoy the thrill of finding the unexpected, then pay Imperial Reservoir a visit.

RED BLUFF LAKE

To the north, at the Texas–New Mexico boundary, the Pecos River has been dammed to create Red Bluff Lake, by far the largest body of water in the Trans-Pecos. Although reasonably accessible from Interstate 20, the Guadalupe Mountains, or Carlsbad, New Mexico, the lake has been very lightly birded and its birds are poorly known. The chances for a significant find are good. Pacific Loon, Roseate Spoonbill, Parasitic Jaeger, and Black-legged Kittiwake have been reported in recent years, along with some sizable waterbird concentrations. The lake sits in some very stark oilfields, and adjacent areas will hold few birds.

Exit Interstate 20 in Pecos (exit 42), and head north on US-285 to the tiny town of Orla (40.0 miles). (You may notice on maps what appears to be a large lake—Lake Toyah—just south of Pecos. This "lake" is now, and is generally, a dry alkali flat, but has had water in wet years.) Orla is practically deserted; do not count on any services. Carlsbad, New Mexico, is 45 miles to the north, and, by taking FM-652 to the west, the Guadalupe Mountains are just over an hour away.

The land is nearly all private, and access to the lake is limited. Continue north from Orla on US-285 to FM-447 (2.7 miles). Turn right here to the dam (2.7 miles). As you approach the dam, look for a handpainted sign for a "Sand Beach." A right turn here leads to a beach on the east side from which the southern end of the lake can be scoped. Another option is to head to the dam, then left through a gate to some picnic tables. You may be charged a nominal fee here, but the south end can be examined. A scope is essential for this large lake.

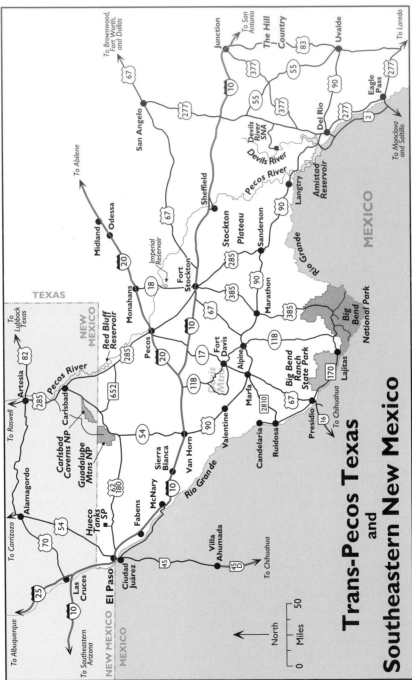

Trans-Pecos Texas
and
Southeastern New Mexico

TRANS-PECOS TEXAS

AND SELECTED NEW MEXICO SITES

The region of Texas west of the Pecos River is called the Trans-Pecos. The Chihuahuan Desert comprises most of this part of the state. Desert mountain ranges dominate the landscape down the center of this vast region, while the mixture of desert, grassland, and woodland gives this part of Texas an incredible diversity of habitats and, thus, birdlife.

The Chihuahuan Desert might appear barren and hostile at first glance, but a closer look reveals a markedly diverse avifauna. Granted, much of the desert is dominated by open creosote flats, not supporting much in the way of bird life. In contrast, however, riparian corridors and the mixed desert scrub growing along arroyos and in other protected areas offer excellent birding opportunities. In addition, mid-elevation grasslands provide habitat to an entirely different suite of birds. Unfortunately, there are no large tracts of grassland habitat open to the public, but roadside birding can usually provide you with an opportunity to observe most of its specialties. Finally, the mountains serve as islands of woodland habitats, each mountain range sheltering a slightly different avifauna. Big Bend and Guadalupe Mountains National Parks provide ready—if not always effortless—access to these montane habitats.

Trans-Pecos climate is dry and temperate, with a rainy season stretching from July into September. The amount of rainfall varies greatly from year to year, directly affecting the quality of birding throughout the entire year—wet summers mean lush vegetation in the fall, the primary blooming period for most plants, and that moisture translates into the quality of the winter food crop.

During summer it is not uncommon to find temperatures of 100 degrees or more from the Lower Valley to El Paso. If you can withstand these high temperatures, the late summer is an excellent time to visit Big Bend National Park to bird the Chisos Mountains. The temperatures in the mountains are usually in the upper 80s to low 90s. This is a great time to see the spectacular fall hummingbird migration and is the time to look for post-breeding wanderers from nearby mountain ranges in Mexico.

In general, fall migration starts with shorebirds in mid-July, reaching its peak in September and October. In the Trans-Pecos fall is often better than spring for observing passerine migrants. Large concentrations of birds are not so common as in spring, but your chances of finding rare and out-of-place species are greater.

Many western montane species found in the Trans-Pecos are not regular anywhere else in Texas. Colima Warbler is the only Trans-Pecos species that does not occur elsewhere in the United States. The Chisos Mountains in Big Bend National Park harbor the northernmost population of this warbler. Other montane species of interest include Montezuma Quail, Band-tailed Pigeon, Flammulated Owl, Whip-poor-will, Blue-throated and Broad-tailed Hummingbirds, Cordilleran Flycatcher, Plumbeous and Hutton's Vireos, Steller's and Mexican Jays, Mountain Chickadee, Pygmy Nuthatch, Western Bluebird, Grace's Warbler, Painted Redstart, Hepatic and Western Tanagers, Spotted Towhee, and Black-headed Grosbeak.

MARATHON

In the 1880s settlers began moving into the expansive grasslands of the Marathon Basin. With the arrival of the railroad, a booming cattle industry developed. The community of Marathon soon became well established as a rail stop, and cattle from all over the Big Bend region passed through its stockyards. A cattle baron, Alfred Gage, built the Gage Hotel in 1927 as the headquarters for his 600-section ranch, the largest landholding in Texas at the time. Legend has it that over a million head of cattle were bought and sold in the lobby of the Gage Hotel. Today, the restored hotel offers a welcome rest and West Texas dining for visitors to the Big Bend area.

To visit a small county park (locally referred to as The Post), turn south onto a paved road one-half mile west of the intersection of US-90 and US-385 to the entrance (5.0 miles). (Pavement gives way to dirt after about 4 miles.) Before reaching the park, the road crosses a creek. This area can be productive, particularly in winter. Look for Ring-necked Duck, Sora, Eastern Phoebe, Marsh Wren, and Common Yellowthroat. Inside the park the creek is dammed to form a small pond. There are numerous cottonwood trees in the park as well as manicured grounds and a small amount of desert scrub. This site is worth checking during migration and in winter. During breeding season look for Golden-fronted Woodpecker, Black Phoebe, Vermilion Flycatcher, Cactus Wren, and Lark and Black-throated Sparrows. In winter Yellow-bellied and Red-naped Sapsuckers, Marsh Wren, Brown Creeper, and numerous sparrows can be found. There have even been documented records from this site of Northern Jacana, Groove-billed Ani, and Lawrence's Goldfinch.

Before leaving Marathon for Big Bend, make sure that you have plenty of gasoline. The park entrance at Persimmon Gap is 42 miles south on US-385. The visitors center (park headquarters) at Panther Junction is 26 miles farther.

BIG BEND NATIONAL PARK

Halfway between El Paso and Laredo, the Rio Grande swings southward to form a large bend that now holds Big Bend National Park. (See map on page 104.) The park was established in 1944 and covers some 801,163 acres or about 1,252 square miles. The Chisos Mountains are the centerpiece of Big Bend. The woodlands of their upper elevations give way to desert grasslands which, in turn, give way to the open desert. During much of the year the desert can be extremely harsh and dry, but summer rains transform the landscape into green hillsides covered with wildflowers. This flush of growth coincides with fall bird migration; it is also the best time to search for vagrants coming out of the nearby Sierra del Carmen and other mountain ranges farther into Mexico.

Despite this harshness the park offers unforgettable scenery. The open desert is dissected with arroyos, and mountains rise majestically over the rocky terrain. The Rio Grande has carved a magnificent canyon with walls towering hundreds of feet above the river. One cannot begin to experience this vast park on a single visit.

Your first stop is the Visitors Center (open 8 AM–6 PM) at Panther Junction. There is a $10/week entrance fee as well as exhibits and books covering local history and natural history topics. The park staff can be very helpful in getting you oriented. You might want to buy a few books, road and trail guides, topographic maps, and checklists of the reptiles, mammals, and birds. A wildlife-sightings book is maintained at the front desk. You may contribute to the book by filling out sighting cards available from the personnel on duty. These cards are archived and their data have been used, for example, to form the backbone of Ro Wauer's *A Guide to the Birds of Big Bend*.

Gasoline can be a problem. Be sure to fill up before leaving Alpine or Marathon, or at the service stations just outside the park at Study Butte. The only gas stations in the park are located at Panther Junction and Rio Grande Village. They are open seven days a week, but normally only during regular business hours. You will find campgrounds, as well as small convenience stores offering limited supplies of food and campers' supplies, at Rio Grande Village, in The Basin, and at Castolon. For non-campers, there is a modern lodge, dining room, and stone cottages in The Basin. Advance reservations are required during most of the year; phone 915/477-2291.

Over 448 species of birds (57 of which are on the hypothetical list) have been recorded in Big Bend National Park, along with 75 species of mammals and 67 species of reptiles and amphibians. The avifauna of the mountains is very different from that of the desert, and the best birding spots are widely scattered in this vast park. A good strategy for the first-time visitor might be to visit birding areas at various elevations. Many of the most productive and regularly birded spots are detailed below, but there are literally dozens of little springs and canyons that may yield good birds. Study a map of the park, read one or more of the excellent bird-oriented natural history books (see

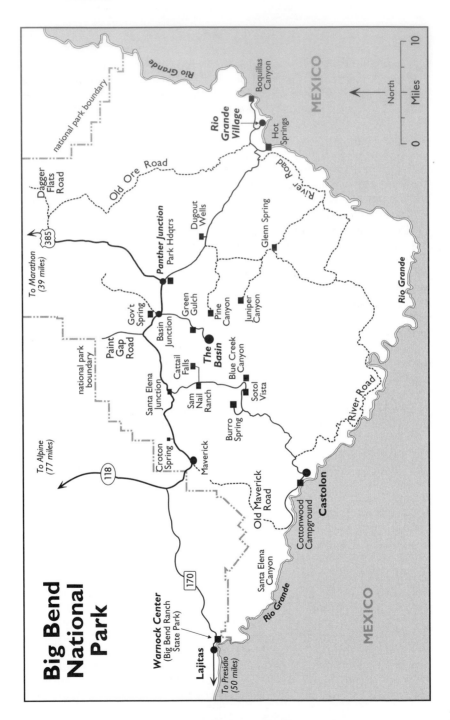

Big Bend National Park

References), and determine which areas you are interested in visiting. Then, in keeping with your vehicle's capability and your own stamina, explore some places not mentioned here!

Rio Grande Village—This area usually provides good year-round birding. The best place to start is at the little store. Walk into the cottonwood grove behind the store, making sure to check the boat ramp at the river.

Among the trees you may find White-winged and Inca Doves, Common Ground-Dove, Greater Roadrunner, Western Screech-Owl (night), Great Horned Owl, Golden-fronted and Ladder-backed Woodpeckers, Vermilion Flycatcher, Black-tailed Gnatcatcher, Northern Mockingbird, Brown-headed Cowbird, House Finch, and Lesser Goldfinch. In summer look for Gray Hawk, Yellow-billed Cuckoo, Elf Owl (night), Black-chinned Hummingbird, Western Kingbird, Summer Tanager, Blue Grosbeak, Painted Bunting, Bronzed Cowbird, and Orchard Oriole. In winter watch for Yellow-bellied and Red-naped Sapsuckers, Northern (Red-shafted) Flicker, Blue-gray Gnatcatcher, American Robin, Ruby-crowned Kinglet, Orange-crowned and Yellow-rumped Warblers, Green-tailed and Spotted Towhees, Dark-eyed Junco, and American Goldfinch. During migration an amazing variety of eastern and western species has been found here. Yellow-green Vireo has been recorded on three occasions, and many other rarities have made an appearance, including Ruddy Ground-Dove, Tufted Flycatcher, Thick-billed Kingbird, Tropical Parula, and Black-vented Oriole. The Sennett's race of Hooded Oriole found here is almost red about the face, however these birds can often be difficult to locate.

The road to the right of the store goes past the RV campsites to the river (0.7 mile). Upon reaching the parking area check the thickets along the river and surrounding the cottonwood stand, all of which can be productive. The species here are the same as those listed above. This is usually the best location for finding Gray Hawk, and Great Horned Owls are almost always present. Keep an eye overhead for Zone-tailed Hawks. In winter look for a variety of sparrows, including Swamp and White-throated. Check the small pond behind the northwest corner of the cottonwood stand for Common Yellowthroat, which is present year round. The resident subspecies of Common Yellowthroat is very bright and slightly larger than the migratory subspecies that winter in the park. This is also a good place for Black Phoebe, swallows, and waterbirds, such as Pied-billed Grebes and herons. Shorebirds (if mudflats are present) and Sora are often about during migration. Least Grebe has been found on a couple of occasions. An interesting plant that is common in this area, as well as in other parts of the park, is Screwbean Mesquite (*Prosopis pubescens*). The tightly-corkscrewed seed pod is among the most interesting fruit of any plant in the park.

The road to the left of the store also leads to the river. There is a small pond down a service road on the right just before the entrance to the campground where you should look for Pied-billed Grebe, American Coot, or Ring-necked Duck; this area also can be productive for passerines year round. This pond is home of the world's native population of *Gambusia affinis*; the water swarms with this tiny mosquitofish. Verdin, Canyon Towhee, Pyrrhuloxia, and, in summer, Bell's Vireo can be found in mesquite thickets.

Go back and carefully check the campground. Elf Owls are sometimes found using cavities in utility poles carved by Ladder-backed Woodpeckers. In general, though, you should find the same species here as mentioned for the area around the store.

A short nature trail starts opposite campsite #18. From the boardwalk, among the tangle of willows and Carrizo Cane, you may spot Yellow-billed Cuckoo, Bell's Vireo, Painted Bunting, Orchard Oriole, and many migrants in season. The trail ends on a high point above the river. From this vantage point scan the cattail-filled ponds and surroundings, watching for Belted Kingfisher, Common Yellowthroat, and Yellow-breasted Chat. This is an excellent spot for migrants. Shorebirds can sometimes be found along the shoreline of the river, and, in summer, the air may be filled with Northern Rough-winged, Cliff, and Barn Swallows. Cave Swallows also have been seen in this area, though they are fairly rare in the park.

Boquillas Canyon (*Bow-KEY-yas*)—This canyon is a spectacular sight, but it is better for photography than for birds. White-throated Swifts and Canyon Wrens can be found along the cliffs, and Rock Wrens and Black-throated Sparrows can usually be found along the trail to the canyon. On summer nights Common Poorwills are usually common along the entrance road. Sage Thrashers are sporadic winter visitors in the park, but can often be found in the mesquite flats up canyon during fall and early winter.

Hot Springs—Hot Springs is located toward Panther Junction from Rio Grande Village. A rather rough 2-mile-long road leads to an abandoned village. From there it's a one-mile hike to the springs, one of the more picturesque spots along the river. Say's Phoebes have nested about the ruins of the old motel, and Hooded Orioles nest in the cottonwoods. Bell's Vireos and Verdins frequent the mesquite thickets, while Black-tailed Gnatcatchers flit around in the dry washes.

River Road—This primitive road crosses the southern end of the park from Rio Grande Village to Castolon—a high-clearance vehicle is required. However, it takes less time to go to Castolon by way of Panther Junction on the paved road, so do not take this road if your time is limited, and do not go at any time of year other than winter. The way is long, hot, dry, and rough, but geologists and botanists will find it fascinating. The display of Big Bend Bluebonnets in February can be breathtaking.

Dugout Wells—This little oasis can be good during migration and early in the morning during dry periods, in part because there is a still functioning windmill here. Resident species are Scaled Quail, Greater Roadrunner, Ladder-backed Woodpecker, Northern Mockingbird, and Black-throated Sparrow. Bell's Vireos nest; listen for their two-part song that seems to ask a question and then answers itself. The surrounding creosote flats are good for finding Verdin and Black-tailed Gnatcatcher. There are well-documented records of such rare species as Yellow-green Vireo and Rufous-capped Warbler from this location.

Pine Canyon—The turn-off, located on graveled Glenn Spring Road, is about 2.5 miles south of the main road. The primitive road goes up the canyon another 5 miles, but the last few are steep, rocky, and sometimes impassable. At road-end is the old Wade Ranch, from which a short trail leads to a waterfall. During the rainy season, the cascade can be impressive.

The upper part of the canyon is well-wooded and full of birds. Here, among the Arizona Cypress, Arizona and Mexican Pinyon Pines, Douglas-fir, Texas Madrone, Big-toothed Maple, and Emory and Grave's Oaks, look in summer for Black-chinned and Broad-tailed Hummingbirds, Ash-throated Flycatcher, Hutton's Vireo, Mexican Jay, Tufted (Black-crested) Titmouse, Bushtit, Bewick's Wren, Blue-gray Gnatcatcher, Hepatic Tanager, Spotted Towhee, Rufous-crowned Sparrow, and Black-headed Grosbeak. In August and early September many of the higher-elevation species can be found in the upper reaches of this canyon, including Colima Warbler. In recent years this canyon has produced some real rarities, including Dusky-capped and Sulphur-bellied Flycatchers and Flame-colored Tanager (first state record).

Juniper Canyon—A good birding area, but difficult to reach. The turn-off is 4.4 miles beyond the Pine Canyon Road turn-off on the Glenn Spring Road. From here a very rough and primitive road leads another 7.5 miles into the canyon. A 6.5-mile hiking trail continues upcanyon to the cabin at Boot Spring. It is a rough hike, but you should see numerous birds.

Green Gulch—The first 5 miles of the 7-mile road leading into The Basin go through Green Gulch. In the desert scrub at the bottom, you can expect Scaled Quail, Greater Roadrunner, Verdin, Black-tailed Gnatcatcher, Curve-billed Thrasher, and Black-throated Sparrow. As the brush gets thicker, look for Ladder-backed Woodpecker, Bell's Vireo, Phainopepla, Pyrrhuloxia, and Varied Bunting. When you see the first Drooping Junipers, start watching for flowering agaves. Their tall flower-stalks furnish a banquet for White-winged Dove, Lucifer and Black-chinned Hummingbirds, and Scott's Oriole. After the agaves quit blooming in summer, the hummingbirds move up into the mountains to take advantage of the late-summer and fall bloom at these higher elevations. There are convenient pull-outs for parking along this road.

Lost Mine Trail—The road up Green Gulch passes through Panther Pass (El. 5,800 ft) on the way into The Basin. Here you will find the start of the Lost Mine Trail (see map on following page). The view into Juniper Canyon at the end of this two-mile trail is one of the finest in the park, but most hikers settle for the magnificent view at the end of the first mile. Buy a pamphlet for the self-guided tour at the trailhead; following it will give you a better understanding of the area. During late summer and fall this trail can be excellent for hummingbirds and other fall migrants. At any time of year the

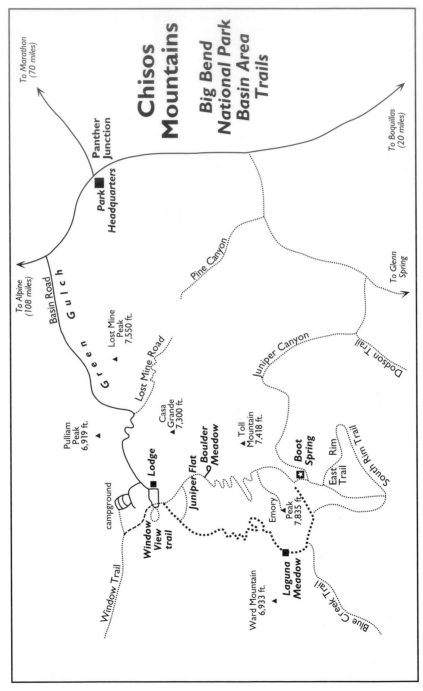

Chisos Mountains

Big Bend National Park Basin Area Trails

To Marathon (70 miles)

To Boquillas (20 miles)

Panther Junction

Park Headquarters

To Alpine (108 miles)

Basin Road

Green Gulch

Pine Canyon

To Glenn Spring

Lost Mine Peak 7,550 ft.

Lost Mine Road

Juniper Canyon

Dodson Trail

Pulliam Peak 6,919 ft.

Casa Grande 7,300 ft.

Toll Mountain 7,418 ft.

Boulder Meadow

Boot Spring

Rim Trail

South Rim Trail

Lodge

Juniper Flat

East Trail

campground

Emory Peak 7,835 ft.

Window View trail

Window Trail

Ward Mountain 6,933 ft.

Laguna Meadow

Blue Creek Trail

oak woodlands can produce Hutton's Vireo, Mexican Jay, Bushtit, Summer Tanager, and Black-headed Grosbeak among other mid-elevation montane species.

The Basin—This large bowl-shaped valley sits in the very center of the Chisos Mountains at about 5,400 feet elevation. The beauty of the surrounding peaks and the relatively cooler, highland climate makes this a favorite spot for both birds and people in summer. Chisos Lodge and a large campground (fee) are located here. Mexican Jay, Cactus Wren, and Canyon Towhee are often abundant. The area about the hotel and campground is very good for Black-chinned Sparrow and Lesser Goldfinch. Elf Owls and Common Poorwills can be heard on summer nights. The best birding is along the trails that emanate from the Basin Trailhead. There are 32 hiking trails in the park totaling more than 150 miles. These are listed in the *Hiker's Guide* published by the Big Bend Natural History Association, available at park headquarters or from the ranger station at The Basin.

The Window Trail—This 5.2-mile round-trip trail starts at The Basin Trailhead across the parking lot from the lodge, but it is a mile shorter if you catch it along the southwest edge of the campground. You cross a brushy grassland interspersed with oaks, pinyon, and juniper, where in early morning you could see Ladder-backed Woodpecker, Say's Phoebe, Cactus and Bewick's Wrens, Canyon Towhee, Rufous-crowned and Black-chinned Sparrows, Pyrrhuloxia, Blue Grosbeak, and Scott's Oriole. Black-capped (scarce) and Gray Vireos breed in the scrub habitat below the sewer pond. This is also a good area to look for Varied Bunting. There is even a winter record of Elegant Trogon. Blooming *Anisacanthus* along the bottom half-mile of the trail is the best place in the park to find Lucifer Hummingbird.

Boot Spring—In summer this is the most exciting area for birding in the park. Colima Warbler is the main attraction, but there are other tantalizing possibilities. When you are this close to the border, who knows what may wander up from Mexico! Some of the rarities that have been documented include Berylline Hummingbird, Elegant Trogon, Greater Pewee, Aztec Thrush, Red-faced Warbler, and Yellow-eyed Junco. Most of these birds have only been found once or twice, but the potential for vagrants from Mexico is readily apparent.

The hike to the spring is strenuous. All of the routes into Boot Canyon require long hikes. The most direct route is up Pinnacles Trail via Boulder Meadow and Pinnacle Pass (El. 7,100 ft). It is a steep 3.5-mile climb to the top of the pass, after which the trail descends another mile into Boot Canyon.

The 10-mile loop-route used by most birders goes up the Laguna Meadow Trail from the Basin Trailhead, across the Colima Trail, and heads back down the Boot Canyon Trail and Pinnacles Trail through Boulder Meadow. Following this route, it is 5.5 miles to the spring, but the hiking is much easier. (A good point to remember is that Colima Warblers can be present all summer at Laguna Meadow. If this is your only target bird, you may not have to go the whole loop-route, though the Boot Spring area itself is excellent for

Colima Warbler
Narca Moore-Craig

many other birds as well.) The trail from Pinnacle Pass to Boulder Meadows is very steep. There are 22 switch-backs and the hike down can be difficult.

There is no drinking water at Boot Spring. Be sure to take along plenty. This is usually a long, hot trip, but it is sometimes cool, particularly after the rainy season starts.

Mid-April through mid-June is the best time to find the breeding birds of the lower elevations, but some of the highland species do not start to nest until the summer rains begin in early July. By late June many of the lowland birds have moved into the mountains, and by late August there are post-breeders from the Rockies present.

As soon as you leave the Basin Trailhead, start watching for Ash-throated Flycatcher, Bewick's Wren, and Rufous-crowned Sparrow. Crissal Thrasher and Black-chinned Sparrow have nested on the brushy hillsides at Laguna Meadow (3.5 miles). When the red-flowered Mountain Sage and the yellow-flowered Century Plant are in bloom, this meadow is a great spot for Black-chinned Hummingbird and Scott's Oriole. Watch for post-nesting Lucifer and Rufous Hummingbirds as well.

Above Laguna Meadow you enter the woodlands of deciduous oaks and maples that are preferred by Colima Warblers. In early summer the new leaves of the oaks stand out in sharp contrast to the surrounding vegetation, making it easy to pick out clumps where warblers might be found. The birds can sometimes be found at lower elevations when they first arrive in mid-April or just before they leave in mid-September, but the nesting sites (nests are built on the ground) are all above 5,900 feet elevation.

Although this warbler responds well to squeaks, pishes, and owl calls, it can be hard to see. It is usually located by its trilling song, which is suggestive of that of a Pine Warbler or a Chipping Sparrow. Luckily, the males are persistent singers from late April to about mid-June. The females can often be found by their sharp *psit* call-notes.

At the start of the South Rim Trail, 0.5 mile above Laguna Meadow, there is a trail junction. The trail to the right continues along the rim and joins the Southeast Rim Trail, which eventually comes back to the Boot Canyon Trail after 3 miles. To the left is the Boot Canyon Trail; this portion of the trail is called the "Colima Trail." It is 1 mile to the cabin at the spring, which is located in about the middle of the canyon. Boot Canyon is well wooded with Arizona Cypress, Arizona Pine, Douglas-fir, Texas Madrone, Big-tooth Maple, and Emory and Grave Oaks, and offers some of the best birding in the Chisos. Another area that should be carefully birded is the first few hundred yards of the South Rim Trail above Boot Spring. The mixture of maples and oaks makes this another prime birding area.

Colima Warblers are fairly common and can be found throughout this area, including all of Boot Canyon and along all of the trails emanating from the cabin. Also watch for Band-tailed Pigeon, and Blue-throated, Magnificent (rare), and Broad-tailed Hummingbirds. During fall migration, hundreds of Black-chinned, Broad-tailed, and Rufous Hummingbirds can be seen daily. Keep a careful watch for less common species, such as Lucifer, Calliope, and Ruby-throated Hummingbirds. Male Calliopes move through in July followed by females and immatures during August. It is not unusual to see seven species of hummingbirds during an August hike in the Chisos. Watch for Acorn Woodpecker, Cordilleran Flycatcher, Hutton's Vireo, Mexican Jay, Violet-green Swallow, Tufted (Black-crested) Titmouse, Bushtit, White-breasted Nuthatch, Painted Redstart (some summers), and Hepatic Tanager. Warbler migration, particularly in the fall (mid-August to early October), can be fabulous. Orange-crowned, Yellow-rumped, Townsend's, Black-and-white, and Wilson's are the most common migrant warblers. Usually there are also a few Virginia's, Black-throated Gray, and Hermit Warblers around. Nashville and MacGillivray's Warblers are found as high as Boulder Meadow, but are more usual at lower elevations. Red-faced Warbler was documented almost annually in the Chisos during the 1990s; most records are from August and in most years only one bird has been located. A Slate-throated Redstart was seen here in spring 1990. If you camp here overnight, you should hear Flammulated Owl, Western Screech-Owl, and Whip-poor-will.

About one-half mile below the cabin on your way back to The Basin, you will find the Boot, a volcanic spire shaped like an upside-down cowboy boot.

In the same area, is the Emory Peak Trail, which goes one mile to the top of the highest peak (El. 7,835 ft) in the park. There are not many birds on the mountain, but the view is terrific.

One-half mile below the Emory Peak Trail is Pinnacle Pass (El. 7,100 ft), from which you can get a fine view of The Basin far below. From this high vantage point, you can see Turkey Vultures, Red-tailed Hawks, an occasional Golden Eagle, and White-throated Swifts. This is also a great place to watch for Zone-tailed Hawk. Carefully check all of the vultures to make sure that none has a bright-yellow cere and black-and-white-banded tail.

A 1.5-mile series of steep switchbacks brings you to the floor of The Basin at Boulder Meadow, only 1.5 miles from the lodge. This slope is also excellent birding, with Colima Warblers possible along the upper half of this stretch. You may be too tired after the long walk to Boot Spring to bird this area, but if you come back another day, you will find it to be a good spot. Lucifer Hummingbirds are sometimes common in summer about the agaves.

Government Spring—This spring is on the left side of the road to the Grapevine Hills (0.3 mile west of Basin Junction) about one-half mile north of the main road from Panther Junction to Maverick. When the spring is flowing, birds come here to drink. Look for Scaled Quail, Canyon Towhee, Black-throated Sparrow, Pyrrhuloxia, Varied Bunting, and migrants. Many wintering sparrows feed at the horse corral. Early in the morning, or just at dusk, you can often see Mule Deer, Collared Peccary, Coyote, and Desert Cottontail coming to the spring, and you might see a Common Gray Fox, a Bobcat, or even a Mountain Lion. Be on the lookout for rattlesnakes in summer.

The rest of the road to the Grapevine Hills is scenic, but is usually not as productive as other areas in the park. There is good habitat for Lucifer Hummingbirds along the arroyos found throughout this grassland. The same may be said of the Paint Gap Road. Croton Spring can be good for mammals, but the spring is not so productive since it was "improved" a few years ago.

Sam Nail Ranch—The parking area for the ranch is 3 miles south of Santa Elena Junction. Most of the buildings are gone, but the windmill still creaks out a trickle of water that lures numerous birds and mammals. In season, it is an excellent migrant trap, with the birds concentrated in a very small area. By spending an hour or two in this peaceful spot (a bench in the shade is provided for your comfort), you may see Yellow-billed Cuckoo, Lucifer and Black-chinned Hummingbirds, Bell's Vireo, and Painted Bunting. Orange-crowned, Nashville, Virginia's, Yellow, and Wilson's Warblers are frequently found in migration. There are also records of migrant Blackburnian and Prairie Warblers from this location. Look for Yellow-breasted Chat, Summer Tanager, Black-throated Sparrow, Northern Cardinal, Pyrrhuloxia, Blue Grosbeak, Scott's Oriole, and House Finch. Crissal Thrasher and Varied Bunting are frequently seen here, particularly the bunting. They come to the water, particularly during spring and early summer when water is scarce elsewhere, but are often seen in the area between the parking area and the old buildings.

Cattail Falls—Cattail Creek starts on the north side of Ward Mountain, flowing westward. During periods of heavy rain, it actually crosses the highway just north of Sam Nail Ranch. To reach the falls, go east on Oak Canyon Road, which starts almost opposite the Sam Nail Ranch parking area. The dirt road soon bears left to cross the dry bed of Cattail Creek. Park and walk up the creekbed, looking for the same species as at Sam Nail Ranch.

Blue Creek Canyon—On the left, near the highest point on the Santa Elena Road, is Blue Creek Overlook, from which a trail drops into the canyon and climbs 5.5 miles up to Laguna Meadow. About a mile above the old Wilson Ranch, and near a spectacular formation of red rock spires, a narrow canyon branches off to the north. A rare red oak (*Quercus graciliformis*) occurs far up the canyon. This canyon is particularly good for Lucifer Hummingbird, Gray Vireo, Crissal Thrasher, and Varied Bunting in April and May. Black-capped Vireos also occur in this canyon.

Sotol Vista—This view is terrific, though the Sotol-dominated grassland surrounding the parking area is usually not very productive for birds. Wintering grassland sparrows can sometimes be found at this location.

Burro Spring—This is one of the better springs in the desert areas of the park, and it attracts many animals. The one mile trail to it starts from the road that leads to the Burro Mesa Pour-off. There is another trail that goes to the pour-off, but the spring is the better birding spot.

The spring attracts the usual mammals, such as Mule Deer, Collared Peccary, and Coyote, but you may also see Burro. Most of the Burros have just wandered up from Mexico, but they have adapted quickly and well to the hostile environment. The tourists may consider these hardy animals to be cute, but they can be very detrimental to the fragile habitat and to the native mammals.

Castolon (25 miles from Santa Elena Junction)—The weedy fields near Castolon are at their best in early winter, when you can find great flocks of sparrows. The common sparrows are Clay-colored, Brewer's, Vesper, and White-crowned. With a little more effort, you may find Cassin's, Chipping, Field, Savannah, Grasshopper, Song, Lincoln's, Swamp, and White-throated.

Cottonwood Campground is located here (fee, primitive). This is currently an excellent birding location, but this area will be slowly undergoing change. The cottonwoods require regular watering and care by the park service personnel. As these cottonwoods die, they will be replaced with lower maintenance, desert adapted species. Greater Roadrunners are tame here and White-winged Doves are abundant. Migrant warblers such as Yellow-rumped (Audubon's) are common in spring. Other nesting species include Mourning and Inca Doves, Western Screech-Owl (common in this area), Great Horned Owl, Common Poorwill, Ash-throated Flycatcher, Western Kingbird, Black-tailed Gnatcatcher, Summer Tanager, and Orchard

Oriole. Black Vultures can be seen in this area of the park. Thick-billed Kingbirds nested here from 1988 to 1991, and Tropical Kingbirds nested in 1996–1998. One of the main attraction of this campground is that it is one of the best places in Texas to see Lucy's Warbler. The warblers, which usually arrive in early March and remain through early July, are found in the mesquite woodlands surrounding the campground.

The mesquite thickets and willows along the river might yield Ladder-backed Woodpecker, Vermilion Flycatcher, Common Yellowthroat, and Canyon Towhee. Other birds to be found in summer are Yellow-billed Cuckoo, Black-chinned Hummingbird, Bell's Vireo, Yellow-breasted Chat, Summer Tanager, Blue Grosbeak, Painted Bunting, and Orchard Oriole. Lucy's Warbler is also found in the mesquite thickets from Castolon to Santa Elena Canyon.

Between Castolon and Cottonwood Campground watch for a road on the left leading to the river-crossing for Santa Elena, Mexico. This maintained dirt road offers excellent birding in stands of cottonwoods along arroyos in several locations along the road. All of the species listed for the campground campground can be found here, as well as Gray Hawks, which have nested in the cottonwood stands.

Santa Elena Canyon—You might want to visit this very scenic spot, but it is not particularly good for birds. However, you will be impressed by the Peregrine Falcons and White-throated Swifts that zoom up and down the canyon, and who can forget the Canyon Wrens, whose beautiful songs echo down from the cliffs? The 1.7-mile round-trip trail into the canyon has markers identifying the plants and features. Be on the alert for rarities; on at least two occasions Rufous-capped Warblers have made an appearance in this canyon.

Old Maverick Road—This 14-mile gravel road leading from Santa Elena Canyon to Maverick (west entrance to park) can be good for hawks at all seasons and nightjars on summer evenings. It also makes an interesting alternative to retracing your way back up the main road. At the turn of the century, this was prime grassland with cottonwood-lined streams. By the end of World War I, overgrazing and drought had reduced it to its present state.

TX-118 to Alpine—Of all of the routes into the park, this one offers the best opportunities for birding. In winter the grasslands along the way abound with sparrows and Lark Buntings. About midway a wooded rest area should be checked for migrants and resident Golden-fronted Woodpeckers. North of that is Calamity Creek, which sometimes attracts a few birds. As the road climbs toward Alpine it enters an open oak-juniper woodland, an excellent area for Townsend's Solitaire, and Western and Mountain Bluebirds during good winters. The abundance of these species varies greatly from year to year.

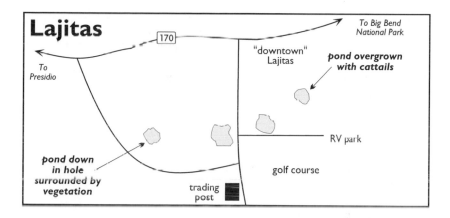

Lajitas–Big Bend Ranch State Park–Presidio Route—The route to US-90 via FM-170 and US-67—ending at Marfa—is longer and rougher than heading north on TX-118 to intersect US-90 at Alpine, but it offers a scenic trip along the river. The headquarters for Big Bend Ranch State Park (16.0 miles from the FM-170/TX-118 junction) is on the south side of the road. Stop here at the Barton Warnock Environmental Education Center for information on this new state park.

In Lajitas (1.2 miles) turn south (toward the river) at the center of town where there are signs advertising the trading post, golf course, and RV campground. Down this dirt road there are four ponds, two on each side of the road (0.1 mile). The two closest to the road are the least productive. The other two have vegetation all around them and are difficult to see; however, they are worth the time to check. A Ruddy Ground-Dove spent a month here in 1990. Resident species which you may find include "Mexican Duck" Mallard, White-winged and Inca Doves, Black-throated Sparrow, and House Finch. Lucifer Hummingbird is a rare breeder in this area. In winter also look for Green Heron, Swamp Sparrow, and Lesser Goldfinch. Migrants include various western warbler species, Grasshopper Sparrow, and Lazuli Bunting. Several unusual sightings include Swallow-tailed Kite, Sora, and Common Grackle.

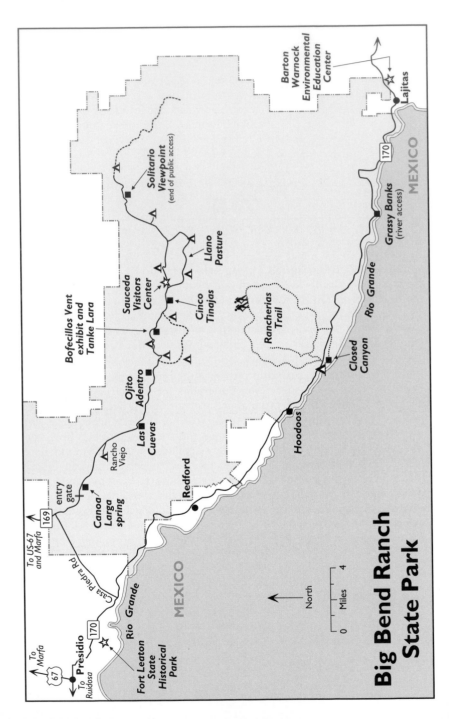

Big Bend Ranch
State Park

Barton Warnock Environmental Education Center

Lajitas

170

MEXICO

Grassy Banks
(river access)

Solitario Viewpoint
(end of public access)

Rio Grande

Llano Pasture

Sauceda Visitors Center

Cinco Tinajas

Rancherias Trail

Bofecillos Vent exhibit and Tanke Lara

Closed Canyon

Ojito Adentro

Hoodoos

Las Cuevas

Rancho Viejo

Redford

entry gate

Canoa Larga spring

To US-67 and Marfa

169

MEXICO

Casa Piedra Rd.

North

Miles
0   4

Rio Grande

To Marfa

67

To Ruidosa

170

Presidio

Fort Leaton State Historical Park

BIG BEND RANCH STATE PARK

Big Bend Ranch State Park (entrance fee $3/person) is the largest state park in Texas and one of the largest in the U.S. Approximately 280,000 acres in size, it stretches more than 45 miles from the southeast corner of the park to the northwest corner. The park can be divided into four fairly distinct units: the Barton Warnock Environmental Education Center near Lajitas, the river corridor along FM-170 between Presidio and Lajitas, Fort Leaton State Historical Park near Presidio, and Sauceda in the interior of the park in an area accessible to the public (the Bofecillos Mountains/Plateau). The majority of this vast park lacks the roads and other infrastructure to allow public access at this time.

Birds of the area are typical of those found in the general region and in the northern portions of the Chihuahuan Desert. Habitats include riparian woodlands and thickets, canyons, desert scrub, and desert grasslands. Elevations range from approximately 2,200 feet near Lajitas to 5,135 feet at Oso Mountain's summit. The river corridor is open to the general public, but permits are required if you leave the highway right-of-way. To access Sauceda in the interior, you must get a permit and gate combination at either Fort Leaton or the Warnock Center at Lajitas. Day-trips are permitted in the interior; overnight accommodations include primitive camping at one of ten designated areas, bunkhouse-style lodging, and lodging in the main ranch house. Campers may shower at the Sauceda Visitors Center.

Environmental conditions at the park are extremely harsh at times. Temperatures exceeding 100° F. can occur between March–October. Most plants are armed with thorns, several species of animals can inflict painful bites or stings, and several species of snakes are venomous. Backcountry areas of the park are vast, remote, and irregularly patrolled—getting lost would potentially risk one's life. If you are going to bird remote portions of the park, always consult the park staff in advance and advise them of your plans. At the Warnock Center near Lajitas, you can walk through a desert garden to become familiar with many of the desert plants found at the park. The garden's water pond and feeders attract a variety of desert birds as well as migrants.

Several areas along the river are suitable introductions to your birding adventure at Big Bend Ranch State Park. West of Lajitas (approximately 8 miles) stop at Grassy Banks. Bird along the dirt roads and the river in mesquite and Tamarisk (salt cedar) habitat. You can usually find Ladder-backed Woodpecker, Black and Say's Phoebes, Vermilion Flycatcher, Verdin, Black-tailed Gnatcatcher, Crissal Thrasher and Pyrrhuloxia at this location. This area can be very productive during spring and fall migrations; during winters subsequent to a wet summer and fall season the area can be especially good. Typical winter birds include Spotted Sandpiper, White-throated Swift, Northern Rough-winged Swallow, Ruby-crowned Kinglet, Blue-gray Gnatcatcher, Hermit Thrush, American Pipit,

Orange-crowned and Yellow-rumped Warblers, Green-tailed and Spotted Towhees, Chipping, Brewer's, Savannah, Lincoln's and White-crowned Sparrows, Dark-eyed Junco, and Lesser Goldfinch. Gray, Dusky, and Ash-throated Flycatchers, Lucy's and Townsend's Warblers, Blue Grosbeak, Varied Bunting, and Scott's Oriole have also been observed in winter.

Numerous other sites along the river road provide birding opportunities in similar habitats. Two major trails lead off of the highway: one is the 18-mile-long Rancherias Loop and the other is the Rancherias Canyon Trail, which is available for day-hikes. Because summer seasons are excessively hot, the best time to visit is from October through April. On the steep bluffs of Colorado Canyon, and at one additional site upstream in the vicinity of the Hoodoos (approximately 15 miles), look for the usually present Peregrine Falcons. Summer birds expected along this corridor are typical of those occupying riparian habitat zones throughout the region and include Turkey Vulture, White-winged Dove, Lesser Nighthawk, Black-chinned Hummingbird, Ash-throated Flycatcher, Western Kingbird, Bell's Vireo, Cliff Swallow, Yellow-breasted Chat, Summer Tanager, Blue Grosbeak, Varied and Painted Buntings, Bronzed Cowbird, Orchard, Hooded, Bullock's and Scott's Orioles, and Lesser Goldfinch.

As you continue along FM-170 toward Presidio, agricultural activities begin to become more evident where the flood plain of the Rio Grande widens near Redford (about 23 miles from Grassy Banks). In summer you can find Yellow-breasted Chat, Northern Cardinal, and Varied and Painted Buntings.

A potentially good birding stop is Alamito Marsh, located just west of and including the Alamito Creek bridge on the highway (8.5 miles). Between the road and the Rio Grande is a small marshy area that can be loaded with migrant waterfowl and shorebirds. Most of the shorebirds will be Least Sandpipers, but Westerns are also common, and there will be some Baird's. The marsh can yield Green Heron, various rails, Marsh Wren, Common Yellowthroat, Swamp Sparrow, and Red-winged Blackbird.

Fort Leaton State Historical Park, located 3 miles south of Presidio on FM-170, serves as the western visitor-services station for Big Bend Ranch State Park. Bird among the cottonwood trees and the thorn scrub-mesquite woodland located behind Fort Leaton, excellent especially during spring and fall migrations.

If you have decided to explore the interior of Big Bend Ranch State Park (after obtaining the proper permits at Fort Leaton), turn around and proceed south (toward Lajitas) on FM-170 for 5 miles, turning left onto Casa Piedra Road. This county-maintained dirt road leads northeast for some 26.5 miles to Sauceda Visitors Center. Approximately 6.9 miles down Casa Piedra Road take the right fork of the road and proceed 2.4 miles ahead to the locked-gate entrance to the park. Just a short distance into the park (just past the Botella turn-off where wayside exhibit #1 is located) is Canoa Larga, a desert spring. Look in the thickets to the right of the road to find where the spring flows into a water trough. The combination of thick cover and water attracts a variety of typical low-desert birds and migrants; Gray Vireo has wintered at this location.

Wayside exhibit #2 near Rancho Viejo (13.2 miles from FM-170) offers another opportunity to look for typical desert birds. Ahead another 2.5 miles is Las Cuevas wayside exhibit (#3). The yellow bluffs of volcanic tuff located here beg to be photographed. The road then crosses Bofecillos Creek and its woodland thickets, but be careful to confine your birding to the main road because the area off-road is restricted to guided tours only.

Two and one-half miles ahead (18.2 miles from FM-170) is one of your best birding opportunities in the interior. Stop at the Ojito Adentro wayside (#4) and walk the short trail (less than one-half mile) down to the beautiful woodland tucked into the head of the canyon. This cottonwood-willow-hackberry woodland gallery is typical of many such sites on the park where permanent surface water exists. A beautiful 30-foot high waterfall is located at the end of the trail. Find a spot where birds are coming to drink at the surface water of the stream, sit quietly in the shade, and observe. This site can be particularly productive during migration and likewise during some winters. Anna's and Rufous Hummingbirds, Dusky Flycatcher, and Varied Bunting have been seen here in winter. Numerous species of flycatchers, vireos, warblers (including Painted Redstart), tanagers, and orioles have been observed at this location during migration. Continue eastward on the main road for just over a mile; at the top of the steep hill is Cuesta Prima, which provides a scenic overlook of Bofecillos Canyon and, in the distance, Presidio and the Rio Grande.

Just past wayside exhibit #6 (Bofecillos Vent), approximately 23 miles from the highway, is Tanke Lara. The earthen tank can be productive when water is present. During winter a number of waterfowl species use the pond; look for shorebirds during migration. In summer, a special treat is the evening flight of Lesser and Common Nighthawks, as well as a number of bat species. Almost 3 miles ahead is wayside exhibit #7 (Cinco Tinajas, five waterholes). Levya Canyon cuts a narrow slot through the volcanic mountains creating secluded pools of semi-permanent to permanent water in the solid rock bottom of the creek. Black Phoebes should be active at the pools; Rock and Canyon Wrens serenade from the bluffs of the canyon.

Sauceda Visitors Center and Ranch Complex is only 0.6 mile ahead. At times, excellent birding opportunities exist about the grounds and along Levya Creek just west of the complex. In this typical desert habitat, summer birds include Elf Owl, Common Nighthawk, Common Poorwill, Golden-fronted Woodpecker, Say's Phoebe, Vermilion and Ash-throated Flycatchers, Cassin's Kingbird, Loggerhead Shrike, Cliff, Cave, and Barn Swallows, Verdin, Cactus and Bewick's Wrens, Curve-billed Thrasher, House Finch, and Lesser Goldfinch. During migration, Red-winged, Yellow-headed, and Brewer's Blackbirds, Bronzed and Brown-headed Cowbirds, and an occasion Great-tailed Grackle are usually found in the corrals. Look for numbers of sparrows of several species in winter.

From Sauceda, you can take a loop drive through Llano Pasture (8.5 miles round-trip). To begin, go east past the airport and turn to the south 3 miles from Sauceda. Desert grassland habitats can be found all along this route and can be very productive at times, especially after the wetter late-summer and fall rainy periods. A high-clearance vehicle is recommended. Look for excellent sparrow diversity in winter: Black-throated Sparrow is a common resident, Sage Sparrow is usually uncommon in winter, and Cassin's Sparrow can be abundant in spring and summer. These grassland flats have also harbored Prairie Falcon, Gambel's Quail, Green-tailed Towhee, and Chestnut-collared and McCown's Longspurs at times. If you can find a desert waterhole (look behind the numerous erosion control berms in the drainages), find a shady spot to sit quietly and watch the water. You will be rewarded with good looks at almost every species of bird in the vicinity and, at times, other species of wildlife.

On the main park road, 9 miles east of Sauceda, the public access ends at the Fresno Canyon-Solitario overlook (wayside exhibit #10). Here you can get a spectacular vista of Fresno Canyon and The Solitario (a collapsed volcano 8–10 miles in diameter). Enjoy the view and the solitude—you are 35 miles from the highway.

TWO ROUTES FROM PRESIDIO TO MARFA

Presidio is said to be the oldest settlement in the United States. The Indians inhabited this region long before Spaniards arrived in the sixteenth century. At Presidio you have a choice: you can turn north to Marfa on US-67 or continue northwest on River Road FM-170 to Ruidosa. (See chapter map on page 100.)

If you choose to follow US-67, turn north. An interesting stop might be the ghost town of Shafter (19.0 miles), where some $18,000,000 worth of silver was mined. Western Scrub-Jays and Phainopeplas are rather common around cottonwoods and junipers. All land off the road is private; do not trespass.

Just before you reach Marfa (40.0 miles), one mile south, on the east side of US-67 you will find an area flooded with water from the sewage treatment plant. Here you should see Snow Goose (winter), "Mexican Duck" Mallard, other dabbling ducks, migrant White-faced Ibis and shorebirds (yellowlegs, peep, etc.), and Yellow-headed Blackbird. There are usually Pronghorns around.

If you choose to continue upriver, you'll find the road to Ruidosa (36 miles) to be narrow and undulating. Drive carefully because loose cattle and other livestock are common. Along the way watch for Turkey Vulture,

Greater Roadrunner, White-winged and Mourning Doves, Verdin, Cactus Wren, and Crissal Thrasher. Black Vultures are rather common here, part of a small population in the Ruidosa-Candelaria area. Harris's Hawk is resident, and you may begin to see Gambel's Quail.

The best birding is beyond Ruidosa along the road to Candelaria (12.0 miles). Along this stretch watch the skies carefully. Common Black-Hawk, Zone-tailed Hawk, and Peregrine and Prairie Falcons have all nested in the vicinity. Golden Eagles are fairly common, especially in migration. Near Candelaria an oxbow of the river can be alive with spring migrant waterfowl and shorebirds. In the sandy draws and in the trees look for migrating warblers and Lazuli Buntings. In summer such species as Ladder-backed Woodpecker, Bell's Vireo, Common Yellowthroat, Yellow-breasted Chat, Summer Tanager, Varied Bunting, and Hooded and Scott's Orioles may be present. From mid-March to early June listen for the high-pitched trill of a singing Lucy's Warbler. This area around Candelaria is one of the few reliable places in Texas where this bird nests. In winter numerous species of sparrows are found.

This road ends at Candelaria, so return to Ruidosa, and if you are really adventurous—rather than returning to Presidio to take paved US-67—take Ranch Road 2810 to the left over the Chinati Mountains (not recommended for low-clearance vehicles) to Marfa (52.0 miles). This road is dirt and narrow, but very scenic. The road travels through Pinto Canyon, which is unfenced private property. *Do not leave the roadway.* (*Note:* There are no bridges on 2810. If it is raining or has recently rained, watch out for low-water crossings, which may be washed out.) After going over the pass, the road is paved for the last 32 miles.

Upon reaching Marfa there is a choice of three routes. If you are going to the Davis Mountains take TX-17 north from Marfa, or travel east to Alpine, or north toward Valentine and Van Horn.

US-90—MARFA TO VALENTINE

A vast grassland extends from Marfa northward along US-90, an excellent area to look for raptors in winter. Red-tailed and Ferruginous Hawks, American Kestrel, Merlin (scarce), and Prairie Falcon can usually be found along this stretch. An Aplomado Falcon spent the winter of 1991–1992 near Valentine. There is a considerable population of Aplomados just across the border in northern Chihuahua and this species is likely to be found here again. A great variety of sparrows, as well as McCown's and Chestnut-collared Longspurs, can be abundant in winter. Pronghorns are commonly seen along this route. FM-505 (6.7 miles south of Valentine) connects US-90 with the scenic loop around the Davis Mountains.

US-90—MARFA TO ALPINE

The prairies along US-90 between Marfa and Alpine are good for Golden Eagle, an occasional Prairie Falcon, Horned Lark, Eastern and Western (winter only) Meadowlarks, and, in winter, flocks of sparrows and McCown's and Chestnut-collared Longspurs. Occasionally, Swainson's Hawks nest on power poles along the way. The resident Eastern Meadowlarks are of the very pale *lilianae* subspecies. These birds appear similar to a Western Meadowlark, but sound like an Eastern. Are you confused now?

Between Marfa and Alpine there is an expansive grassland that has become famous for a phenomenon known as the Marfa Lights. On most nights there are definitely unexplained lights on the horizon. The lights appear to be in the foothills of Chinati Peak some 20 miles away in a southwesterly direction. They look like a lantern or bonfire, which brightens, flickers, fades, and brightens again. They even seem to move around. Some people think that these are the lights of a distant car, but there are no roads in that area. A hundred years ago, when the light was first observed, there were no cars.

Several explanations for the light have been offered, but none verified. Unromantic and scientific types explain them away as a phosphate deposit that glows on dark nights after a rain, but they can be seen on moonlit nights in dry weather. Local legends say that it is the ghost of Alsate, an ancient Indian chief, looking for his lost wives.

Many people have tried to find the lights. But they do not stay in one spot. Cowboys and tourists have covered the area on foot and by horseback and have found nothing unusual. Better-organized groups have spent months trying to triangulate the light from different directions, but to no avail.

The State Highway Department has opened a sizable picnic area as the official Marfa Light viewing position.

ALPINE

You may think of Alpine (population 5,700, elevation 4,484 ft) as a small town, but it is the largest town in the largest county (5,935 square miles) in Texas. It is the home of Sul Ross State University, named after a former governor and Civil War general. To most travelers Alpine is only a rest stop, a role it has played for centuries because several old Indian trails passed this way. Cabeza de Vaca, the first European to cross Texas, camped about a mile north of the present town in 1532.

Going north from Alpine on TX-118 on the way to Fort Davis, you will find a large pond (16.0 miles) next to the road. View it from the stone wall. *Do not cross the fence.* In winter you should find various ducks, including Gadwall, "Mexican Duck" Mallard, Cinnamon Teal, Northern Shoveler, Ring-necked Duck, Bufflehead, and others. There are two records for Common Goldeneye. Look for Eastern Phoebes and Eastern Bluebirds. In summer you can expect to see Black Phoebe, Vermilion and Ash-throated Flycatchers, Phainopepla, Summer Tanager, and Black-headed and Blue Grosbeaks. In migration look for Osprey, *Empidonax* flycatchers, five species of swallows, House Wren, warblers such as Yellow, Yellow-rumped, Wilson's, MacGillivray's, and Common Yellowthroat, Western Tanager, and Indigo Bunting.

A picnic area/rest stop is just 1.5 miles up the road. A traveler can overnight here. Early in the morning or late in the evening, Wild Turkey, Mule Deer and Collared Peccary (Javelina) can be seen in large pasture along the right side of the highway here. Wild Turkeys strut in this pasture during April.

DAVIS MOUNTAINS

Open grasslands surround the Davis Mountains. The range is much larger than the Chisos or Chinati Mountains and has a higher average rainfall, which results in a well-developed oak-juniper woodland in the foothills. These foothills are rounded and well-vegetated, not rugged and bare like those of the Chisos. Palisade rock formations are very evident around Fort Davis and in many of the surrounding canyons.

Mount Livermore (El. 8,382 ft) is the highest peak in the Davis Mountains and the second highest in Texas. In fact, there is not a higher mountain east of this point until one reaches the Alps in Europe. The upper parts of the peak are privately owned and closed to public access. This is regrettable from a birder's point of view, because the forests of Gambel Oak, Ponderosa and Limber Pines, and aspen on top are a relic of another era when the climate was wetter and the flora of the Rocky Mountains extended farther south.

Rich birding areas around the lower parts of the mountain are accessible from the 74-mile scenic loop that encircles the peak. The starting point for this trip is 24 miles north of Alpine at Fort Davis, which has all the services a traveler needs—stores, motels, cafes, and service stations.

This little town has only 900 people, but it is the largest in Jeff Davis County. The county's other town, Valentine, has only 330. The entire county has a population of about one person for each of its 2,363 square miles. Cattle, sheep, deer, and Pronghorns far outnumber people.

Although this area is off the beaten path today, during the last half of the 19th century it was not. After the discovery of gold in California, thousands migrated west via the San Antonio/El Paso Trail, which passed this way to take advantage of the abundance of grass and water. The wagon trains and cattle of the migrants were prime targets for the raiding Mescalero Apaches and Comanches. To provide protection, the United States Army, in 1854, established Fort Davis, named after Jefferson Davis, then Secretary of War. The fort was used off and on until 1891. In 1963 it was made a National Historical Site, open now 8 AM–5 PM all year, except Christmas and New

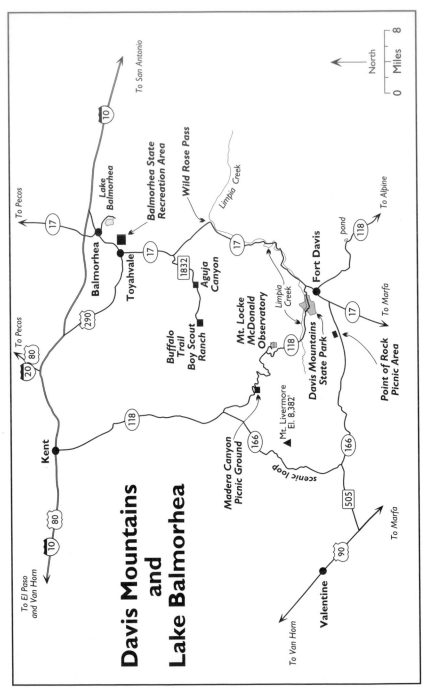

Davis Mountains and Lake Balmorhea

North

0 Miles 8

To San Antonio

10

To Pecos

17

Lake Balmorhea

Balmorhea State Recreation Area

Wild Rose Pass

Limpia Creek

Balmorhea

Toyahvale

17

17

290

17

To Alpine

118

pond

Fort Davis

To Pecos

20 80

1832

Aguja Canyon

Buffalo Trail Boy Scout Ranch

Mt. Locke McDonald Observatory

Limpia Creek

118

Davis Mountains State Park

17

To Marfa

Point of Rock Picnic Area

Kent

118

Madera Canyon Picnic Ground

166

Mt. Livermore El. 8,382'

scenic loop

166

505

To El Paso and Van Horn

80

10

80

90

Valentine

To Van Horn

To Marfa

Year's Day. It encompasses 460 acres, offers several miles of hiking trails, and a pleasant shaded picnic area.

Check the area by the gate or along the Tall Grass Nature Trail for Horned Lark, Cassin's Sparrow, and Eastern and Western (winter only) Meadowlarks. Look for Rock and Canyon Wrens, Canyon Towhee, and Rufous-crowned Sparrow by the rocky cliffs. In summer Cassin's Kingbirds and Orchard Orioles nest in the trees along the highway.

There are three distinct birding areas in the Davis Mountains: the Scenic Loop around the mountains, Limpia Creek, and Aguja Canyon. Although many birds are common to all three, each has a few species that are not seen elsewhere in the mountains. Some 235 species of birds have been recorded in Jeff Davis County, and the Davis Mountains Christmas Counts average over 100 species. All of these birds are seen from the roadsides, because *West Texas birders make it a rule never to trespass on private property. Visitors should behave accordingly.*

THE SCENIC LOOP

To follow this 74-mile loop, drive north from Fort Davis on TX-17. Travel in a counter-clockwise direction, turning left at both TX-118 (1.0 mile) and TX-166 (29.0 miles) until returning to Fort Davis. The first few miles of TX-118 follow Limpia Creek, which will be discussed later.

After leaving Limpia Creek behind, I X-118 traverses grassy hillsides with scattered clumps of Gray and Emory Oaks, Pinyon Pine, and Alligator and One-seeded Junipers. Especially note the Alligator Juniper with its conspicuous squarish bark-scales, which resemble the hide of an alligator. During June, another feature of this segment of the loop is the 12-foot stalks of yellow-blossomed Century Plants. When these are in bloom, watch for Black-chinned Hummingbirds and Scott's Orioles about the flowers. Another favorite of the hummingbirds is Scarlet Bouvardia, which blooms most of the summer. It is an attractive shrub with neat foliage and clusters of bright red, honeysuckle-like flowers.

Davis Mountains State Park (2.8 miles) (1,869 acres) is located in the foothills between the grassland and the mountains (entrance fee $3/person). The park maintains an excellent campground (fee) and Indian Lodge (Box 786, Fort Davis, TX 79734; phone 915/426-3254). The lodge has a good dining room, comfortable rooms, and a heated pool. It is a great spot to spend a few days; advance reservations are highly recommended. An elevation of 4,900 to 5,500 feet provides mild winters and cool summers, with average rainfall of 19 inches. A 4.5-mile hiking trail connects the park with Fort Davis. A checklist showing the habitat preference of each species recorded in Jeff Davis County can be purchased at the park.

Campers are usually awakened by noisy Cassin's Kingbirds and Western Scrub-Jays. Other birds encountered in the campground and along the highway are White-winged Dove, Acorn and Ladder-backed Woodpeckers, Say's Phoebe, Tufted (Black-crested) Titmouse, Bushtit, Rock and Bewick's Wrens, Western Bluebird, Phainopepla, Chipping Sparrow, and House Finch. In summer look for Common Poorwill, White-throated Swift, Summer and Western Tanagers, Canyon Towhee, Cassin's and Lark Sparrows, Pyrrhuloxia, Black-headed Grosbeak, and Orchard Oriole. In winter, in addition to the above residents, you should be able to find Red-naped Sapsucker, Green-tailed and Spotted Towhees, and Dark-eyed Junco. There is only one record of Williamson's Sapsucker from the park, though they probably are annual in the upper elevations of the mountains.

Montezuma Quail are a park specialty, although it may take some patience to find them. The campground host, whose trailer is parked across the road from the entrance to the campground, operates a feeding station. In early morning and late afternoon the quail stop by for seed and water. Watch for them also in and along the dry wash, which runs through the middle of the campground, or along the road to Indian Lodge and in the canyon behind the lodge. They often sit motionless when cars approach them along the highway; however, sharp-eyed birders may find them by driving slowly and watching closely. The best location is along TX-118 on either side of the Mount Locke Road (11.3 miles) during the two hours before dark. The quail seem to be most common during the year following a wet year.

Montezuma Quail
Narca Moore-Craig

Those interested in astronomy should take the trip up the steepest and highest road in the state of Texas to McDonald Observatory atop Mount Locke (1.5 miles) (El. 6,802 ft). The facility is operated by the University of Texas. Tours are given each afternoon year round (also in the mornings in summer), and the view from the top is excellent. In the residential area at the base of the mountain, you may find Montezuma Quail.

Beyond the Mount Locke Road, the highway soon passes the mile-high marker, staying above that elevation for several miles. This higher country is more forested, and the birdlife changes. The best birding is at Lawrence E. Wood Picnic Grounds in Madera Canyon. Plan to spend an hour or so in the vicinity. Do not cross any fences—all land around the picnic area is privately owned.

Band-tailed Pigeons might be spotted anywhere in the high country, and flocks of Bushtits can be found. Acorn Woodpeckers nest in the dead pines across the creek, while Violet-green Swallows nest in the old woodpecker holes. Hepatic Tanagers and Black-headed Grosbeaks nest in the Ponderosa Pines. Grace's Warblers nest farther up the canyon and can occasionally be seen in the picnic grounds. On June nights Western Screech-Owls and Common Poorwills are heard. Steller's Jays and Mountain Chickadees sometimes wander down from their home on the slopes of Mount Livermore after the nesting season or in winter, when you can also find Mountain Bluebird, Townsend's Solitaire, and Dark-eyed Junco. In migration Yellow-rumped, Townsend's, and Wilson's Warblers pass through. If Pinyon Jays are in the neighborhood, they will make themselves known by their raucous cries. Also, in winter, watch for Williamson's and Red-naped Sapsuckers, and Golden Eagles overhead.

After a few more miles of high country, the scenic loop turns left onto TX-166 (14.0 miles from the Mount Locke Road) to drop into lower, more open country. Pronghorn are frequently seen along this section. You also might spot White-tailed and Mule Deer, Rock Squirrel, Black-tailed Jack Rabbit, Eastern Cottontail, and Mexican and Spotted Ground Squirrels. At night there may be Spotted, Striped, Hooded, and Common Hog-nosed Skunks, Raccoon, Common Gray Fox, Coyote, Bobcat, and Porcupine. In winter this open stretch is the most favorable spot for seeing Ferruginous Hawk, Golden Eagle, and McCown's and Chestnut-collared Longspurs. Zone-tailed Hawks (rare) are summer residents in the Davis Mountains and might be seen in the air from almost any location. Other birds of this area are Prairie Falcon, Say's Phoebe, Cassin's Sparrow, and Western Meadowlark.

At Point of Rock roadside picnic area (5.0 miles) you can easily hear the down-the-scale song of Canyon Wrens, and may possibly be able to find one with your binoculars. The grasslands along the return to Fort Davis could harbor a few Mountain Plovers (nesting records) and lots of McCown's and Chestnut-collared Longspurs in winter. Watch for Pronghorns.

Limpia Creek

It is worth the $1 picnicking fee to have the privilege of birding among the cottonwoods and willows about the private campground on Limpia Creek at the junction of TX-17 and TX-118. In winter at least 40 species can be found in two hours, including Black Phoebe, Vermilion Flycatcher, Eastern, Western, and Mountain Bluebirds, Song, Swamp, Lincoln's, and White-throated Sparrows, and Lesser Goldfinch. In summer Western Wood-Pewee and Summer Tanager are among the nesting birds. For several years a pair of Common Black-Hawks has nested in the cottonwoods farther up the creek. *Do not cross the fence* where the Common Black-Hawks are found.

After birding the campground, go northeast on TX-17, which follows Limpia Creek all the way to Wild Rose Pass. After 0.8 mile stop at the Litter Barrel sign. Common Black-Hawks nest in the tall cottonwood across Limpia Creek. Stop at each bridge and beside all oak groves and thickets. In summer Cliff Swallows nest under the bridges and in winter Green-tailed and Spotted Towhees are common in the brush. Canyon Towhees and Rufous-crowned Sparrows are present all year, but Common Ground-Doves and Inca Doves are seen only occasionally in the fields. Some 15 species of sparrows winter in the grassy areas, and small flocks of Lark Buntings sometimes find their way this far into the mountains.

Where the canyon narrows and the road approaches the palisade-like cliffs, Canyon Wrens may be heard singing at almost any time of year. Great Horned Owls sit in crevices and hawks soar above the cliffs. Red-tailed Hawk is the most common, but in winter watch for Ferruginous as well.

Aguja Canyon

After crossing Wild Rose Pass (22.6 miles), continue north on TX-17 to the sign indicating FM-1832 to the Buffalo Trail Boy Scout Ranch (12.1 miles). Turn left (west) and drive through typical foothill brush country. This paved road has lots of room, so you can pull over to birdwatch.

This is the habitat of such typical desert species as Greater Roadrunner, Western Kingbird, Ash-throated Flycatcher, Verdin, Cactus Wren, Sage and Curve-billed Thrashers, Brewer's and Black-throated Sparrows, and Pyrrhuloxia. After 8.5 miles the road enters a wide-mouthed canyon, the scrub giving way to larger trees.

At the first place where the road fords the creek, look in summer in the stream-side thickets for White-winged Dove, Bell's Vireo, Summer Tanager, and Varied and Painted Buntings, but do not leave the highway. *All of the land along this road is private.* At the second ford look in winter for Black-chinned Sparrow. At the entrance to the Boy Scout Ranch, watch along the cliffs for the White-throated Swifts, which are present year round and may be seen even in winter on warm days.

The first few miles of this road are often one of the best places to study sparrows in the Davis Mountains. Chipping, Clay-colored, Brewer's, Field, Vesper, Black-throated, Lark Bunting, Savannah, and White-crowned Sparrows are almost always present during migration and winter. There are even several documented records of Baird's Sparrow from this area.

Return to TX-17, go north to the town of Toyahvale and US-290 (7.0 miles), and turn right. Just beyond is Balmorhea State Recreation Area, a fine place for birding (entrance fee $3/person; camping and showers available). (Accommodations are available at San Solomon Springs Courts, Box 15, Toyahvale TX 78786; phone 915/375-2370). The park is noted for the 26-million-gallon per day artesian San Solomon Spring, around which is built a natural-appearing swimming-pool. These spring waters are home to two very rare, endangered desert fishes, the Comanche Spring Pupfish and the Pecos Mosquitofish. Cave Swallows nest under the eaves of the entrance station and other buildings along with Cliff and Barn Swallows.

In 1996 Texas Parks and Wildlife, in cooperation with the Reeves County Water District and the Texas Department of Transportation, restored a cienega within the park. The cienega, or desert wetland, was constructed to preserve the endangered fish as well as to create educational opportunities. The marsh also provides a great birding opportunity. The restoration project includes planting native plants around the marsh. The potential of this area for birds is really unknown, but Wood Duck, Greater Scaup, Red-breasted Merganser, and Sora have already been noted. Marsh Wrens and Swamp Sparrows are common in winter.

Resident birds in the remainder of the park include Scaled Quail, White-winged and Inca Doves, Greater Roadrunner, Ladder-backed Woodpecker, Black and Say's Phoebes, Loggerhead Shrike, Cactus Wren, Curve-billed Thrasher, Canyon Towhee, Black-throated Sparrow, Pyrrhuloxia, Eastern Meadowlark, Common (uncommon) and Great-tailed Grackles, and House Finch. Other nesters are Black-chinned Hummingbird, Cassin's and Western Kingbirds, Bewick's Wren, and Blue Grosbeak. In winter look for Northern Flicker, Marsh Wren, Ruby-crowned Kinglet, Hermit Thrush, Cedar Waxwing, Yellow-rumped Warbler, Green-tailed and Spotted Towhees, Chipping, Clay-colored, Brewer's, Vesper, Savannah, Song, Lincoln's, and White-crowned Sparrows, Lark Bunting, Dark-eyed Junco, and Western Meadowlark. Migrations should bring Wilson's Warbler, Summer Tanager (spring), and Orchard and Bullock's (uncommon) Orioles.

LAKE BALMORHEA

In the town of Balmorhea (4.0 miles), turn right at the sign for Lake Balmorhea onto Houston Street and drive to the lake (2.6 miles). Check in at the store; there is a charge of $2/day for birdwatching, fishing, and primitive camping at this private lake. The water in the lake, which is a storage area for irrigation projects, comes from San Solomon Spring at the State Recreation

Area. Lake Balmorhea is one of the premier places in all of the Trans-Pecos for waterbirds in migration and winter.

Some 40 species of waterbirds winter here, including "Mexican Duck" Mallard. This duck is most often seen in the irrigation canals leading into or out of the lake. Western and Clark's (10 percent) Grebes winter here in large numbers. In recent years individuals of both species have begun summering on the lake. The great fluctuation in water levels on the lake during the summer is not conducive to breeding, but the first nesting record for *Aechmophorus* grebes in Texas was recorded here in 1991.

Many shorebirds can be seen during spring and fall migrations, including American Avocet, Long-billed Curlew, Pectoral and Stilt Sandpipers, Wilson's (Common) Snipe (also winters), and Wilson's and Red-necked Phalaropes. The lake is well-known for its nesting Snowy Plovers. Black-necked Stilts also nest in good numbers. Neotropic Cormorants have become regular in the fall. Rarities include Red-throated, Pacific, and Yellow-billed (2 records) Loons, Brown Pelican, Tricolored Heron, Reddish Egret, Ross's Goose, all three scoters, and Sabine's Gull.

The lake is not large (573 acres), but it is big enough to require a telescope to observe birds out on the water. It is not uncommon to encounter windy conditions which create waves large enough to make birds in the center of the lake difficult to see. The dirt roads around the lake can be rough driving and are often impassable after rains. Many raptors can be found wintering around the lake or migrating through, including Osprey, Northern Harrier, Ferruginous and Rough-legged (rare) Hawks, Golden Eagle (rare), American Kestrel, and Prairie Falcon. A bird checklist available at the State Recreation Area includes the lake and the town. Lesser and Common (rare) Nighthawks and Common Poorwill can also be found around the lake in spring and summer. Ash-throated and Scissor-tailed Flycatchers breed in the area. Western Wood-Pewee and Willow, Least, and Dusky Flycatchers are regular but rare migrants. Common Ravens are resident. American Pipit is common in winter. Verdins are resident in the surrounding fields.

Return to Balmorhea via Houston Street. At TX-17 turn north (right) and continue 1.9 miles to CR-315. Turn left onto CR-315 and follow it under Interstate 10 for about 1.6 miles to open range. CR-315 passes under the interstate at a very low bridge—perhaps too low for RVs. However this road can be reached from the frontage road paralleling the interstate. This open desert grassland might appear very barren in drought years, but offers excellent sparrow habitat during the winter. This is a consistent location for Sage Sparrow, Lark Bunting, and many other sparrow species.

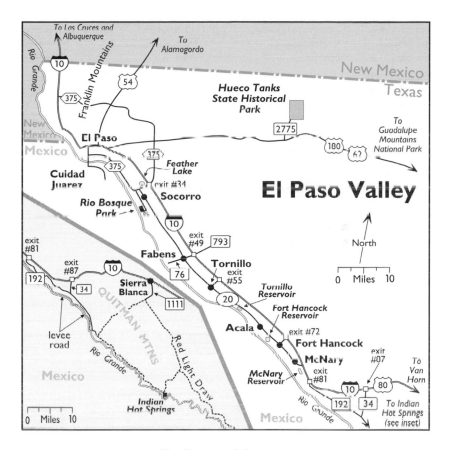

EL PASO VALLEY

To continue west after your visit to Lake Balmorhea and the Davis Mountains, take Interstate 10 to Van Horn (68.0 miles). At the junction with I X-54, you have a choice of continuing west to El Paso or driving north to the Guadalupe Mountains. If you opt for El Paso, continue west on Interstate 10 to Sierra Blanca (33.0 miles). About 28 miles west of Sierra Blanca, you can leave busy Interstate 10 at the McNary turn-off (exit 78) to follow old TX-20 through the farmlands of the El Paso Valley. Most of the little towns along the way are practically deserted now, but the road is in good shape and there's little traffic. There are a few good birding spots in this oasis, and you're sure to find the green cotton fields to be a pleasant relief from the desert.

The first missionaries came through the valley in 1581, but the first mission was not established until 1659. On Socorro Road (FM-258) near Clint, you can see San Elizario Mission and several historic buildings. One is the original

El Paso County Courthouse, and another is reported to be the oldest building in Texas. This is also the site of the first introduction by Europeans of domestic animals into the United States. They were brought here in 1598 when Don Juan de Oñate established the first military garrison.

The Spaniards, on entering this area in the 16th century, found large and prosperous settlements occupied by the Tigua Indians, whose ancestors built the famous cliff houses of Mesa Verde. They had developed a complex irrigation system, some of which is still in use today. Their principal crops were maize and squash.

INDIAN HOT SPRINGS

An interesting section of the Rio Grande, the next readily accessible stretch of river west of Candelaria, can be reached by exiting Interstate 10 at exit 87 (FM-34). From exit 87, go south on FM-34 to the intersection with FM-192 (2.4 miles). Alternately, this intersection can be reached from the west by leaving the freeway at exit 81 (FM-2217) and driving east for 7.9 miles. FM-2217 becomes FM-192 1.2 miles from Interstate 10.

Continue east on FM-192 from this intersection. The road is paved for the next 11.7 miles, but the birding here is not great. Look for Harris's Hawk, which is resident. Two miles before the pavement ends, look for the levee of the Rio Grande on the right. Although signs may suggest otherwise, you are permitted to drive on the levee west toward McNary and Fort Hancock. This section is one of the most reliable areas near El Paso for Vermilion Flycatcher.

By proceeding east on the now gravel road, you will reach the **Indian Hot Springs** in another twenty miles. This former cavalry post is now privately owned, and visits are by invitation only. The best birding is along the road before reaching the hot springs. The hot springs still flow, and a foot bridge links the springs with a tiny Mexican village. The white buildings of the springs are visible from a hilltop about a mile to the west. At this point it is time to head back toward Interstate 10.

The best birding starts when the road reaches the Rio Grande 6.2 miles after the pavement ends. The river is unleveed here and very narrow. It is surrounded by dense Tamarisk stands. For the next 13.2 miles (until the hot springs come into view), the road meanders between the river and barren desert hills, affording a number of close approaches. The best spot is a large pond 19.6 miles from the end of the pavement. Since the river is unleveed here, water levels in this pond and several other smaller ones are unpredictable.

This area has been very lightly birded, and affords very real opportunities for discovery. Great Blue Heron, Great Egret, Snowy Egret, Green Heron, and Black-crowned Night-Heron are found at the ponds, along with a variety of dabbling ducks in winter. Cinnamon Teal may be seen here in midwinter when it is absent farther north and west. Harris's Hawk might be seen throughout, and Gambel's Quail is fairly common. Regular breeders include Yellow-billed Cuckoo, Black Phoebe (resident), Vermilion Flycatcher (resident), Ash-throated Flycatcher, Bell's Vireo, Verdin (resident), Bewick's Wren (resident), Northern Mockingbird, Lucy's Warbler, Yellow-breasted Chat, Summer Tanager, Lark Sparrow, Blue Grosbeak, Painted Bunting, and Orchard and Bullock's Orioles. Black Vulture is possible; Green Kingfisher and Varied Bunting have not been recorded here, but should be kept in mind.

Although the dirt road is good, caution is necessary due to its isolated nature. Be sure to take water, and to watch for loose livestock and Mule Deer. Car trouble could mean a long wait or a long hike. All land here is private, so birding must be done from the road. Another way to reach this area is to exit Interstate 10 in Sierra Blanca at exit 107 (FM-1111). Go south on FM-1111 before turning right at the end of the pavement (4.8 miles). (A left turn here would follow Red Light Draw some 25 miles to a very poorly known area of the Rio Grande.) After turning right and then veering left (3.0 miles), one can continue on a passable dirt road across the Quitman Mountains to meet up with FM-192 near where the pavement ends. The Quitmans hold desert birds such as Ladder-backed Woodpecker, Verdin, Cactus and Rock Wrens, and Pyrrhuloxia.

MCNARY RESERVOIR

The best birding location in the valley east of El Paso is **McNary Reservoir**. (See map on following page.) Exit Interstate 10 at exit 78 (TX-20). The overpass has a small colony of Cave Swallows, present here since at least 1984. There are numerous other colonies nearby, but this location is a convenient one. Cave Swallow, present from mid-February through October, is second only to Barn Swallow as the most common breeding swallow in the area.

Continue west on TX-20 for 0.2 mile, before turning left onto FM-192. Follow this road through desert scrub until you reach the McNary Reservoir dike on the left (1.7 miles). The quickest way to bird this fairly large body of water is to park along FM-192 about halfway down the dike, then walk onto the dike. *Absolutely do not drive onto the dike, even if the gates (at either end) are open.* Despite No Trespassing signs on the gates, birders are permitted to bird on foot on the dike parallel to FM-192. Do not act in any way that might cause birders to lose access to this spot.

The list of attractions here is long. Clark's Grebes bred in the summer of 1997 (2 pairs) for the first pure nesting of *Aechmophorus* grebes in Texas. (A mixed Western/Clark's pair bred at Lake Balmorhea in 1991.) Both species are resident, with combined numbers approaching fifty in recent winters. Since 1994—the reservoir was created in the fall of 1993—the flooded trees on the north side have hosted a sizable rookery of Double-crested Cormorants, Snowy and Cattle Egrets, and Black-crowned Night-Herons.

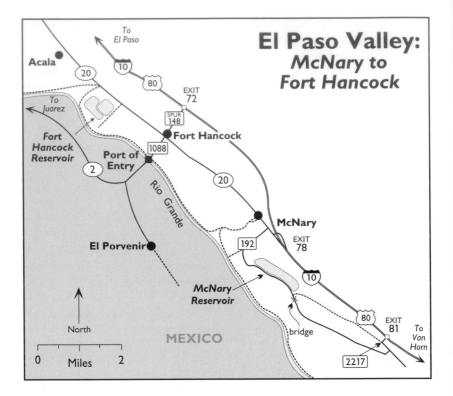

El Paso Valley: McNary to Fort Hancock

Acala

To El Paso

To Juarez

Fort Hancock Reservoir

Port of Entry

Fort Hancock

McNary

El Porvenir

McNary Reservoir

North

0 Miles 2

MEXICO

Rio Grande

bridge

To Van Horn

Increasing numbers of Neotropic Cormorants bred in 1996 and 1997, and a few at least can be expected year round, although most field guides do not accurately represent their status in the area.

Ross's Goose is regular in winter, as are Snow Goose and Canada Goose. All regularly occurring waterfowl can be found here. Common Mergansers generally winter by the hundreds; close scrutiny will typically reveal several Hooded and Red-breasted Mergansers. Osprey is to be expected in migration. The water levels are usually too high to provide much shorebird habitat, but Wilson's Phalaropes can dot the surface in migration. If there is any exposed mud to be found, it will be at the far west end. Ring-billed Gulls winter here in good numbers, usually with a Herring Gull or two. Franklin's and Bonaparte's Gulls are fairly common migrants, as are Forster's and Black Terns. A large Cave Swallow colony nests near the west end of the reservoir under a bridge in front of a small white house. Seven swallow species could be seen at McNary in migration. The brushy ditch parallel to FM-192 has breeding Green Herons and Blue Grosbeaks, and a few sparrows in winter.

McNary Reservoir has hosted a fascinating array of rarities in its brief history. These include Pacific Loon, Brown Pelican, Tricolored Heron, Reddish Egret, Yellow-crowned Night-Heron, Surf Scoter, Long-tailed Jaeger,

Laughing Gull, California Gull, Sabine's Gull (in May and July!), Caspian Tern, Least Tern, and Purple Martin. Texas' first fully documented Arctic Tern was found here 5–7 June 1997.

Previous editions of this book refer to an 'old' McNary Reservoir, reached by going east 0.2 mile from the east end of the current reservoir, then turning left just before a bridge. Formerly it was possible to go 1.0 mile here, then left 0.6 mile to a row of Tamarisks and Screwbean Mesquite. Increasingly, however, cattle have decimated this area and access is spotty. It may still be possible to find local breeders like Painted Bunting, Lark Sparrow, and Orchard Oriole here. One can continue east on FM-192 to connect with FM-2217 just east of Interstate 10 exit 81. Brief stops at abandoned ranch sites (2.5 and 3.0 miles east of the aforementioned bridge) may yield a few birds. *Bird these sites from the road—the land is private.*

RIO GRANDE LEVEE ROAD

The levee road of the Rio Grande offers some interesting birding. Signs will read Not Authorized for Public Use, but you are allowed to drive on this good gravel road. One of the most productive stretches of levee can be accessed at McNary. In 'downtown' McNary—just west of the TX-20/FM-192 junction turn south from TX-20 onto a dirt road. Take this to the levee road (1.4 miles), which then can be traveled east about twenty miles to its eastern terminus with FM-192, or west about six miles to the Fort Hancock port of entry with Mexico. You can continue west of here for another four miles or so until the levee road connects with TX-20 less than a mile west of Fort Hancock Reservoir. The levee is safe, and you are likely to encounter few others, aside from a dove hunter or two in season. Be aware that U.S. Border Patrol may find you interesting and stop to chat. Many birds can readily be seen in Mexico from the levee.

The levee passes through agricultural fields good for raptors in winter, including uncommon species like Ferruginous Hawk, Merlin, and Prairie Falcon. Long-billed Curlew is a possibility in winter or migration, and look especially for Upland Sandpipers in cut alfalfa fields in August and September. You may see Burrowing Owls in summer. The river will yield some dabbling ducks, and, with low water, waders like Killdeer, Black-necked Stilt, American Avocet, both yellowlegs, and Least Sandpiper on the sandbars. Any Mallard seen in summer will likely be a "Mexican Duck." Other birds to look for include Gambel's Quail, Greater Roadrunner, Black Phoebe, Say's Phoebe, Vermilion Flycatcher (rare), Ash-throated Flycatcher (summer), Western Kingbird (summer), Bell's Vireo (summer), Verdin, Crissal Thrasher, Phainopepla, Loggerhead Shrike, Yellow-breasted Chat (summer), Pyrrhuloxia, Painted Bunting (summer), a variety of wintering sparrows, and breeding Orchard and Bullock's Orioles. To the west, in the area covered by this book, Bell's Vireo, Painted Bunting, and Orchard Oriole become scarce quickly.

FORT HANCOCK AREA

If you have chosen not to drive along the Rio Grande levee to Fort Hancock, continue west on TX-20 from Interstate 10 exit 78. After about six miles you will reach the TX-20/Spur 148 junction in Fort Hancock. Alternately, this corner can be reached by leaving Interstate 10 at exit 72 (Fort Hancock/Spur 148) and going south through town. Fort Hancock has a small

motel and several stores, gas stations, and cafes. Most of the other 'towns' along TX-20—McNary, Acala, Alamo Alto—are practically deserted and offer no services.

A dirt road leads north from Interstate 10 at exit 72. The desert scrub here in the first mile or so can yield Sage Sparrows in winter, as well as resident Black-tailed Gnatcatchers, a very local species in extreme west Texas and south-central New Mexico. Side roads branching from

Sage Sparrow
Mark W. Lockwood

residential Fort Hancock can be worth brief exploration in winter. A small pencil cholla grows in dense clumps here and, when laden with fruit, can be attractive to Sage (winter), Curve-billed, and Crissal Thrashers, and Pyrrhuloxia. Northern Mockingbird is an abundant breeder in desert habitats, but in winter it retreats almost entirely into urban areas. A few are usually around town in winter.

For those interested in birding in Mexico, there is a port of entry at the end of FM-1088, which intersects TX-20 just 0.8 mile east of the TX-20/Spur 148 junction. Traffic here is light, no visa, passport, or car papers are needed, and hassles are unlikely. Once in Mexico, continue straight ahead on the paved road. Within several miles there will be a fork—left leads to the village of El Porvenir, right is Route 2 which takes you back to Juarez. This road gets crowded and slow, and aside from winter flocks of American Crows about thirty miles farther west, offers little notable birding. As you head from the port of entry to the fork mentioned above, watch on your right for a small "1 KM" post. Turn right here onto a dirt road; a concrete-lined channel will be on your left. This road, connecting with Route 2 in several miles, offers fairly good birding. Check any flooded fields for dabbling ducks and shorebirds. White-faced Ibis is likely in migration, and Long-billed Curlew is possible in winter. The birds here are similar to those on the Texas side, but, due to different agricultural practices, there are more trees and brush here. Return to Texas at the Fort Hancock port of entry.

The best birding near Fort Hancock is at **Fort Hancock Reservoir**. To reach it go west from Fort Hancock on TX-20 for 2.2 miles. Park on the left at the west end of the dirt dike. Vehicle traffic is not permitted around the reservoir; *do not drive in even if the gates happen to be open*. Birders are allowed to walk in, as at McNary Reservoir.

Typically, there is more exposed mud here than at McNary Reservoir. As the water level lowers, mudflats appear first at the near, northwest corner, occasionally extending over half of the reservoir. Often, however, there will be no exposed mud. Water levels are subject to irrigation needs and can change dramatically from day to day. When mudflats are present, look for Great Blue Heron, Great and Snowy Egrets, White-faced Ibis (migration), and a variety of shorebirds. Killdeer, Black-necked Stilt, American Avocet, both yellowlegs, Spotted, Western, Least, Baird's, and Stilt Sandpipers, Long-billed Dowitcher, Wilson's (Common) Snipe, and Wilson's Phalarope are the most common migrants. All but Lesser Yellowlegs, Baird's Sandpiper, Stilt Sandpiper, and Wilson's Phalarope might be seen in winter, but Western Sandpiper is rare at that season. Black-bellied, Snowy, and Semipalmated Plovers, Willet, Long-billed Curlew, Marbled Godwit, Pectoral Sandpiper, and Red-necked Phalarope migrate through in much smaller numbers.

Western and Clark's Grebes occur in low numbers and might be seen at any season. Ross's and Snow Geese winter, as do many ducks, mostly dabblers. Common Merganser winters here in good numbers. Both Double-crested and Neotropic Cormorants are usually present; they especially like to loaf on an old dock and pilings in the southwest corner of the reservoir. Ring-billed Gull is common in winter; a wide assortment of gulls has occurred here. Several colonies of Cave Swallows breed nearby, coming to hawk insects over the water. In recent years, the reservoir has attracted many rarities including Brown Pelican, Eurasian Wigeon, Black Scoter, Hudsonian Godwit, Dunlin, Laughing, Mew, California, and Thayer's Gulls, Black-legged Kittiwake, and Least Tern. Be aware that light conditions, especially in the morning, can be frustratingly poor.

Continue driving west on TX-20. A left turn (0.8 mile) leads to the levee road which can be taken east; another left turn (0.1 mile) also leads to the levee road. You can drive the levee road west about 20 miles to the Fabens port of entry, however, you are better off birding the levee around McNary.

The land here is heavily agricultural with the principal crops being cotton, chiles, and alfalfa. Harris's Hawk is perhaps more reliable along the next ten miles of TX-20 than anywhere else around El Paso. In winter look for Northern Harrier, Red-tailed Hawk, Ferruginous Hawk, American Kestrel, Say's Phoebe, Loggerhead Shrike, Pyrrhuloxia, and Lark Bunting (numbers variable). Brewer's and White-crowned are the most common wintering sparrows along the roadsides. Western Kingbird and Northern Mockingbird are conspicuous breeders.

A grove of a dozen or so mistletoe-infested cottonwoods at a roadside rest (7.8 miles) west of the Fort Hancock Reservoir is worth investigation.

Breeding birds here may include Harris's Hawk (resident; look also in the row of trees extending westward on the north side of TX-20), Black-chinned Hummingbird, Ladder-backed Woodpecker (resident), Western Kingbird, Bell's Vireo, Verdin (resident), Northern Mockingbird, Yellow-breasted Chat, Summer Tanager, Pyrrhuloxia (resident), Painted Bunting, and Orchard (rare) and Bullock's Orioles. Western Bluebird occurs some winters, and there are usually Phainopeplas. This site takes only a few minutes to cover, and at times is not even worth that brief amount of time. However, as the largest grove for miles around, it has the potential to lure migrants.

TORNILLO RESERVOIR

A short distance (1.1 miles) farther west on US-20 is Tornillo Reservoir Park on the left. As with Fort Hancock and McNary Reservoirs, birding on foot only is allowed on the dike. In general, this is the least productive of the three reservoirs, because the shores are all crushed stone, and only very rarely are water levels low enough to attract many shorebirds. Western and Clark's Grebes might be here in winter, but are not always around in summer. Eared Grebe is common in winter, and Pied-billed Grebe is a common non-breeding resident.

Tornillo Reservoir usually hosts large numbers of wintering waterfowl, including a few Ross's or Snow Geese. Very large numbers of wintering (Green-winged) or migrant (Blue-winged or Cinnamon) teal can be present, along with all other regular waterfowl. Great and Snowy Egrets are present all year, but are rarer in winter; neither is to be expected north or west of this location in winter. Barrow's Goldeneye and Heermann's Gull have been recorded here.

The brushy ditch between the reservoir and TX-20 can produce Verdin, Cactus and Bewick's Wrens, Ruby-crowned Kinglet (winter), Crissal Thrasher, Pyrrhuloxia, Painted Bunting (summer), Green-tailed and Spotted Towhees (winter), and wintering sparrows such as Brewer's, Song, Lincoln's, Swamp, and White-crowned. Culverts here have a few pairs of Cave Swallows. Strong spring winds, mostly in March and April, can raise whitecaps and cause blowing dust. Birding the reservoirs under these conditions can be unpleasant.

At this point, the next good birding opportunities are in El Paso. Your best bet is to continue west on TX-20 to Tornillo, about five miles, before turning right onto O.T. Smith Road to connect in several miles with Interstate 10 at exit 55. The town of Fabens is about twelve miles west of the reservoir. A right turn here at the traffic light (FM-76, which soon becomes FM-793) will also take you north, in several miles, to Interstate 10 (exit 49). Fabens offers a far wider variety of services than does Tornillo.

EL PASO AREA

El Paso County is located at the western extremity of Texas. The city of El Paso lies in the valley of the Rio Grande at the base of the Franklin Mountains, in the heart of the Chihuahuan Desert. El Paso is a growing city of 600,000, offering the traveler a multitude of dining and lodging options. An average annual rainfall of about eight inches falls mostly in brief, intense thunderstorms between July and September. El Paso's birdfinding habitats are varied, though somewhat limited—finding birds here means finding water. Nevertheless, El Paso County has accumulated an impressive list of over 400 species of birds, about ninety of which are regular breeders. In addition, a stunning array of rarities has been found here.

Some of the resident and nesting birds include "Mexican Duck" Mallard, Swainson's Hawk (summer), Scaled and Gambel's Quail, Common Moorhen, White-winged and Inca Doves, Greater Roadrunner, Burrowing Owl, Lesser Nighthawk (summer), Common Poorwill (summer), White-throated Swift, Say's Phoebe, Ash-throated Flycatcher (summer), Chihuahuan Raven, Verdin, Cactus, Rock, and Canyon Wrens, Crissal Thrasher, Phainopepla, Black-throated Sparrow, and Scott's (summer) and Hooded (rare and local in summer) Orioles.

HUECO TANKS STATE PARK

Hueco Tanks State Historical Park (WAY-co) ($2/person plus camping fee) is an excellent place to study the Chihuahuan Desert. To reach the 86-acre park from downtown El Paso take Interstate 10 exit 23B (Paisano/US-62/US-180) and drive east to FM-2775 (21.8 miles). Turn left here to the park (8.0 miles). Alternately, exit Interstate 10 at exit 34 (Americas Avenue/Loop 375) and go north to US-62/US-180 (7.5 miles). Turn right and go east to FM-2775. (You can continue north on Loop 375 to cross US-54 [exit 9] on El Paso's northeast side before crossing the Franklin Mountains to reconnect with Interstate 10 [exit 6] on El Paso's extreme northwest side. US-62/US-180 continues east to Guadalupe Mountains and Carlsbad Caverns National Parks.)

Hueco Tanks State Historical Park, created to preserve Native American rock art, is excellent for birds. There are six small ponds (or tanks) in wet winters, and some trees (mostly oak, willow, and hackberry with a few cottonwoods) around the impressive rocky outcrops. The largest pond (but often dry) is over the dike behind the Old Ranch House, right across the road from the entrance station. Two other ponds are located in Mescalero Canyon, in the park's center between East Mountain and West Mountain. This is typically the best birding area. A small flock of Lawrence's Goldfinches was enjoyed here by many Texas birders in the winter of 1996–1997.

At any season you should find Red-tailed Hawk, Scaled Quail, Greater Roadrunner, Great Horned Owl, White-throated Swift, Ladder-backed Woodpecker, Say's Phoebe, Loggerhead Shrike, Verdin, Cactus, Rock, and Canyon Wrens, Crissal Thrasher, Canyon Towhee, Rufous-crowned and Black-throated Sparrows, and Pyrrhuloxia. In summer, watch for Swainson's Hawk, Lesser Nighthawk, Common Poorwill, Black-chinned Hummingbird, Ash-throated Flycatcher, Western Kingbird, Cliff and Barn Swallows, Northern Mockingbird, Cassin's Sparrow, Blue Grosbeak, Eastern Meadowlark, and Scott's Oriole. Winter is often the best time to visit the park. Not only is it cooler, but also there may be water in the ponds. At this season look for Northern Harrier, American Kestrel, Long-eared Owl (rare), Western Scrub-Jay, Western and Mountain Bluebirds (sporadic), Townsend's Solitaire (sporadic), Sage Thrasher (sporadic), Green-tailed and Spotted Towhees, Chipping, Brewer's, Black-chinned, Vesper, Sage, Savannah, Song, Lincoln's, and White-crowned Sparrows, Dark-eyed Junco, Western Meadowlark, and American Goldfinch. In irruptive winters the park can be good for Steller's Jay, Mountain Chickadee, and Red-breasted and White-breasted Nuthatches. Migration can be productive, with a variety of flycatchers, Warbling Vireo, swallows, warblers including Orange-crowned, Virginia's, Black-throated Gray, Townsend's, MacGillivray's, and Wilson's, Western Tanager, Black-headed Grosbeak, and Lazuli Bunting.

If birding is slow in the warmer months, you can look for lizards—Southwestern Earless Lizard, Crevice Spiny Lizard, Fence Lizard, Big Bend Tree Lizard, Texas Horned Lizard, Round-tailed Horned Lizard, several whiptails, and Great Plains Skink. Rock Squirrel and Texas Antelope Squirrel frequent the rocks, and Common Gray Fox and Ringtail are common enough to sometimes be seen in the daytime. Be aware that rockclimbing here is very popular and the park and campground can be full in winter. In addition, the entrance road is closed by a gate from dark until eight in the morning.

Due to continued vandalism of rock art, dramatic changes in visitorship policies took effect in September 1998. These include needing advance arrangements for camping, a $5 entry fee per person, and now nearly all of the park can be visited only if visitors are escorted by park personnel. It is unknown at the time of this publication if these changes will be permanent, or if exceptions will be granted.

FEATHER LAKE

Feather Lake is a marshy pond on El Paso's east side, protected and managed by the El Paso/Trans-Pecos Audubon Society, which is responsible for the fence and the No Trespassing signs. The society has worked very hard in recent years to restore native vegetation and otherwise improve this formerly neglected stormwater basin. Feather Lake is open (free) October–April from 8 AM–noon every Saturday and from 2 PM–dusk on Sundays. The site is closed from May through September. Call 915/545-5157 or 532-9645 to try to arrange a visit at times when the site is normally closed.

Feather Lake
and
Rio Bosque
Park Area

To reach Feather Lake, exit Interstate 10 at Americas Avenue/Loop 375 (exit 34) and go south 1.2 miles, turning right onto North Loop Road. Go 0.4 mile to the parking area on the left.

Feather Lake has resident Pied-billed Grebe, "Mexican Duck" Mallard, Common Moorhen, and American Coot. In summer look for Least Bittern (rare), Great, Snowy, and Cattle Egrets, and Green Heron. A variety of ducks, mostly dabblers, winters here, and Eurasian Wigeon has been seen several times. In migration, immense numbers of White-faced Ibises, sometimes numbering over 2,000, roost at Feather Lake. Cottonwoods surround some of the lake and may provide refuge to migrant passerines.

RIO BOSQUE PARK

Continue south on Americas Avenue (Loop 375) from the junction with North Loop Road. After crossing Socorro Road (1.2 miles), look for signs for the Zaragosa Bridge. Follow these signs, but make a U-turn under the overpass just before reaching the bridge so that you are heading back northward on Loop 375. Turn right onto Southside Road (0.2 mile), driving east. Immediately after crossing the Riverside Canal (1.0 mile), you can turn right or left onto the dirt road parallel to the canal. (Do not continue straight into the Bustamante Wastewater Treatment Plant.) A right turn leads to the Rio Grande (0.6 mile), where the brush may have some birds, and a marshy basin across the canal might be worth a look. The U.S. Border Patrol is very active in this area.

A left turn along Riverside Canal leads to Rio Bosque Park (0.7 mile), a 277-acre city park. Rio Bosque Park is currently undergoing a major facelift, managed by the University of Texas-El Paso's Center for Environmental Resource Management with financial and strategic input from Ducks Unlimited, among others. Dense, unproductive stands of Tamarisk have been cleared, leaving scattered Screwbean Mesquites. Plans call for the planting of cottonwoods and feed crops for waterfowl. One major objective is to provide nesting habitat for "Mexican Duck" Mallards. Several canals now criss-cross the park, and ponds have been dug.

The park can be explored on a network of dirt roads. Water for the park comes from the wastewater plant and "belongs" to the local irrigation district, with the park getting it primarily during the nongrowing season—mid-October through mid-March.

This exciting, collaborative venture promises excellent birding. Currently, look in winter (assuming some water) for Pied-billed Grebe, Great Blue Heron, various ducks—especially dabblers, Northern Harrier, Red-tailed Hawk, Gambel's Quail, Greater Roadrunner, Black and Say's Phoebes, Loggerhead Shrike, American Crow (local in the El Paso area), and sparrows. The park holds great potential as a migratory hotspot. In summer look for Great and Snowy Egrets, Green Heron, Black-crowned Night-Heron, Lesser Nighthawk, Ash-throated Flycatcher, Bell's Vireo, Cliff and Barn Swallows, Northern Mockingbird, Yellow-breasted Chat, Lark Sparrow, Blue Grosbeak, Painted Bunting, and Bullock's Oriole.

Future plans call for a parking area, observation towers, and foot-access from the northeast corner of the park, which can be reached by driving east from Americas Avenue on Socorro Road for 3.0 miles to the entrance of an abandoned sewage treatment plant on the right. When this entrance is opened, access via Southside Road may be denied. Notice the Socorro Mission on your left 1.5 miles east of Americas Avenue. This mission was founded in 1682 for Piro Indians fleeing the Pueblo Revolt in what is now New Mexico, and is the oldest active church building in the United States. The Ysleta Mission, founded in 1682, can be reached by taking Socorro Road west from Americas Avenue for about one mile. These missions lie along the Camino Real, or Royal Road, which linked Chihuahua, Mexico, with Santa Fe. Contact the El Paso Convention and Visitors Bureau (phone 915/534-0696) for more information about the missions.

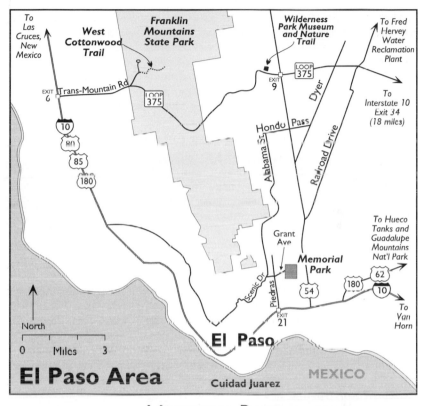

To
Las
Cruces,
New
Mexico

West
Cottonwood
Trail

Franklin
Mountains
State Park

Wilderness
Park Museum
and Nature
Trail

To Fred
Hervey
Water
Reclamation
Plant

West Cottonwood Trail

Trans-Mountain Rd

EXIT
6

LOOP
375

EXIT
9

LOOP
375

To
Interstate 10
Exit 34
(18 miles)

Hondo Pass

Dyer

Railroad Drive

Alabama St

10

80

85

180

To Hueco
Tanks and
Guadalupe
Mountains
Nat'l Park

Grant
Ave

Memorial
Park

62

Scenic Dr

Piedras

54

180

10

To
Van
Horn

North

EXIT
21

El Paso

0   Miles   3

El Paso Area   Cuidad Juarez   MEXICO

MEMORIAL PARK

This city park, located near downtown El Paso, is a favorite with local birders. To reach it from Interstate 10, drive north on Piedras Avenue (exit 21) for seven blocks before turning right onto Grant Avenue and going 0.3 mile to the park. Resident and breeding birds include White-winged and Inca Doves, Black-chinned Hummingbird (summer), Ladder-backed Woodpecker, Western Kingbird (summer), American Robin, Northern Mockingbird, Great-tailed Grackle, Bullock's Oriole (summer), and House Finch. Spring migration can be great for western warblers including Orange-crowned, Virginia's, Yellow, Yellow-rumped, Black-throated Gray, Townsend's, MacGillivray's, and Wilson's. Also look in migration for Western Wood-Pewee, Plumbeous, Cassin's, and Warbling Vireos, Western Tanager, and Black-headed Grosbeak. A variety of eastern warblers has been seen here. *Empidonax* flycatchers are present in spring and fall—Willow, Least (rare), Hammond's, Gray (rarer in spring), Dusky, and Cordilleran—if you can identify the silent ones. Also, in fall and winter look for a possible Flammulated Owl (fall) along with Williamson's and Red-naped Sapsuckers, Steller's Jay, Western Scrub-Jay, Red-breasted, White-breasted, and Pygmy

Nuthatches, Mountain Chickadee, Golden-crowned Kinglet, and Red Crossbill. A few of these montane species can be expected most winters (Red-naped Sapsucker, Western Scrub-Jay, and Red-breasted Nuthatch), but the others will be completely absent most years. Expect to see wintering Ruby-crowned Kinglet, Orange-crowned Warbler (uncommon), Yellow-rumped Warbler, White-crowned Sparrow, Dark-eyed Junco (mostly Oregon/pink-sided types with a few Gray-headeds), and perhaps Pine Siskin, Lesser Goldfinch, or American Goldfinch.

FRANKLIN MOUNTAINS

The Franklin Mountains, towering above the El Paso to the north, look very dry and barren, but they do harbor some desert species such as Scaled Quail, Verdin, Cactus, Rock, and Canyon Wrens, Rufous-crowned and Black-throated Sparrows, and Scott's Oriole (summer). There is good birding in several of the canyons off TransMountain Road (Loop 375) which crosses the mountains. To reach Loop 375, drive west on Interstate 10 from downtown about 15 miles to exit 6, or go north on US-54 for 9 miles to exit 9. From Interstate 10 exit 6 proceed east to Franklin Mountains State Park on the left (3.3 miles). This is a fee area—$2/day, with picnicking, and primitive camping by permit only (call 915/566-6441). The gate is open daily from 8 AM to 5 PM.

Follow the paved road through the archway for 1.0 mile, parking at the picnic area on your right. Walk the wide, rocky path up the large canyon to the isolated clump of cottonwoods one-half mile to the east. This is **West Cottonwood Spring**, a great area in fall migration (mid-July through mid-September) for Calliope, Broad-tailed, and Rufous Hummingbirds. Warblers such as Orange-crowned, Virginia's, Black-throated Gray, Townsend's, and MacGillivray's—and even rare ones like Hermit Warbler and Painted Redstart—have been found here. Western Scrub-Jays occur in fall and winter, along with Black-chinned Sparrows, which may occasionally also be found in summer. Resident birds include Scaled Quail, White-throated Swift, Cactus, Rock, Canyon, and Bewick's Wrens, Crissal Thrasher, Canyon Towhee, and Rufous-crowned and Black-throated Sparrows.

Return to the entrance of the park and continue driving east on Loop 375. Previous editions of this book discuss Whispering Springs Canyon and Indian Springs Canyon. In summer 1998 the U.S. Army, which owns the land along the eastern slope of the Franklin Mountains, began denying all access to these canyons. *Any entry into the canyons is strictly prohibited.*

The Wilderness Park Museum, ahead on the left (6.6 miles), has exhibits on Native Americans and a nature trail good for sparrows and desert species, as well as both meadowlarks. Listen from any pull-off for Common Poorwill after dark in the warmer months.

From the Wilderness Park Museum, continue east to US-54 (0.6 mile), which can be taken south about ten miles to downtown. If you want to visit the **Fort Bliss Sewage Ponds**—actually called the Fred Hervey Water Reclamation Plant—continue east on Loop 375 to Railroad Drive (3.0 miles). Turn left on Railroad to the entrance road on your right (3.6 miles). (Loop 375 continues east to connect with Interstate 10 [exit 34] in 18.2 miles.) Drive across the railroad tracks, and follow the paved road to the buildings. Do not enter the plant proper (permission is not necessary), but turn right before the gate onto the gravel road and drive toward the trees. This will put you at the south end of three large ponds (one or more may be entirely dry), the dikes around which can be driven or walked. Be aware that the roads can be a real mess when wet and that vegetation can be thick by late summer. The trees are the most extensive here at the south end, making this an excellent spot to pish out passerines. Water levels, and thus shorebird and waterbird habitat, vary.

The ponds are quite birdy all year and can be exceptional during migration. Fully one-half (some 310 species) of the Texas state list has been seen here, making this one of the best vagrant traps in the Southwest. Resident birds include Pied-billed and Eared Grebes, Mallard, "Mexican Duck" Mallard, Ruddy Duck, American Kestrel, Scaled and Gambel's Quail, Common Moorhen, American Coot, Killdeer, Mourning Dove, Greater Roadrunner, Ladder-backed Woodpecker, Say's Phoebe, Loggerhead Shrike, Verdin, Cactus Wren, Crissal Thrasher (very reliable here), Black-throated Sparrow, and Pyrrhuloxia. Additional summer nesters are Swainson's Hawk, Black-necked Stilt, American Avocet, Lesser Nighthawk, Western Kingbird, Blue Grosbeak, and Bullock's Oriole. Winter brings in a variety of waterfowl, raptors (Harris's Hawk is a rare possibility at any season), Northern Flicker, Marsh Wren, Green-tailed and Spotted Towhees, and an assortment of sparrows including Swamp.

The ponds contain no fish, so although numerous gulls and herons have been seen, they generally do not linger. If mudflats are present, shorebirding can be exceptional. Over 35 species of shorebird have been seen, including the first Red-necked Stint for Texas in July 1996. Anything is possible in migration, and up to one hundred species have been seen in one day. At least a partial list of the incredible assortment of rarities deserves mention: Brown Pelican, Reddish Egret, Glossy Ibis, Oldsquaw, White-winged Scoter, Masked Duck, Gray Hawk, Piping Plover, Red Knot, Ruff, Western Gull, Caspian Tern, Spotted Owl (specimen), Downy Woodpecker, Yellow-throated Vireo, Golden-winged, Magnolia, Blackburnian, and Palm Warblers, Varied Bunting, Eastern Towhee, Bobolink, and Lawrence's Goldfinch.

In the warmer months look for lizards including Longnose Leopard Lizard, Twin-spotted Spiny Lizard, Texas Horned Lizard, and several species of whiptails. Be careful if you decide to wander off the roads—Prairie Rattlesnakes are common in the brush. On another cautionary note, illegal shooting occurs here frequently, and it is common to find spent shotgun shells along the roads.

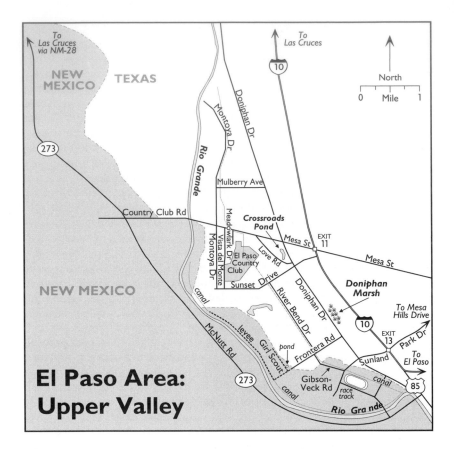

To
Las Cruces
via NM-28

NEW
MEXICO   TEXAS

To
Las Cruces

10

North

0   Mile   1

273

Rio Grande

Doniphan Dr

Montoya Dr

Mulberry Ave

Country Club Rd

Meadowlark Dr
Vista del Monte
Montoya Dra

Crossroads Pond

Mesa St

EXIT 11

Mesa St

El Paso Country Club

Love Rd

Sunset Drive

River Bend Dr

Doniphan Dr

Doniphan Marsh

To Mesa Hills Drive

10

NEW MEXICO

canal

levee

Girl Scout

pond

Frontera Rd

EXIT 13

Park Dr

To El Paso

McNutt Rd

273

Gibson-Veck Rd

canal

race track

Sunland

canal

85

Rio Grande

El Paso Area: Upper Valley

UPPER VALLEY

The Rio Grande valley on El Paso's northwest side is known locally as the Upper Valley, and it offers some of the most interesting and varied birding in the area. Established residential neighborhoods are a reasonable facsimile of woodland, and are excellent in migration and winter. In addition to these neighborhoods and the Rio Grande itself, riparian thickets, ponds, canals, and agricultural fields intermix in this area. For the state lister, the geography is a bit baffling. The Texas/New Mexico state line does not follow the current course of the Rio Grande. There are areas of New Mexico to the east of the river, and portions of Texas to the west. A city map is the best way to sort out the situation.

Access is from Interstate 10 exit 11 (Mesa Street) or exit 13 (Sunland Park Drive). From exit 13, go west on Sunland Park Drive. Just after crossing a canal, turn left into a small gravel lot (0.85 mile). You are now in New Mexico, looking at the pond at the Sunland Park Racetrack. For a better view of the pond, walk down the levee that borders the canal. The primary attraction is the gull flock in winter. Between December and March a flock of several hundred to a thousand Ring-billed Gulls roosts at dusk after spending the day at a nearby landfill. Numbers vary from week to week. A careful search will typically reveal a California Gull or two, and often a Herring Gull. Laughing, Franklin's, Bonaparte's, Mew, and Thayer's Gulls have been seen in recent winters. Sabine's Gull has occurred twice in September. There can be a decent assortment of waterfowl (Eurasian Wigeon and Surf Scoter have been seen), and a small flock of Snow Geese (usually with a Ross's or two) winters in nearby fields. A few shorebirds and perhaps a Black Tern may be present in migration.

If the gull flock is not at the racetrack, check the nearby Keystone Reserve, also known as Doniphan Marsh. Head north on Doniphan Drive from its intersection with Sunland Park Drive. Just after passing Frontera Drive (0.4 mile) on your left, turn right onto a paved drive, then bear left across the gravel. You will soon see the marsh. Park at the south end and walk, or drive along the western boundary. Do not explore the east side of the marsh or the brush to its south. The marsh and adjacent Native American settlement remains were recently purchased by a local preservationist coalition.

The gull flock often spends much of the day roosting and bathing in the water at the south end and the birds can be closely approached. Resident species include Pied-billed Grebe, Ruddy Duck, Common Moorhen, American Coot, and Killdeer. Summer brings nesting Black-necked Stilts (occasionally lingering into winter) and, often, American Avocets. Although not a great area for shorebirds, a decent variety is found in migration. Greater Yellowlegs is regular in winter along with Least Sandpiper. Great Blue Heron, Great and Snowy Egrets, and Green Heron are usually present, although the latter three can be missing in winter. Hundreds of migrant White-faced Ibises come in at dusk to roost. Immense numbers of Yellow-headed Blackbirds, almost entirely adult males, winter in west El Paso. Thousands can be seen here at dusk when they cover the power lines and cattail beds. It makes for quite an impressive spectacle. This site has not been great for rarities, but Little Blue Heron, Tricolored Heron, Mew Gull, and Lesser Black-backed Gull have been recorded. [*The above site was added for the 2003 reprinting to replace a previously described site that is now unsuitable for birding.*]

Several excellent spots can be reached by exiting Interstate 10 at Mesa Street, exit 11. Go west on Mesa (after 0.6 mile it is called Country Club Road) for 1.05 miles and turn left onto Love Road. Park on the left by a fence (0.6 mile). The small pond here, known as Crossroads Pond, is reliable in winter for Pied-billed Grebe, Gadwall, American Wigeon, Mallard, Northern Shoveler, Green-winged Teal, Canvasback, Redhead, Ring-necked Duck, Bufflehead, and Ruddy Duck. Wood Duck and Hooded Merganser are rarer possibilities. Green Heron is usually present in summer.

Return to Country Club Road and head west toward the Rio Grande (1.0 mile). Notice cross streets such as Meadowlark, Vista del Monte, and Montoya. The richly wooded neighborhoods for a mile to the north and south offer good birding in migration and in winter. Unless otherwise posted, the dirt roads along the numerous irrigation canals can be walked. Once again, a city map will be helpful. Look between Doniphan Drive on the east, Sunset Drive to the south, Mulberry to the north, and the Rio Grande to the west. Although the residents here are accustomed to some birding activity, these are among El Paso's most exclusive neighborhoods—*respect the property and privacy of the homeowners, please.*

Resident and breeding birds to look for are Mississippi Kite (summer), American Kestrel, White-winged, Mourning, and Inca Doves, Monk Parakeet (a small population has been here for close to twenty years), Yellow-billed Cuckoo (rare in summer), Lesser Nighthawk (summer), Black-chinned Hummingbird (summer), Ladder-backed Woodpecker, Black Phoebe, Western Kingbird (summer), American Robin, Northern Mockingbird, Phainopepla, and Bullock's Oriole (summer). Winter is often the best time, with Sharp-shinned and Cooper's Hawks, Belted Kingfisher, Yellow-bellied (rare) and Red-naped Sapsuckers, Northern Flicker, Plumbeous and Cassin's Vireos (both rare), Ruby-crowned Kinglet, Cedar Waxwing (irregular), Orange-crowned and Yellow-rumped Warblers, Spotted Towhee, White-crowned Sparrow, Dark-eyed Junco, and American Goldfinch.

Irregular montane invaders in fall and winter add spice to the scene: Western Scrub-Jay, Red-breasted Nuthatch, Western Bluebird, and Pine Siskin are nearly annual and can be common some years. The following species are more highly irregular and are completely absent most years, but are occasionally present: Steller's Jay, Mountain Chickadee, White-breasted and Pygmy Nuthatches, Eastern Bluebird, Townsend's Solitaire, Cassin's Finch, Red Crossbill, and Evening Grosbeak. Expect the unexpected in migration. Rarities from all directions have sought refuge in these "woodlands" in recent years. These include Northern Goshawk, Band-tailed Pigeon, Ruddy Ground-Dove, Ruby-throated Hummingbird, Lewis's, Acorn, Downy, and Hairy Woodpeckers, Juniper Titmouse, Bushtit, Carolina Wren, Gray Silky-flycatcher, Red-faced Warbler, Golden-crowned Sparrow, Yellow-eyed Junco, and Lawrence's Goldfinch.

Once you are at the Rio Grande, it is possible to walk the west levee to good birding spots in either direction. A ten-minute walk to the north (Texas) leads to a small grove and some brush. Various sparrows will be present in winter, along with a few ducks on the river. A more extensive area of cottonwoods, canals, and brush is reached after a ten-minute walk to the south (New Mexico). Wood Duck is regular here, and migrants can abound. Expect to see Gambel's Quail and Crissal Thrasher. In recent years, increased residential construction and frequent use of the area as a campsite by human transients have made this area less productive, and, at times, a bit creepy to bird alone.

The most direct route to Las Cruces, New Mexico, is to return to Interstate 10 via Country Club Road. Another possibility is to continue west for 1.0 mile to NM-273, McNutt Road. Turn right here. In about 6 miles you will hit the intersection with NM-28, which can be followed north through agricultural fields and Pecan orchards to Las Cruces. Cave Swallows breed under bridges 5.1 and 5.5 miles north of this intersection for their only known breeding in New Mexico away from the Carlsbad Caverns area. Flooded fields can hold shorebirds; check the edges of the Pecan groves (private and generally fenced) for migrants.

Before you reach NM-28, note a turn to Airport Road 1.7 miles after turning onto McNutt Road. Turn left here and go to the stop sign (2.3 miles). Turn left onto NM-136 and go 2.5 miles. A right turn here will take you west on good paved roads (NM-9) to Portal, Arizona, about 170 miles. This recently opened road, not on most maps, is the most direct and scenic route from El Paso to Arizona. Services are few and far between but gas is available in Columbus and in Animas, New Mexico. Pancho Villa State Park in Columbus can be hopping during migration, and the nearby fields can host large wintering flocks of Snow Geese and Sandhill Cranes.

LAS CRUCES, NEW MEXICO

Las Cruces is a growing city of about 75,000 located in the valley of the Rio Grande some 40 miles north of El Paso. (See map on following page.) It is here that this book bids farewell to the Rio Grande, having followed the river some 1,300 miles from the Gulf of Mexico. For the birder traveling west on Interstate 10, the Arizona state line is only 140 miles distant. En route, a visit to the Gila River at Redrock, north of Lordsburg, can yield "Arizona" specialties such as Gila Woodpecker and Abert's Towhee. If you are traveling north on Interstate 25, a side trip into the Black Range west of Hillsboro via NM-152 (exit 63) might yield Zone-tailed Hawk (uncommon), Band-tailed Pigeon, Flammulated Owl (summer), Steller's Jay, Mountain Chickadee, Bridled and Juniper Titmice, Pygmy Nuthatch, Olive Warbler (uncommon in summer), Grace's Warbler (summer), Red-faced Warbler (summer), and Painted Redstart (summer). Percha Dam State Park and Caballo Lake (exit 59), and Bosque del Apache National Wildlife Refuge (exit 139), are well worth visiting at any season. (See References for birdfinding guides covering all of these areas.)

As well as offering a wealth of nice restaurants and hotels, the Las Cruces area is close to some fine birding spots, including the nearest Ponderosa Pine woods to El Paso. One of the best spots is known as the **Old Refuge**, a remnant of thickets and trees along this very heavily cultivated stretch of the Rio Grande. To reach Old Refuge, leave Interstate 10 at the Mesilla Park/NM-28 exit (exit 140). Go south on NM-28 for 1.0 mile, then turn right onto NM-359 (Calle del Norte) at the north edge of Mesilla. Continue west for 1.0 mile before turning left onto Snow Road (NM-372). Proceed south on Snow for 2.6 miles to NM-374. Turn right here and go 1.0 mile to the Rio Grande. Jog left on the levee, then right over the bridge, followed immediately by another left-right jog over a second, smaller bridge. You are

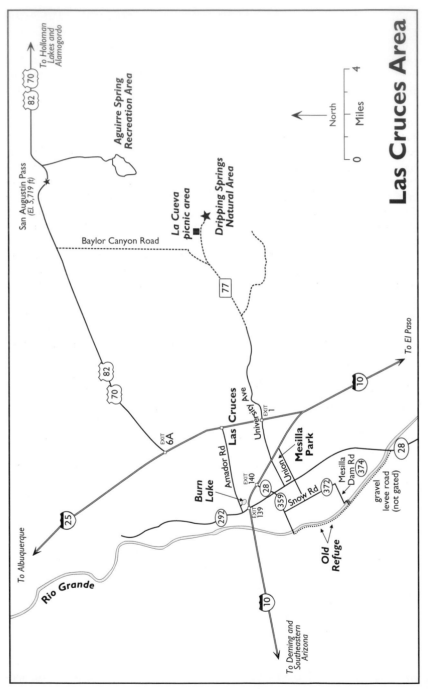

Las Cruces Area

now on the west side of the river. Proceed north, paralleling the river on the rutted dirt road, which can become nearly impassable when wet. After a mile or so the road ends at the south end of a canal, which can be walked to the north. Alternately, this canal also can be reached from the north. From the NM-359/Snow Road junction, continue west on NM-359 for another mile to the river. Walk south on the west levee—it is rarely open to vehicles here—for a mile to the aforementioned canal.

Look for residents such as Great Blue Heron, American Kestrel, Gambel's Quail, Common Moorhen, White-winged Dove, Greater Roadrunner, Ladder-backed Woodpecker, Black and Say's Phoebes, Loggerhead Shrike, Verdin, Bewick's Wren, Crissal Thrasher, Pyrrhuloxia, and House Finch. In winter, check mistletoe-infested cottonwoods for Eastern (rare) and Western Bluebirds—both are irregular. Long-eared Owls have wintered in dense thickets along the canal. Barn Owls are resident here. A few dabbling ducks will be in the river. Look for Least Sandpiper and American Pipit on the sandbars. Other wintering birds are Northern Harrier, Sharp-shinned, Cooper's, and Ferruginous Hawks, Belted Kingfisher, Western Scrub-Jay (irregular), American Crow, Marsh Wren, Ruby-crowned Kinglet, Yellow-rumped Warbler, Green-tailed and Spotted Towhees, and Chipping, Brewer's, Vesper, Savannah, Song, Lincoln's, Swamp, White-throated (rare), and White-crowned Sparrows. Breeders include Yellow-billed Cuckoo, Lesser Nighthawk, Black-chinned Hummingbird, Western Kingbird, Ash-throated Flycatcher, Yellow-breasted Chat, Blue Grosbeak, and Bullock's Oriole. Migration can be very birdy. It should be noted that human transients sometimes camp in the thickets, and dirt bikes, illegal shooting, and other activities can detract from the birding appeal.

A different nearby habitat is the wooded residential neighborhoods of Mesilla Park. Like neighborhoods in El Paso, the trees attract an interesting assortment of wintering birds, especially montane species like nuthatches, corvids, and finches. In addition, the abundant vegetation, ornamental plantings, and relatively warm microclimates can hold lingerers into winter. The following rarities have occurred in recent winters: Yellow-bellied Sapsucker, Hammond's Flycatcher, Hutton's Vireo, Mountain Chickadee, Pygmy Nuthatch, Olive Warbler, and Hepatic Tanager. A careful search in winter should turn up a Plumbeous or Cassin's Vireo, along with Orange-crowned Warbler.

To reach Mesilla Park, go south on NM-28 from Interstate 10 for about 2 miles to NM-373 (Union Avenue). Turn left on Union to McDowell; park here. The best areas can be canvassed by walking north on McDowell to Conway, east to Bowman, and then south back to Union. Mississippi Kite has bred here a time or two, and White-winged Dove cannot be missed at any season. *Confine your birding to the roads and respect the property and privacy of the residents.*

Another local spot is worth a brief mention. Burn Lake is a small fishing lake with steep, sterile dirt banks. It can be reached by leaving Interstate 10 at exit 139 (NM-292/Motel Boulevard) and going north to the first right, Amador Road. Turn right onto Amador, and then make another right in a mile or so at the sign for Burn Lake. The lake is not worth a special trip, but stop by if you are in the neighborhood. It can be thoroughly birded in ten minutes. Wintering waterfowl may include Canvasback, Redhead, Ring-necked Duck, Lesser Scaup, and Bufflehead. Expect Pied-billed and Eared Grebes in winter; Western or Clark's Grebes are rarer possibilities. The large domestic goose contingent may include a habituated Snow or Ross's Goose. Rare species such as Pacific Loon, Brown Pelican, and White-winged Scoter have been recorded.

ORGAN MOUNTAINS, NEW MEXICO

The dominant feature on the Las Cruces horizon is the imposing Organ Mountains just east of town. This rugged range is crossed by only one road, and explorations must be made on foot. An excellent site is **Dripping Springs Natural Area**, (entrance fee $3/car) jointly administered by the Bureau of Land Management and The Nature Conservancy. To reach Dripping Springs, exit Interstate 25 at exit 1 (University Avenue), heading east on University. Continue east after the road turns to gravel (4.9 miles) to the lot for the A.B. Cox Visitors Center (5.3 miles), open seven days a week year round, from 8 AM to dusk. Sign in here, pick up a trail map, and check the chalk-board showing recent wildlife sightings. The desert en route is good for desert residents, including the local Black-tailed Gnatcatcher. Sage Sparrow is possible in winter. Hummingbird feeders at the visitors center could have Calliope, Broad-tailed, and Rufous Hummingbirds from mid-July through September. Broad-billed and Magnificent Hummingbirds have been recorded in recent years.

Begin your 30-minute, easy hike to Dripping Springs from the south end of the parking lot. The crumbling remains of several turn-of-the-century ventures—a hotel and a tuberculosis clinic—are clustered in the oaks and hackberries near the springs. The trail follows a wash before passing through an open area with scattered junipers. Resident and breeding birds include Turkey Vulture (summer), Red-tailed Hawk, Golden Eagle, American Kestrel, Mourning Dove, White-throated Swift, Black-chinned Hummingbird (summer), Ladder-backed Woodpecker, Ash-throated Flycatcher (summer), Violet-green Swallow (summer), Cactus, Rock, and Canyon Wrens, Curve-billed Thrasher, Phainopepla, Canyon Towhee, Rufous-crowned and Black-chinned Sparrows, Blue Grosbeak (summer), and Scott's Oriole (summer). This is a very good place for Black-chinned Sparrow, which can be common in winter.

Winter birding can be slow. Much depends on the supply of hackberries, which can attract Eastern, Western, and Mountain Bluebirds, Townsend's Solitaire, Hermit Thrush, American Robin, and Sage Thrasher some years. Other montane species—Steller's Jay, Western Scrub-Jay, Mountain

Chickadee, Juniper Titmouse, Bushtit, nuthatches, Cassin's Finch, and Evening Grosbeak—may be present in occasional winters, but are usually absent. Expect to see Ruby-crowned Kinglet, Green-tailed and Spotted Towhees, and various sparrows. Long-eared Owls sometimes flush from the dense trees.

On your drive back to Las Cruces, note the La Cueva picnic area on your right about one-half mile west of the visitors center. This, too, is part of the natural area, and a trail meanders between it and the visitors center. Long-eared Owls sometimes roost in winter in this brushy ravine. This can be a good spot for Black-tailed Gnatcatcher. Native Americans inhabited caves (*cuevas* in Spanish) at the base of the beautiful red cliffs. If you are headed to Aguirre Spring, you might want to turn right on Baylor Canyon Road (about 2 miles west of the visitors center) and take this road north to US-70/82 at a point about 10.6 miles east of Interstate 25. Desert birds can easily be found along Baylor Canyon Road.

AGUIRRE SPRING RECREATION AREA, NM

Aguirre Spring Recreation Area (entrance fee $3/day; fee for camping) on the east side of the Organ Mountains offers access to oak/juniper woodland with Ponderosa Pines at higher elevations. This is the closest location to El Paso for a handful of montane breeding species. Leave Interstate 25 in Las Cruces at exit 6A and take US-70/82 east to San Augustin Pass (El. 5,719 ft) (13.7 miles). Continue east to the turn for Aguirre Spring (1.1 miles). Take the paved road south to the camping area and trailheads (5.5 miles). The gate opens daily at 8 AM to non-campers.

The scenery here is beautiful. The broad Tularosa Basin to the east is home to the White Sands Missile Range and White Sands National Monument. Across the basin rise the Sacramento Mountains with extensive areas of coniferous forest above 8,500 feet elevation. To the northeast is the towering cone of Sierra Blanca, southern New Mexico's highest peak at 12,003 feet. Collared Lizards are fairly common at Aguirre Spring, and Chihuahuan Spotted Whiptail is abundant along the trails in summer.

Park on the left across from the trailhead for the Pine Tree Trail. This 4.5-mile loop will take several hours at least, and has a considerable elevation gain. Pack water at any season, and be prepared in winter for the potential of abrupt temperature changes or cold, snowy conditions. The trail passes through open Ponderosa Pine woodland at the top.

Resident and breeding birds around the trailhead are White-throated Swift (rare in winter), Black-chinned and Broad-tailed Hummingbirds (summer), Acorn Woodpecker, Western Wood-Pewee (summer), Cassin's Kingbird (summer), Gray Vireo (irregular in summer), Violet-green Swallow (summer), Juniper Titmouse, Bushtit, Rock, Canyon, and Bewick's Wrens, Hepatic Tanager (summer), Rufous-crowned and Black-chinned Sparrows, Black-headed Grosbeak (summer), Scott's Oriole (summer), and Lesser

Goldfinch. Campers should listen for Western Screech-Owl and Common Poorwill. On the upper reaches of the trail look for breeding Western Wood-Pewee, Cordilleran Flycatcher, Plumbeous Vireo, White-breasted Nuthatch (resident), Virginia's Warbler (in thickets of Gambel Oak), Black-throated Gray Warbler (rare in the oaks), Grace's Warbler, and Hepatic Tanager. Recent explorations suggest that Hutton's Vireo and Mountain Chickadee breed as well. Northern Pygmy-Owl has been sighted here several times, and Band-tailed Pigeon, possible at any season, may breed.

Winter birding is highly variable and can often be slow. Typically this is a good area for frugivores like bluebirds, Townsend's Solitaire, and Sage Thrasher, but these can be completely absent some winters. In rare winters, jays, nuthatches, and finches like Cassin's Finch, Red Crossbill, and Evening Grosbeak are present.

If you are heading east on US-70/82 toward Alamogordo, be sure to stop at Holloman Lakes, an excellent spot for shorebirds and waterbirds with breeding Snowy Plovers. This site is reached by turning left onto a dirt road just past an alkali flat, 39.0 miles east on US-70/82 from the turn-off to Aguirre Spring. [*Note added for 2003 reprinting:* Since the events of 9/11/2001, the entrance gate has frequently been shut.]

GUADALUPE MOUNTAINS NATIONAL PARK

Birders who are trying to build up their Texas list will find that a visit to the Guadalupe Mountains is a must. This is the only place in the state where some Rocky Mountain species reliably can be found. To reach this interesting area, drive east from Hueco Tanks on US-62/180 for 88 miles (the park is 110 miles east of El Paso). Watch especially for Pronghorn along the middle sections of this drive. *If you are coming from Van Horn, head north on US-54 for some 60 miles.* This 76,293-acre park was created in 1972, but is intended to have only limited development. There is a primitive campground and a number of trails. Stop at the visitors center for more information. Pick up a bird checklist as well as maps, books, and other literature.

Approaching from the south, the most impressive view of the Guadalupe Mountains is the towering cliffs of El Capitan (El. 8,085 ft), perhaps the most-photographed natural landmark in Texas. This majestic peak marks the southern end of Capitan Reef, an ancient limestone formation that was laid down beneath the oceans of long ago. From El Capitan the reef rises to the top of Guadalupe Peak (El. 8,749 ft), the highest point in Texas, and then slopes downward into New Mexico like the prow of a colossal ship rising from the land. The edges of the reef have been eroded into deep canyons. The center has been partially dissolved to form huge caves such as those of Carlsbad Caverns, which are in the northern part of the reef.

The visitors center and headquarters is located at **Pine Springs**, the first road to the left as you drive north from the south park-boundary sign (0.9

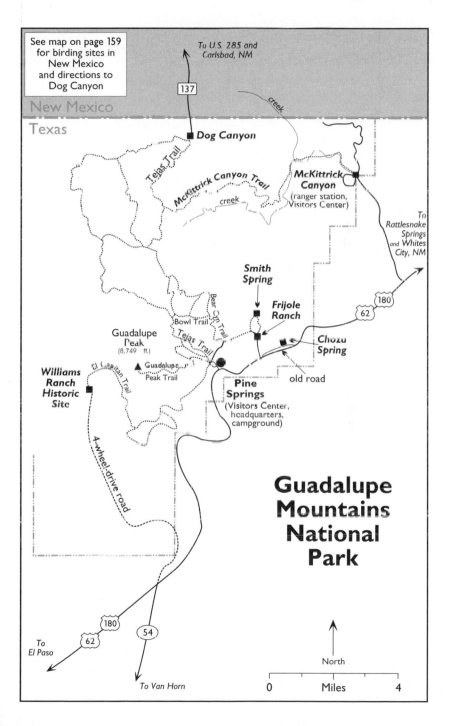

See map on page 159 for birding sites in New Mexico and directions to Dog Canyon

To U.S. 285 and Carlsbad, NM

137

New Mexico

Texas

Dog Canyon

Tejas Trail

McKittrick Canyon Trail

creek

creek

McKittrick Canyon (ranger station, Visitors Center)

To Rattlesnake Springs and Whites City, NM

180

62

Smith Spring

Frijole Ranch

Bear Cyn Trail

Bowl Trail

Guadalupe Peak (8,749 ft.)

Tejas Trail

Chozu Spring

Williams Ranch Historic Site

El Capitan Trail

Guadalupe Peak Trail

old road

Pine Springs (Visitors Center, headquarters, campground)

4-wheel-drive road

Guadalupe Mountains National Park

180

62

54

To El Paso

To Van Horn

North

0   Miles   4

mile). The campground is located nearby at the trailhead for El Capitan and Guadalupe Peak. To really see Guadalupe Mountains National Park, one must be prepared to hike. There are 80 miles of hiking trails.

There are over 250 species of birds in the park, and most are seen only by hiking, although some are found at the campground and several other places to which one can drive. Resident birds around Pine Springs are Red-tailed Hawk, Golden Eagle, American Kestrel, Scaled Quail, Mourning Dove, Greater Roadrunner, Western Screech-Owl, Great Horned Owl, Common Poorwill (not in winter), Acorn and Ladder-backed Woodpeckers, Phainopepla, Green-tailed (rare in summer), Spotted, and Canyon Towhees, Rufous-crowned, Chipping, Black-chinned, Lark (summer), and Black-throated Sparrows, and Pyrrhuloxia. In winter look also for Mountain Chickadee, Western Bluebird, Sage Thrasher, Dark-eyed Junco, and Lesser and American Goldfinches.

Continuing north on US-62/180, turn left at the road (1.2 miles) leading to **Frijole Ranch** (0.7 mile). The old ranch house has a spring in the yard with Pecans and Chinkapin Oaks. A trailhead to Smith and Manzanita Springs (2.3-miles round trip) is also located here. In winter rare woodpeckers, such as Red-headed Woodpecker, Lewis's Woodpecker, and Williamson's Sapsucker, have been found here. All three bluebirds can be rather common some winters, both in the yard and the surrounding junipers. Look also for Townsend's Solitaire, Western Scrub-Jay, resident Juniper Titmouse, and, in good years, American Robin and Cassin's Finch. Juniper-clad mountain slopes such as these are particularly attractive to frugivores, but numbers vary from one winter to the next.

MCKITTRICK CANYON

Possibly the prettiest spot in the park is **McKittrick Canyon**, which is reached by continuing on US-62/180 for some 5 miles to the turn-off on the left, and then to the end of the road (4.4 miles). This is a day-use only area. There is a small ranger station and visitors center here. The trail starts in the low desert, but as you climb higher, the canyon closes in and the walls get higher and higher, reaching over 2,000 feet in places. The canyon eventually forks. The north fork is rugged and much drier. The south fork has a permanent supply of water, which is first encountered as scattered puddles, then as a quiet brook, and finally as a rushing, rock-hopping stream.

In the desert brushland at the mouth of the canyon, you should find Scaled Quail, Greater Roadrunner, Ladder-backed Woodpecker, Verdin, Cactus and Rock Wrens, Curve-billed and Crissal Thrashers, Canyon Towhee, Rufous-crowned and Black-throated Sparrows, Pyrrhuloxia, and House Finch. In winter look for Sage Thrasher, Spotted Towhee, and numerous sparrows, including Chipping, Brewer's, Song, Lincoln's, and White-crowned. You may also see Desert Cottontail, Black-tailed Jack Rabbit, Texas Antelope

Squirrel, Rock Squirrel, Porcupine, American Badger, Striped and Common Hog-nosed Skunks, Bobcat, and Mule Deer.

Farther upcanyon the talus slopes become covered with dense brush, and the streamside forest of Alligator Juniper, Gray Oak, Black Walnut, Velvet Ash, and Texas Madrone gets thicker. The canyon is well known for the vivid fall colors of its Bigtooth Maples. Scattered throughout are huge Faxon Yuccas, an endemic species that may reach 20 feet in height. An unforgettable sight is to see Scott's Orioles feeding in the yucca's six-foot stalks of snowy-white flowers. The yucca in lower grassy flats with thinner, floppier leaves is Soaptree Yucca.

In spring the canyon rings with the songs of Gray, Plumbeous, and Warbling Vireos and Black-headed Grosbeaks. It is an excellent location for Black-chinned Sparrows. Every stunted Yellow Pine may seem to have a Grace's Warbler singing from its tip, and you might see a Hepatic Tanager, Wild Turkey, or Zone-tailed Hawk. However, the one sound which dominates the canyon is the song of the Canyon Wren, tripping down from every ledge and cliff.

Other birds to look for in McKittrick Canyon are White-throated Swift, Blue-throated (rare) and Black-chinned Hummingbirds, Acorn and Ladder-backed Woodpeckers, Say's Phoebe, Ash-throated Flycatcher, Cassin's Kingbird, Western Scrub-Jay, Cliff Swallow, Bushtit, Bewick's Wren, Virginia's Warbler, Western Tanager, Spotted and Canyon Towhees, Rufous-crowned Sparrow, Blue Grosbeak, Hooded Oriole (rare), and Lesser Goldfinch. Many of these species are breeders only. In winter look for Cooper's and Sharp-shinned Hawks, Golden Eagle, Steller's Jay, Mountain Chickadee, Golden-crowned Kinglet, and Hermit Thrush. There are two recent records of American Dipper, and in one recent winter a Yellow-eyed Junco stayed the season.

The upper reaches of the canyon have never been open to cattle, thanks to the far-sighted conservation attitude of its owners, J. C. Hunter, Jr. and Wallace Pratt. These men realized that the fragile balance of nature would have been destroyed by grazing. Because of their enlightened vision, the park has a canyon that is little changed from its pristine condition.

The high country along the top of McKittrick Ridge is well-forested with Douglas-fir, Limber and Ponderosa Pines, and even Quaking Aspen. In this forested area you should find Band-tailed Pigeon, Hairy Woodpecker, Steller's Jay, Mountain Chickadee, White-breasted and Pygmy Nuthatches, Brown Creeper, Western Bluebird, Hermit Thrush, Dark-eyed Junco, Red Crossbill (irregular), and Pine Siskin. In summer there may be Blue-throated (rare), Magnificent (rare), Black-chinned, and Broad-tailed Hummingbirds, Olive-sided and Cordilleran Flycatchers, Western Wood-Pewee, Violet-green Swallow, Blue-gray Gnatcatcher, Orange-crowned, Virginia's, and Yellow-rumped Warblers, Hepatic and Western Tanagers, and Black-headed Grosbeak. Also watch for Gray-footed Chipmunk, Porcupine, Mule Deer, and Elk.

THE BOWL

North of Guadalupe Peak is a highland, forested depression rimmed on three sides by the sharp edges of the reef. Fittingly, it is known as **The Bowl**. One way to reach the highland forests is to hike. The 4-mile trail to the top of Guadalupe Peak is popular and offers an excellent view. The Bowl can be reached by a roundabout trail via Pine Canyon, or by the 2.5-mile trail up Bear Canyon. Each originates near the park's main visitors center.

Most birders use the Bear Canyon Trail, but it has one little drawback. Although relatively short, it goes almost straight up the side of the escarpment. Be sure to get an early start and take lots of water. As you rest at the top of each switchback, enjoy the magnificent view and scan the sky for Golden Eagles and Zone-tailed Hawks. Near the top of the trail, if you are very lucky, you may flush a Spotted Owl, but you will have to stay overnight to see or hear Flammulated Owl, Western Screech-Owl, Common Nighthawk, and Whip-poor-will. Most of the birds found in The Bowl are similar to those listed above for McKittrick Ridge.

Hikes to The Bowl should not be taken lightly. Camping is primitive and one must carry in all supplies, including water. Strong winds in excess of 50 miles per hour are not unusual in the Guadalupes and are especially prevalent in the spring. Strong thunderstorms with heavy lightning can materialize quickly in summer and early fall. In addition, sudden temperature swings are possible at any season.

A less physically challenging way to reach forested areas in the Guadalupe Mountains is to drive to **Dog Canyon**. This means traveling into New Mexico. Drive north on US-62/180 to the New Mexico line and beyond about 16 miles to Whites City. Here is the entrance to Carlsbad Caverns National Park. Continue north for another 9.5 miles before turning left onto FR-408 (Dark Canyon Road). After 22.6 miles, turn left onto NM-137 and follow it into Dog Canyon. The road is paved all the way except for the last half-mile into Dog Canyon. By the way, Dog Canyon is back in Texas, so you should keep your state lists properly shuffled. The campground here has water and modern restrooms, and there is a trailhead for several trails with relatively easy grades.

In this forested area of junipers, pines, maples, and oaks look for Band-tailed Pigeon, Hairy Woodpecker, Steller's Jay, Mountain Chickadee, Pygmy Nuthatch, and Dark-eyed Junco. In summer there should be Broad-tailed Hummingbird, Olive-sided and Cordilleran Flycatchers, Warbling Vireo, Violet-green Swallow, Western Bluebird, Hermit Thrush, Yellow-rumped Warbler, Hepatic and Western Tanagers, Black-headed Grosbeak, and Red Crossbill (irregular).

After exploring the Dog Canyon area, you may wish to bird the North Rim Road (FR-540) for wonderful views down into North McKittrick Canyon. Birds of this area will include many of the same species seen in The Bowl and

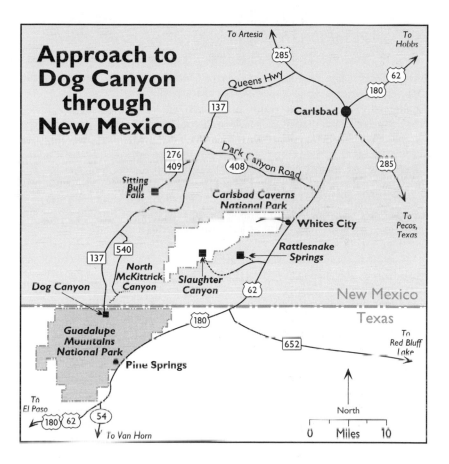

Approach to Dog Canyon through New Mexico

other higher park elevations. The North Rim trail eventually crosses back into Texas and ends at the escarpment overlooking the mouth of McKittrick Canyon. *Do not descend into the canyon.* This is an extremely fragile area and each hiker's passage carries the potential of increasing the damage that it has already sustained.

A detour to Sitting Bull Falls on FR-409 on the way out of the area is a wonderful way to spend an afternoon. The falls are impressive, and the climb into the cool caves behind them is worth the effort. Birding is excellent in the riparian area above the falls where the stream feeds the falls themselves. There are several deep pools for swimming. A rough trail to the top of the falls leaves from the parking area and follows switchbacks to the top. It is fairly easy, is short, and promises many of the same species found in McKittrick Canyon.

CARLSBAD CAVERNS NATIONAL PARK, NM

On your way to and from Dog Canyon you will pass Carlsbad Caverns National Park. The spectacular caverns are worth a visit, and one site in the park, **Rattlesnake Springs**, offers excellent birding.

From Whites City go south on US-62/180 for 5.4 miles to CR-418 (Washington Ranch Road). This intersection is 10.3 miles north of the Texas/New Mexico line. Head west on CR-418 for 2.3 miles to the stop sign. Turn right for 0.15 mile, then left into Rattlesnake Springs. Straight ahead before this last turn will take you to Washington Ranch, a facility for the mentally handicapped. In recent years a trickle of birders has birded the wooded grounds. If you ask permission at the office, park out of the way, and are quiet and unobtrusive, you will likely be able to bird the property. The birds here are similar to those at Rattlesnake Springs, and migration can be exciting.

Rattlesnake Springs is a must during migration. The area is fairly small and can be thoroughly birded in several hours. The cottonwoods and dense brush surrounding the damp, grassy swales—all in the midst of arid surroundings—make it a fabulous migrant trap. A Piratic Flycatcher was photographed here in September 1996, and a Yellow-green Vireo was once collected here. Nearly every eastern warbler and passerine has been recorded. Expect to see an eastern warbler or two during any visit in the first half of May. Fall migration is more diffuse, but equally interesting. Expect the unexpected.

In summer it's hard to miss breeders such as White-winged Dove, Yellow-billed Cuckoo, Vermilion Flycatcher, Cassin's and Western Kingbirds, Cliff and Barn Swallows, Common Yellowthroat, Yellow-breasted Chat, Summer Tanager, Blue Grosbeak, and Orchard and Bullock's Orioles. Be alert for more local and uncommon breeders like Bell's Vireo, Northern Cardinal, Painted Bunting, and Hooded Oriole.

Winter brings a variety of sparrows, as well as montane invaders some years. Brown Thrasher and Field Sparrow are rare but regular here at the western edge of their winter ranges. Wild Turkey is often seen, especially early in the morning, and Scaled Quail is common in adjacent arid areas.

You may have noticed signs for Slaughter Canyon Cave on your way in from US-62/180. The cave is reached by heading south on CR-418—following signs and several road changes—for another 9.0 miles, and can be entered only by guided, prearranged tours. Although Cave Swallows can be seen at the mouth, it is not worth a special birding visit. The road ends before the trees appear in the canyon, and a lengthy hike is needed to reach the birdy areas.

Lastly, there are a few good birds to be had along the main road into Carlsbad Caverns. From Whites City head west on NM-7 toward the headquarters and caverns entrance (7.0 miles). Cave Swallows are abundant around the cave mouth. Along the road check in brushy areas on the canyon floor for Varied Bunting, a rare and local breeder. It will be hard to miss Canyon Wren, Canyon Towhee, Rufous-crowned Sparrow, and other common desert birds. Just before reaching the headquarters, note the entrance on the right to the 9.5-mile wildlife drive. The one-way gravel loop passes through the arid brush typical of much of the park and is not especially birdy. Look for Green-tailed Towhee from fall through spring, along with numerous sparrows. Mountain Bluebird and Sage Thrasher are more sporadic, but can be abundant at times. Gray Vireos nest along the road about 6 to 7 miles in; listen for their songs in areas of heavier juniper growth. Varied Bunting is a possibility here as well.

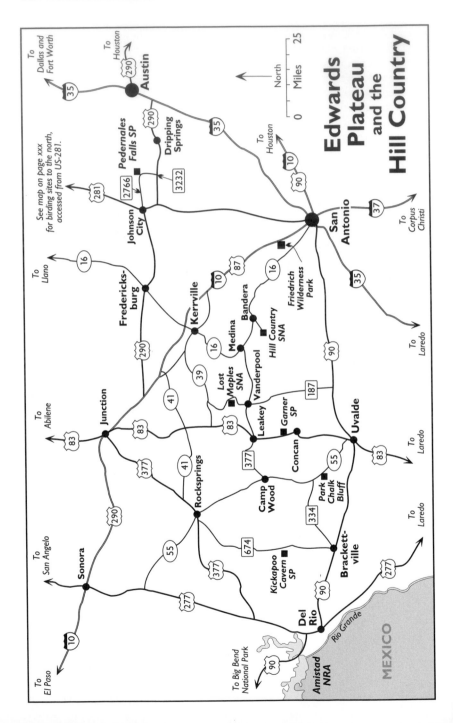

Edwards Plateau and the Hill Country

North
Miles
0 25

To Dallas and Fort Worth

To Houston

Austin
290
35

290
Pedernales Falls SP
Dripping Springs

See map on page xxx for birding sites to the north, accessed from US-281.

281
2766
3232
35

To Houston
10
90

San Antonio
37
To Corpus Christi

Johnson City

To Llano
16

Fredericks-burg
290

Kerrville
10
87

Bandera
16

Friedrich Wilderness Park

35
To Laredo

Medina
16
Vanderpool
Hill Country SNA

Lost Maples SNA
39

Junction
41

To Abilene
83
83

Leakey
83
Garner SP

187
90

Uvalde
83
To Laredo

377
41
Concan
55
Park Chalk Bluff

To San Angelo
290

Rocksprings
Camp Wood
334

Sonora
55

377
674
Kickapoo Cavern SP

Bracket-ville
90
277
To Laredo

To El Paso
10

277

Del Rio

Rio Grande

90

Amistad NRA

MEXICO

To Big Bend National Park
90

THE EDWARDS PLATEAU

If you are generally following the route in this book, you might want to reach the Edwards Plateau by leaving the Rio Grande Valley at Laredo and traveling north on Interstate 35. As an alternative, you could go as far north as Del Rio and travel east on US-90. Although there are birding opportunities to be enjoyed on the Edwards Plateau at any time of year, spring through early summer is definitely the time most birders will want to visit this beautiful area.

The Edwards Plateau is the southernmost extension of the Great Plains, characterized by its rolling terrain honeycombed with caves and sinkholes. This distinct region is a well-defined formation of Cretaceous limestone that slopes from northwest to southeast. The northwestern and central regions of the plateau are characterized by broad, relatively level uplands between deep canyons. To the north, the plateau gradually grades into the Rolling Plains, but on the south it is bounded by the Balcones Escarpment (*Ball-CO-nes*, Spanish for "balconies"). The escarpment is particularly steep along the southern boundary of the region. The deeply dissected portion adjacent to the escarpment is known as the Balcones Canyonlands—this is the true "Hill Country" of Texas. In this region it is not uncommon to see stream valleys that lie over 200 feet lower than the surrounding ridges. To the west, the plateau is separated from the geologically similar Stockton Plateau by the Pecos–Devils River divide.

The arid western end of the plateau (annual rainfall of 12 inches) still retains some of its former shortgrass prairies, but overgrazing has heavily modified many of them. The worst areas look like rocky wastelands. The eastern end is much wetter (annual rainfall of 33 inches) and is characterized by wooded hills, valleys, and clear, sparkling streams.

Much of the Edwards Plateau is occupied by sheep and goat ranches, although some of the land is set aside for recreation sites such as parks, guest ranches, and hunting preserves. The most important function of the plateau is that of an aquifer. The limestone collects vast amounts of water, which is slowly released along its innumerable springs. Many of these springs are home to endemic species of fish, amphibians, and even a few aquatic plants. The Aquarena Springs in San Marcos is home to both the world's population of Texas Wild Rice and the Fountain Darter (a small fish). There are at least six species of aquatic salamanders endemic to the plateau, each found in only one, or sometimes a few, of the springs of the Edwards aquifer.

Because this is an overlap area for eastern and western species, the plateau offers excellent birding. Many western species reach the eastern limits of their ranges here, while many eastern species reach their western limits. However, most birders plan to visit the Edwards Plateau in search of three birds: Golden-cheeked Warbler, Black-capped Vireo, and Cave Swallow.

GOLDEN-CHEEKED WARBLER

The entire breeding range of the Golden-cheeked Warbler lies within Texas. This striking bird is Federally listed as an Endangered Species. Golden-cheeks are found exclusively in diverse juniper-oak woodlands. They are dependent on the presence of Ashe Juniper (*Juniperus ashei*). These birds use only strips of bark from mature trees to construct their nests. The nest may be placed in any type of tree, but there must be mature junipers in the vicinity. It is because of this obligate relationship with the juniper, and the fact that much of its habitat has been cleared for agriculture and urbanization, that this species is endangered.

To have the best chance of seeing this limited-range species one must be in the right habitat at the right time. The birds arrive by mid-March, and the males soon begin to actively defend territories. By late July and early August most of the warblers have departed for southern Mexico and Guatemala. The best time to find one is from mid-March to late May, when the males are singing. Luckily, males frequently sing from conspicuous perches, and from mid-March to mid-April territorial males often sing through much of the day. In late April the first broods of the season fledge; from this time forward the adults become more difficult to locate. Being familiar with the bird's song is a must, but you should have no trouble locating a Golden-cheeked Warbler without using a tape. *As with the endangered Black-capped Vireo, use of tapes to arouse and attract Golden-cheeked Warblers is inappropriate.*

BLACK-CAPPED VIREO

The endangered Black-capped Vireo is considerably harder to see than the Golden-cheeked Warbler. Although widespread, this is not a common bird, and it is rather shy. Trying to lure one out into the open for a good look is a very difficult task at best. It responds well to pishing and squeaking, but will often stay hidden in the middle of a bush. Being familiar with its song is almost required.

The best way to see this bird is to find a singing male and quietly wait for it to come into view. There are many colonies on publicly accessible lands. However, many colonies are also found in preserves with strict access control or on private property. *Trespassing on any of these sites or entering private lands without permission is a very serious transgression.* Please pay special attention to directions and warnings given on sites for this species in the following pages.

Black-capped Vireos prefer fairly open shrublands where the foliage of the shrubs reaches the ground. The species composition of the habitat is not what is important—the structure, or profile, of the vegetation is what determines vireo habitat. On the eastern Edwards Plateau, habitat is often the result of disturbance (e.g., fire, removal of livestock after overgrazing). In the more arid western parts of the species' range this habitat type may be the normal climax community. This is the case on south- and west-facing slopes of the western plateau and in the Devils River drainage. Habitat may be found on alluvial flats, in canyons, or on hillsides. Black-caps are found from southwestern Oklahoma south across the plateau to Big Bend and Coahuila. Overbrowsing by sheep, goats, and the native White-tailed Deer has heavily impacted vireo habitat over much of its range.

Black-capped Vireos arrive on the southern parts of the plateau by the last week in March and depart in early September. They are very active singers from the time they arrive until early July. Males frequently sing all day during most of this time period, even during the hottest times of day.

CAVE SWALLOW

Cave Swallows historically nested in just 16 limestone caves and sinkholes ranging from Kerrville to New Mexico's Carlsbad Caverns. Within the last 15 years the species has begun using highway bridges. This has resulted in an incredible expansion of its range, bringing them into direct competition with Barn and Cliff Swallows for nesting sites. Cave Swallows can now be found over much of the Edwards Plateau, southward on to the South Texas Plains, and west through parts of the Trans-Pecos. The Edwards Plateau remains a prime area for finding Cave Swallows.

Cave Swallows arrive very early at nest sites, often by the end of February. Most sites are occupied by the first of April. As Cave Swallows have enlarged their breeding range, they also seem to be expanding their winter range into South Texas. It is now the expected wintering swallow south of the Balcones Escarpment.

The route outlined below will give you a chance of finding all three specialties plus many other species. It will also show you some of the most beautiful scenery in Texas. The layout of this section of the guide is in four parts: birding sites near the three metropolitan areas and sites scattered throughout the rest of the plateau. The route generally follows from east to west across the plateau.

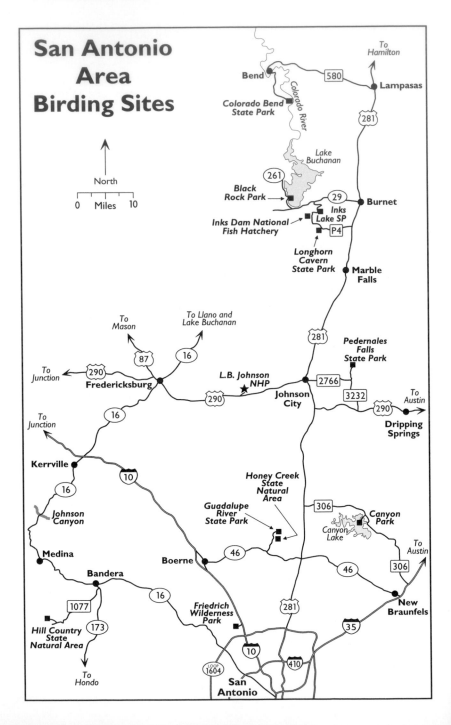

San Antonio Area Birding Sites

North

0   Miles   10

To Hamilton

Bend

580

Lampasas

Colorado Bend State Park

Colorado River

281

Lake Buchanan

261

Black Rock Park

29

Burnet

Inks Lake SP

Inks Dam National Fish Hatchery

P4

Longhorn Cavern State Park

Marble Falls

To Mason

To Llano and Lake Buchanan

87

16

To Junction

290

Fredericksburg

281

Pedernales Falls State Park

L.B. Johnson NHP

2766

Johnson City

3232

To Austin

290

290

Dripping Springs

To Junction

16

Kerrville

10

Honey Creek State Natural Area

16

Johnson Canyon

Guadalupe River State Park

306

Canyon Park

Canyon Lake

To Austin

Medina

Boerne

46

Bandera

16

46

306

New Braunfels

1077

Friedrich Wilderness Park

281

35

Hill Country State Natural Area

173

10

410

To Hondo

LOOP 1604

San Antonio

SAN ANTONIO

San Antonio is a great city in which to spend a day or more. In addition to the Alamo and other historic missions, the zoo, and the River Walk, you may also enjoy birding in some of the city parks, especially **Friedrich Wilderness Park**.

To reach these 232 acres of typical Hill Country habitat, preserved by the San Antonio Department of Parks and Recreation, go west on Interstate 10 for about 10 miles beyond Interstate 410. Exit onto Camp Bullis Road (exit #554), cross under the freeway, and drive north on the frontage road for 1.2 miles. Turn left (west) at the Friedrich Wilderness Park sign, and drive one-half mile to the park entrance. The park (free) is open 9 AM–5 PM Wednesday through Sunday, with no admittance after 4 PM.

Golden-cheeked Warblers can be found from 15 March to the first of July in along the north-facing slopes of the central ravine. The habitat is mature Ashe Juniper mixed with Texas Oak, Black Cherry, and Cedar Elm. After the singing slows down in June, the warblers can be harder to find. Black-capped Vireos are no longer found at this location. Habitat for this species on the eastern plateau can be very transitory as the habitat matures into woodland habitats.

One of the better birding areas in the park centers around the parking lot. Other nesting species include Northern Bobwhite, Greater Roadrunner, Black-chinned Hummingbird, Golden-fronted and Ladder-backed Woodpeckers, Ash-throated Flycatcher, White-eyed Vireo, Western Scrub-Jay, Verdin, Bewick's Wren, Blue-gray Gnatcatcher, Yellow-breasted Chat, Painted Bunting, Orchard and Bullock's Orioles, House Finch, and Lesser Goldfinch.

Guadalupe River State Park (1,900 acres; entrance fee $4/person; fee for camping) is located north of San Antonio. To reach the park, travel northwest on Interstate 10 to Boerne (21 miles from intersection of I-10 and Loop 410) and turn right onto TX-46 to Park Road 31 (13 miles), which leads into the park (7 miles). Alternatively, Park Road 31 can also be reached by traveling northeast from San Antonio on US-281 to TX-46 (21 miles from the intersection of US-281 and Loop 410) and then traveling west 8 miles.

The primary birding area in the park is along the Bald Cypress-lined Guadalupe River. Northern Parulas and Yellow-throated Warblers (scarce) nest here. The riparian trees and brushy areas also can be excellent places to find migrant songbirds. Green Kingfishers are often seen flying up and down the river. Other breeding birds that might be found along the river and in the tent-camping area include Eastern Wood-Pewee, Great Crested Flycatcher, Yellow-throated Vireo, and Summer Tanager. The remainder of the park is live-oak savannah with birds such as Western Scrub-Jay, Bewick's Wren, Lark Sparrow, and Painted Bunting.

Neighboring **Honey Creek State Natural Area** (1,825 acres) is currently open only to scheduled guided tours at 9 AM on Saturdays ($2/person; be sure to call the park at 830/438-2656 in advance to confirm the tour). Green Kingfisher, Acadian Flycatcher, Northern Parula, Yellow-throated Warbler, and Louisiana Waterthrush nest along this drainage. Golden-cheeked Warblers are also found in the juniper-oak woodland that overlooks the creek. The guided tours are not designed for birders, but it is worth your time to see this magnificent area and you may have the opportunity to see a few birds in the process.

A side trip from San Antonio (or Austin), worthwhile during the winter months, is **Canyon Lake**. The numerous parks situated around the lake all charge a fee ($3), however the best birding location is along the entrance road to Canyon Park on the north shore. From San Antonio take Interstate 35 north to New Braunfels (21 miles past Loop 410). At exit #188 turn left on FM-306 to Canyon Park (19.5 miles). Immediately upon turning left into the park you will see two fingers of the lake which should be checked. This is one of the most reliable places in central Texas for Greater Scaup. Watch for other ducks, including Ring-necked Duck, Lesser Scaup, and Red-breasted Merganser. Common Loon, Bonaparte's and Ring-billed Gulls, and Forster's Tern can normally be found. Pacific Loon has been seen here at least twice, and in the winter of 1996–1997 three Red-throated and two Pacific Loons were seen regularly from this vantage point. The willows along the lakeshore and the oak woodlands on the hillsides are worth checking for passerines.

If you are going to Kerrville from San Antonio, take TX-16 through Bandera, a very pretty drive. About 12 miles north of Medina is **Johnson Canyon**, where Black-capped Vireos and Golden-cheeked Warblers have been found. Park near the highway sign marked "Hill" and walk down the slope.

At Bandera turn left onto TX-16 on the south edge of town, making a right turn onto FM-1077 to **Hill Country State Natural Area** (11 miles) (5,369 acres; entrance fee $3/person; fee for camping). The park is closed on Tuesdays and Wednesdays. There are few roads within this undeveloped park, so hiking is required to reach most areas. A preliminary bird checklist and a trail map are available at park headquarters.

Steep hills and large canyons dominate the northwestern section of the park. These protected canyons contain deciduous hardwoods surrounded by more open juniper-oak woodland. Golden-cheeked Warblers can be found in these canyons. These woodland habitats can be reached in the Twin Peaks area. From park headquarters go north to the trailhead parking area and follow the trail up the slope. White-eyed Vireo, Carolina Chickadee, Tufted (Black-crested) Titmouse, Blue-gray Gnatcatcher, Black-and-white Warbler, and Summer Tanager are some of the other breeding birds found in this habitat. The wintering avifauna is equally diverse, with Yellow-bellied Sapsucker, Ruby-crowned Kinglet, Hermit Thrush, and Spotted Towhee, among others.

The foothills dominating the landscape in the southern two-thirds of Hill Country SNA consist of a mixture of open grassland with live-oak mottes and mixed scrublands composed primarily of Texas Persimmon, Evergreen Sumac, and other dense-foliaged shrubs. Black-capped Vireos are found in these habitats. There are two main areas to look for the vireo. The first is around Wilderness Camp, where the vireos nest on the escarpment above the camp area as well as on the small hills surrounding it. The other good area is the foothills across the road from "Nacho's House." To reach these areas go east along the entrance road past headquarters for 1.5 miles to the abandoned (Nacho's) house on the left side of the road; park here. To reach Wilderness Camp follow *Trail 1*, which begins directly across the road from the house. Follow this trail for 1.1 miles to reach the camp. During breeding season Mourning Dove, Common Poorwill, Eastern Phoebe, Vermilion Flycatcher, Bewick's Wren, Painted Bunting, and Scott's Oriole can be found here.

West Verde Creek is a perennial stream that runs near the eastern boundary of the park. Remnant riparian woodland habitat here attracts a wide variety of birds. Breeding birds include Red-shouldered Hawk, Yellow-billed Cuckoo, and Blue Grosbeak. Numerous other springs are scattered throughout the park, providing excellent birding opportunities, particularly in summer.

AUSTIN

Austin, the capital of Texas, was named for Stephen F. Austin, colonizer of the first American settlement in the state. This city of over 500,000 offers cultural, educational, and commercial features aplenty. Situated in the wooded hills at the eastern edge of the Edwards Plateau, Austin overlooks the Colorado River. Austin has landscaped the banks of the Colorado with beautiful parks and paths. Many outdoor recreational activities also revolve around nearby Highland Lakes, and even in the midst of the large urban population there are such novelties as the colony of Brazilian Free-tailed Bats which resides beneath the Congress Avenue Bridge. Austin is also home to a population of Monk Parakeets, which build their large stick nests on the lights surrounding the softball fields found in city parks along the Colorado River. One of the best locations for seeing them can be found by traveling west from Interstate 35 on Riverside Drive to the T-intersection at Lamar Boulevard. Cross Lamar and park in the hike-and-bike-trail parking lot. The parakeets can normally be seen around the softball fields.

Known simply as "City Park" to the locals, **Emma Long Metropolitan Park** is the closest place to downtown Austin to find Golden-cheeked Warblers. To reach the park go north on Interstate 35 from downtown Austin and take the exit for US-290 (4.0 miles), turning west onto FM-2222 (Koenig Lane). Go under Loop-1 (3.3 miles) and proceed to Loop-360 (4.0 miles). After passing this, start watching for the small signs marking City Park

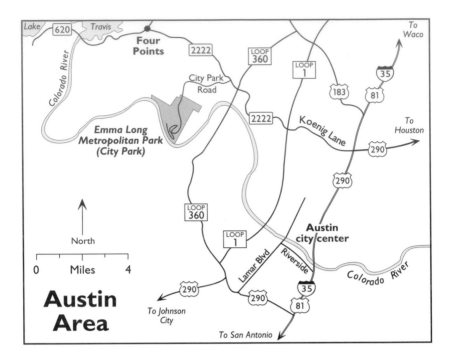

Road (0.5 mile), which is on the left. Turn left and go to the top of the hill. From here to the end of the road (6.0 miles), you will see much prime habitat for the warbler. Unfortunately, the first five miles of this road traverse private property, and developments are consuming more of the habitat each year. Warblers are frequently heard and seen at the several dirt pull-outs where the road skirts the hillside. Perhaps the best location in the park for finding the warbler is near the little rock bridge at the only creek-crossing on the road (4.5 miles). Small foot-paths leading upstream and downstream from this bridge traverse prime warbler habitat.

Travis Audubon Society owns and manages a 600-plus-acre wildlife sanctuary, located about twenty miles northwest of Austin, where Golden-cheeked Warblers nest in fairly good numbers. But, during the nesting season (mid-March to late June) access is allowed only by scheduled guided tours, even to chapter members. Regular tours on Saturdays in spring and summer to see Black-capped Vireos have been organized in recent years. You may call the Austin Area Audubon Alert (phone: 512/926-8751), which maintains a recorded message with the capacity for callers to leave their own messages. Anyone wanting to visit the sanctuary would either be given a name and number to call or could leave a message requesting further information.

Balcones Canyonlands National Wildlife Refuge encompasses a diversity of Hill Country habitats. The refuge covers over 16,000 acres and is located west and northwest of Austin in parts of Travis, Burnet, and Williamson Counties. There is a substantial population of Golden-cheeked Warblers and a few colonies of Black-capped Vireos. Typical Hill Country birds can be observed on the refuge, including some of the easternmost populations of Canyon Towhee and Black-throated Sparrow. Currently, the refuge is not open to the public, except through guided tours, but future plans call for sections of the refuge to be open by spring 1999, as well as for the addition of visitor facilities, including a viewing stand in Black-capped Vireo habitat. This will be the closest location to Austin where this bird may be seen. Call the refuge office (phone: 512/339-9432) for further information.

Starting from Austin, go west on US-290 toward Fredricksburg. (See San Antonio area map on page 166.) After passing Dripping Springs (21.0 miles), start watching on the right for FM-3232 (8.0 miles), which leads to **Pedernales Falls State Park** (6.3 miles) (entrance fee $4/person; fee for camping). The 5,200-acre park stretches along both banks of the Pedernales River, although there is no need to cross the river. Bald Cypresses and sycamores line the riverbanks while Ashe Juniper and oaks cover the uplands. A seasonal checklist is available at park headquarters.

There is a large population of Golden-cheeked Warblers at this park. One of the best, and most accessible, places to find the bird is along the **Hill Country Nature Trail**. The trail starts between campsites 19 and 21. Warblers normally can be found between the trailhead and the overlook at Twin Falls. Also look for Golden-cheeks in the area around the amphitheater (next to campsite 33). Another area where this species may be found is in the mixed woodlands west of the falls parking lot at the north end of the park. Once you have parked your car, walk back down the main road about one-quarter mile to a dirt road on the right. Take the right fork of this dirt road and follow it another quarter-mile until it forks again. There are several pairs of warblers in the area between the road and the Pedernales River.

Other birds to be found include Golden-fronted and Ladder-backed Woodpeckers, Eastern Phoebe, Ash-throated and Great Crested Flycatchers, Western Kingbird, White-eyed and Yellow-throated Vireos, Cliff Swallow, Carolina Chickadee, Tufted (Black-crested) Titmouse, Verdin, Bushtit, Canyon, Carolina, and Bewick's Wrens, Summer Tanager, Canyon Towhee, Rufous-crowned and Black-throated Sparrows, Blue Grosbeak, Painted Bunting, and Lesser Goldfinch.

As you leave the park, turn right onto FM-2766. At Johnson City (9.0 miles) either travel north on US-281 to visit the Lake Buchanan area (see below) or continue west on US-290 toward Kerrville.

LAKE BUCHANAN REGION

Although the Lake Buchanan region offers another opportunity to observe Golden-cheeked Warblers, this area is better known as offering some of the best waterbirding on the Edwards Plateau. As a result, it is best visited from October to March.

From Johnson City travel north on US-281 past Marble Falls (23 miles) to Park Road 4 (9 miles). Turn left onto Park Road 4 and proceed 6 miles to **Longhorn Cavern State Park**. The park is small (639 acres) and currently there is no fee to picnic or for walking the hiking trails. There is a fee to enter the cavern, which has a long, and interesting past, including having a dance floor installed in the cave during the 1930s. Birding at this site is limited to oak-juniper woodland habitat; consequently the diversity of birds is not high, however Golden-cheeked Warblers can be found along the hiking trails between mid-March and early June. Other residents include Ladder-backed Woodpecker, Canyon Wren, Bushtit, Rufous-crowned Sparrow, and Northern Cardinal. Breeding species also include Ash-throated Flycatcher, Summer Tanager, and Painted Bunting.

Continue west on Park Road 4 to **Inks Dam National Fish Hatchery** (4.2 miles). The hatchery is worth checking for migrating shorebirds and wintering ducks, and is open from 8 AM–4 PM Monday through Friday only. The brushy areas between the hatchery and the Colorado River are a good place to look for Eastern Phoebe, Carolina Chickadee, Carolina Wren, Hermit Thrush, Spotted Towhee, Northern Cardinal, and a variety of wintering sparrows. Return to Park Road 4 and continue 2.4 miles to **Inks Lake State Park** (1,201 acres: entrance fee $4/person; fee for camping). The park sits on the shore of Inks Lake, an excellent place to find wintering Common Loon, Pied-billed, Horned, and Eared Grebes, and Red-breasted Merganser. There are over seven miles of hiking trails in the park. Golden-fronted Woodpecker, Western Scrub-Jay, Tufted (Black-crested) Titmouse, and Bewick's Wren, among other typical Hill Country species, can be found in the park. A seasonal checklist which includes Longhorn Cavern State Park is available at park headquarters.

Return to Park Road 4, continuing toward **Lake Buchanan**. At TX-29 (3.6 miles) turn left toward the dam (3 miles). The overlook from the dam can reveal many of the species listed for Inks Lake, particularly Common Loon. Another good vantage point is **Black Rock Park** ($3/person). To reach this park continue west on TX-29 to TX-261 (1.5 miles), turning right to the park (2.7 miles). Black Rock Park sits on a peninsula that offers an excellent vantage point from which to scope the lake. Common Loon, Horned Grebe, Red-breasted Merganser, and Bonaparte's, Ring-billed, and Herring Gulls are usually visible from the point. The remainder of the park is small and primarily a picnic area, with a few scattered live oaks and other trees. Tufted (Black-crested) Titmouse, Ruby-crowned Kinglet, Northern Mockingbird, Yellow-rumped Warbler, and Chipping and Savannah Sparrows can usually be found in winter. There is little reason to visit this site during the breeding season. A Llano County park (no admission fee) is located next to Black Rock Park, however this park encircles a cove and only a small portion of the lake can be viewed from it.

Lake Buchanan is also the winter home to Bald Eagles. The best way to observe these birds is by taking the Vanishing Texas River Cruise (PO Box 901, Burnet, Texas 78611; phone: 512/756-6986) from late November to March. The cruise covers part of the lake and up the Colorado River.

From Lake Buchanan, travel to Burnet via TX-29 (13 miles), making a left (north) turn onto US-281 to Lampasas (22 miles). Proceed through town until you see the sign for **Colorado Bend State Park** (5,328 acres; entrance fee $3/person; fee for camping). Turn left onto North Street, following it to a T-intersection at FM-580; turn right and drive to Bend (22.0 miles). At Bend the road crosses the Colorado River, where there is a large colony of Cliff Swallows nesting under the bridge where FM-580 abruptly turns right (stop sign). At the stop sign turn left and follow the signs down a well-maintained gravel road to the park entrance (6 miles). The park office and best birding are both found at the far end of the park at the Colorado River. Hiking trails lead upstream from the upper end of the camping area and downstream from the boat-ramp parking area. Golden-cheeked Warblers can be found along both trails, which also are excellent places to look for migrants. The upstream trail follows the river, taking the hiker through a mixed gallery forest where a wide variety of

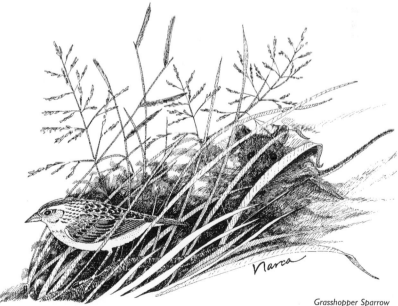

Grasshopper Sparrow
Narca Moore-Craig

birds can be found. During spring and summer look for Red-shouldered Hawk, Yellow-billed Cuckoo (after 1 May), Golden-fronted Woodpecker, Acadian Flycatcher (rare), Great Crested Flycatcher, White-eyed, Yellow-throated, and Red-eyed Vireos, Western Scrub-Jay, Carolina Chickadee, Canyon and Carolina Wrens, and Summer Tanager. This trail eventually enters open grassland—about 100 yards wide by one-half mile long—where wintering Vesper, Savannah, and Grasshopper Sparrows can be found. Other wintering species along the river corridor include Hermit Thrush, Spotted Towhee, and Chipping, Song, Lincoln's, White-throated, and White-crowned Sparrows.

The downstream trail turns up into Spicewood Canyon, a beautiful area well worth the hike. Golden-cheeks can be seen anywhere from the parking area to upper Spicewood Canyon. The species listed for the previous trail are basically the same ones that can be observed here. A few large Pecan trees next to the parking area attract nesting Orchard Orioles and also can be excellent for woodpeckers, including Golden-fronted and Downy, year round, and Yellow-bellied Sapsucker and Northern Flicker in winter. There are generally a few nesting pairs of Indigo Buntings found along this trail before it reaches Spicewood.

Upland areas of the park have a different avifauna. A nature trail that leads from the main park road down to the Colorado River traverses the drier uplands and can produce Ash-throated Flycatcher, Bushtit, Bewick's Wren, and Rufous-crowned, Field, and Black-throated Sparrows.

A seasonal checklist is available at park headquarters. The park provides guided tours to Gorman Falls on weekends. The 60-foot-high falls are the highest on the Edwards Plateau and are well worth the $2/person fee for the tour.

KERRVILLE

From Johnson City (see also San Antonio area map on page 166) travel west on US-290 to FM-1 (10.9 miles), which leads to the LBJ Ranch. To visit the ranch, park at the state park on the south side of the road and board one of the tour buses, which takes you to Johnson's birthplace, the cemetery, and for a short tour of the ranch. The main ranch house is not open to the public.

At Fredericksburg (14.0 miles), renowned for its German-style cooking, turn left onto TX-16 toward Kerrville (24.0 miles).

Kerrville (population 15,276, elevation 1,645 feet) is the hub of the vacation activities in the Hill Country. Motels, guest ranches, and campgrounds abound. After seeing this pretty little town on the beautiful Guadalupe River, you may not want to go any farther. Birding can be good almost anywhere in the area. **Louise Hayes Park**, just across the river from the downtown area, has some tall trees that can be good for warblers and other migrants.

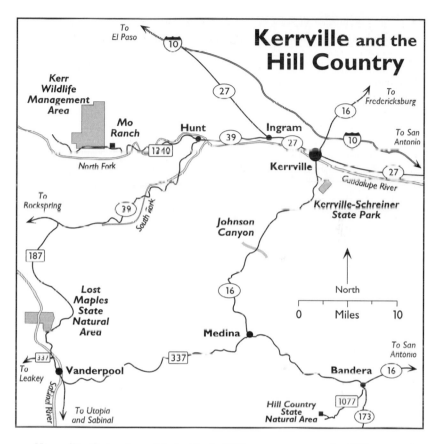

Kerrville and the Hill Country

To
El Paso

10

Kerr
Wildlife
Management
Area

27

To
Fredericksburg

16

Mo
Ranch

Hunt

39

Ingram

27

10

To San
Antonio

1340

North Fork

Kerrville

Guadalupe River

27

To
Rockspring

39

South Fork

Johnson
Canyon

Kerrville-Schreiner
State Park

187

Lost
Maples
State
Natural
Area

16

North

0   Miles   10

Medina

To San
Antonio

337

337

To
Leakey

Vanderpool

Bandera

16

Sabinal River

To Utopia
and Sabinal

Hill Country
State
Natural Area

1077

173

Kerrville-Schreiner State Park (517 acres; entrance fee $3/person; fee for camping) is just south of town. Take TX-16 to TX-173 (0.5 mile) and turn left to the park (2.5 miles). The best birding is normally on the hillside above the camping area. Wild Turkeys may be foraging here among the oaks. Some common resident species include Inca Dove, Greater Roadrunner, Belted Kingfisher, Golden-fronted and Ladder-backed Woodpeckers, Eastern Phoebe, Western Scrub-Jay, Carolina Chickadee, Tufted (Black-crested) Titmouse, Carolina and Bewick's Wrens, Eastern Bluebird, Northern Mockingbird, Northern Cardinal, Brown-headed Cowbird, and House Finch. Other summer nesters are Green Heron, Yellow-billed Cuckoo, Chimney Swift, White-eyed Vireo, Cliff and Barn Swallows, Summer Tanager, and Bronzed Cowbird. Yellow-throated Warbler is an uncommon nester.

Johnson Canyon, good for Golden-cheeked Warbler, crosses TX-16 some 12 miles south of Kerrville (or 12 miles north of Medina). Park near the highway sign which reads "Hill" and walk down the highway. The birds may be

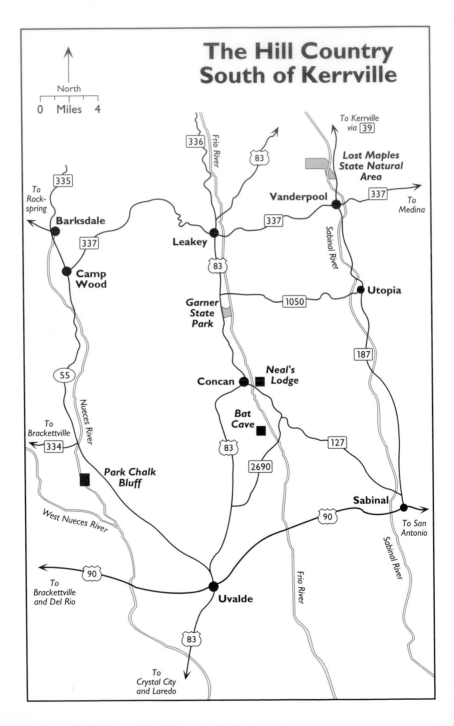

The Hill Country
South of Kerrville

found anywhere in the stands of oak. Of course, they are most active early in the morning.

THE HILL COUNTRY SOUTH OF KERRVILLE

To reach the very heart of the Hill Country, drive northwest from Kerrville on TX-27 to Ingram (7.0 miles). Turn west onto TX-39, which runs along the Guadalupe River. At Hunt turn right onto FM-1340 to explore a beautiful stretch of the North Fork of the Guadalupe River. After a couple of blocks, watch on the left for a house with sugar-water feeders, which swarm with Black-chinned Hummingbirds in summer.

The area along the river is great for Wood Duck, Cliff Swallow, Eastern Phoebe, Yellow-throated Vireo, Canyon Wren, and many other species. Green Kingfisher might be found here in summer if you look hard enough. This small, shy bird is easily overlooked because it perches close to the water on rocks or low, overhanging limbs. Your best bet is to stop as often as possible to scan the river.

Mo Ranch Church Camp (10.7 miles) on the right is a delightful place to bird. Accommodations can be arranged during off-seasons. **Kerr Wildlife Management Area** (2.0 miles) (6,439 acres) is home to Golden-cheeked Warblers and Black-capped Vireos. There are approximately 20 pairs of the endangered warbler and over 100 pairs of Black-capped Vireos within the WMA. Aggressive management activities have produced vireo habitat and, as a result, the birds are doing well and increasing in numbers. Their preferred habitat is live-oak thickets with a low, thick understory. Take the 4.5-mile interpretive driving tour, picking up a copy of the guide booklet at the registration booth. Northern Bobwhites and Wild Turkeys are relatively common here. To see the warbler and vireo requires a visit to the WMA office. Office hours are 8 AM–5 PM weekdays; WMA personnel will direct you to appropriate areas.

Beyond this point the road leaves the river to cross open ranchland. Turn around, go back to Hunt, and continue west on TX-39, now following the South Fork of the Guadalupe River—just as pretty and birdy as the North Fork.

Eventually, the road leaves the river to cross grasslands dotted with Shin Oak. Watch for Wild Turkey, Greater Roadrunner, Great Horned Owl, Golden-fronted Woodpecker, Western Scrub-Jay, Common Raven, Carolina Chickadee, Tufted (Black-crested) Titmouse, Verdin, Bushtit, Rock, Canyon, Carolina, and Bewick's Wrens, Eastern Bluebird, Canyon Towhee, Cassin's, Rufous-crowned, Chipping, Field, Lark, and Black-throated Sparrows, Eastern Meadowlark, House Finch, and Lesser Goldfinch. In summer look for Common Nighthawk, Common Poorwill, Chuck-will's-widow, Eastern Phoebe, Vermilion, Ash-throated, and Great Crested Flycatchers, Western Kingbird, Scissor-tailed Flycatcher, White-eyed, Bell's, and Red-eyed Vireos, Grasshopper Sparrow, Blue Grosbeak, Painted Bunting, and Orchard and

Scott's Orioles. In migration you may see large concentrations of Mississippi Kites and Swainson's Hawks, and in winter, Clay-colored, Vesper, Lark Bunting, Savannah, Fox, Lincoln's, White-throated, and White-crowned Sparrows. Keep an eye out for the black morph of Rock Squirrel.

At FM-187 (20.0 miles) turn left. For the next few miles watch the utility wires for Cave Swallows, particularly in late afternoon. On the right, there is a windmill with a water trough (1.5 miles), where the swallows often come to

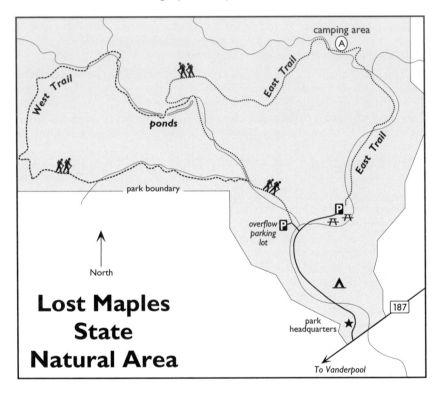

drink. If you do not see them here, check the utility wires between the buildings of the former Bonnie Hills Ranch (2.8 miles) on the right.

LOST MAPLES STATE NATURAL AREA

One of Texans' favorite spots for viewing fall colors is Sabinal Canyon, where an isolated stand of Big-toothed Maples turns a brilliant red. This remote area is in **Lost Maples State Natural Area** (9.8 miles) (2,174 acres; entrance fee $4/person; $5 during October and November; fee for camping). Not only is this a very scenic spot, but it is also a good birding area. A seasonal bird checklist is available at park headquarters.

Lost Maples has one of the largest populations of Golden-cheeked Warblers on publicly accessible lands. Black-capped Vireos can also be found at this location. Golden-cheeks can be seen from any of the main trails. East Trail makes a long loop covering the eastern section of the natural area. The trail can be accessed from either the picnic area or the overflow parking lot. Many warbler territories are located along the trail between the picnic area and primitive camping area A (1.7 miles). Hiking the other end of the loop, starting at the overflow parking area and walking to the pond, also takes you through an excellent area (1.1 miles). This segment of the trail is better for Black-capped Vireos. The vireos are found on brushy west- and south-facing hillsides, areas that are not easily accessible, so seeing the birds can be particularly difficult. The lower slope next to the pond is one of the best places to look. Being familiar with the songs of these two birds will make finding them much easier. *Please stay on the trails; it is against park regulations to leave the trails.* The park staff is knowledgeable about these birds' locations and can usually direct visitors to places where they can be observed.

Keep an eye out for Zone-tailed Hawks while you are in the park and the nearby area. There are scattered breeding pairs in the vicinity and they can sometimes be seen flying up and down the canyons or over the surrounding hills. Other nesting species include Greater Roadrunner, Green Kingfisher, Ladder-backed Woodpecker, Acadian Flycatcher, Black Phoebe, Ash-throated and Great Crested Flycatchers, White-eyed, Yellow-throated, and Red-eyed Vireos, Western Scrub Jay, Common Raven, Bushtit, Black-and-white Warbler, Louisiana Waterthrush, Canyon Towhee, Northern Cardinal, Painted Bunting, Orchard Oriole, and Lesser Goldfinch. The waterthrush is normally found along the many small streams in the park. West Trail is a more strenuous walk, but a good place look for these birds.

During summer and fall take some time to see what is coming to the hummingbird feeder at park headquarters. Normally there are just Black-chinned Hummingbirds, but there also may be Ruby-throats and Rufous in fall. Such rarities as Green Violet-ear (1995) and Blue-throated Hummingbird (1996) have been documented at this feeder.

GARNER STATE PARK

Continue south on FM-187 through Vanderpool (4.7 miles) to Utopia (10.5 miles). Turn right (west) onto very scenic FM-1050 to US-83 (15.0 miles). Turn left after about one mile to Garner State Park (1,419 acres; entrance fee $5/person; fee for camping). Birding is often productive along the Frio River and along the park's six miles of hiking trails. The park can be exceptionally crowded on weekends in spring and anytime during summer.

The clear, spring-fed Frio River has large Bald Cypresses lining its banks. Birding along the river can yield Green Kingfisher, Black Phoebe, and Yellow-throated Warbler (in the cypresses). Golden-cheeked Warblers are found in the oak-juniper woodlands in the southwestern portion of the park.

The hillsides there are very steep, which makes finding the warblers difficult, however leaving the trail is strongly discouraged. One segment of the trail, formerly serving as the entrance to the park, is paved, and this is probably the best place to look for the birds. There is a small parking area on the right, at the top of the hill, where the main park road leads to the extreme southern camping area in the park. If you see the pavilion and miniature golf course, you have passed the trailhead.

Resident are Western Scrub-Jay, Common Raven, Verdin, Bushtit, Cactus, Canyon, Carolina, and Bewick's Wrens, Canyon Towhee, Rufous-crowned Sparrow, and Pyrrhuloxia. White-winged Dove, Vermilion Flycatcher, Black-and-white Warbler, and Scott's Oriole occur during the breeding season.

NEAL'S LODGE

Continuing south on US-83, turn left onto TX-127 at Concan (7.3 miles). Neal's Lodge (0.6 mile) (PO Box 165, Concan 78838; phone 830/232-6118), on the left, is on the beautiful Frio River. This attractive vacation spot, operating since 1927, has rooms, many housekeeping cabins, a cafe, and a grocery store available year round.

Birds are abundant about the 300-acre grounds. White-winged and Inca Doves, Canyon, Carolina, and Bewick's Wrens, Eastern Phoebe, Hooded Oriole, and Rufous-crowned Sparrow can be found about the buildings. At night you may hear Common Nighthawk, Common Poorwill, and Chuck-will's-widow. By walking up the road and across the cattle-guard behind the store, you reach a dry hillside covered with cacti and thorny brush. Look here for Say's Phoebe, Vermilion and Ash-throated Flycatchers, Verdin, Cactus Wren, Curve-billed Thrasher, Canyon Towhee, Pyrrhuloxia, and Black-throated Sparrow. Unless there are lots of campers, a hike along the river might produce Black Phoebe and possibly a Green Kingfisher or a Yellow-throated Warbler. There is even a chance for Black-capped Vireo on the hill behind the store. The trail going up starts behind cabin #15, or you can take the road behind the store. If this area is crowded, try the trail on the other side of the river, reached from the highway. Ask at the office for directions.

FRIO BAT CAVE

If you are staying at Neal's Lodge, or are in the area in late evening, you may want to see bats. Drive east on TX-127 to FM-2690 (4.4 miles). Turn right and start checking the swallows, especially at the low-water crossing on the Frio River (0.1 mile). In the hills off to the right is a cave that harbors some 500 to 600 Cave Swallows and about 17 million Brazilian Free-tailed Bats. Although the cave is not open to the public, the swallows can usually be seen flying around, particularly in the evening. If you set up a spotting scope at the wooden gate on the right (1.6 miles), you can see the bats come swirling up like a stream of smoke just at dark.

CAMP WOOD ROAD

Return to US-83 and drive north past Garner State Park to the little town of Leakey (17.0 miles from Concan), where you will find restaurants, stores, and cabins. Turn left in the heart of town onto Camp Wood Road (FM-337), which runs along a ridge through stands of scrub oak. Over the years, this has been one of the better spots for Zone-tailed Hawks, and the only way to find one is to check all of the vultures. In flight, even at close range, the Zone-tailed can look similar to a Turkey Vulture. The hawk's black and white tail-bands often can be seen only with the aid of binoculars. By looking at enough Turkey Vultures, you will find, sooner or later, a Zone-tailed Hawk.

At Camp Wood (20.7 miles) you have a choice of routes. The shortest option is to turn south onto TX-55 toward Uvalde—and the birding can be good. At the Nueces River (3.6 miles) check the area below the dam for Green Kingfishers. For several years a pair nested on the east side of the road in a small bank on the north side of the stream. Cave Swallows have attempted to nest in the road culverts (12.0 miles), but the nests are usually wiped out by high water. At FM 334 (2.5 miles) you either can turn right toward Brackettville (30 miles) to continue your trip up the Rio Grande or continue south on TX-55 to Park Chalk Bluff (22.6 miles).

PARK CHALK BLUFF

Park Chalk Bluff (entrance fee $2/person during winter, $3/person during remainder of year) is a private facility along the Nueces River. Many species that are usually found farther south on the South Texas Plains can be seen here. The river, lined with sycamores and Bald Cypresses, has been a reliable location in recent years to find Ringed and Green Kingfishers. Green are resident, and Ringed have been seen year round, although winter is the best time to find them. The park contains some remnant riparian habitat as well as live-oak mottes above the floodplain. Year-round residents include Golden-fronted Woodpecker, Western Scrub-Jay, Cactus, Carolina, Canyon, and Bewick's Wrens, Long-billed Thrasher, Olive Sparrow, Rufous-crowned, Field, and Black-throated Sparrows, Northern Cardinal, and Pyrrhuloxia. During spring and summer look for Common Ground-Dove, Black Phoebe, Ash-throated and Brown-crested Flycatchers, Couch's Kingbird, Yellow-breasted Chat, Indigo and Painted Buntings, Hooded Oriole, and Lesser Goldfinch. Zone-tailed Hawks nest in the area and are often seen in the vicinity. A Rufous-capped Warbler spent the summer of 1995 at this park.

During winter Chalk Bluff is home to an impressive array of sparrows, including the resident species listed above plus Chipping, Vesper, Savannah,

Song, Lincoln's, Swamp, White-throated, White-crowned, and Dark-eyed Junco. Other wintering species frequently found here include Yellow-bellied Sapsucker, Ruby-crowned Kinglet, Hermit Thrush, Orange-crowned and Yellow-rumped Warblers, Spotted Towhee, and American Goldfinch.

A longer route (see chapter map on page 162) is to turn north at Camp Wood onto TX-55 toward Rocksprings (29.0 miles). From Rocksprings go south on US-377 to FM-674 (3 miles), a scenic road along the West Nueces River that leads to Kickapoo Cavern State Park (34 miles). The entrance to the park faces to the south and is easily missed. It is located one-half mile north of the Edwards–Kinney county line.

KICKAPOO CAVERN STATE PARK

Kickapoo Cavern State Park (6,400 acres; entrance fee $2/person; fee for camping) is an undeveloped, understaffed park, so advance reservations are required (phone: 830/563-2342). It is recommended that reservations be made at least two weeks prior to the date you wish to visit the site, although last-minute visits often can be arranged. Kickapoo Cavern is a great place to spend a day or two. Spring and early summer offer the best birding, but this scenic park has good birding opportunities at all seasons. The park's location on the southwestern corner of the plateau provides for a unique assemblage of birds. Species normally associated with the Edwards Plateau, the Trans-Pecos, and the South Texas Plains can be found here. The starting point for all birding is at the center of the park at the old hunting lodge. The park staff will lead you to this point, and all of the birds found on the park can be located by walking the roads that radiate from this point. A good bird checklist is avilable if you ask for it. The area surrounding the lodge is one of the best places to find Vermilion Flycatcher and Hooded Oriole. During dry periods, or in midsummer, the water troughs around the lodge attract many birds, including Varied Buntings.

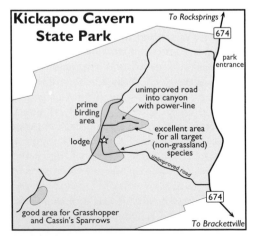

Kickapoo's claim to fame is a large population of Black-capped Vireos. Censuses have recorded more than 100 pairs of this endangered species within the boundaries of the park. Other breeding species include Wild Turkey, Common Ground-Dove (scarce), Common Poorwill, Vermilion Flycatcher, Bell's and Gray Vireos, Cave Swallow, Yellow-breasted

Chat, Pyrrhuloxia, Varied and Painted Buntings, Cassin's, Black-throated, and Grasshopper Sparrows, and Hooded and Scott's Orioles.

Black-capped and Gray Vireos arrive and are on territory by the first of April. Black-caps are easily heard, and with some patience seen, in the clumps of Texas Persimmon along the roads leading from the lodge. The park staff surveys for these birds and can point you to areas where territorial vireos are present. *It is important to remain on the roads so that the vireos are not disturbed.* Some of the best places are along the roads leading directly north and south from the lodge. It is not uncommon to hear singing males from the lodge's parking area

Gray Vireo is far more difficult to find. As with the Black-cap, being familiar with the bird's song is the key to finding them. Gray Vireos defend large territories, so finding them takes a little bit of luck, but as with most vireos, the males sing almost constantly through spring and early summer. Be sure to ask the park staff if any have been seen recently.

One of the best birding spots in the park is within easy walking distance of the lodge. Walk north along the entrance road past the first creek crossing (dry except after heavy rains) to a old two-track road leading off to the right. This road enters a canyon with a power line running down it. This is one of the best places in the park for Varied Bunting and Scott's Oriole. The songs of Painted and Varied Buntings are similar, so check every bunting you hear. Black-capped and Gray Vireos are also found in this canyon. While at Kickapoo during spring and summer, watch for Zone-tailed Hawks. There are at least three pairs in the area and they are frequently seen on the park.

A sight not to be missed is the emergence of Brazilian Free-tailed Bats from Green Cave. Between early April and September there are frequent tours to see this spectacular bat flight. Before the bats begin to emerge there is ample time to study the colony of Cave Swallows that reside in the entrance to the cave. After watching the bat flight, drive slowly around the park roads to see Common Poorwills. Eastern Screech-Owl and Great Horned Owl are common on the park, and there are usually a few Elf Owls in residence as well, but these tiny owls are more often heard than seen.

Fall and winter are great seasons to study sparrows at Kickapoo. Look for Rufous-crowned, Chipping, Field, Vesper, Black-throated, Savannah, Song, Lincoln's, and White-crowned. Check the old cleared pastures that are now grass-covered for Le Conte's and Grasshopper among the numerous Savannah and Vesper Sparrows.

Upon leaving the park turn right (south) toward Brackettville (22.5 miles). Before reaching Brackettville the road crosses the escarpment and leads down onto the South Texas Plains, where the habitat changes dramatically. Watch for Scaled Quail, Harris's Hawk, and Crested Caracara along the roadside. At dusk this road, as well as US-90, is a good place to see Lesser and Common Nighthawks. After dark, if there is not much traffic, nighthawks and Common Poorwills land on the pavement. In Brackettville turn left on US-90 toward Del Rio.

BIRDS OF THE REGION

With this edition of *A Birder's Guide to the Rio Grande Valley* there are some fundamental changes to this section of the book. An annotated checklist replaces the standard bar-graph checklist that is so familiar to users of the various guides in this ABA series. The avifaunas of the three major regions covered in this guide obviously have common components, but they are more different than they are similar. The differences in latitude and longitude between El Paso and Brownsville strongly affect the average arrival times of migrants, winter residents, and breeding species. In carefully reviewing the bar-graphs accompanying the previous edition it became clear that in order to produce a valuable and accurate component of the book, three or four lines of bars would be needed for many species. An annotated checklist seemed the best way to overcome this obstacle. Basically, the *Specialties of the Region* section of previous editions has been expanded to include every species that has been documented within the area covered by this guide. For species with fewer than five records, every record is included. The names of the species that would have been in the *Specialties of the Region* section are highlighted here in all capital letters.

For each species there are three components to the checklist. The **relative abundance** of each species is included. The seven terms used to describe abundance are:

abundant always present with a very high probability of being observed; expect large numbers in proper habitat and season

common should be encountered in proper habitat and season; numbers may vary from high to low

fairly common normally encountered in proper habitat and season; usually not found in large numbers

uncommon usually present in proper habitat and season but may easily be overlooked; rarely occurs in large numbers

rare not always present but can often be found with persistent searches; may occur in a narrow time frame within a season or in very specialized habitats

casual irregular and unpredictable; more than 10 accepted records in a century

accidental very rare and not to be expected; fewer than 10 accepted records in a century

184

The **normal range** for each species in the annotated checklist is described. The **proper habitat** is included for many species, primarily permanent residents, breeding species, and a few winter residents. Migrants are often found in a variety of habitat types, and for that reason no specific habitats are included for those birds.

This checklist is a brief overview; locally-produced checklists for specific sites will provide you with more locally-accurate information and should be used whenever possible.

Nomenclature and taxonomic sequence follow the American Ornithologists' Union The A.O.U. Check-list of North American Birds, 7th edition, June 1998. Many of the common and scientific names used in this guide do not correspond with those in even the most recent bird field guides. Please refer to the table on pages 12–13 to help reconcile the differences.

Red-throated Loon *(Gavia stellata)*—Casual fall and winter visitor to reservoirs in the Trans-Pecos and eastern Edwards Plateau. Most records (four) are from Lake Balmorhea, but also one documented record each from El Paso, Pecos, Comal, and Bexar Counties.

Pacific Loon *(Gavia pacifica)*—Casual fall and winter visitor to reservoirs of the Trans-Pecos and eastern Edwards Plateau. More than ten records overall with the majority being in late fall and early winter. One recent spring record from Laguna Madre, Cameron County in April 1998.

Common Loon *(Gavia immer)*—Uncommon winter resident (late October–early April) on large reservoirs on eastern Edwards Plateau and along the coast and Falcon Reservoir in South Texas. Rare to casual migrant and winter visitor at reservoirs in Trans-Pecos.

Yellow-billed Loon *(Gavia adamsii)*—Accidental winter visitor. Two documented records exist (25 November–10 December 1993; 21 December 1996–2 January 1997), both from Lake Balmorhea.

LEAST GREBE *(Tachybaptus dominicus)*—Uncommon to locally common resident of freshwater ponds in south Texas; irregular from Del Rio to the Gulf. Look for at the resaca at Sabal Palm Grove and at both Willow and Pintail Lakes at Santa Ana NWR. This species is known to wander in fall and winter, where they occasionally show up in the in the Trans-Pecos (along the Rio Grande near Big Bend National Park). Rare breeder in the Austin area (Bastrop County).

Pied-billed Grebe *(Podilymbus podiceps)*—Common winter resident (September–April) throughout. Uncommon as a breeding species over much of the region, but may be locally common.

Horned Grebe *(Podiceps auritus)*—Rare to very uncommon migrant and winter visitor (October–March) to larger reservoirs throughout. More records from late fall than other seasons.

Eared Grebe *(Podiceps nigricollis)*—Fairly common migrant and winter resident (October–April) throughout. Most often seen on larger reservoirs or along coast. Breeds locally in the El Paso area, especially at Fort Bliss Sewage Ponds.

Western Grebe *(Aechmophorus occidentalis)*—Fairly common to uncommon migrant and winter resident (October–April) to larger bodies of water throughout the Trans-Pecos. Casual in the Lower Valley. Irregular in summer in Reeves, Hudspeth, and El Paso Counties. Has interbred with Clark's Grebe on two occasions in the region. Look for at Lake Balmorhea, McNary Reservoir, and Fort Hancock Reservoir.

Clark's Grebe *(Aechmophorus clarkii)*—Uncommon to rare migrant and winter resident (October–April) to larger bodies of water in the western Trans-Pecos. Rare, but increasing in summer with documented breeding at McNary Reservoir and Lake Balmorhea.

Yellow-nosed Albatross *(Thalassarche chlororhynchos)*—There are just two accepted records of this species for Texas, both from the Lower Valley coast: from Port Isabel, 14 May 1972, and from South Padre Island, 28 October 1976. The latter bird was held at Gladys Porter Zoo in Brownsville until its death on 19 April 1977. The specimen is locacated at the University of Texas–Pan American University in Edinburg.

Cory's Shearwater *(Calonectris diomedea)*—Rare to uncommon offshore of Port Isabel in summer and fall; very rare at other seasons.

Sooty Shearwater *(Puffinus griseus)*—Very rare offshore and along the Texas coast in all seasons, although more numerous in spring and summer. Of the ten state records, there is only one from the Lower Valley coast at Boca Chica, 6 January 1992.

Audubon's Shearwater *(Puffinus lherminieri)*—Rare in summer and fall off Port Isabel in the Lower Valley. This species is found on most deep-water pelagic trips north of our coverage area (Freeport, upper coast, and Port O'Connor, central coast).

Leach's Storm-Petrel *(Oceanodroma leucorhoa)*—Rare summer and fall visitor off Port Isabel in the Lower Valley. There are over a dozen records for the state, most of them coming from recent pelagic birding trips off Port O'Connor.

Band-rumped Storm-Petrel *(Oceanodroma castro)*—Rare but regular offshore from spring through fall. After tropical storms, this species has been found along the coast and inland. There are two inland records occurring far from the coast: in Lower Valley at Edinburg, 25 June 1954 and at San Antonio, 14 June 1984.

Red-billed Tropicbird *(Phaethon aethereus)*—There are two Texas specimen records, both from unusual localities: Houston (Upper Coast) on 13 November 1985 and Zapata (along the Rio Grande) on 29 April 1989. A recent sighting off Port O'Connor on 21 September 1996 is currently being reviewed by the Texas Bird Records Committee.

Masked Booby *(Sula dactylatra)*—Rare to uncommon migrant and nonbreeding summer resident off the Lower Valley coast (seen fairly regularly on offshore birding trips from Port Isabel); very rare to rare offshore in winter. Very rarely seen along the coast.

Blue-footed Booby *(Sula nebouxii)*—Two records for Texas: Lower Valley coast at South Padre Island, 5 October 1976; Edwards Plateau at Lake L.B. Johnson, 2 June 1993–6 October 1994. The latter bird was relocated at Lake Bastrop, 10 December 1994–12 April 1995.

Brown Booby *(Sula leucogaster)*—Very rare along the Lower Valley coast: Boca Chica, 20 December 1987; Laguna Madre, 24 September 1988.

Northern Gannet *(Morus bassanus)*—Uncommon migrant and winter visitor along the Lower Valley coast and offshore, occasionally seen in large numbers. Best viewing spots on the lower coast are from the South Padre Island and Boca Chica jetties.

American White Pelican *(Pelecanus erythrorhynchos)*—Common migrant and winter resident along Lower Valley coast, on many inland lakes and reservoirs, and along the Rio Grande to Falcon Dam; uncommon to rare through much of the Trans-Pecos. Nonbreeding birds are very rare to locally uncommon in summer along the coast and on some inland reservoirs, where they may sometimes occur in numbers.

Brown Pelican *(Pelecanus occidentalis)*—Uncommon to locally common resident along the Lower Valley coast; vagrant along the Rio Grande near Falcon Dam, at scattered inland reservoirs, and in the Trans-Pecos. Best spot in the region is at Boca Chica Beach, from the jetties to the mouth of the Rio Grande.

NEOTROPIC CORMORANT *(Phalacrocorax brasilianus)*—Fairly common to uncommon permanent resident (though more numerous in summer) along the Rio Grande from Del Rio south. Generally easy to find at Falcon Dam and Santa Ana National Wildlife Refuge. Less numerous north along the river. Irregularly uncommon to rare through much of the Trans-Pecos with most sightings from summer. Increasing at all seasons in El Paso and Hudspeth Counties where it bred at Fort Hancock and/or McNary reservoirs from 1995–1998.

Double-crested Cormorant *(Phalacrocorax auritus)*—Common winter resident (late September–April) in the Lower Valley and the eastern Edwards Plateau. Year-round resident at various lakes in the El Paso area. Currently, there is a breeding colony at McNary Reservoir.

Anhinga *(Anhinga anhinga)*—Fairly common spring migrant and locally uncommon winter resident along the Lower Valley coast and most of the Lower Rio Grande Valley, becoming rare around Falcon Dam, uncommon summer resident along the coastal plain and rare inland to the Edwards Plateau. Often seen at both Willow and Pintail Lakes at Santa Ana NWR and along resacas in the Brownsville area.

Magnificent Frigatebird *(Fregata magnificens)*—Uncommon summer visitor along the Lower Valley coast and offshore, becoming rare inland to about Brownsville and accidental farther west in the Falcon Dam area; very rare along coast in winter. Vagrant to Austin and San Antonio. Best spot is along Boca Chica Beach during summer or after tropical storms. Also seen frequently from offshore birding trips.

American Bittern *(Botaurus lentiginosus)*—Uncommon to rare in winter and migration (late September–April) along the eastern Lower Valley; rare to very rare visitor in the remainder of the region.

Least Bittern *(Ixobrychus exilis)*—Uncommon resident in coastal areas and cattail-lined resacas (Brownsville) in the Lower Valley. Uncommon summer resident west to Santa Ana NWR; rare as far west as Falcon Dam. There is a small breeding population in marshes along the Rio Grande south of Presidio. Rare in summer around El Paso where this species may breed as well. This secretive species may be more widespread along the Rio Grande than is currently known.

Great Blue Heron *(Ardea herodias)*—Common resident on the Edwards Plateau and south Texas where habitat exists. Uncommon summer visitor in the Trans-Pecos where there are very few breeding records, becoming more common in migration and winter.

Great Egret *(Ardea alba)*—Common to fairly common at all seasons in the Lower Valley. Nests locally along coast. Less numerous upriver where the species is a fairly common to uncommon and local visitor through much of the Trans-Pecos and Edwards Plateau. Recent breeding at McNary Reservoir provides the only nesting records for the Trans-Pecos.

Snowy Egret *(Egretta thula)*—Common to fairly common at all seasons in the Lower Valley. Nests locally along the coast. Less numerous and more localized upriver. Breeds locally around El Paso and Las Cruces. A fairly common migrant elsewhere in the Trans-Pecos and Edwards Plateau near water. Rare in those regions in winter.

Little Blue Heron *(Egretta caerulea)*—Uncommon resident in the Lower Valley; very rare and irregular post-breeding wanderer as far west as El Paso.

Tricolored Heron *(Egretta tricolor)*—Common resident along Lower Valley coast becoming uncommon in Falcon Dam area; rare to occasional visitor inland.

Reddish Egret *(Egretta rufescens)*—Locally common resident along the Lower Valley coast where it is found in the almost exclusively in saltwater environs. Rare to occasional visitor inland. Often seen in the Laguna Madre, especially along the bayshore of South Padre Island. Two good spots are at the S.P.I. Convention Center boardwalk and among the Black Mangroves where the causeway debouches onto South Padre Island.

Cattle Egret *(Bubulcus ibis)*—Common to uncommon migrant throughout. Breeds locally along coast in Lower Valley and around El Paso and Las Cruces. Less numerous in winter along western stretches of the Rio Grande.

Green Heron *(Butorides virescens)*—Fairly common migrant and summer resident along most of river and in the Edwards Plateau. Less numerous in winter when it may be quite difficult to find in much of the Trans-Pecos. Often found along vegetated canals, small ponds, or along the banks of the Rio Grande.

Black-crowned Night-Heron *(Nycticorax nycticorax)*—Locally common resident along the Lower Valley coast. Locally common to rare migrant and summer resident in the rest of the region, with breeding reported west to El Paso County. Locally uncommon to rare winter resident inland. Black-crowned Night-Herons roost in large numbers in Black Mangroves at the mouth of the Rio Grande at Boca Chica. McNary Reservoir (Hudspeth County) has a fairly large rookery, with scattered breeding in the Tamarisk-lined canals along the river.

Yellow-crowned Night-Heron (*Nycticorax violacea*)—Uncommon resident in the Lower Valley and eastern Edwards Plateau; casual and irregular post-breeding wanderer as far west as El Paso.

White Ibis (*Eudocimus albus*)—Locally common resident along the Lower Valley coast; nesting reported at several inland locales. Regular post-breeding wanderer inland to Travis and Bexar Counties just off the Edwards Plateau. Very rare straggler to the Trans-Pecos (four records).

Glossy Ibis (*Plegadis falcinellus*)—Rare visitor to many parts of the state; most records are concentrated along the upper and central coasts. In the Lower Valley, there are records from Brownsville, McAllen, and Santa Ana NWR; photographic record from El Paso, May 1992. Although Glossy Ibis has been seen in all months, it is most reliably identified in alternate plumage from March through June.

White-faced Ibis (*Plegadis chihi*)—Fairly common to common migrant and winter resident in the Lower Valley. Some local breeding along the coast with birds present throughout summer at various Lower Valley locations. Fairly common to uncommon migrant (March–May; August–October) through the Trans-Pecos and eastern Edwards Plateau. Rare in winter. A few scattered breeding records from the El Paso/Las Cruces area.

Roseate Spoonbill (*Ajaia ajaja*)—Locally common resident along the Lower Valley coast, becoming somewhat less common in winter; occasionally wanders inland to Falcon Dam. Regular post-breeding wanderer inland to Travis and Bexar Counties. Accidental in the Trans-Pecos.

Jabiru (*Jabiru mycteria*)—Of the five Texas records, one comes from the Lower Valley near Bentsen-Rio Grande Valley State Park, 5–8 August 1985; another from just outside our coverage area near Encino, north of McAllen, 29 October 1979. There is also a recent sighting from Laguna Atascosa NWR, 11 August 1997, currently being reviewed by the Texas Bird Records Committee.

Wood Stork (*Mycteria americana*)—Uncommon post-breeding visitor in Lower Valley in summer and fall, becoming rare in the Falcon Dam area; no recent records in the Trans-Pecos. Wood Storks are also very rare along the Lower Valley coast in winter.

Black Vulture (*Coragyps atratus*)—Common resident on the Edwards Plateau southward to the Lower Valley. Uncommon and local along the Rio Grande in the Big Bend region.

Turkey Vulture (*Cathartes aura*)—Abundant to common summer resident and migrant (mid-March–October) throughout. Absent from much of the Trans-Pecos in winter (November–February), but still common at that season in the Lower Valley and Edwards Plateau

BLACK-BELLIED WHISTLING-DUCK (*Dendrocygna autumnalis*)—Common resident, more localized in winter, throughout most of the Lower Valley. Fairly numerous at Falcon Dam from April–October; rare there in winter. Local in summer on southern Edwards Plateau; vagrant in Trans-Pecos. Easy to find along the banks of many of Brownsville's resacas (especially the resaca on Central Boulevard ½ mile south of FM-802), where 100+ individuals often congregate in winter; also easy at Santa Ana NWR.

FULVOUS WHISTLING-DUCK *(Dendrocygna bicolor)*—Uncommon spring migrant and summer resident in the Lower Valley from the coast to about Santa Ana NWR; occasionally found in winter. Rare post-breeding wanderer inland to Travis and Bexar Counties. Accidental in the Trans-Pecos. Easiest to find in late spring and early summer at Willow and Pintail Lakes, Santa Ana NWR. Although difficult to find in winter, check for the occasional Fulvous in the Black-bellied flocks in Brownsville (see above).

Greater White-fronted Goose *(Anser albifrons)*—Rarely encountered migrant over eastern Edwards Plateau. Fairly common winter resident (November–March) in agricultural areas of the Lower Valley. Rare, but increasing, winter visitor and migrant to reservoirs in the Trans-Pecos.

Snow Goose *(Chen caerulescens)*—Uncommon to rare migrant and winter resident (October–early April) throughout. Most numerous along coast (where locally common) and in the vicinities of El Paso and Las Cruces. Scarce on the Edwards Plateau and in the Big Bend region. Occasional stragglers in summer.

Ross's Goose *(Chen rossii)*—Very uncommon to rare winter visitor and migrant in the Trans-Pecos. Most likely to be found at reservoirs southeast of El Paso, where the species seems to be increasing in recent years. Rare winter visitor coastally in the Lower Valley.

Canada Goose *(Branta canadensis)*—Uncommon to rare migrant and winter resident (October–April) throughout. Presumed escapees thought to be responsible for recent breeding at Feather Lake near El Paso.

Brant *(Branta bernicla)*—Very rare migrant and winter visitor to Texas; one record in the Lower Valley near Vernon (Willacy County), 28 December 1956.

Trumpeter Swan *(Cygnus buccinator)*—Accidental. One just north of Las Cruces 14–21 December 1985 and another along the Rio Grande below Falcon Dam 28 December 1989–14 January 1990.

Tundra Swan *(Cygnus columbianus)*—Occasional to accidental winter visitor (November–March) throughout with perhaps more records for the Trans-Pecos than elsewhere. Generally found in singles or, less regularly, small groups.

MUSCOVY DUCK *(Cairina moschata)*—These ducks have been present on the lower Rio Grande River since 1984, where they are rare to uncommon residents in the Falcon Dam area (from Frontón to San Ygnacio), becoming very rare east to Santa Ana NWR. Most often seen flying up and down the river at Santa Margarita Ranch, Chapeño, Salineño, and below Falcon Dam from April through September; scarcer during winter months. Apparently this species has been increasing recently in northeastern Mexico, responding to a Ducks Unlimited of Mexico nest-box program. First nesting evidence was at Bentsen-Rio Grande Valley State Park in July 1994.

Wood Duck *(Aix sponsa)*—Uncommon and local resident along portions of the Rio Grande and in the Edwards Plateau. Breeds regularly along the river below Falcon Dam, around El Paso and Las Cruces, and in the Hill Country. Irregular elsewhere with more records for winter than for other seasons. Seems to be on the increase in portions of its range.

Gadwall *(Anas strepera)*—Fairly common to common migrant and winter resident (September–April) throughout. Rare summer visitor.

Eurasian Wigeon *(Anas penelope)*—Occasional migrant and winter visitor (November–early May) throughout with about fifteen records overall. Interestingly, ten of these records are from El Paso and Hudspeth Counties in the far western Trans-Pecos. Should be looked for wherever large concentrations of American Wigeons occur.

American Wigeon *(Anas americana)*—Fairly common to common migrant and winter resident (September–April) throughout. Rare straggler in summer with no evidence of breeding.

Mallard *(Anas platyrhynchos)*—Genuine Mallards (wild birds not of the "Mexican Duck" race) are uncommon to common wintering birds (September–April) and somewhat rare breeders in the Trans-Pecos. They are generally uncommon in the Edwards Plateau, and basically absent altogether from the Lower Valley.

"MEXICAN DUCK" MALLARD *(Anas platyrhynchos novimexicanus)*—Now considered conspecific with Mallard. Fairly common to uncommon permanent resident of rivers, ponds, and irrigation canals from Lake Balmorhea and Big Bend National Park westward. Most numerous along the river southeast and north of El Paso, but is fairly widespread. Regular in the Falcon Dam area in winter and migration, where their numbers seem to be increasing. Occasionally seen side by side with Mottled Ducks for comparison in that area.

MOTTLED DUCK *(Anas fulvigula)*—Locally common resident along the Lower Valley coast and west along Rio Grande to about Falcon Dam. Regular post-breeding wanderer inland to Travis and Bexar Counties. Often seen at the Sabal Palm Grove resaca, Willow and Pintail Lakes at Santa Ana NWR, in freshwater coastal wetlands, and along the Rio Grande in the Falcon Dam area.

Blue-winged Teal *(Anas discors)*—Common to fairly common migrant (late March–May; August–October) throughout, decreasing in numbers westward. Fairly common in winter in Lower Valley, while basically absent from the Trans-Pecos at that season. Summer lingerers are very uncommon to rare throughout, with documented breeding only in El Paso County.

Cinnamon Teal *(Anas cyanoptera)*—Common to uncommon migrant (March–May; August–October) in the Trans-Pecos. Generally less numerous in mid-winter. Uncommon to rare and localized breeder in the western Trans-Pecos. Non-breeding summer lingerers are occasionally seen throughout. Locally uncommon in Lower Valley in winter; some years mostly absent except for Santa Ana NWR, where there are usually small numbers present.

Northern Shoveler *(Anas clypeata)*—Common migrant and winter resident (September–May) throughout. Very uncommon to rare and local as a nesting species in the Trans-Pecos. Non-breeding summer lingerers are occasionally seen throughout.

White-cheeked Pintail *(Anas bahamensis)*—One documented record for Texas: Laguna Atascosa NWR, 20 November 1978 to 15 April 1979.

Northern Pintail *(Anas acuta)*—Fairly common to common fall migrant and winter resident (September–early March) throughout. Less numerous in spring as most tend to depart northward by March. Rare summer visitor with verified breeding only at El Paso.

Garganey *(Anas querquedula)*—Accidental in spring. A male was found in Presidio County 29 April–6 May 1994. It eventually died of undetermined causes and the specimen is now at Texas A&M University.

Green-winged Teal *(Anas crecca)*—Fairly common to abundant migrant and winter resident (September–early May) throughout. Rare summer visitor with no evidence of breeding.

Canvasback *(Aythya valisineria)*—Uncommon to fairly common winter resident (October–March) throughout. Scarce later in spring and earlier in fall migration (September/April). Casual summer visitor.

Redhead *(Aythya americana)*—Fairly common to uncommon migrant and winter resident (October–March) throughout. Most numerous along the coast. An uncommon and localized breeding species mostly in the vicinity of El Paso. A rare straggler to other areas in summer.

Ring-necked Duck *(Aythya collaris)*—Fairly common to uncommon migrant and winter resident (late September–April) throughout. Casual summer visitor.

Greater Scaup *(Aythya marila)*—Rare to casual winter visitor (November–March). Perhaps more numerous along the coast than elsewhere. One summer record from El Paso in June 1998.

Lesser Scaup *(Aythya affinis)*—Common to uncommon migrant and winter resident (late September–April) throughout. Casual summer visitor.

Harlequin Duck *(Histrionicus histrionicus)*—Two documented records for Texas: Lower Valley coast at South Padre Island, 30 January–4 February 1990; out of our coverage area in northeast Texas at Lake Tawakoni, 5 January 1995.

Surf Scoter *(Melanitta perspicillata)*—Rare to casual migrant and winter visitor along the Lower Valley coast, Edwards Plateau, and Trans-Pecos.

White-winged Scoter *(Melanitta fusca)*—Accidental fall migrant and winter visitor along the Lower Valley coast, Edwards Plateau, and Trans-Pecos.

Black Scoter *(Melanitta nigra)*—Rare winter visitor along the central and upper coasts (not yet recorded in the Lower Valley); very rare fall migrant inland.

Oldsquaw *(Clangula hyemalis)*—Rare to casual migrant and winter visitor in the Lower Valley along the Rio Grande, Edwards Plateau, and Trans-Pecos.

Bufflehead *(Bucephala albeola)*—Fairly common to uncommon winter resident throughout (late October–March). Rare later in spring or earlier in fall migration. Accidental summer visitor.

Common Goldeneye *(Bucephala clangula)*—Very uncommon to very rare winter resident (November–March) throughout. More numerous in western Trans-Pecos than elsewhere.

Barrow's Goldeneye *(Bucephala islandica)*—Accidental winter visitor to Trans-Pecos (El Paso County); one male was photographed at Tornillo, 20 December 1995.

Hooded Merganser *(Lophodytes cucullatus)*—Rare winter visitor throughout (November–March). Somewhat regular in very small numbers on larger Trans-Pecos reservoirs.

Common Merganser *(Mergus merganser)*—Uncommon winter resident (November–March) on larger reservoirs in much of the Trans-Pecos. Generally scarce to absent elsewhere. Some years large flocks of several hundred grace reservoirs such as McNary, Fort Hancock, and Red Bluff. Accidental summer visitor around El Paso.

Red-breasted Merganser *(Mergus serrator)*—Uncommon winter resident (November–March) along coast. Scarce inland, although somewhat regular in small numbers on Trans-Pecos reservoirs and reservoirs on eastern Edwards Plateau (Lake Buchanan and Canyon Lake) in late fall and early winter.

MASKED DUCK *(Nomonyx dominicus)*—Rare and irregular on the Lower Valley coastal plain northward beyond our region to Brazos Bend State Park and Anahuac NWR. Absent in some years, locally uncommon in others, and generally more common in wet years. This species has occurred several times at Santa Ana NWR. Masked Ducks prefer freshwater ponds with emergent vegetation, especially rushes. They can be quite shy and skulking.

Ruddy Duck *(Oxyura jamaicensis)*—Common to uncommon migrant and winter resident (September–April) throughout. Very uncommon and localized breeding species in portions of the Trans-Pecos; most easily found then at the Fort Bliss Sewage Ponds.

Osprey *(Pandion haliaetus)*—Fairly common migrant and winter visitor (August–May) to the Lower Valley. Rare to uncommon migrant in the remainder of the region. Rare in summer in Lower Valley

HOOK-BILLED KITE *(Chondrohierax uncinatus)*—Rare resident in the Lower Valley from Santa Ana NWR to the Falcon Dam area. This species is most often seen at Santa Ana NWR, Anzalduas County Park, Bentsen SP, and along the Rio Grande at Chapeño and below Falcon Dam. Although this raptor is occasionally spotted in early morning, it is more often seen soaring from about 10 AM–1 PM. Pairs are occasionally seen soaring over breeding territories in spring and early summer.

Swallow-tailed Kite *(Elanoides forficatus)*—Rare migrant in the Lower Valley, more common on the coastal plain (late March through April). Very rare on the Edwards Plateau.

WHITE-TAILED KITE *(Elanus leucurus)*—Uncommon to locally common resident of coastal prairies and farmlands in the Lower Valley; rare visitor to southwestern Edwards Plateau and the Trans-Pecos. Good spots are along TX-4 toward Boca Chica Beach and along FM-511 between US-77 and the Port of Brownsville. Also seen frequently on entrance road to Sabal Palm Grove. Look also for this attractive raptor over open habitats around Santa Ana NWR and Anzalduas County Park.

Snail Kite *(Rostrhamus sociabilis)*—One recent photographic record (May 1998) from along the Rio Grande in Hidalgo County (Lower Valley). If accepted by the Texas Bird Records Committee, it will constitute just the second record for Texas.

Mississippi Kite *(Ictinia mississippiensis)*—Fairly common to uncommon migrant along the Rio Grande and in the Edwards Plateau. Less numerous as one moves westward. A fairly common, but extremely localized, nesting species in older established neighborhoods of El Paso and occasionally Las Cruces. Should be looked for in migration at Santa Ana NWR or Bentsen State Park (often with migrant Broad-winged Hawks) or in breeding season (May–August) in wooded neighborhoods of west El Paso.

Bald Eagle *(Haliaeetus leucocephalus)*—Rare to casual winter visitor (November–March) at larger reservoirs and rivers in the Trans-Pecos and Edwards Plateau. Most regular at Lake Buchanan where uncommon. Generally absent from the Lower Valley.

Northern Harrier *(Circus cyaneus)*—Fairly common to common migrant and winter resident (September–April) to open country throughout. Rare summer visitor with one historical nesting record in the Trans-Pecos.

Sharp-shinned Hawk *(Accipiter striatus)*—Fairly common to uncommon migrant and winter resident (September–April) to all areas. Very rare in summer with historical nesting in Big Bend, the Edwards Plateau, Hidalgo County, and possibly the Guadalupe Mountains.

Cooper's Hawk *(Accipiter cooperii)*—Fairly common winter resident (September–April) throughout. Local breeder on Edwards Plateau and in mountains of the Trans-Pecos.

Northern Goshawk *(Accipiter gentilis)*—Accidental winter visitor (November–January) to the Trans-Pecos, eastern Edwards Plateau, and Las Cruces. Two records for Big Bend National Park (29–30 December 1982 and 20 January 1989), one for El Paso (13 November 1989), one for Las Cruces (20 December 1992), and one from Austin (11 November 1995). Many other unverified reports from scattered localities.

Crane Hawk *(Geranospiza caerulescens)*—One documented record for Texas: Lower Valley at Santa Ana NWR, 20 December 1987–9 April 1988. First record for the ABA Area.

GRAY HAWK *(Asturina nitida)*—Local summer resident (March–August) along the Rio Grande in Big Bend National Park and in the Lower Valley. More common in winter (October–March) in the Lower Valley.

COMMON BLACK-HAWK *(Buteogallus anthracinus)*—Local summer resident (March–August) in the Davis Mountains, best observed along Limpia Creek near Davis Mountains State Park. Very rare migrant in the El Paso area as well as Big Bend National Park, but recently found nesting near Rio Grande Village. There are scattered summer records from other areas of the Trans-Pecos and Edwards Plateau. Irregular winter visitor to Lower Valley, primarily along the Rio Grande in the Falcon Dam area.

HARRIS'S HAWK *(Parabuteo unicinctus)*—Common to fairly common resident of brushlands of South Texas as far north as the Edwards Plateau. Especially common from Rio Grande City to Laredo along US-83. Also common near the old manager's residence at Santa Ana NWR. Often seen perched atop utility poles, especially along FM-511 (Brownsville) from US-77 to the Port of Brownsville. Rarely found on the Edwards Plateau proper. Generally uncommon and localized in the Trans-Pecos with known nesting near El Paso and in the Big Bend region. Look for this species along US-90 east of Del Rio and along US-20 between Fort Hancock and Tornillo.

Roadside Hawk *(Buteo magnirostris)*—Three accepted records for Texas, all from the Lower Valley: Cameron County, 2 April 1901; Rancho Santa Margarita, 7 January 1979; Bentsen SP, 7 October 1982–mid-February 1983.

Red-shouldered Hawk *(Buteo lineatus)*—Common resident in riparian and other mixed hardwood woodland on the Edwards Plateau. Uncommon winter resident and rare in summer in the Lower Valley (not known to breed).

Broad-winged Hawk *(Buteo platypterus)*—Common to abundant migrant in the Lower Valley and on Edwards Plateau (October, late March/April); rare and irregular in the Trans-Pecos.

Short-tailed Hawk *(Buteo brachyurus)*—Seven records for the state since 1989, five of which have come from the along the Rio Grande at Santa Ana NWR, Bentsen SP, and Santa Margarita Ranch (March through October). Accidental on Edwards Plateau at Lost Maples SNA and near Dripping Springs.

Swainson's Hawk *(Buteo swainsoni)*—Common to fairly common migrant (mid-March–May; August–October) throughout. Often seen in large concentrations around recently plowed fields. A common breeder in grasslands and mesquite brushlands throughout much of the Trans-Pecos (except for Big Bend country), and open areas bordering the Edwards Plateau south to about Falcon Dam. Accidental in the Lower Valley in winter.

WHITE-TAILED HAWK *(Buteo albicaudatus)*—Uncommon, local resident of coastal plain of Lower Valley; fairly common just north of the Lower Valley on Highway 77 along the King Ranch (south of Kingsville to Raymondville). Accidental on Edwards Plateau. Also one documented record for the Trans-Pecos Uncommon but regular near Brownsville along FM-511 between US-77 and Port of Brownsville. Occasional at coastal areas like TX-4 to Boca Chica.

ZONE-TAILED HAWK *(Buteo albonotatus)*—Uncommon summer resident (April–September) in the mountains of the Trans-Pecos and southwestern Edwards Plateau; irregular migrant and rare winter visitor to the Lower Valley. This species is completely absent in the extreme western end of the Trans-Pecos. There are no records from El Paso or Hudspeth Counties. Look for at Kickapoo Cavern State Park, Big Bend National Park, and the Davis Mountains. Best spots in the Lower Valley are at Falcon Dam spillway and Anzalduas County Park.

Red-tailed Hawk *(Buteo jamaicensis)*—Fairly common to common permanent resident throughout. Generally more numerous in winter, in some areas markedly so, with the influx of wintering birds from the north. Breeding birds in west Texas usually lack the belly band often associated with this species. "Harlan's" race of Red-tailed Hawk is a rare winter visitor to the Trans-Pecos region and Lower Valley.

Ferruginous Hawk *(Buteo regalis)*—Uncommon winter resident through much of the Trans-Pecos and areas surrounding the Edwards Plateau. Much scarcer to nearly absent in the Lower Valley. Best looked for from late October through early March in grasslands around the Davis Mountains or along the Rio Grande from Fort Hancock to Las Cruces.

Rough-legged Hawk *(Buteo lagopus)*—Rare to casual winter visitor (November–March) to grasslands of the Trans-Pecos and perhaps elsewhere. Numbers may fluctuate from one year to the next.

Golden Eagle *(Aquila chrysaetos)*—Uncommon permanent resident of the mountains of the Trans-Pecos. More common and widespread in winter (October–March), when it reaches the Edwards Plateau and elsewhere. Accidental in Lower Valley. Your best bet for finding this bird in summer is probably either in Big Bend National Park or in the Franklin Mountains (especially Trans-Mountain Road) of El Paso, where a couple of pairs breed annually. In winter good locations include the Davis Mountains, along US-90 west of Alpine, and along Interstate 10 between Fabens and El Paso.

Collared Forest-Falcon *(Micrastur semitorquatus)*—One documented record for Texas: Lower Valley at Bentsen SP, 22 January–24 February 1994. First record for the ABA Area.

CRESTED CARACARA *(Caracara plancus)*—Fairly common to uncommon permanent resident in the brush country of South Texas north to the eastern edge of the Edwards Plateau. A rare visitor to the Edwards Plateau itself and to the eastern Trans-Pecos. Accidental in the central and western Trans-Pecos. Most easily seen from the Falcon Dam area north to Del Rio.

American Kestrel *(Falco sparverius)*—Common to abundant winter resident and migrant (September–April) throughout. A fairly common to uncommon breeding species in the Trans-Pecos and perhaps portions of the Edwards Plateau.

Merlin *(Falco columbarius)*—Uncommon to rare migrant (March–April; September–October) throughout. Less numerous in mid-winter. Probably more common along the coast than elsewhere.

APLOMADO FALCON *(Falco femoralis)*—Formerly a rare summer resident in the Lower Valley and Trans-Pecos. A recent record from the Trans-Pecos was accepted as a wild bird. Small populations occur in Chihuahua, Mexico within 100–150 miles of El Paso, principally near the villages of Coyame and Villa Ahumada. These are certainly the source of the handful of recent records near Las Cruces, NM, as well as Valentine, TX. See box on following page.

Peregrine Falcon *(Falco peregrinus)*—Rare summer resident in Big Bend National Park and in the Guadalupe Mountains. Most common as a migrant along the coast especially in fall (Octover/November), but may be encountered anywhere in the region as a very uncommon to rare migrant and winter visitor.

Prairie Falcon *(Falco mexicanus)*—Rare to very uncommon permanent resident of the mountains of west Texas. Nests in Big Bend National Park, the Davis Mountains, and at least formerly at Hueco Tanks State Park. More numerous and widespread in winter, when often found in grasslands or agricultural areas. At that season check especially in grasslands surrounding the Davis Mountains (the Valentine area along US-90 seems particularly good) or along the river levees southeast of El Paso. Rare winter visitor to the Lower Valley.

PLAIN CHACHALACA *(Ortalis vetula)*—Locally common resident of the Lower Valley; found in thorn scrub and riparian habitats from Falcon Dam to the Gulf. Abundant along the trailer loop at Bentsen SP. Other good spots include the feeders at Sabal Palm Grove and Santa Ana NWR.

Ring-necked Pheasant *(Phasianus colchicus)*—Rare resident around Rattlesnake Springs, NM. Formerly an uncommon resident in the agricultural areas near Balmorhea northward toward Pecos. Has not been reported in recent years.

Wild Turkey *(Meleagris gallopavo)*—Fairly common resident on the Edwards Plateau and the central mountains of the Trans-Pecos. This species is fairly common just north of the Lower Valley at the King Ranch. Often seen from highways.

SCALED QUAIL *(Callipepla squamata)*—Fairly common to common permanent resident of arid brushlands from the Falcon Dam area westward. Perhaps easiest to find in Big Bend National Park, but look also in desert areas above Saliñeno and Santa Margarita Ranch, at Lake Balmorhea, Hueco Tanks State Park, and the lower slopes of the Franklin Mountains in El Paso.

GAMBEL'S QUAIL *(Callipepla gambelii)*—Common to fairly common permanent resident along the Rio Grande from Las Cruces south to Presidio. Less numerous in desert arroyos and brushy canyons of the western Trans-Pecos away from the river. Rare as far south as Big Bend National Park.

Northern Bobwhite *(Colinus virginianus)*—Common resident in the Lower Rio Grande Valley northward to the Edwards Plateau and rare to uncommon as far west as Balmorhea.

APLOMADO FALCON

With long wings and tail, broad white supercilium, black chest band, and cinnamon thighs, the Aplomado Falcon is unmistakable. Although not gregarious, mated Aplomado pairs hunt cooperatively when chasing avian prey.

Historically, Aplomado Falcons nested locally in desert grasslands and coastal prairies from south Texas to southeastern Arizona, but the species has been extirpated from the United States since the 1940s. In South Texas, habitat alteration (conversion of open grassland to farmland) and pesticide use were contributing factors in the decline. The falcons were officially listed as endangered in 1986. The following year a cooperative program was initiated between the Peregrine Fund, the Mexican government (SEDUE/SEDESOL), and USF&WS to reestablish the Aplomado Falcon in the southwestern United States and Mexico.

Since four birds were introduced onto King Ranch back in 1985, there have been over 100 birds released in South Texas (the vast majority at Laguna Atascosa NWR). In 1995, after a 50-year absence, Aplomados again nested in the Brownsville area. Look for these banded falcons between Brownsville and the coast in grassland habitats dotted with mesquites and Spanish dagger. The best spots have been near the Port of Brownsville, along Old Port Isabel Road, at the Brownsville Sanitary Landfill, on TX-4 toward Boca Chica, and around Laguna Atascosa NWR.

MONTEZUMA QUAIL *(Cyrtonyx montezumae)*—Common, but secretive, resident in the Davis Mountains and surrounding mountain ranges. Relict population exists on the southwestern Edwards Plateau. Easiest to see at Davis Mountains State Park.

Yellow Rail *(Coturnicops noveboracensis)*—Very rare migrant and winter resident along the Lower Valley coast, with recent sightings from the South Padre Island Convention Center boardwalk (Cameron County). Accidental on Edwards Plateau.

Black Rail *(Laterallus jamaicensis)*—Very rare migrant and winter resident along the Lower Valley coast; up to two birds have been seen and heard recently from the South Padre Island Convention Center boardwalk.

Clapper Rail *(Rallus longirostris)*—Common resident in salt marshes along the Lower Valley coast; vagrant inland.

King Rail *(Rallus elegans)*—Common resident in freshwater marshes of the Lower Valley; rare to uncommon migrant along Edwards Plateau and eastern Trans-Pecos. Recent summer records from the eastern Trans-Pecos (Lake Balmorhea) suggest breeding.

Virginia Rail *(Rallus limicola)*—Fairly common to rare migrant (April–mid-May; August–September) throughout. Uncommon to rare and localized in winter. Breeding sporadic and very localized in the El Paso area.

Sora *(Porzana carolina)*—Fairly common to uncommon migrant (April–mid-May; mid-August–mid-October) throughout. An uncommon winter resident at least in the Lower Valley and El Paso. Has bred sporadically in the El Paso area.

Purple Gallinule *(Porphyrula martinica)*—Rare to uncommon migrant in the Lower Valley from the coast to about Bentsen SP (April and August). Rare to uncommon summer resident in the Lower Valley. Regular post-breeding wanderer inland to Travis and Bexar Counties. Very rare in Trans-Pecos.

Common Moorhen *(Gallinula chloropus)*—Fairly common permanent resident in the Lower Valley and the El Paso/Las Cruces area. Rare and local on the Edwards Plateau. Prefers reed-choked ponds or drainage canals near the river. A rare migrant in most other areas.

American Coot *(Fulica americana)*—Abundant to common winter resident throughout. Somewhat less common and more localized as a breeding species in the Lower Valley, eastern Edwards Plateau, around El Paso and Las Cruces, and occasionally in the Big Bend region.

Sandhill Crane *(Grus canadensis)*—Uncommon to rare migrant and winter resident (late September–mid-March). Most likely to be seen near the coast or in the El Paso area.

Black-bellied Plover *(Pluvialis squatarola)*—Common to abundant migrant and winter resident along the Lower Valley coast; uncommon migrant farther inland in the Lower Valley. Migrant inland to Travis and Bexar Counties. Rare migrant in Trans-Pecos.

American Golden-Plover *(Pluvialis dominica)*—Common spring migrant and rare fall migrant in the Lower Valley (March–April, August–October). Regular migrant inland to Travis and Bexar Counties. Accidental spring migrant and very rare fall migrant in Trans-Pecos.

Collared Plover *(Charadrius collaris)*—One documented record for Texas: Edwards Plateau at Uvalde, 9–12 May 1992. A first record for the ABA Area.

Snowy Plover *(Charadrius alexandrinus)*—Uncommon summer resident along the Lower Valley coast (April–August); rare in winter. Fairly common to rare migrant throughout Trans-Pecos; uncommon and very localized breeding species at Balmorhea, Imperial Reservoir, Red Bluff Lake, and Lake Amistad. Accidental on Edwards Plateau and in Trans-Pecos in winter. Look for along the bayshore mudflats of South Padre Island and the open coast at Boca Chica.

Wilson's Plover *(Charadrius wilsonia)*—Uncommon to locally common summer and rare winter resident along the Lower Valley coast. Look for along the bayshore mudflats of South Padre Island and the open coast at Boca Chica.

Semipalmated Plover *(Charadrius semipalmatus)*—Fairly common to uncommon migrant and winter resident (August–early May) to coastal portions of the Lower Valley. Uncommon to rare migrant (April–mid May; August–September) to remainder of region.

Piping Plover *(Charadrius melodus)*—Locally common winter resident along the Lower Valley coast (September–April). Uncommon migrant along Edwards Plateau. Vagrant in Trans-Pecos. Look for along the bayshore mudflats of South Padre Island and the open coast at Boca Chica.

Killdeer *(Charadrius vociferus)*—Common to fairly common permanent resident throughout.

Mountain Plover *(Charadrius montanus)*—Rare and localized migrant and winter resident in some portions of the Lower Valley and eastern Edwards Plateau. A very rare breeder in small numbers in grasslands of the Davis Mountains. A casual migrant to sod farms in the El Paso/Las Cruces area.

American Oystercatcher *(Haematopus palliatus)*—Uncommon local resident along the Lower Valley coast. More common along the bayshore of the Laguna Madre at South Padre Island; rare along the open coast at Boca Chica.

Black-necked Stilt *(Himantopus mexicanus)*—Common to uncommon breeding bird in the Lower Valley and the El Paso area. Fairly common to uncommon in winter in the Lower Valley; rare and localized, but seemingly increasing, at that season in El Paso. A fairly common to uncommon migrant to other areas.

American Avocet *(Recurvirostra americana)*—Common to fairly common migrant (March–May; August–October) throughout. Common in winter along the coast, becoming much less numerous inland; a casual winter visitor to the El Paso area. A fairly common breeding bird around El Paso; scarce as a breeding species along coast.

Northern Jacana *(Jacana spinosa)*—Irregular and rare visitor in the Lower Valley from Brownsville to Falcon Dam; most sightings have come from Santa Ana NWR (6 records). Accidental along the Edwards Plateau and Trans-Pecos.

Greater Yellowlegs *(Tringa melanoleuca)*—Fairly common to uncommon migrant (March–early May; mid-July–October) throughout. Fairly common in winter in the Lower Valley, but becoming less numerous as one moves farther inland. A very uncommon though regular wintering species in El Paso.

Lesser Yellowlegs *(Tringa flavipes)*—Common to fairly common migrant (mid-March–early May; mid-July–October) throughout. Fairly common in Lower Valley in winter, but rare inland at that season.

Solitary Sandpiper *(Tringa solitaria)*—Fairly common to uncommon migrant (April–May; July–mid-October) throughout region. Uncommon, but regular, in winter in the Lower Valley.

Willet *(Catoptrophorus semipalmatus)*—Abundant to common resident along coast in Lower Valley. Fairly common to very uncommon migrant (April–May; July–September) through rest of region, decreasing in abundance westward.

Spotted Sandpiper *(Actitis macularia)*—Common to fairly common migrant (March–May; July–October) throughout. Less numerous in winter when it ranges from fairly common in Lower Valley to very uncommon and local in the Trans-Pecos.

Upland Sandpiper *(Bartramia longicauda)*—Common to uncommon migrant (late March–early May; late July–September) over the Edwards Plateau southward to the Lower Rio Grande Valley. More uncommon and primarily a fall migrant over much of the Trans-Pecos.

Eskimo Curlew *(Numenius borealis)*—Status uncertain, possibly extinct. Nine specimen records from the Lower Valley in Brownsville between 1889–1894. All records are from 13 March to 2 April. One specimen from the Edwards Plateau at Boerne, 17 March 1880.

Whimbrel *(Numenius phaeopus)*—Uncommon migrant in the Lower Valley, more common on the coast (April, September); locally uncommon to rare winter resident (October–March) and rare straggler in summer on the coast; rare migrant along Edwards Plateau and casual in Trans-Pecos.

Long-billed Curlew *(Numenius americanus)*—Common migrant and winter resident (August–April) in Lower Valley. Fairly common to uncommon migrant to remainder of region. Rare and local in winter around El Paso. A rare and local breeder along coast in Cameron County. One historical nest record for the Trans-Pecos from 1936 in Jeff Davis County.

Hudsonian Godwit *(Limosa haemastica)*—Occasional spring migrant along the Lower Valley coast (April), less common farther inland to about the McAllen Sewer Ponds. Very rare spring migrant over Edwards Plateau; accidental to Trans-Pecos.

Marbled Godwit *(Limosa fedoa)*—Fairly common winter resident and migrant (August–April) along coast in Lower Valley. Uncommon to rare migrant (April–May; July–September) in rest of region.

Ruddy Turnstone *(Arenaria interpres)*—Common migrant and winter resident along the Lower Valley coast; uncommon visitor during summer. Rare and migrant inland.

Red Knot *(Calidris canutus)*—Common migrant along the Lower Valley coast (April, September), rare and local inland. Rare and local winter resident along the coast.

Sanderling *(Calidris alba)*—Abundant migrant and winter resident along the Lower Valley coast, uncommon in summer. Rare to uncommon migrant inland. Occasional spring migrant and rare fall migrant in Trans-Pecos.

Semipalmated Sandpiper *(Calidris pusilla)*—Uncommon migrant (April–May; July–September) over the eastern Lower Rio Grande Valley northward to the Edwards Plateau. Rare fall migrant and casual spring migrant in the Trans-Pecos.

Western Sandpiper *(Calidris mauri)*—Common to fairly common migrant (late March–mid-May; July–October) throughout. Common along coast in winter, but decreasingly numerous as one moves inland at that season. Casual in mid-winter anywhere in the Trans-Pecos.

Red-necked Stint *(Calidris ruficollis)*—Accidental fall migrant. One adult at the Fort Bliss Sewage Ponds 17–22 July 1996 represented a first Texas record.

Least Sandpiper *(Calidris minutilla)*—Abundant to common migrant (March–early May; mid-July–October) throughout. Common to fairly common wintering bird in most of the region.

White-rumped Sandpiper *(Calidris fuscicollis)*—Uncommon to rare, primarily spring migrant (May) over the eastern Edwards Plateau and Lower Valley. Very rare spring migrant in Trans-Pecos.

Baird's Sandpiper *(Calidris bairdii)*—Fairly common to rare spring (April–May) and fairly common to uncommon fall (July–mid-October) migrant. In the Trans-Pecos seen far more often in fall than spring. Often seen away from water on sod farms amd golf courses.

Pectoral Sandpiper *(Calidris melanotos)*—Fairly common to rare migrant (mid-March–mid-May; late July–October) throughout region. Most numerous in Lower Valley, rarest in the Trans-Pecos (where the majority of records are in the fall).

Purple Sandpiper *(Calidris maritima)*—Vagrant to the Lower Valley and Edwards Plateau; prefers man-made rock structures. There are two records from opposite ends of the Lower Valley: Falcon Dam, 15–16 December 1975; Boca Chica (28 February–10 March 1991). One record from Edwards Plateau: Austin, 29–30 March 1976.

Dunlin *(Calidris alpina)*—Common migrant and wintering species (August–April) along the coast at South Padre Island and Boca Chica. Uncommon migrant inland; very rare in the Trans-Pecos.

Curlew Sandpiper *(Calidris ferruginea)*—Accidental; two records for region, 3–7 May 1994 and 22 May 1996, both from Santa Ana NWR.

Stilt Sandpiper *(Calidris himantopus)*—Fairly common migrant (April–May; mid-July–October) and uncommon winter resident in Lower Valley. Uncommon to rare migrant in the rest of the region. Near El Paso this species is fairly common in fall, but quite rare in spring.

Buff-breasted Sandpiper *(Tryngites subruficollis)*—Rare to uncommon migrant in the Lower Valley, becoming very rare on the Edwards Plateau (April, August/September).

Ruff *(Philomachus pugnax)*—Casual fall migrant and winter visitor (July–March). Eight overall records, most from Travis and Bexar Counties just off of the Edwards Plateau. One Trans-Pecos record from El Paso County and one coastal record in Cameron County.

Short-billed Dowitcher *(Limnodromus griseus)*—Common migrant and wintering species (August–April) along the coast at South Padre Island and Boca

Chica. Fairly rare migrant inland, accidental spring migrant and rare fall migrant in the Trans-Pecos.

Long-billed Dowitcher *(Limnodromus scolopaceus)*—Common to fairly common migrant (March–May; July–October) throughout. Common in winter in Lower Valley. Uncommon to rare elsewhere at that season.

Wilson's (Common) Snipe *(Gallinago delicata)*—Fairly common to uncommon migrant and winter resident (September–early May) throughout region.

American Woodcock *(Scolopax minor)*—Local and difficult to find winter resident (November–February) on the eastern Edwards Plateau. Occasionally found as far west as Del Rio; accidental farther west and south.

Wilson's Phalarope *(Phalaropus tricolor)*—Abundant to uncommon migrant (April–May; July–mid-October). Most numerous in western Trans-Pecos where groups of many hundreds, if not thousands, can be found in migration. Less numerous in Lower Valley and eastern Edwards Plateau. Late spring or early fall migrants can be seen virtually throughout the summer. In winter, very rare in Lower Valley and accidental in El Paso.

Red-necked Phalarope *(Phalaropus lobatus)*—Rare spring (April–May) and uncommon to rare fall (mid-August–October) migrant throughout. Most common around El Paso and Las Cruces in September and October when the species is often found in numbers. Scarcest in the Lower Valley.

Red Phalarope *(Phalaropus fulicaria)*—Casual fall (mid-September–early November) and accidental spring (May) migrant. One winter record. Most records from the El Paso area and Travis and Bexar Counties just off the Edwards Plateau proper. One Lower Valley record from 15 July 1978.

Pomarine Jaeger *(Stercorarius pomarinus)*—Rare migrant and winter visitor along Lower Valley coast and offshore waters; very rare in summer. Very rare inland, usually after hurricanes.

Parasitic Jaeger *(Stercorarius parasiticus)*—Rare migrant and winter visitor along Lower Valley coast and offshore waters; very rare in summer. Very rare inland, not necessarily after hurricanes.

Long-tailed Jaeger *(Stercorarius longicaudus)*—Accidental. One in Austin 16 August 1975, singles at Port Isabel 8 June 1989 and 17 June 1992, and another at McNary Reservoir 12–14 June 1996.

Laughing Gull *(Larus atricilla)*—Abundant resident along Lower Valley coast, becoming uncommon to rare inland to Falcon Dam; recent breeding records at Lake Amistad. Very rare to rare in Edwards Plateau and Trans-Pecos, mostly in late summer and fall.

Franklin's Gull *(Larus pipixcan)*—Common to uncommon migrant (late March–May; September–mid-November) throughout. Probably most numerous along coast in Lower Valley, but readily found in the eastern Edwards Plateau and the Trans-Pecos as well. The Brownsville Dump can be an excellent place for seeing numbers of this species. Casual mid-winter, and mid-summer straggler throughout region.

Bonaparte's Gull *(Larus philadelphia)*—Fairly common to uncommon migrant and winter resident along coast. Less numerous inland, but still regular in the eastern Edwards Plateau and Trans-Pecos (where most numerous in fall).

Heermann's Gull *(Larus heermanni)*—Accidental. One photographed 1 April 1984 south of Las Cruces. Another record is currently under review by the TBRC from Tornillo Reservoir (El Paso County) 5 April 1997. A third record from Big Lake (Reagan County) 2–4 December 1975 just outside of the coverage area.

Mew Gull *(Larus canus)*—Casual winter visitor (late November–early March) with about 9 total records. All records to date from either Travis and Bexar Counties just off of the Edwards Plateau or far western Trans-Pecos.

Ring-billed Gull *(Larus delawarensis)*—Abundant to fairly common migrant and winter resident throughout. Most numerous coastally and least numerous in Trans-Pecos. Nonbreeders regularly oversummer along coast or large reservoirs.

California Gull *(Larus californicus)*—Occasional visitor, mostly in winter, to far western Trans-Pecos, Travis and Bexar Counties just off the Edwards Plateau, and Lower Valley. Most often found on large reservoirs or at dumps. Records concentrated between November and March, but every month represented except September/October.

Herring Gull *(Larus argentatus)*—Common migrant and winter resident along the Lower Valley coast, locally uncommon farther inland; rare winter visitor to reservoirs throughout. Uncommon summer visitor along the coast and inland lakes and reservoirs; absent in summer in Trans-Pecos. One breeding record in coastal Lower Valley (Laguna Madre) in 1990.

Thayer's Gull *(Larus thayeri)*—Occasional winter visitor (December–March) to coastal Lower Valley, Travis and Bexar Counties just off of the Edwards Plateau, and far western Trans-Pecos. Ten or eleven overall records, most from large reservoirs, dumps, or coastal beaches. Nearly all are of first-winter birds.

Iceland Gull *(Larus glaucoides)*—One documented record for Texas: along Lower Valley coast at South Padre Island, 15 January–12 February 1977.

Lesser Black-backed Gull *(Larus fuscus)*—Rare but regular winter resident along the Lower Valley coast, less common inland. There are three documented records in Trans-Pecos from Lake Balmorhea and El Paso. The species seems to be increasing in numbers in Texas.

Slaty-backed Gull *(Larus schistisagus)*—One documented record for Texas: Lower Valley at Brownsville Municipal Landfill, 7–22 February 1992.

Western Gull *(Larus occidentalis)*—Accidental. Two accepted state records: one at Fort Bliss Sewage Ponds (El Paso County) 14 May 1985 and the other at Boca Chica (Cameron County) 6 April 1995.

Glaucous Gull *(Larus hyperboreus)*—Rare migrant and winter resident along the Lower Valley coast; very rare inland at landfills and reservoirs.

Great Black-backed Gull *(Larus marinus)*—Two records for the Lower Valley: South Padre Island, 27 February 1990; Brownsville Landfill, 5 February 1996.

Sabine's Gull *(Xema sabini)*—Very rare to occasional fall migrant (September–October) throughout. Over twenty records for the region. Two exceptional records at McNary 6 May 1995 and 13–15 July 1996.

Black-legged Kittiwake *(Rissa tridactyla)*—Occasional winter visitor throughout (November–March). Thirteen records widely scattered over the region.

Gull-billed Tern *(Sterna nilotica)*—Common resident along the Lower Valley coast, less numerous in winter. A small population breeds on Falcon Reservoir. Rare visitor to central Texas. Often seen along TX-4 toward Boca Chica hawking insects over shortgrass prairie inland from the open Gulf.

Caspian Tern *(Sterna caspia)*—Common resident along the coast; locally common to uncommon on freshwater resacas in Lower Valley. Rare migrant and winter visitor on Edwards Plateau. Occasional visitor to Trans-Pecos in summer and fall.

Royal Tern *(Sterna maxima)*—Common resident along the Lower Valley coast. Reported as far west as Zapata and Edwards Plateau, usually after tropical storms.

Elegant Tern *(Sterna elegans)*—Accidental. One photographed at Lake Balmorhea 23 December 1985 represents one of only two accepted Texas records.

Sandwich Tern *(Sterna sandvicensis)*—Common summer resident and uncommon winter resident along the Lower Valley coast. Reported as far west as Zapata and Edwards Plateau, usually after tropical storms.

Common Tern *(Sterna hirundo)*—Fairly common migrant (April–May; August–October) along coast in Lower Valley. Increasingly rare westward. Only a casual spring and rare fall migrant in the Trans-Pecos. Formerly bred along coast in Lower Valley. Non-breeding stragglers occasionally seen throughout.

Arctic Tern *(Sterna paradisaea)*—Accidental. The first documented state record from McNary Reservoir (Hudspeth County) 5–6 June 1997.

Forster's Tern *(Sterna forsteri)*—Common along the coast at South Padre Island and Boca Chica. Uncommon migrant (April–May; August–September) inland throughout the region. Regular in small numbers during winter (December–February) on the highland lakes on the Edwards Plateau.

Least Tern *(Sterna antillarum)*—Common summer resident (April–September) along the coast at South Padre Island and Boca Chica. Uncommon breeding species at Falcon Reservoir and Lake Amistad. Irregular, but increasing migrant and summer visitor to lakes in the Trans-Pecos. May occasionally breed at some of these locations.

Bridled Tern *(Sterna anaethetus)*—Rare summer visitor in Lower Valley offshore waters. Recent deepwater pelagic trips suggest that this species may be more common and regular than previously thought in Texas waters. Very rare vagrant on coast following tropical storms. Recorded from both South Padre Island and Boca Chica following Hurricane *Gilbert* in September 1988.

Sooty Tern *(Sterna fuscata)*—Rare and local summer resident along the lower coast; breeds in the lower Laguna Madre. Rare to uncommon visitor to offshore waters during summer months. Many records along the coast and at scattered inland locations following tropical storms, including the Trans-Pecos.

Black Tern *(Childonias niger)*—Fairly common to uncommon migrant (mid-April–early June; July–mid-October) throughout. Occasional stragglers in mid-summer and early winter.

Brown Noddy *(Anous stolidus)*—Four accepted records for Texas, of which two are from Lower Valley coast: along South Padre Island in the wake of Hurricane *Gilbert*, 18 September 1988; offshore of Port Isabel, 12 September 1992.

Black Skimmer *(Rynchops niger)*—Locally common resident along the Lower Valley coast; rare inland to Falcon Dam area, especially in summer and fall. Vagrant to Trans-Pecos (Lake Balmorhea), mostly following tropical storms.

Rock Dove *(Columba livia)*—Abundant permanent resident of cities and larger towns. Less numerous in smaller towns and rural areas.

White-crowned Pigeon *(Columba leucocephala)*—One sight record for Texas on the Lower Valley coast at Green Island, 24 June and 2 July 1989.

RED-BILLED PIGEON *(Columba flavirostris)* Rare to uncommon summer resident in the Lower Valley from Santa Ana NWR upriver to San Ygnacio; very rare farther west along the Rio Grande to near Del Rio. Rare winter resident in much the same area; vagrant to coastal Lower Valley in winter. Best spots are along the Rio Grande at Santa Margarita, Salineño, Chapeño, and below Falcon Dam.

BAND-TAILED PIGEON *(Columba fasciata)*—Fairly common summer resident of the higher, forested mountains of the Trans-Pecos. Sporadic in winter. Casual away from breeding areas in migration. Easiest to see along the Boot Spring Trail in Big Bend National Park, at The Bowl in Guadalupe Mountains National Park, or along the scenic loop in the Davis Mountains. In late spring when the mulberries are ripe, it may be seen in Fort Davis.

Eurasian Collared-Dove *(Streptopelia decaocto)*—This species appears to be rapidly expanding westward across the southeastern United States and into Texas. There are recent records from five counties on the eastern and one from the western Edwards Plateau and El Paso. Currently there are records from at least 30 counties in Texas, and nesting has been noted in seven of these counties. This species will likely continue to increase and may become a common resident in urban areas across the state.

WHITE-WINGED DOVE *(Zenaida asiatica)*—Common to abundant summer resident of brushlands and towns along the entire river and in the Edwards Plateau. Away from urban areas the majority seem to depart in winter, but they still can be found at that season (in some cities abundantly so) in Brownsville, McAllen, San Antonio, Austin, Las Cruces, and El Paso.

Mourning Dove *(Zenaida macroura)*—Abundant to common permanent resident throughout. Somewhat less numerous in the Trans-Pecos in winter.

INCA DOVE *(Columbina inca)* Fairly common to common resident in larger towns and cities throughout. Less frequently in smaller towns and around farms. Its no hope call is often heard in residential areas and parks.

Common Ground-Dove *(Columbina passerina)*—Fairly common resident on brushlands and farmlands of the Lower Rio Grande Valley northward to the southern edge of the Edwards Plateau. Becoming more localized in the Trans-Pecos where it is most often found in Big Bend National Park with scattered spring and fall records elsewhere.

Ruddy Ground-Dove *(Columbina talpacoti)*—Occasional visitor (about twelve records overall) along the entire length of the river from Brownsville to Las Cruces. Most records are between October and early May. This species has been documented south of Las Cruces, in El Paso, in Big Bend National Park, and in the Lower Valley. Occurrences in the west seem to be on the increase.

Caution: confusion with brightly colored male Common Ground-Doves in south Texas has led to many misidentifications in the past.

WHITE-TIPPED DOVE *(Leptotila verreauxi)*—Common resident in the Lower Valley; accidental in eastern Trans-Pecos. Easy to find at Sabal Palm Grove feeders, anywhere at Santa Ana NWR, along trailer loop at Bentsen SP, and in riparian woodlands in the Falcon Dam area.

Ruddy Quail-Dove *(Geotrygon montana)*—One record for Texas: Lower Valley at Bentsen SP, 2–6 March 1996.

Monk Parakeet *(Myiopsitta monachus)*—A large population of this exotic parakeet is present in Austin. Can be found nesting in the light standards at softball fields all along the Colorado River. Usually easy to see at the city park at the intersection of Lamar and Riverside Avenues.

GREEN PARAKEET *(Aratinga holochlora)*—Although the origin of both Green Parakeet and Red-crowned Parrot flocks is indeterminable, their populations appear to be stable or increasing in the Lower Valley, due in part to successful nesting. Green Parakeets are year-round residents centered principally (but not exclusively) in urban areas, including Brownsville and McAllen. Over 300 individuals have been recently reported in winter at Fort Brown in Brownsville.

RED-CROWNED PARROT *(Amazona viridigenalis)*—This species has been reported in the Lower Valley for decades. In recent years, flocks of several dozen to one hundred or more are seen in Brownsville, San Benito, Harlingen, Weslaco, and McAllen. With the onset of the nesting season in early April, Red-crowned Parrots begin to disperse from their large winter aggregations. Nesting occurs in each of the cities listed above. Best spots to look are at the intersection of Honeydale and Los Ebanos in Brownsville, at the K-Mart near the intersection of Morgan and Grimes in Harlingen, and on the east end of Dallas Avenue (near Mockingbird Street) in McAllen. Best times are dawn and dusk. Both Red-crowns and Green Parakeets are fairly common in adjacent northeast Mexico, where habitat loss has been extensive, suggesting that some of the birds may be displaced wild birds. Severe freezes in the late 1980s that reached into northern Mexico might have induced that natural dispersal of some birds; large numbers of parrots turned up in the wake of these hard freezes. However, the origin of any individual or flock is indeterminable. There are scattered reports of Red-crowned Parrots in central Texas (Austin and San Marcos). Both Red-crowned Parrot and Green Parakeet were added to the *Checklist of the Birds of Texas* (TOS) in 1995.

Exotic Parrots of the Lower Rio Grande Valley—Red-crowned Parrots are by far the most likely Amazona parrot species encountered in the Lower Valley, yet other species are around as well. Both Red-lored (*A. autumnalis*) and Yellow-headed (*A. oratrix*) Parrots are occasionally mixed in with the large Red-crowned Parrot flocks in Brownsville, Harlingen, and McAllen. Although these birds are resident just 200 miles south of the Valley, their origin is uncertain due to the illicit parrot trade along the Texas–Mexico border. Both species are popular cage birds, intentional releases are known, and any birds you see should be presumed to be escaped cage birds. Other exotics include Lilac-crowned (*A. finschi*) and White-fronted (*A. albifrons*), which are native to western and southern Mexico, and White-crowned Parrot (*Pionus senilis*), a smaller parrot from east Mexico and Central America.

Black-billed Cuckoo *(Coccyzus erythropthalmus)*—Uncommon migrant (late April–early May; August) in the eastern Lower Valley. Rare to very rare in the remainder of the region.

Yellow-billed Cuckoo *(Coccyzus americanus)*—Common migrant and summer resident (late April–September) in the Lower Valley and Edwards Plateau becoming more uncommon and local (riparian woodlands) in the Trans-Pecos, particularly in the El Paso region.

Dark-billed Cuckoo *(Coccyzus melacoryphus)*—One state record (specimen): the bird was delivered alive (and unidentified) to a Lower Valley bird rehabilitation center near Weslaco, 10 February 1986. It died shortly thereafter and was sent to Louisiana State University where it was subsequently identified as a Dark-billed Cuckoo. This South American species is capable of long distance migration, having also been recorded in Panama and Mexico. This is the first-ever record north of Mexico.

Mangrove Cuckoo *(Coccyzus minor)*—Six records for Texas, of which three are from the Lower Valley: Santa Ana NWR, 26–27 August 1982; Laguna Atascosa NWR, 11 June 1991; Laguna Atascosa, 25 April–late July 1992.

Greater Roadrunner *(Geococcyx californianus)*—Fairly common to common permanent resident of brushlands, desert, farmlands, and foothills (up to about 5,500 feet) throughout. Fairly easy to find at Falcon State Park and Big Bend National Park, among other areas.

GROOVE-BILLED ANI *(Crotophaga sulcirostris)*—Common summer resident in the Lower Valley west to Laredo; rare on southwestern Edwards Plateau and Trans-Pecos. Rare in winter in the Lower Valley. One of the best spots in spring and summer is near the old manager's residence at Santa Ana NWR. Anis can be found anywhere along the Rio Grande in this season. They are sometimes seen on migration on bayshore woodlots on South Padre Island. In winter the best spot is near the resaca at Sabal Palm Grove.

Barn Owl *(Tyto alba)*—Fairly common to uncommon permanent resident throughout region. Prefers open country and brushlands to densely wooded areas. Utilizes old buildings, holes in embankments, and palm trees as roosting and nesting sites.

Flammulated Owl *(Otus flammeolus)*—Fairly common to uncommon summer resident in upper elevations of the Chisos, Davis, and Guadalupe Mountains. A very uncommon to rare migrant, mostly in fall, away from breeding areas in the western Trans-Pecos.

Western Screech-Owl *(Otus kennicottii)*—Fairly common permanent resident of riparian habitat and the oak zone of mountains in west Texas. A rare and local resident on the western Edwards Plateau, east to Kerrville. Occasionally in other habitats. Easiest to find in Big Bend NP and the Davis Mountains.

Eastern Screech-Owl *(Otus asio)*—Common resident in Lower Valley and on Edwards Plateau west to Pecos River. Rare and local in the eastern and southern Trans-Pecos.

Great Horned Owl *(Bubo virginianus)*—Common to uncommon permanent resident throughout. Uses a wide variety of habitats and elevations from coastal plain to desert to forested areas.

Northern Pygmy-Owl *(Glaucidium gnoma)*—Accidental in mountains of the Trans-Pecos and Dona Ana County in New Mexico. Two accepted record from Big Bend National Park: 12 August 1982 and 25 April 1993. Three sightings at Aguirre Springs in the Organ Mountains near Las Cruces. A specimen listed as taken in El Paso in 1918 cannot be located. Various other undocumented sightings from Big Bend and the Guadalupe Mountains.

FERRUGINOUS PYGMY-OWL *(Glaucidium brasilianum)*—Rare resident in the Lower Valley, primarily in the riparian woodlands below Falcon Dam. Locally common just north of the Lower Valley in Kenedy County (El Canelo, Kenedy, and King Ranches).

Elf Owl *(Micrathene whitneyi)*—Uncommon to fairly common summer resident (mid-March–September) in the Lower Valley and Big Bend Region; less numerous in the Davis Mountains; rare summer resident on the southwestern Edwards Plateau and Guadalupe Mountains. Accidental in the El Paso area.

Burrowing Owl *(Athene cunicularia)*—Fairly common to uncommon and local summer resident (April–August) through much of the Trans-Pecos. Most depart in winter, but a few can still be found in and around El Paso and Las Cruces. A very uncommon to rare migrant and winter visitor to the eastern Edwards Plateau and the Lower Valley.

Mottled Owl *(Ciccaba virgata)*—One documented record for Texas: photograph of a roadkill in Lower Valley near Bentsen SP, 23 February 1983. First record for the ABA Area.

Spotted Owl *(Strix occidentalis)*—Rare and extremely local permanent resident in the Guadalupe and Davis Mountains. Seldom encountered anywhere. Accidental visitor around El Paso with three winter/spring records.

Barred Owl *(Strix varia)*—Fairly uncommon resident in riparian woodlands on the eastern Edwards Plateau. Also a local resident along drainages into the Rio Grande between Eagle Pass and Del Rio.

Long-eared Owl *(Asio otus)*—Irregular, and difficult to find, winter visitor to much of the region, including the Lower Valley. Uncommon to rare migrant and winter visitor (mid-October–mid-April) throughout El Paso/Las Cruces area.

Stygian Owl *(Asio stygius)*—Two documented records for Texas. Both sightings came from Bentsen SP (9 December 1994 and 26 December 1996) and represent the only records for the ABA Area.

Short-eared Owl *(Asio flammeus)*—A very rare to casual winter visitor (November–March) throughout. This species has declined significantly in the western Trans-Pecos in the past two decades.

Northern Saw-whet Owl *(Aegolius acadicus)*—Casual migrant and winter visitor throughout the Trans-Pecos. Apparently a very rare summer resident in upper elevations of the Guadalupe and Davis Mountains.

Lesser Nighthawk *(Chordeiles acutipennis)*—Common summer resident (April–September) from Falcon Dam northward to the Balcones Escarpment and westward to El Paso. Less common in the remainder of the Lower Valley, but numerous at Laguna Atascosa. Fairly common to uncommon migrant on the Lower Valley coast.

Common Nighthawk *(Chordeiles minor)*—Fairly common, but locally decreasing breeder (May–September) on Edwards Plateau, Lower Valley, and Davis and Guadalupe Mountains. Fairly common to very uncommon migrant throughout

COMMON PAURAQUE *(Nyctidromus albicollis)*—Common resident in South Texas. Best found along the outer loop at Bentsen SP at dusk. Can also be seen at dusk on the entrance road to Sabal Palm Grove and at Santa Ana NWR.

COMMON POORWILL *(Phalaenoptilus nuttallii)*—Fairly common to common breeder (March–October) in dry, rocky habitats in the Trans-Pecos and Edwards Plateau; uncommon in the Lower Valley east to the Falcon Dam/Santa Margarita Ranch area. A few winter records; regular then in the southwestern Edwards Plateau, as at Kickapoo Caverns. Look for it in Big Bend, the Franklin Mountains, and state parks on the Edwards Plateau.

Chuck-will's-widow *(Caprimulgus carolinensis)*—Common summer resident (April–September) of the eastern Edwards Plateau becoming uncommon to scarce in the western plateau. Uncommon migrant through the Lower Rio Grande Valley, particularly in the eastern half. Can be heard easily at the state parks on the eastern half of the plateau as far west as Garner State Park.

Whip-poor-will *(Caprimulgus vociferus)*—Common summer resident (April–September) at upper elevations of the Guadalupe, Davis, and Chisos Mountains. Regular, but seldom detected, migrant over the extreme eastern portions of the Edwards Plateau and Lower Valley. Casual migrant in El Paso.

Black Swift *(Cypseloides niger)*—Accidental; an accepted sight record from El Paso (22 August 1985).

White-collared Swift *(Streptoprocne zonaris)*—Four accepted records for the state, three of them at coastal locales north of the Lower Valley (December–March); one record (with photograph) from Brownsville (18 May 1997).

Chimney Swift *(Chaetura pelagica)*—Common migrant through the Lower Valley and Edwards Plateau. Rare and local summer resident in the Lower Valley, particularly around Edinburg. Common resident (April–October) in urban areas on the eastern plateau. This species becomes less common westward to Alpine and Fort Davis. A casual migrant west to El Paso. Vaux's and Black Swifts have not been documented in Texas, however both species are potential migrants through the western Trans-Pecos and should be looked for and carefully documented.

White-throated Swift *(Aeronautes saxatalis)*—Common summer resident of cliffs and mountain peaks in west Texas east to the Devils River. Less numerous, but still present throughout the winter in most areas. On warm winter days often seen feeding over the Rio Grande from at least Big Bend westward. Easy to find in Boquillas and Santa Elena Canyons and around the Pinnacles in Big Bend National Park, McKittrick Canyon in the Guadalupe Mountains, and at Hueco Tanks State Park.

Green Violet-ear *(Colibri thalassinus)*—There are 22 documented Texas records since 1961 (April–September) of this tropical hummer. Most are from the Lower Rio Grande Valley and the Edwards Plateau. There are also several records from the coast.

Green-breasted Mango *(Anthracothorax prevostii)*—Five fall records for Texas, all since 1988; three are from Lower Valley: Brownsville, 14–23 September 1988; Santa Ana NWR, 18–20 August 1993; Harlingen, 17–20 August 1996. So far all birds have been immatures, likely the result of post-breeding dispersal from northern Mexico.

Broad-billed Hummingbird *(Cynanthus latirostris)*—Casual visitor in all seasons throughout. A majority of these records are from the Trans-Pecos, but there are a few Lower Valley and Edwards Plateau records as well.

White-eared Hummingbird *(Hylocharis leucotis)*—Accidental summer and fall visitor to the Chisos Mountains and El Paso. In recent years has become a rare, but regular, summer visitor in localized portions of the Davis Mountains with breeding at least suspected. One Starr County record, 14–16 July 1990.

Berylline Hummingbird *(Amazilia beryllina)*—Accidental late summer visitor with single records from Big Bend National Park (18 August 1991) and from the Davis Mountains (17 August–4 September 1997).

BUFF-BELLIED HUMMINGBIRD *(Amazilia yucatanensis)*—Uncommon to locally common summer resident of the Lower Valley, becoming rare in winter; found locally at hummingbird feeders, especially at the Sabal Palm Grove visitors center. These hummingbirds are especially fond of the small red blooms of Turks Cap *(Malvaviscus arboreus)*. Also easy to see most of the year at feeders and flowers around the visitors center and old manager's residence at Santa Ana NWR.

Cinnamon Hummingbird *(Amazilia rutila)*—Accidental. One west of El Paso in southern Dona Ana County, New Mexico, 18–21 September 1993. This bird represented only the second ABA Area record.

Violet-crowned Hummingbird *(Amazilia violiceps)*—Accidental visitor to El Paso (2–14 December 1987), Big Bend National Park (30–31 March 1996), and Val Verde County (31 October 1996)—all accepted Texas records.

Blue-throated Hummingbird *(Lampornis clemenciae)*—Uncommon to fairly common breeder in the Chisos Mountains; rare in the Davis Mountains and Guadalupes. Occasional visitor to lowlands throughout, including Lower Valley.

Magnificent Hummingbird *(Eugenes fulgens)*—Rare to uncommon breeder in the Chisos, Davis, and Guadalupe Mountains. Accidental visitor elsewhere, mostly in the Trans-Pecos.

LUCIFER HUMMINGBIRD *(Calothorax lucifer)*—Uncommon summer resident (mid-March–October) in Big Bend National Park and regular post-breeding wanderer to the Davis Mountains in late summer and early fall. Look for it at blooming agaves at all elevations in the spring and summer. The Window Trail (especially at blooming *Anisacanthus* on lower portion of trail), Laguna Meadows, and along the trail to Boulder Meadows are usually good places to look. In late summer and fall the large patches of flowers along the South Rim Trail are worth carefully checking.

Ruby-throated Hummingbird *(Archilochus colubris)*—Common migrant (late March–early May; July–September) over Edwards Plateau southward to the

Lower Valley. In recent years has been detected with increasing frequency in the Davis and Chisos Mountains. Accidental in El Paso.

Black-chinned Hummingbird *(Archilochus alexandri)*—Common summer resident (March–September) on the Edwards Plateau and the Trans-Pecos. Uncommon to rare migrant and breeder in the Lower Valley, more common westward.

Anna's Hummingbird *(Calypte anna)*—Rare to uncommon winter resident (late September–March) of the Trans-Pecos; occasional farther east. Rare in fall in the western Lower Valley (Falcon Dam/Salineño). Bred once in the Davis Mountains.

Costa's Hummingbird *(Calypte costae)*—Accidental visitor to extreme west Texas and the Las Cruces area. Three documented records for El Paso County (March–December) plus several records from the Las Cruces area.

Calliope Hummingbird *(Stellula calliope)*—Uncommon to rare fall migrant (mid-July–September) in the western half of the Trans-Pecos. Casual farther east to the Edwards Plateau. Easiest to find at feeders in El Paso and the Davis Mountains or in canyons of the Franklin Mountains. Also seen with some regularity in Big Bend National Park. There are two winter records from El Paso.

Broad-tailed Hummingbird *(Selasphorus platycercus)*—Uncommon summer resident in the Davis, Chisos, Guadalupe, and Organ Mountains. Fairly common to uncommon elsewhere in west Texas in migration, particularly in El Paso. Can be found along the Boot Spring Trail in Big Bend National Park, at The Bowl in the Guadalupe Mountains, and along the Pine Tree Trail in the Organ Mountains. A rare migrant on the western Edwards Plateau and a very rare migrant and winter resident in Lower Valley. There are two winter records at feeders in El Paso.

Rufous Hummingbird *(Selasphorus rufus)*—Common to very common fall migrant (mid-July–mid-October) in the Trans-Pecos; uncommon to rare eastward. Occasional spring migrant in the Trans-Pecos, and rare to uncommon (Brownsville area) winter visitor throughout.

Allen's Hummingbird *(Selasphorus sasin)*—Accidental fall migrant and winter visitor throughout. Numerous reports, but few are acceptably documented. Some of the unaccepted records are of fully green-backed males and are likely valid.

Elegant Trogon *(Trogon elegans)*—Accidental; two documented records from Lower Valley (14 September 1977 and 25–31 January 1990) and three from the Chisos Mountains, Big Bend National Park (29 April 1993, 28 November–8 January 1996, and 16 June 1996).

RINGED KINGFISHER *(Ceryle torquata)*—Locally common resident along the Lower Rio Grande, west to about Laredo; rare to Del Rio and the southern Edwards Plateau. Vagrant elsewhere along Edwards Plateau and Lower Trans-Pecos. Often seen along the Rio Grande at Santa Margarita Ranch, Salineño, Chapeño, and below Falcon Dam. Can also be found at Santa Ana NWR, Anzalduas County Park, Bentsen SP, and occasionally on utility wires near roadside ponds in Lower Valley.

Belted Kingfisher *(Ceryle alcyon)*—Common to fairly common winter resident (September–April) throughout. Local summer resident on the eastern Edwards Plateau; rare straggler to the Lower Valley and the El Paso area at this season.

GREEN KINGFISHER *(Chloroceryle americana)*—Uncommon resident along the Rio Grande from the Lower Valley northward, becoming rare west of the mouth of the Pecos. Uncommon resident on the Edwards Plateau. Look for this species below Falcon Dam, at Lost Maples SNA and Bentsen-Rio Grande Valley and Garner State Parks.

Lewis's Woodpecker *(Melanerpes lewis)*—Casual winter visitor (September–May) to Trans-Pecos and western Edwards Plateau. Not seen every year.

Red-headed Woodpecker *(Melanerpes erythrocephalus)*—Rare, primarily winter (October–April), visitor to the eastern edge of the Edwards Plateau occasionally wandering as far west as El Paso.

Acorn Woodpecker *(Melanerpes formicivorus)*—Fairly common permanent resident of oak woodlands in the Chisos, Davis, Guadalupe, and Organ Mountains. Very local and rare resident near Kerrville on the western Edwards Plateau. Casual in fall and winter away from breeding areas. Can be found anywhere in the Chisos Mountains in Big Bend National Park and at the Madera Canyon Picnic Area in the Davis Mountains.

GOLDEN-FRONTED WOODPECKER *(Melanerpes aurifrons)*—Common resident from the Rio Grande north to the Edwards Plateau, and only in the Trans-Pecos in the Del Norte (Davis) Mountains (along Calamity Creek), Big Bend NP (Rio Grande Village and Cottonwood Campground), and Alamito Creek (between Big Bend NP and Presidio). Easily found in wilderness and residential areas throughout the Lower Coast.

Red-bellied Woodpecker *(Melanerpes carolinus)*—Rare resident/visitor on the extreme eastern edge of the Edwards Plateau. Common in Austin and eastward, but generally replaced by Golden-fronted Woodpecker on the plateau. Also an accidental straggler to the Lower Valley west to about Santa Ana NWR.

Williamson's Sapsucker *(Sphyrapicus thyroideus)*—Rare, but probably overlooked, migrant and winter resident (September–April) of the Trans-Pecos, especially in montane conifers. Most regular in the Davis Mountains. Accidental elsewhere.

Yellow-bellied Sapsucker *(Sphyrapicus varius)*—Uncommon to locally common migrant and winter resident in the region, except in the western Trans-Pecos where it is rare.

Red-naped Sapsucker *(Sphyrapicus nuchalis)*—Uncommon migrant and rare to uncommon winter resident in the Trans-Pecos (October–April); very rare on the Edwards Plateau and Lower Valley. May breed in the Guadalupes.

Ladder-backed Woodpecker *(Picoides scalaris)*—Common to fairly common resident throughout, except for the highest Trans-Pecos elevations.

Downy Woodpecker *(Picoides pubescens)*—Local resident in riparian woodlands on the eastern Edwards Plateau. Rare in winter in the Guadalupe Mountains and western Edwards Plateau, accidental elsewhere in the region.

Hairy Woodpecker *(Picoides villosus)*—Fairly common resident in the Guadalupe Mountains and rare winter visitor to the Davis Mountains. Accidental on the Edwards Plateau and at El Paso.

Northern Flicker *(Colaptes auratus)*—Common migrant and winter resident (October–March) in the Trans-Pecos and Edwards Plateau. Rare in winter in the Lower Valley and a very rare to rare and irregular migrant there. Locally uncommon to rare breeder in the Trans-Pecos and the Edwards Plateau. "Red-shafted" forms predominate in the Trans-Pecos.

Pileated Woodpecker *(Dryocopus pileatus)*—Accidental; one record from Colorado Bend State Park (2–31 May 1997).

NORTHERN BEARDLESS-TYRANNULET *(Camptostoma imberbe)*—Rare to locally uncommon resident in the Lower Valley; most often seen at Santa Ana NWR, Anzalduas County Park, and Bentsen SP trailer loop. Very rare on the Lower Valley coast and in the Falcon Dam area. Best located by voice—usually a slightly nasal *peeEEt* or a short, plaintive *dee-dee-dee*.

Tufted Flycatcher *(Mitrephanes phaeocercus)*—Accidental visitor to west Texas. One record from Big Bend National Park (3 November 1991–17 January 1992) and another from Pecos County (2–5 April 1993), representing the only ABA Area records.

Olive-sided Flycatcher *(Contopus cooperi)*—Uncommon to fairly common migrant (May–early June; late July–September) throughout. Uncommon breeder in the Guadalupes and rare in the Davis Mountains.

Greater Pewee *(Contopus pertinax)*—Accidental visitor to the Trans-Pecos and eastern Edwards Plateau with records from Big Bend National Park (17 August 1991), the Davis Mountains (20 May 1992), San Antonio (7 April 1991), and El Paso (5–14 December 1996). One bird tape-recorded and photographed in Davis Mountains 21–24 June 1998.

Western Wood-Pewee *(Contopus sordidulus)*—Common migrant (May–early June; late July–September) in the Trans-Pecos; uncommon to very rare eastward (western Edwards Plateau). Accidental in Lower Valley (Hidalgo County). Fairly common to common breeder in the Davis, Guadalupe, and Organ Mountains.

Eastern Wood-Pewee *(Contopus virens)*—Fairly common summer resident (late April–September) in riparian woodlands on the Edwards Plateau west to the Pecos River. Uncommon migrant (late April–May; late August–September) through the Lower Valley (more common along coast) and Edwards Plateau. Accidental as far west as Big Bend Ranch State Park.

Yellow-bellied Flycatcher *(Empidonax flaviventris)*—Uncommon to common migrant in Lower Valley and eastern Edwards Plateau (late April–May, October); very rare in Trans-Pecos.

Acadian Flycatcher *(Empidonax virescens)*—Common migrant in Lower Valley and on Edwards Plateau (late April–May, September). Local summer resident in mesic canyons with well-developed woodlands. Look for at Lost Maples State Natural Area.

Alder Flycatcher *(Empidonax alnorum)*—Uncommon to locally common migrant in Lower Valley and eastern Edwards Plateau (late April–May, September).

Willow Flycatcher *(Empidonax traillii)*—Rare to fairly common migrant throughout (late April–May, September); formerly bred in western Trans-Pecos.

Least Flycatcher *(Empidonax minimus)*—Common migrant (late April–May; late August–September) through the Lower Valley northward through the Edwards Plateau and eastern Trans-Pecos; very uncommon to rare as far west as El Paso. More common in the fall in the Trans-Pecos.

Hammond's Flycatcher *(Empidonax hammondii)*—Rare to uncommon migrant (April–May; August–September), and rare to casual winter resident, in the Trans-Pecos.

Gray Flycatcher *(Empidonax wrightii)*—Rare to uncommon migrant (April–May; August–September) in the Trans-Pecos. Rare to very uncommon in winter around Big Bend; uncommon and extremely localized breeder in the Davis Mountains.

Dusky Flycatcher *(Empidonax oberholseri)*—Uncommon to fairly common migrant (April–May; August–October) in the Trans-Pecos. Rare suspected breeder in the Guadalupe Mountains. Occasional to rare in winter around Big Bend.

Pacific-slope Flycatcher *(Empidonax difficilis)*—Accidental. One calling bird was identified by sonogram 17–23 December 1995 at Old Refuge, Las Cruces, NM. Not on official Texas list, though at least two late fall and winter records in the Big Bend area may pertain to this species. Any aseasonal "Western" Flycatcher should be scrutinized carefully and tape-recorded if possible.

Cordilleran Flycatcher *(Empidonax occidentalis)*—Uncommon summer resident of the higher forests of the Chisos, Davis, Guadalupe, and Organ Mountains. An uncommon to fairly common migrant at lower elevations elsewhere in west Texas. Easiest to find near Boot Spring in Big Bend National Park or at The Bowl in the Guadalupe Mountains.

Black Phoebe *(Sayornis nigricans)*—Uncommon permanent resident near water from the western Edwards Plateau through west Texas. Can often be found along the Rio Frio at Neal's Lodge, or anywhere along the Rio Grande from Big Bend National Park to Las Cruces. Winters sporadically around Falcon Dam, and very rare in that season elsewhere in the Lower Valley.

Eastern Phoebe *(Sayornis phoebe)*—Fairly common migrant and winter resident (September–April) through South Texas. Resident on the Edwards Plateau becoming less common in winter. Uncommon to very rare migrant and winter visitor in the Trans-Pecos, decreasing westward.

Say's Phoebe *(Sayornis saya)*—Fairly common to uncommon permanent resident of the Trans-Pecos. More widespread in winter and migration, when it reaches, in small numbers, the Lower Valley and Edwards Plateau. Often nests about old buildings or rocky cliff faces. Look for it around the Chisos Lodge in Big Bend National Park and at Hueco Tanks State Park.

Vermilion Flycatcher *(Pyrocephalus rubinus)*—Common, but somewhat localized resident over much of the Trans-Pecos and Edwards Plateau. Generally withdraw from the Edwards Plateau in winter and become less common in the Trans-Pecos. Uncommon migrant and winter resident in Lower Valley.

Dusky-capped Flycatcher *(Myiarchus tuberculifer)*—Casual spring and summer visitor (April–September) to the Trans-Pecos. Possibly a rare nester in upper elevations of the Davis Mountains. Records for Big Bend National Park, the Davis Mountains, and El Paso.

Ash-throated Flycatcher *(Myiarchus cinerascens)*—Common to fairly common summer resident from the Falcon Dam area to El Paso and the Edwards Plateau. Rare in migration in coastal Lower Valley. Occurs in a variety of habitats from desert scrub to lower oak foothills. Easy to find at Big Bend National Park, the Davis Mountians, Hueco Tanks State Park, and Aguirre Springs. Casual in winter in the Big Bend region.

Great Crested Flycatcher *(Myiarchus crinitus)*—Uncommon migrant through South Texas. Fairly common migrant and summer resident (April–September) in riparian woodlands on the Edwards Plateau. A rare to casual migrant through the Trans-Pecos. Found in more mesic habitats than Ash-throated Flycatcher.

Brown-crested Flycatcher *(Myiarchus tyrannulus)*—Common summer resident in the Lower Valley, becoming uncommon to rare north to the southern Edwards Plateau (April–August); rare to very rare in Trans-Pecos. Very rare winter resident in the Lower Valley.

GREAT KISKADEE *(Pitangus sulphuratus)*—Common resident in the Lower Valley, becoming locally common in counties just north and west of the Lower Valley. Vagrant in Trans-Pecos (one record from Big Bend NP). Usually noisy and conspicuous. Easily found along wooded resacas, especially on Willow and Pintail Lakes at Santa Ana NWR and at Sabal Palm Grove.

Social Flycatcher *(Myiozetetes similis)*—One Texas sight record: Lower Valley at Anzalduas County Park, 17 March–5 April 1990.

Sulphur-bellied Flycatcher *(Myiodynastes luteiventris)*—Accidental. One to two birds were present at Santa Margarita Ranch in spring and/or summer of 1975–1977. One at Pine Canyon, Big Bend NP, 28 July–10 August 1997.

Piratic Flycatcher *(Legatus leucophaius)*—Accidental. One was photographed 2–7 September 1996 at Rattlesnake Springs, NM. A well-documented April 1998 report from Big Bend is pending review.

TROPICAL KINGBIRD *(Tyrannus melancholicus)*—The status of this species in Texas has changed in recent years. Before 1991 there was just one record documented by specimen: Lower Valley at Brownsville, 5 December 1909. Since 1991, Tropical Kingbirds have become rare to locally uncommon permanent residents in the Lower Valley (9 records), primarily in the Brownsville area east to Port Isabel and west to about Santa Ana NWR; records for Falcon Dam, 26 June 1991 and Trans-Pecos at Big Bend NP (Cottonwood Campground), 24 June–3 August 1996. Breeding well documented in Cameron County. Best spots are in the Brownsville area (see text).

COUCH'S KINGBIRD *(Tyrannus couchii)*—Common summer resident in the Lower Valley to Del Rio; uncommon and irregular in winter. Rare in summer along the eastern Trans-Pecos. Accidental on southwestern Edwards Plateau. Can be found in forest areas and disturbed habitats throughout the Lower Valley. Frequently seen on utility lines and other high perches in residential areas and along highways. Generally nests in more wooded areas than Tropical or Western Kingbirds.

TROPICAL AND COUCH'S KINGBIRDS

Because Tropical and Couch's Kingbirds are virtually identical in appearance, voice becomes essential in distinguishing the two species. The calls of Couch's Kingbirds include sharp *kip* notes, often followed by a breezy *breeer*. The dawn song of Couch's (which may run long into the daylight hours) often begins with a series of *breeer* notes followed by *s'wee s'wee s'wee s'wee s'wee-i-chu.*

Conversely, Tropical Kingbirds have little variation in their vocalizations. Their calls are a series of sharp, staccato *pip-pip-pip-pip* notes that accelerate toward the end. This trill usually lasts between 2–5 seconds before repeating and often occurs in flurries. The song is softer and more repetitious. Both kingbird species can be silent for extended periods, so be patient.

From April through October, Couch's Kingbirds far outnumber Tropical Kingbirds in the Valley; but in winter, when many Couch's withdraw southward into Mexico, their numbers are more equal. If you see a non-vocalizing bird during spring, summer, or fall (away from known Tropical Kingbird breeding territories), then you can be fairly certain that it is a Couch's you're looking at. However, during winter all bets are off!

Cassin's Kingbird *(Tyrannus vociferans)*—Fairly common summer resident of woodlands of the Davis Mountains and at Rattlesnake Springs. Less regular in other areas of the Trans-Pecos. An uncommon migrant through most of west Texas. Accidental in fall and winter in Lower Valley.

Thick-billed Kingbird *(Tyrannus crassirostris)*—Very rare and sporadic summer resident along the Rio Grande in Big Bend National Park. Nested for several years in a row at Cottonwood Campground during the late 1980s. Not expected most years.

Western Kingbird *(Tyrannus verticalis)*—Common to fairly common, though somewhat local, summer resident in open areas of theTrans-Pecos, Edwards Plateau, and portions of the Lower Valley (locally common in Brownsville). Easiest to find around El Paso and Las Cruces where almost impossible to miss from mid-April through August.

Eastern Kingbird *(Tyrannus tyrannus)*—Common migrant (April–May; August–September) throughout the Lower Valley northward through the Edwards Plateau. A very rare migrant through most of the Trans-Pecos. Local summer resident on the eastern Edwards Plateau.

SCISSOR-TAILED FLYCATCHER *(Tyrannus forficatus)*—Common migrant and summer resident (March–October) from the Lower Valley northward through the Edwards Plateau. Become more uncommon and somewhat localized in the Trans-Pecos as far west as Marfa and Pecos. A casual migrant to El Paso. Rare in winter in the Lower Valley, especially near the coast.

Fork-tailed Flycatcher *(Tyrannus savana)*—Accidental; two records from the Lower Valley (4 February 1961 at Edinburg and 17 December–16 January 1985 near Rio Hondo).

Rose-throated Becard *(Pachyramphus aglaiae)*—Formerly a rare resident in the Lower Valley, now only a rare winter visitor. Most recent sightings have come from Santa Ana NWR, Anzalduas County Park, and Bentsen SP; also records from Salineño, December 1987–January 1988, and Trans-Pecos near Fort Davis, 18 July 1973.

Masked Tityra *(Tityra semifasciata)*—One documented record for Texas: Lower Valley at Bentsen SP, 17 February–10 March 1990. First record for ABA Area.

Loggerhead Shrike *(Lanius ludovicianus)*—Common resident over all but the Lower Valley, less common and more localized in summer. In the Lower Valley this species is common throughout except in summer, when it is rare in the western half and absent in the eastern half.

Northern Shrike *(Lanius excubitor)*—Accidental to occasional winter visitor to the Trans-Pecos. Absent most years. Most birds seen this far south are immatures.

White-eyed Vireo *(Vireo griseus)*—Common migrant and summer resident (mid-March–September) on the Edwards Plateau westward to the Pecos River and southward to Lower Valley. Most withdraw from plateau in winter.

Bell's Vireo *(Vireo bellii)*—Fairly common and somewhat local summer resident (April–September) of dense mesquite brushland, foothills, and riparian edge in the Trans-Pecos and Edwards Plateau. In the Trans-Pecos, found mostly along the Rio Grande and adjacent drainages. Rare migrant to Lower Valley and rare and irregular summer resident in the Falcon Dam area. Most numerous in Big Bend and the Hill Country.

BLACK-CAPPED VIREO *(Vireo atricapillus)*—Uncommon and often difficult to see, summer resident (mid-March–August) of shrublands on the Edwards Plateau ranging westward locally to Big Bend National Park. This species is very sensitive to over-browsing by White-tailed Deer and domestic goats. Most common on the western and central Edwards Plateau. Some of the better locations to find this species include Kickapoo Cavern State Park, Devils River State

Natural Area, and the Chandler Ranch/Independence Creek Preserve. Once the vireo observation platform is open at Balcones Canyonlands National Wildlife Refuge, it will be added to this list of sites.

Gray Vireo *(Vireo vicinior)*—Uncommon to scarce summer resident (March–September) in brushy canyons of the Chisos, Guadalupe, and Organ Mountains and the western Edwards Plateau. Very localized with much seemingly suitable habitat unoccupied. Rare in winter in Big Bend National Park. Virtually unknown as a migrant. Best found at Kickapoo Cavern State Park, along the Window Trail or in Blue Creek Canyon in Big Bend, McKittrick Canyon in the Guadalupe Mountains, or at Aguirre Springs in the Organ Mountains.

Yellow-throated Vireo *(Vireo flavifrons)*—Uncommon migrant over Lower Valley northward to Edwards Plateau. Uncommon and local summer resident (late March–August) in riparian woodlands on the Edwards Plateau west to the Pecos River. Rare migrant in Trans-Pecos west to the Davis Mountains. Casual to El Paso.

Plumbeous Vireo *(Vireo plumbeus)*—Fairly common to uncommon nesting species in the Davis, Guadalupe, and Organ Mountains. Rare nester at Big Bend. A fairly common migrant throughout the Trans-Pecos. A rare winter visitor, particularly to lower elevation riparian areas.

Cassin's Vireo *(Vireo cassinii)*—Uncommon migrant to at least the western portions of the Trans-Pecos. Somewhat more numerous in fall than in spring. A few winter records from the El Paso area, Big Bend National Park, and the Guadalupe Mountains. Recent winter sightings from Lower Valley as well. Migrant traps in the vicinity of El Paso and Las Cruces would probably be your best bet for finding this newly split species.

Blue-headed Vireo *(Vireo solitarius)*—Common migrant (April–early May; September) throughout the Edwards Plateau southward through the Lower Valley. Common winter resident south of the plateau, occasionally occurring on the plateau during mild winters. Rare migrant and casual wintering species in the Trans-Pecos.

Hutton's Vireo *(Vireo huttoni)*—Common to uncommon summer resident of oak woodlands in the Chisos, Davis, and Organ Mountains. Less numerous in winter. Scattered records for the Guadalupe Mountains where breeding has not been substantiated. Casual in migration and winter to lower elevations.

Warbling Vireo *(Vireo gilvus)*—Uncommon to fairly common migrant (April–May; August–September) over Lower Valley and eastern Edwards Plateau as well as the Trans-Pecos. Rare migrant over western plateau. Uncommon summer resident (April–August) in riparian and pine-oak woodlands in the mountains (Guadalupes and possibly Davis) of the Trans-Pecos.

Philadelphia Vireo *(Vireo philadelphicus)*—Uncommon spring and rare fall migrant along the Lower Valley and Edwards Plateau, more common on the coast (April, September). Occasional spring and very rare fall migrant in Trans-Pecos.

Red-eyed Vireo *(Vireo olivaceus)*—Fairly common summer resident (April–September) in riparian woodlands on the Edwards Plateau locally westward to the Pecos River. Fairly common migrant over the plateau and South Texas becoming increasing rare westward.

Yellow-green Vireo *(Vireo flavoviridis)*—Very rare summer resident in the Lower Valley: six Lower Valley records range from Brownsville to near the coast (at Laguna Atascosa NWR). Look for near Sabal Palm Grove in late spring and summer. Accidental in Trans-Pecos. One record from the Austin area.

Black-whiskered Vireo *(Vireo altiloquus)*—Accidental. A dozen records for Texas, mostly from the upper and central Texas coasts. The lone Lower Valley record is from Brownsville, 25 May 1991.

Steller's Jay *(Cyanocitta stelleri)*—Locally fairly common to uncommon resident in the higher parts of the Guadalupe and Davis Mountains. In some winters may move into lowlands throughout the western portion of the Trans-Pecos. Best found at The Bowl in the Guadalupe Mountains.

Blue Jay *(Cyanocitta cristata)*—Uncommon resident, primarily in urban areas, on the Edwards Plateau west to Rocksprings. Somewhat irruptive into woodland habitats throughout the plateau and occasionally wandering to the Lower Valley and the Trans-Pecos where the species is casual to accidental.

GREEN JAY *(Cyanocorax yncas)*—Common resident in the Lower Valley west to about Laredo. Uncommon and local winter visitor as far north as Del Rio and Uvalde. Easy to see at Bentsen SP, Santa Ana NWR, and Sabal Palm Grove. Easily found in wooded areas throughout, especially at feeders. Best spots are along trailer loop at Bentsen SP and the feeding stations at Santa Ana NWR, Sabal Palm Grove, and Laguna Atascosa NWR.

BROWN JAY *(Cyanocorax morio)*—Rare to uncommon and very local in the Lower Valley along the Rio Grande between Rio Grande City and San Ygnacio. Most often found along the Rio Grande at Salineño, Chapeno, and woodlands below Falcon Dam. The best winter spot of late has been the feeders at the El Rio RV Park at Chapeño.

Western Scrub-Jay *(Aphelocoma californica)*—Common permanent resident of brushlands on the Edwards Plateau. Fairly common to common resident in parts of the Trans-Pecos such as the Davis and Guadalupe Mountains. Largely absent from the Big Bend region. In the El Paso area, present most winters in varying numbers depending on the intensity of the montane invasion in a given year. Look for at Edwards Plateau state parks and Davis Mountains SP.

MEXICAN JAY *(Aphelocoma ultramarina)*—Common resident in oak woodlands in mid and upper elevations of the Chisos Mountains.

Pinyon Jay *(Gymnorhinus cyanocephalus)*—Occasional to rare and irregular visitor (September–May) in the Trans-Pecos. May be more regular around Dog Canyon in the Guadalupes.

Clark's Nutcracker *(Nucifraga columbiana)*—Casual and highly irregular visitor (September–January mostly) to the Trans-Pecos.

Black-billed Magpie *(Pica pica)*—Accidental visitor to the Trans-Pecos (September–May). Most of the handful of reports are from the El Paso area, and there is an accepted record from there (4–6 and 17 February 1990). It nests south to about Albuquerque in New Mexico.

American Crow *(Corvus brachyrhynchos)*—Irregular in occurrence along the eastern edge of the Edwards Plateau. Very common just to the east of the plateau. Winters (October–March) from Fabens north to Las Cruces near large pecan groves. Numbers vary annually, but at times there may be thousands of birds.

TAMAULIPAS CROW *(Corvus imparatus)*—Locally common to uncommon winter resident in the Brownsville area, primarily at the Brownsville Municipal Landfill; first reported in 1968. Rare in summer in the Brownsville area, where it has nested. Best spots in spring and summer are the Port of Brownsville area and the NOAA Weather Station near Brownsville International Airport.

Chihuahuan Raven *(Corvus cryptoleucus)*—Common to fairly common resident in grasslands, mesquite brushlands and other desert habitats through much of the Trans-Pecos and South Texas. Numbers decline in winter in much of the Trans-Pecos. Generally absent from the Big Bend region. Replaced by Common Raven on the Edwards Plateau and in montane habitats in the Trans-Pecos.

Common Raven *(Corvus corax)*—Uncommon on the Edwards Plateau and fairly common in montane habitats in the central Trans-Pecos. Absent from the El Paso/Las Cruces area. Descends to lower elevations in the Trans-Pecos in winter.

Horned Lark *(Eremophila alpestris)*—Fairly common to common winter resident (October–March) and an uncommon and local breeder throughout.

Purple Martin *(Pronge subis)*—Common migrant and summer resident (February–August) from the Lower Valley northward through the Edwards Plateau as far west as Del Rio. Rare to casual migrant through the Trans-Pecos.

Gray-breasted Martin *(Pronge chalybea)*—Accidental. Two documented records by specimen, both at Lower Valley locales: Rio Grande City, 25 April 1880; Hidalgo County, 18 May 1889.

Tree Swallow *(Tachycineta bicolor)*—Common migrant (February–May; August–October) throughout. Rare to occasional in winter throughout.

Violet-green Swallow *(Tachycineta thalassina)*—Fairly common to uncommon summer resident of higher elevations of the Chisos, Davis, Guadalupe, Franklin, and Organ Mountains. A fairly common migrant through at least the western half of the Trans-Pecos, becoming scarce farther east. Accidental as a migrant to the Lower Valley. Often seen along the Window Trail or near the Pinnacles in Big Bend National Park, in the Davis Mountains, along Trans-Mountain Drive in the Franklin Mountains, and at Aguirre Springs.

Northern Rough-winged Swallow *(Stelgidopteryx serripennis)*—Fairly common to common migrant (February–May; August–October) throughout; an uncommon and local breeder. Rare to uncommon in winter upstream to Big Bend, and occasional elsewhere.

Bank Swallow *(Riparia riparia)*—Uncommon migrant (April–May; August–September) over entire region. Local and irregular breeding species over much of the region.

Cliff Swallow *(Petrochelidon pyrrhonota)*—Common migrant and summer resident (March–September) over the entire region. Cave Swallows are in direct competition for nesting areas over much of the region. The effect this will have on the Cliff Swallow is not clearly understood.

CAVE SWALLOW *(Petrochelidon fulva)*—Common to fairly common summer resident (late February–early October) throughout much of the Trans-Pecos, the Edwards Plateau, and south into the Lower Valley. Winters in some numbers in the Lower Valley. Largely absent from the Big Bend region and the Davis Mountains. Though virtually unkown from West Texas or the Lower Valley 20 years ago, this species has undergone an amazing expansion by using culverts, bridges, and overpasses as nesting sites. Historically Cave Swallows nested only in limestone caves and sinkholes on the Edwards Plateau and at Carlsbad Caverns. Easy to see at Kickapoo Caverns SP, among many other places.

Barn Swallow *(Hirundo rustica)*—Common to abundant migrant and breeder throughout (March–October). Rare in the Lower Valley in winter; occasional elsewhere.

Carolina Chickadee *(Poecile carolinensis)*—Common resident in mixed woodland on the Edwards Plateau west to the Nueces River drainage. Accidental in the Lower Valley.

Black-capped Chickadee *(Poecile atricapillus)*—Accidental. One old El Paso specimen (10 April 1881) represents the only accepted Texas record. It nests south along the Rio Grande in New Mexico to about Albuquerque.

Mountain Chickadee *(Poecile gambeli)*—Fairly common in the coniferous forests at the higher elevations of the Davis and Guadalupe Mountains. Sporadic as a breeder in the Organ Mountains. In montane invasion years may also be found in fall and winter (October–March) at lower elevations in the western portion of the Trans-Pecos.

Juniper Titmouse *(Baeolophus griseus)*—Uncommon permanent resident in the oak-juniper zone of the Guadalupe and Organ Mountains. Accidental in the El Paso area. Look for at Frijole Ranch in Guadalupe Mountains National Park or at Aguirre Springs in the Organ Mountains.

Tufted Titmouse *(Baeolophus bicolor)*—The Black-crested form is a common to abundant resident throughout South Texas, the Edwards Plateau and the Davis and Chisos Mountains. Accidental in the Guadalupe Mountains.

Verdin *(Auriparus flaviceps)*—Uncommon to common resident of desert and lower woodlands throughout.

Bushtit *(Psaltriparus minimus)*—Fairly common resident in oak-juniper habitats over much of the Edwards Plateau and the mountains of the Trans-Pecos. Casual away from the breeding areas in fall and winter. Most populations contain "black-eared" individuals, at least in late summer and fall.

Red-breasted Nuthatch *(Sitta canadensis)*—Rare to common, but highly irregular, winter visitor to the Trans-Pecos and Edwards Plateau (September–May). Locally or completely absent some years. Rare in the Lower Valley. A rare resident (has bred) in the Guadalupes.

White-breasted Nuthatch *(Sitta carolinensis)*—Fairly common resident in pine-oak and riparian woodlands in the mountains of the Trans-Pecos. Rare and irregular in winter away from resident populations.

Pygmy Nuthatch *(Sitta pygmaea)*—Fairly common permanent resident of mature pine forests at higher elevations in the Davis and Guadalupe Mountains. Casual visitor elsewhere in west Texas in fall and winter. Can be found at The Bowl in the Guadalupe Mountains.

Brown Creeper *(Certhia americana)*—Uncommon to rare winter resident and migrant throughout (October–April). A rare to uncommon resident in the Guadalupe Mountains, and likely the Davis Mountains.

montane invaders—In the Trans-Pecos, each winter brings a different cast of characters in terms of invading montane species. Most years species such as Red-breasted Nuthatch and Western Scrub-Jay invade lower elevations in varying numbers. Some years these species are joined by less regular invaders such as Acorn Woodpecker, Steller's and Pinyon Jays, Clark's Nutcrackers, Mountain Chickadees, and Pygmy and White-breasted Nuthatches. Occasionally no montane species invade at all. On the average it seems that a major montane invasion (probably brought on by massive food crop failures in the mountains to the north) occurs about once every five years. Frugivores such as bluebirds, solitaires, and Sage Thrashers are also irregular and sporadic in their winter movements in west Texas. One year may bring hundreds of Mountain Bluebirds to widespread parts of the region and then there may be two or three years without any at all.

Cactus Wren *(Campylorhynchus brunneicapillus)*—Common to fairly common permanent resident of desert habitats, brushlands, and lower foothills throughout. Noisy and conspicuous. Easy to find in Falcon State Park, Big Bend National Park, and Hueco Tanks State Park, among other places.

Rock Wren *(Salpinctes obsoletus)*—Common to fairly common permanent resident of dry rocky areas from west Texas to the Edwards Plateau. Some movement to lower elevations in winter, including sporadically south to the Falcon Dam area. Easy to find at Hueco Tanks, in the Franklin Mountains, and in Big Bend National Park.

Canyon Wren *(Catherpes mexicanus)*—Fairly common to common resident of the Trans-Pecos and Edwards Plateau. Easily found, and heard, in rocky canyons such as in Big Bend, Franklin Mountains, Hueco Tanks, McKittrick Canyon, and many other places.

Carolina Wren *(Thryothorus ludovicianus)*—Common resident from the Lower Valley northward through the Edwards Plateau and westward to the Devils River. Local resident along the Rio Grande as far west as the Big Bend region. Accidental west to El Paso. Found primarily in mesic habitats on the plateau and westward.

Bewick's Wren *(Thryomanes bewickii)*—Fairly common to common resident of woodlands throughout. Often local as a breeder, and more common in winter.

House Wren *(Troglodytes aedon)*—Uncommon to fairly common migrant throughout. Uncommon in winter in South Texas. A somewhat local and irregular winter visitor to most of the Edwards Plateau and Trans-Pecos. Local summer resident in the Davis and Guadalupe Mountains in pine-oak woodlands.

Winter Wren *(Troglodytes troglodytes)*—Irregular winter visitor (October–March) to the eastern Edwards Plateau, becoming rarer south to the Lower Valley. Very rare in South Texas and the eastern Trans-Pecos. Accidental to El Paso.

Sedge Wren (*Cistothorus platensis*)—Uncommon migrant and winter resident (September–May) along the coast in extreme South Texas. Very rare to accidental throughout the remainder of the region.

Marsh Wren (*Cistothorus palustris*)—Uncommon to common migrant and winter visitor (September–May) throughout. One documented breeding from El Paso County in 1938.

American Dipper (*Cinclus mexicanus*)—Accidental. Five documented records: November 8–16, 1984, Franklin Mountains, El Paso; 12 March 1906, Big Bend, 5 March 1994, Austin; and two Guadalupe Mountains records from the winters of 1987–1988 and 1988–1989.

Golden-crowned Kinglet (*Regulus satrapa*)—Rare to fairly common, irregular, winter resident (October–March) throughout. Most common in the Edwards Plateau, and rare to occasional in Lower Valley and much of the Trans-Pecos.

Ruby-crowned Kinglet (*Regulus calendula*)—Fairly common to abundant winter resident (October–March) throughout. Less common in September and April–early May.

Blue-gray Gnatcatcher (*Polioptila caerulea*)—Common migrant (mid-March–April; September) from the Lower Valley and Edwards Plateau west to the central Trans-Pecos. Rare migrant farther west. Uncommon in winter in the Lower Valley and southern Trans-Pecos, occasionally in other areas. Fairly common to common summer resident on the Edwards Plateau and the Chisos Mountains of Big Bend National Park.

Black-tailed Gnatcatcher (*Polioptila melanura*)—Fairly common permanent resident of mesquite brushlands and desert scrub in the Big Bend region. Less common and localized throughout the remainder of the Trans-Pecos and south along the river to about Rio Grande City. Look for in desert margins around Rio Grande Village, at Dugout Wells, and at Sam Nail Ranch in Big Bend NP.

Northern Wheatear (*Oenanthe oenanthe*)—One documented record for Texas: Lower Valley at Laguna Atascosa NWR, 1–6 November 94.

Eastern Bluebird (*Sialia sialis*)—Uncommon and local summer resident (late April–September) on the Edwards Plateau. More common and widespread from the central mountains of the Trans-Pecos eastward in winter. Rare in the Lower Valley and El Paso.

Western Bluebird (*Sialia mexicana*)—Uncommon to fairly common, irregular, winter resident (October–April) in the Trans-Pecos. Likes mistletoe-infected cottonwoods and the pinyon/juniper belt of mountains, such as at Aguirre Spring in the Organs or Frijole Ranch in the Guadalupes. Uncommon to fairly common breeder in the Davis and Guadalupe Mountains. Occasional eastward.

Mountain Bluebird (*Sialia currucoides*)—Rare to fairly common, highly irregular, winter resident (November–March) in the Trans-Pecos and western Edwards Plateau. May be numerous and widespread some winters. Very rare in the Lower Valley. There is a nesting record from the Davis Mountains.

Townsend's Solitaire (*Myadestes townsendi*)—Rare to uncommon, irregular, winter resident (late September–April) in the Trans-Pecos and Edwards Plateau. Very rare in the Lower Valley. Look especially in areas with junipers.

Orange-billed Nightingale-Thrush *(Catharus aurantiirostris)*—One documented record for Texas: Lower Valley at Laguna Atascosa NWR, 8 April 1996. First record for the ABA Area.

Veery *(Catharus fuscescens)*—Uncommon migrant in the Lower Valley becoming rare on the Edwards Plateau and west to the Pecos River. Casual in Trans-Pecos.

Gray-cheeked Thrush *(Catharus minimus)*—Rare to uncommon migrant in Lower Valley and eastern Edwards Plateau; most common along the coast. Very rare elsewhere in the region.

Swainson's Thrush *(Catharus ustulatus)*—Common, primarily spring, migrant (April–May; October) from the Lower Valley north to the Edwards Plateau. Rare migrant in the eastern Trans-Pecos, very rare west to El Paso.

Hermit Thrush *(Catharus guttatus)*—Uncommon to common migrant and winter resident (September–May) throughout. Fairly common breeder in high elevations of the Guadalupes and the Davis Mountains.

Wood Thrush *(Hylocichla mustelina)*—Uncommon, primarily spring, migrant (April–May; October) in the eastern half of the Lower Valley. Rare migrant on the eastern Edwards Plateau. Very rare on the western plateau and the Trans-Pecos.

CLAY-COLORED ROBIN *(Turdus grayi)*—Rare visitor in the Lower Valley, mostly in winter; breeding has been recorded. One record at San Ygnacio, 21 February 1988. Most reports are from the trailer loop at Bentsen SP and along the "B" Trail at Santa Ana NWR. Some years this species is more numerous and can even be found in residential areas of Brownsville and McAllen. Also to be looked for at Anzalduas County Park.

White-throated Robin *(Turdus assimilis)*—Accidental to the Lower Valley in winter: One at Laguna Vista (18–25 February 1990), two at Bentsen SP (1 February–3 April 1998), and two at Santa Ana NWR (1–12 March 1998).

Rufous-backed Robin *(Turdus rufopalliatus)*—Casual fall and winter visitor. Three records for the Trans-Pecos including Val Verde County (11–18 November 1976), the Davis Mountains (9 February 1992), and El Paso (27 October 1993). One below Falcon Dam (29 December 1975). Two additional records from the river valley between El Paso and Las Cruces. Carefully check flocks of American Robins at fruiting hackberries and pyracanthas in west Texas for this species.

American Robin *(Turdus migratorius)*—Uncommon to abundant migrant and winter resident (November–March) over entire region. Numbers of wintering individuals vary greatly. Local breeder, primarily in urban areas, over the Edwards Plateau and in El Paso/Las Cruces. Also is a summer resident at upper elevations in the Davis and Guadalupe Mountains.

Varied Thrush *(Ixoreus naevius)*—Accidental to occasional visitor (October–May) to the Trans-Pecos and Lower Valley.

Aztec Thrush *(Ridgwayia pinicola)*—Accidental. Two accepted records, both from Boot Spring in Big Bend: 21–25 August 1977, and 31 July–7 August 1982. There are other Big Bend records, most likely valid, and it should be looked for in moist canyons in Big Bend in late summer.

Gray Catbird *(Dumetella carolinensis)*—Fairly common migrant (late April–May; September–October) from the Lower Valley northward over the eastern Edwards Plateau. Becomes increasingly rare farther west. Rare winter visitor to the Lower Valley and scattered records of overwintering birds in many other locations over the region.

Black Catbird *(Melanoptila glabrirostris)*—Accidental. One documented (specimen) record for Texas: Lower Valley at Brownsville, 21 June 1892.

Northern Mockingbird *(Mimus polyglottos)*—Common to abundant resident throughout. Trans-Pecos populations are reduced in winter, when most birds either migrate south, or retreat into urban areas or places with abundant fruit.

Sage Thrasher *(Oreoscoptes montanus)*—Uncommon to fairly common migrant (March–April; September–November) to desert habitats, mesquite grasslands, and juniper foothills throughout the Trans-Pecos, and to a lesser extent the western Edwards Plateau (rare in eastern portion) and Lower Valley (where rare and irregular; absent along coast). Less numerous in mid-winter. Numbers fluctuate from year to year with large numbers often coinciding with good bluebird years. Easiest to find at Guadalupe Mountains National Park, Carlsbad Caverns National Park, and at Aguirre Springs.

Brown Thrasher *(Toxostoma rufum)*—Uncommon migrant (April–May; September–October) over the eastern Edwards Plateau; rare farther west. Rare in winter on Edwards Plateau and in the Trans-Pecos. Occasionally wanders as far south as the Lower Valley in winter.

LONG-BILLED THRASHER *(Toxostoma longirostre)*—Uncommon to common resident in South Texas from the Rio Grande north to the southern edge of the Edwards Plateau; rare and local in eastern Trans-Pecos. Vagrant in central Texas. Usually found in dense woodlands and occasionally at feeders at Sabal Palm Grove, Laguna Atascosa NWR, along the trailer loop at Bentsen SP, and along the river at Santa Ana NWR.

Bendire's Thrasher *(Toxostoma bendirei)*—Accidental. One accepted record from the Old Refuge, Las Cruces, NM, on 5 June 1993. Not on the official Texas list. This species is a regular breeder to within 100 miles west of Las Cruces.

Curve-billed Thrasher *(Toxostoma curvirostre)*—Common to uncommon permanent resident of brushlands throughout. Somewhat localized in the Trans-Pecos, where it prefers yucca/mesquite/grassland associations to creosote flats and arroyos. Look for at Falcon State Park and around Panther Junction in Big Bend National Park.

CRISSAL THRASHER *(Toxostoma crissale)*—Fairly common but extremely shy permanent resident of brushy arroyos, Tamarisk thickets, and lower mountain canyons in the western third of the Trans-Pecos. Less numerous in other portions of the Trans-Pecos from Big Bend National Park east to the Pecos River. Best found in February and March when singing. Center of abundance is in the El Paso and Las Cruces areas. Look for at Hueco Tanks, the Fort Bliss Sewage Ponds, and in the Franklin Mountains.

Blue Mockingbird *(Melanotis caerulescens)*—Accidental. One was videotaped 7–8 August 1995 in Las Cruces, NM, in good condition, suggesting a wild bird. Not known from Texas.

European Starling *(Sturnus vulgaris)*—Common to abundant in urban areas throughout the region.

American Pipit *(Anthus rubescens)*—Fairly common to common winter resident and migrant (October–early April) throughout.

Sprague's Pipit *(Anthus spragueii)*—A difficult bird to find anywhere in the region. Locally uncommon winter resident (mid-October–March) to the agricultural areas of the Lower Valley; occasionally found in grasslands of the Trans-Pecos as far west as El Paso. Rare migrant over Edwards Plateau.

Cedar Waxwing *(Bombycilla cedorum)*—Uncommon to common, but irregular and local, winter resident and migrant (October–April) throughout.

Gray Silky-flycatcher *(Ptilogonys cinereus)*—Accidental fall and winter visitor. Observed at Laguna Atascosa National Wildlife Refuge 31 October–11 November 1985 and in west El Paso 12 January–5 March 1995. These represent the only accepted ABA records. This neotropical species is largely fruit-eating and may be prone to seasonal wanderings.

Phainopepla *(Phainopepla nitens)*—Uncommon and localized permanent resident of oak woodlands and riparian areas of the Trans-Pecos. Generally associated with mistletoe-infected trees. Some migrational movement in winter. Scarce in Big Bend and in eastern portions of the Trans-Pecos. A casual visitor to the Edwards Plateau and Lower Valley. Can usually be found in the Davis Mountains and in residential areas along the river in El Paso and Las Cruces.

Olive Warbler *(Peucedramus taeniatus)*—Accidental. Three documented Trans-Pecos records (between 30 April and 7 September) plus three documented records from the Las Cruces, NM, area. Two of these are from December. Breeds uncommonly in the Black Range (60 miles northwest of Las Cruces).

Blue-winged Warbler *(Vermivora pinus)*—Rare to uncommon (coastal Lower Valley) migrant (April–early May; September) through the Lower Valley and Edwards Plateau. Accidental in the Trans-Pecos.

Golden-winged Warbler *(Vermivora chrysoptera)*—Rare to uncommon migrant (April–early May; September) through the Lower Valley and Edwards Plateau. Accidental to occasional in the Trans-Pecos.

Tennessee Warbler *(Vermivora peregrina)*—Common migrant (April–May; September–October) through the Lower Valley, particularly near the coast. Much less common, but regular, migrant over the eastern Edwards Plateau becoming increasingly rare westward. Casual in El Paso.

Orange-crowned Warbler *(Vermivora celata)*—Fairly common to common migrant throughout. Fairly common in winter, except in the Trans-Pecos, where it is increasingly rare and local north and west. An uncommon breeder in high elevation deciduous thickets in the Guadalupes, and rare in the Davis Mountains.

Nashville Warbler *(Vermivora ruficapilla)*—Uncommon migrant (April–early May; September–October) through the Lower Valley west to the El Paso area. Probably the most common migrant wood warbler on the Edwards Plateau. Uncommon winter resident in the Lower Valley.

Virginia's Warbler *(Vermivora virginiae)*—Fairly common to uncommon summer resident of higher elevations of the Guadalupe and Organ Mountains. Rare nester in the Davis Mountains. Prefers brushy slopes and areas with Gambel Oaks. A fairly common to uncommon migrant through the western portions of the Trans-Pecos. A very rare winter visitor to the Lower Valley.

COLIMA WARBLER *(Vermivora crissalis)*—Fairly common summer resident in the oak woodlands of the upper elevations of the Chisos Mountains, Big Bend National Park. They arrive in late April and depart by mid-September. Males are normally easy to find from late April to early June when they are most vocal. The Pinnacles Trail, Boot Springs, the Colima Trail, and Laguna Meadows are among the best places to search.

Lucy's Warbler *(Vermivora luciae)*—Very uncommon summer resident of thickets along the Rio Grande from Big Bend National Park (Cottonwood Campground) westward to about McNary. Prefers dense mesquite, tornillo, and Tamarisk thickets adjacent to the river. Very rare as a migrant away from breeding areas.

Crescent-chested Warbler *(Parula superciliosa)*—Accidental; an accepted sight record from the Chisos Mountains (2 June 1993).

Northern Parula *(Parula americana)*—Fairly common migrant (March–April; September) over the eastern Edwards Plateau and Lower Valley. Rare to casual migrant in the Trans-Pecos. Local summer resident in riparian woodlands on the southeastern Edwards Plateau. Look for at Guadalupe River State Park. Rare winter visitor to the Lower Valley.

TROPICAL PARULA *(Parula pitiayumi)*—Rare resident in the Lower Valley along the Rio Grande between Santa Ana NWR and Bentsen SP, rare but somewhat more widespread in winter; often found in mixed-species flocks in winter. This species is a locally uncommon breeder just north of the Lower Valley, primarily in live oak thickets on the King Ranch (north to Kingsville). Accidental in Edwards Plateau and Trans-Pecos (Big Bend NP). Look for in winter along the trailer loop at Bentsen SP, near the old manager's residence at Santa Ana NWR, and along the forest trail at Sabal Palm Grove. Seems to prefer the moss-covered canopy of large Cedar Elm, Sugar Hackberry, and Texas Ebony trees, however, Tropical Parulas may also be found at lower levels when foraging with mixed species flocks.

Yellow Warbler *(Dendroica petechia)*—Fairly common to common migrant (April–May; mid-August–mid-October) throughout. Rare in winter in the Lower Valley; occasional elsewhere. Nested historically on the Edwards Plateau and along the Rio Grande in west Texas.

"Mangrove" Yellow Warbler *(Dendroica petechia bryanti)*—This distinctive neotropical subspecies has shown up twice in Texas: north of the Lower Valley at Rockport, 26 May 1978; Lower Valley at Boca Chica, 20 March–6 April 1990. The three major subspecies of Yellow Warbler ("Northern Yellow Warbler," "Golden Warbler," and "Mangrove Warbler") were formerly treated as separate species and there is still debate over whether one, two, or three species are involved.

Chestnut-sided Warbler *(Dendroica pensylvanica)*—Fairly common to uncommon migrant (mid-April–mid-May; September–October) through the Lower Valley and rare on the eastern Edwards Plateau. Rarer in fall. Rare to casual westward.

Magnolia Warbler *(Dendroica magnolia)*—Fairly common migrant (mid-April–mid-May; September–October) through the Lower Valley and uncommon on the eastern Edwards Plateau. Rare to casual westward. Very rare in winter in the Lower Valley.

Cape May Warbler *(Dendroida tigrina)*—Rare spring migrant (late April–early May) in Lower Valley and accidental during spring west to El Paso.

Black-throated Blue Warbler *(Dendroica caerulescens)*—Rare migrant, mostly through the Lower Valley. Accidental to casual migrant in the Trans-Pecos (mostly in fall), and in the Lower Valley in winter.

Yellow-rumped Warbler *(Dendroica coronata)*—Common to abundant winter resident and migrant throughout (September–May). Rare to uncommon breeder in the Davis and Guadalupe Mountains. The "Audubon's" form is rare to the east; the "Myrtle" form is rare to the west.

Black-throated Gray Warbler *(Dendroica nigrescens)*—Rare to uncommon migrant (April–mid-May; late August–October) in the Trans-Pecos. Locally uncommon to rare migrant elsewhere, and winter visitor in the Lower Valley. A few may breed in Organ and Guadalupe Mountains on dry oak/pine-oak slopes.

GOLDEN-CHEEKED WARBLER *(Dendroica chrysoparia)*—Uncommon and local summer resident in Ashe Juniper-oak woodlands on the Edwards Plateau. Males normally arrive by 10 March and most of the population has departed by 1 August. At present the best places to find them are Pedernales Falls and Colorado Bend State Parks and Lost Maples State Natural Area.

Black-throated Green Warbler *(Dendroica virens)*—Common to fairly common migrant (mid-April–mid-May; mid-September–mid-October) in the Lower Valley, and uncommon on the eastern Edwards Plateau. Rare to casual westward. Rare to uncommon in the Lower Valley in winter.

Townsend's Warbler *(Dendroica townsendi)*—Uncommon to fairly common Trans-Pecos migrant (April–mid-May; late August–mid-October). More common in fall. Occasional migrant elsewhere, and winter visitor along the Rio Grande throughout.

Hermit Warbler *(Dendroica occidentalis)*—Casual to rare fall migrant (mostly September) in the Trans-Pecos; accidental in the Lower Valley (Anzalduas CP, December 1998). Mostly in mountains. Accidental to occasional in spring.

Blackburnian Warbler *(Dendroica fusca)*—Uncommon migrant (late April–early May; September) in the Lower Valley. Rare migrant on the eastern Edwards Plateau and accidental in the Trans-Pecos.

Yellow-throated Warbler *(Dendroica dominica)*—Uncommon migrant over eastern Edwards Plateau and Lower Valley. Locally common summer resident (March–August) in riparian woodlands on the southeastern Edwards Plateau. Look for at Guadalupe River and Garner State Parks and around Neal's Lodge. Fairly common winter resident, primarily in palms, in the Lower Valley.

Grace's Warbler *(Dendroica graciae)*—Fairly common summer resident of pine forests in the Davis, Guadalupe, and Organ Mountains. Rare migrant to lower elevations. Easiest to find in McKittrick Canyon in late April and May when the males are singing.

Pine Warbler *(Dendroica pinus)*—Rare migrant and winter visitor (October–March) to the eastern Edwards Plateau and South Texas. Accidental as far west as Big Bend National Park.

Prairie Warbler *(Dendroica discolor)*—Uncommon to rare migrant in the Lower Valley, accidental elsewhere in the region.

Palm Warbler *(Dendroica palmarum)*—Uncommon to rare migrant and winter visitor in the Lower Valley, very rare elsewhere in the region.

Bay-breasted Warbler *(Dendroica castanea)*—Fairly common spring migrant and uncommon fall migrant in Lower Valley, more common along the coast (late April–May, September). Occasional migrant on eastern Edwards Plateau. Accidental in Trans-Pecos.

Blackpoll Warbler *(Dendroica striata)*—Uncommon spring migrant and rare fall migrant in Lower Valley, mostly on the coast; casual migrant along Edwards Plateau and Trans-Pecos.

Cerulean Warbler *(Dendroica cerulea)*—Uncommon migrant (late April–early May; September) in the Lower Valley, accidental elsewhere in the region.

Black-and-white Warbler *(Mniotilta varia)*—Common migrant from the Lower Valley northward to the Edwards Plateau. Becoming increasingly uncommon westward where this species is a rare migrant in the El Paso area. Fairly common summer resident (March–September) in mixed woodlands on the Edwards Plateau. Regular in winter in the Lower Valley, occasionally found farther north.

American Redstart *(Setophaga ruticilla)*—Fairly common to common migrant (April–mid-May, late August–early October) in the Lower Valley and uncommon to rare on the eastern Edwards Plateau. Rare migrant in the Trans-Pecos (more common in fall), and in winter in the Lower Valley.

Prothonotary Warbler *(Protonotaria citrea)*—Uncommon migrant (April–early May; September) in the eastern Lower Valley. Rare to very rare migrant on the plateau and casual in the Trans-Pecos.

Worm-eating Warbler *(Helmitheros vermivorus)*—Uncommon migrant (late April–early May; September) in the eastern Lower Valley. Rare to very rare migrant on the plateau and accidental in the Trans-Pecos.

Swainson's Warbler *(Limnothlypis swainsonii)*—Uncommon migrant in the Lower Valley, mostly on the coast. Very rare migrant over eastern Edwards Plateau.

Ovenbird *(Seiurus aurocapillas)*—Uncommon to fairly common migrant (mid-April–mid-May; September mostly) in the Lower Valley and uncommon to rare on the eastern Edwards Plateau. Casual to rare in the Trans-Pecos. Rare in winter in the Lower Valley, casual elsewhere.

Northern Waterthrush *(Seiurus noveboracensis)*—Fairly common migrant (April–early May; late August–October) in Lower Valley and Edwards Plateau. Uncommon to rare in the Trans-Pecos. Rare in winter in the Lower Valley.

Louisiana Waterthrush *(Seiurus motacilla)*—Uncommon migrant (late March–mid-April; September) from the Lower Valley northward to the Edwards Plateau. Accidental in the Trans-Pecos. Local summer resident in mesic canyon on the Edwards Plateau.

Kentucky Warbler *(Oporornis formosus)*—Uncommon migrant (late March–early May; September) in the eastern Lower Valley. Rare to very rare migrant on the plateau and accidental in the Trans-Pecos.

Connecticut Warbler *(Oporornis agilis)*—Accidental; one record of a single bird repeatedly mist-netted near Driftwood, Hays County (3–14 May 1986).

Mourning Warbler *(Oporornis philadelphia)*—Uncommon, but secretive, migrant in the eastern Lower Valley. Uncommon migrant (May; September–early October) on the plateau and accidental in the Trans-Pecos.

MacGillivray's Warbler *(Oporornis tolmiei)*—Fairly common migrant (mid-April–May; mid-August–mid-October) in the Trans-Pecos; uncommon to rare in the Lower Valley and Edwards Plateau.

Common Yellowthroat *(Geothlypis trichas)*—Fairly common to common migrant throughout. Common in winter in the Lower Valley, becoming rare in the western Trans-Pecos. Fairly common (El Paso area/Lower Valley) to rare, and local, breeder along the Rio Grande throughout.

Gray-crowned Yellowthroat *(Geothlypis poliocephala)*—Formerly a rare to uncommon resident in the Lower Valley near Brownsville; there are only four Lower Valley records in the twentieth century: Sabal Palm Grove, 15 February–April 1988; Rancho Viejo, 15 April 1988; Santa Ana NWR, 8 March 1989; Sabal Palm Grove, 21 May–5 July 1989.

Cautionary note about yellowthroats: It seems that almost every year Gray-crowned Yellowthroats are reported from somewhere in the Valley. The identification is pretty straightforward, yet with the variability among immature Common Yellowthroats, there is potential confusion. In a nutshell, Gray-crowned Yellowthroats are bulky, big-headed birds with thick, chat-like bills. They show a distinctive gray forehead and crown, black lores, and eye crescents; they have a habit of swinging their cocked tails from side to side. They also prefer grassy areas (not marshes). If you suspect that you have a good sighting of a Gray-crowned Yellowthroat, please attempt to photograph or videotape the bird and provide a detailed written description. Any photographic or written documentation would be greatly appreciated, and should be sent to the Texas Bird Records Committee: Mark Lockwood, 2001 Fort Davis Hwy #15, Alpine, TX 79830.

Hooded Warbler *(Wilsonia citrina)*—Common migrant (late March–April; late August–September) in the eastern Lower Valley. Rare migrant on the plateau and accidental in the Trans-Pecos.

Wilson's Warbler *(Wilsonia pusilla)*—Common to abundant migrant (April–May; late August–early October) throughout, especially westward. Uncommon in winter in the Lower Valley, and occasional elsewhere.

Canada Warbler *(Wilsonia canadensis)*—Uncommon migrant (late April–early May; September) in the eastern Lower Valley. Rare to very rare migrant on the plateau and accidental in the Trans-Pecos.

Red-faced Warbler *(Cardellina rubrifrons)*—Casual migrant to Big Bend National Park and El Paso. About a dozen total records with more from August than any other month. This species breeds in numbers northwest of El Paso in the Black Range of central New Mexico. One Lower Valley record: 18 August 1985.

Painted Redstart *(Myioborus pictus)*—Rare and sporadic summer resident in upper elevations of the Chisos Mountains. Casual as a migrant in El Paso. Accidental in Lower Valley. Some years may be encountered in the vicinity of Boot Spring in Big Bend.

Slate-throated Redstart *(Myioborus miniatus)*—Accidental. One was photographed in the Davis Mountains, 2 August 1997 and one was present at Boot Spring, Big Bend National Park, 30 April–15 May 1990.

Golden-crowned Warbler *(Basileuterus culicivorus)*—Very rare visitor to the Lower Valley in fall and winter (October through March); records from Sabal Palm Grove, Brownsville, Santa Ana NWR, and Bentsen SP.

Rufous-capped Warbler *(Basileuterus rufifrons)*—Casual. This species was first documented for the United States at Falcon Dam in 1973. Since then there have been 11 additional documented records for Texas, mostly from the southwestern Edwards Plateau and Big Bend National Park. There is the possibility that the species occurs more regularly than previously thought in western Val Verde County where there have been three recent records.

Yellow-breasted Chat *(Icteria virens)*—Fairly common migrant throughout. An uncommon to locally common breeder in the Trans-Pecos and western Edwards Plateau, almost entirely in dense, riparian thickets. Rare in winter in the Lower Valley and casual elsewhere.

Hepatic Tanager *(Piranga flava)*—Uncommon summer resident of pine and oak forests of the Chisos, Davis, Guadalupe, and Organ Mountains. Rare as a migrant away from breeding sites. Accidental in Lower Valley in fall and early winter. Best found just above the Chisos Basin Lodge, at the Madera Canyon Picnic area (Davis Mountains), or at Aguirre Springs (Organ Mountains).

Summer Tanager *(Piranga rubra)*—Uncommon to common migrant and breeder (April—October) throughout, but absent as a breeder in the Lower Valley. Restricted primarily to riparian cottonwoods in the Trans-Pecos. Rare in winter in the Lower Valley.

Scarlet Tanager *(Piranga olivacea)*—Uncommon, primarily spring, migrant (April–early May; September) in the eastern Lower Valley. Very rare migrant on the plateau and accidental in the Trans-Pecos.

Western Tanager *(Piranga ludoviciana)*—Fairly common to uncommon summer resident (May–August) of the coniferous forests of the Davis and Guadalupe Mountains. Widespread and fairly common as a migrant (late April–May; mid-July–October) in the western half of the Trans-Pecos when it may be found at any elevation. Rare in winter and migration south to the Lower Valley. Accidental in winter at El Paso.

Flame-colored Tanager *(Piranga bidentata)*—Accidental visitor to Big Bend. Two documented records: 14–19 April 1996 in Pine Canyon, and 20–22 April 1996 in The Basin.

WHITE-COLLARED SEEDEATER *(Sporophila torqueola)*—Rare and local resident along the Rio Grande from the Falcon Dam area to Laredo; slightly more numerous in winter. Best spots of late seem to be the City Park in Zapata and along the Rio Grande at San Ygnacio. These seedeaters prefer weedy edges and second-growth as well as tall cane *(Phragmites)* along the river.

Yellow-faced Grassquit *(Tiaris olivacea)*—Accidental. One documented record for Texas: Lower Valley at Santa Ana NWR, 22–24 January 1990. First record for the ABA Area.

OLIVE SPARROW *(Arremonops rufivirgatus)*—Common resident in southern Texas west to Del Rio; rare at southern edge of Edwards Plateau. Easily found at Bentsen SP and Santa Ana NWR. Although shy, Olive Sparrows can usually be coaxed out of the brush with squeaking. They are fairly easy to see at feeders at Sabal Palm Grove, Laguna Atascosa NWR, and Santa Ana NWR, as well as along the trailer loop at Bentsen SP and in riparian woodlands in the Falcon Dam area.

Green-tailed Towhee *(Pipilo chlorurus)*—Fairly common to rare winter resident and migrant to riparian areas, desert thickets, and lower brushy canyons throughout the Trans-Pecos and south along the river to at least the Falcon Dam area (occasionally farther east to Brownsville). A sporadic winter visitor to the Edwards Plateau. Generally decreasing in abundance eastward. A rare nester in the high elevations of the Guadalupe and Davis Mountains.

Spotted Towhee *(Pipilo maculatus)*—Uncommon to common in winter (October–April) throughout, but rare in the Lower Valley. A fairly common to common breeder in the Chisos, Davis, and Guadalupe Mountains.

Eastern Towhee *(Pipilo erythrophthalmus)*—Rare winter visitor (November–March) to the eastern Edwards Plateau and South Texas. Accidental in El Paso (one record).

Canyon Towhee *(Pipilo fuscus)*—Fairly common to common permanent resident of canyons, foothills, and arroyos throughout the Trans-Pecos and Edwards Plateau. Some irregular movement to lower elevations in winter. Accidental in Lower Valley. Easy to find along the Window Trail in Big Bend National Park, the Franklin Mountains, and Aguirre Springs in the Organ Mountains among other places.

Cassin's Sparrow *(Aimophila cassinii)*—Common to fairly common though somewhat localized summer resident to grasslands, brushlands, and scrub desert throughout the Trans-Pecos, edges of the Edwards Plateau, and Lower Valley. Watch for skylarking birds in appropriate habitat. In the Trans-Pecos, most vocal in late summer (July–August) during monsoonal rains, but may start singing as early as March (as they do in the Lower Valley). Generally less common and harder to see in winter, but still present through much of the breeding range.

BOTTERI'S SPARROW *(Aimophila botterii)*—Uncommon to locally common summer resident along the Lower Valley coastal plain (April–August); prefers zacahuiste (bunch) grasses from east Brownsville to Laguna Atascosa NWR. One documented breeding record in Trans-Pecos (south of Marfa) in summer 1997. Best spots are along Old Port Isabel Road (Brownsville) and along TX-4 toward Boca Chica. Best searched for early and late in the day; often located by its song, which is a series of chips leading into a bouncing-ball trill.

Rufous-crowned Sparrow (*Aimophila ruficeps*)—Common to fairly common permanent resident of lower slopes and canyons throughout the Trans-Pecos mountain ranges and in the Edwards Plateau. Very rare and local around Falcon Dam area. Often on boulder-strewn slopes with scattered oaks or junipers. Easy to find along the Window Trail in Big Bend National Park, in Franklin Mountains State Park, and at Aguirre Springs in the Organ Mountains.

American Tree Sparrow (*Spizella arborea*)—Accidental to casual winter visitor to the Trans-Pecos.

Chipping Sparrow (*Spizella passerina*)—Fairly common to abundant migrant and winter resident (mid-August–May) throughout. Fairly common to common breeder on the Edwards Plateau and in the Davis and Guadalupe Mountains.

Clay-colored Sparrow (*Spizella pallida*)—Common to uncommon migrant (April–May; September–October) over entire region. Increasingly scarce westward. Sporadic in winter in South Texas and the eastern Trans-Pecos.

Brewer's Sparrow (*Spizella breweri*)—Common to uncommon migrant and winter resident (September–early May) to grasslands and desert brushlands throughout the Trans-Pecos. At times may be abundant. Increasingly common westward. Rare to casual as a winter visitor and migrant east into the Edwards Plateau and upper portions of the Lower Valley. Easiest to find around El Paso at areas such as Hueco Tanks State Park and Franklin Mountains State Park.

Field Sparrow (*Spizella pusilla*)—Common permanent resident in brushy habitats on the Edwards Plateau. More widespread in winter when the species can occasionally be found as far south as Falcon Dam and rare south to Brownsville. This species is a casual winter visitor in the Trans-Pecos.

Black-chinned Sparrow (*Spizella atrogularis*)—Fairly common to uncommon permanent resident of brushy mountain slopes in the Chisos, Davis, Guadalupe, Franklin, and Organ Mountains. Some elevational movement to lower desert flats in winter. Males sing from April to well into the rainy season in August. Best locations include the Basin in Big Bend National Park, McKittrick Canyon in the Guadalupe Mountains, and Aguirre Springs in the Organ Mountains.

Vesper Sparrow (*Pooecetes gramineus*)—Fairly common to common migrant and winter resident (September–April) throughout.

Lark Sparrow (*Chondestes grammacus*)—Fairly common to abundant resident throughout much of the region, except absent November–March from much of the Trans-Pecos, and less common then on the Edwards Plateau. Often local as a breeder throughout.

Black-throated Sparrow (*Amphispiza bilineata*)—Common to abundant resident of desert east to about Falcon Dam and La Joya in the Lower Valley. More local on the Edwards Plateau. Hard to miss in desert areas.

Sage Sparrow (*Amphispiza belli*)—Uncommon and local winter resident (November–March) to western portions of the Trans-Pecos. Prefers areas with sand sagebrush and scattered grass, but can be found in creosote flats as well.

Easiest to find in grasslands near Hueco Tanks State Park and below the Organ Mountains.

Lark Bunting *(Calamospiza melanocorys)*—Common to fairly common migrant and winter resident (late July–late April) to open country throughout. Numbers fluctuate from one year to the next. Can be found in grasslands, pastures, and desert brushlands. Often seen along the roadsides in large flocks. Probably more numerous in the Trans-Pecos than other regions.

Savannah Sparrow *(Passerculus sandwichensis)*—Common to abundant winter resident (October–April) in grasslands and weedy habitats throughout the region.

Grasshopper Sparrow *(Ammodramus savannarum)*—Rare to fairly common migrant and winter resident (October–April) throughout. An uncommon, and local, breeder on the Edwards Plateau and in grasslands surrounding the Davis Mountains.

Baird's Sparrow *(Ammodramus bairdii)*—Very rare migrant and winter resident (late October–early May) to grasslands of the Trans-Pecos. Historical records for the Lower Valley. Perhaps overlooked due to its secretive nature, this species is represented by very few well documented records (about 15 in this region) for the entire state. Best bet would be the grasslands along US-90 in the vicinity of Marfa and Valentine. Confusion with Savannah and Grasshopper Sparrows can lead to misidentification.

Le Conte's Sparrow *(Ammodramus leconteii)*—Uncommon to rare winter resident (mid-October–April) in grasslands on the eastern Edwards Plateau. Fairly rare in South Texas and on the western plateau. Accidental in the Trans-Pecos, however there are several records from the Balmorhea area.

Nelson's Sharp-tailed Sparrow *(Ammodramus nelsoni)*—Rare migrant and winter resident along the Lower Valley coast; accidental west in Trans-Pecos to Lake Balmorhea.

Seaside Sparrow *(Ammodramus maritimus)*—Uncommon to rare resident along the Lower Valley coastal marshes; more common in winter. To be looked for in the Black Mangroves at the mouth of the Rio Grande at Boca Chica.

Fox Sparrow *(Passerella iliaca)*—Eastern or red Fox Sparrow is a fairly common, but somewhat local, winter resident (November–February) on the eastern Edwards Plateau. Fairly rare on the western plateau and in the Trans-Pecos. The slate-colored or intermountain Fox Sparrow is a very rare winter visitor to at least El Paso County and is not well documented for the state.

Song Sparrow *(Melospiza melodia)*—Fairly common to common migrant and winter resident (late September–April) throughout, except for the Lower Valley where rare or absent.

Lincoln's Sparrow *(Melospiza lincolnii)*—Fairly common migrant and winter resident (September–April) throughout.

Swamp Sparrow *(Melospiza georgiana)*—Fairly common winter resident (October–April) in appropriate habitat on the Edwards Plateau and eastern Trans-Pecos. Locally uncommon to rare in in coastal swamps of South Texas. Uncommon winter resident in the El Paso area along the river and pond areas.

White-throated Sparrow *(Zonotrichia albicollis)*—Common winter resident (late October–April) on the Edwards Plateau. Rare in winter in the Trans-Pecos and the Lower Valley.

Harris's Sparrow *(Zonotrichia querula)*—Common winter resident (November–February) on the eastern Edwards Plateau. Rare on the western plateau and accidental in the Trans-Pecos as far west as El Paso.

White-crowned Sparrow *(Zonotrichia leucophrys)*—Common to abundant migrant and winter resident (September–May) throughout, but uncommon to rare in the Lower Valley east to about Falcon Dam and La Joya.

Golden-crowned Sparrow *(Zonotrichia atricapilla)*—Casual visitor (November–April) to the Trans-Pecos and, more rarely, the western Edwards Plateau. Typically found as a single bird, often immature, in a flock of White-crowned Sparrows.

Dark-eyed Junco *(Junco hyemalis)*—Fairly common to common migrant and winter resident (October–April) throughout, except in the Lower Valley where rare. "Slate-colored" forms dominate on the Edwards Plateau and are uncommon to rare westward. "Oregon" and "Gray-headed" (less common) forms dominate in the Trans-Pecos. "Gray-headed" is a fairly common breeder in the Guadalupe Mountains.

Yellow-eyed Junco *(Junco phaeonotus)*—Accidental. Five accepted records, three from the Guadalupe Mountains: 25 November 1987; March–April 1988; and 5 November 1990. The other two are from Big Bend: 17 June 1980 and 25 April–5 May 1990. A January 1997 report from El Paso seems credible.

McCown's Longspur *(Calcarius mccownii)*—Very uncommon to rare fall migrant and winter visitor (late October–March) to grasslands and agricultural areas of the Trans-Pecos and Edwards Plateau. Prefers shortgrass pastures or plowed fields. Often in association with Horned Larks. Not reliable anywhere, but grasslands west of the Davis Mountains and sod farms and agricultural fields near El Paso may be your best shot.

Lapland Longspur *(Calcarius lapponicus)*—Very rare winter visitor (late November–early February) to the grasslands of the Trans-Pecos.

Smith's Longspur *(Calcarius pictus)*—Accidental visitor (November) to the grasslands of the Trans-Pecos.

Chestnut-collared Longspur *(Calcarius ornatus)*—Uncommon to rare migrant and winter resident (early October–late March) to grasslands and agricultural areas in the Trans-Pecos and Edwards Plateau. Numbers may fluctuate from year to year with flocks of several hundred occasionally encountered. Generally prefers taller grassland than does the McCown's. Grasslands west of the Davis Mountains are often good for this species.

Snow Bunting *(Plectrophenax nivalis)*—Accidental. Two accepted records: 9 May 1988 in Big Bend, and 27 November 1993 at Lake Balmorhea.

Crimson-collared Grosbeak *(Rhodothraupis celaeno)*—Very rare visitor, primarily to the Lower Valley; mostly in fall and winter. Of the eight Texas records, seven are from our region: near Laguna Vista (Cameron County), Sabal Palm Grove, Santa Ana NWR, McAllen, Bentsen SP, and Laredo. This northeast Mexico endemic prefers a variety of habitats within its native range, including semiarid woodland and second-growth, which is similar to the thorn scrub forest found in much of South Texas. It can be shy and skulking, often found in lower canopy and on forest floor.

Northern Cardinal *(Cardinalis cardinalis)*—Common to abundant resident throughout, except in the Trans-Pecos, where it is locally common in the eastern part, but only casual in the Guadalupes and the El Paso area.

PYRRHULOXIA *(Cardinalis sinuatus)*—Fairly common to common resident of brushlands and desert in the Trans-Pecos and Lower Valley. Fairly easy to see in the Falcon Dam area, especially at Falcon SP. Less numerous but still resident on southwestern portions of the Edwards Plateau (rare and local in eastern portions). May be more widespread in winter when flocks are often encountered. Fairly easy to find in Big Bend NP, Falcon SP, and at the base of the Franklin Mountains.

Rose-breasted Grosbeak *(Pheucticus ludovicianus)*—Uncommon migrant (April–early May; September–early October) in the Lower Valley. Rare migrant on the plateau and Trans-Pecos.

Black-headed Grosbeak *(Pheucticus melanocephalus)*—Fairly common to common migrant in the Trans-Pecos, and as a breeder in the Chisos, Davis, Guadalupe, and Organ Mountains. Rare migrant elsewhere, and occasional in winter in the Lower Valley.

BLUE BUNTING *(Cyanocompsa parellina)*—Very rare and irregular winter visitor to the Lower Valley. Although this species has been recorded along the Rio Grande from Sabal Palm Grove to Salineño, most sightings are from the trailer loop at Bentsen SP. At Bentsen SP both Blue and Indigo Buntings are attracted to the seed feeders at many trailer sites. Blue Buntings are also occasionally spotted at the water bath at the photo blind (Eagle Pond). Although male Blue Buntings are unmistakable, the identification of females should be made with caution, because bright female Indigos are somewhat similar and occur in winter when Blue Buntings are most likely to occur.

Blue Grosbeak *(Guiraca caerulea)*—Common to uncommon migrant over entire region. Common summer resident (mid-April–August) on the Edwards Plateau and throughout much of the Trans-Pecos. Less common in South Texas.

Lazuli Bunting *(Passerina amoena)*—Uncommon to fairly common migrant (late April–May; August–October) in the Trans-Pecos. Rare to the east (though more common in spring along the coast), and in winter from Big Bend downstream.

Indigo Bunting *(Passerina cyanea)*—Common migrant (April–May; late September–October) from the Lower Valley north to the Edwards Plateau. Far less common in the Trans-Pecos. Local summer resident on the Edwards Plateau in mesic habitats. Rare and very local breeder in the Trans-Pecos. Regular in winter in the Lower Valley.

VARIED BUNTING *(Passerina versicolor)*—Fairly common to uncommon and local resident (late April–August) in brushy canyons and dense thickets in Big Bend National Park and on the southwestern Edwards Plateau east to Kimble and Bandera Counties. Rare in the vicinity of Carlsbad Caverns. Local resident as far south as the western Lower Valley. Appears to be a rare, but regular, migrant along at South Padre Island and other coastal locations. Casual in winter in the Big Bend region. Fairly common at Kickapoo Cavern State Park and at Sam Nail Ranch or along the Window Trail in Big Bend.

Painted Bunting *(Passerina ciris)*—Locally common to uncommon summer resident in portions of the Trans-Pecos (rather spottily distributed away from the river), Edwards Plateau, and Lower Valley. Most often encountered in thickets and riparian edge along the Rio Grande or in the Hill Country. Fairly easy to see from Rio Grande Village in Big Bend National Park west along the river to Hudspeth County and throughout proper habitat in the Hill Country (Kickapoo Caverns State Park is especially good). Migrants, especially in fall, sometimes seen away from breeding areas. It is a fairly common migrant in coastal Lower Valley.

Dickcissel *(Spiza americana)*—Common to uncommon summer resident (mid-April–mid-September) to pastures, farmlands, and thickets in the Edwards Plateau and parts of South Texas. A very uncommon to rare and somewhat sporadic fall (late August–mid-October) and accidental spring (May) migrant throughout the Trans-Pecos. One winter record from Lower Valley.

Bobolink *(Dolichonyx oryzivorus)*—Rare migrant (late April–early May; September) along the coast of extreme South Texas. Accidental in the Trans-Pecos.

Red-winged Blackbird *(Agelaius phoeniceus)*—Common to abundant resident throughout, though less numerous and more local as a breeder.

Eastern Meadowlark *(Sturnella magna)*—Uncommon to common, but often local, resident throughout. The *lilianae* race breeds in the Trans-Pecos, *hoopesi* in south Texas, and *magna* on the eastern Edwards Plateau. Identification difficulties may shroud the knowledge of winter distributions of both meadowlark species.

Western Meadowlark *(Sturnella neglecta)*—Fairly common to common breeder in the northwestern Trans-Pecos and western Edwards Plateau; throughout in winter. Often breeds in agricultural habitats as opposed to the native grassland preferred by Easterns.

Yellow-headed Blackbird *(Xanthocephalus xanthocephalus)*—Fairly common to common migrant and local winter resident (September–April) in Trans-Pecos. Less common on the Edwards Plateau and in the Lower Valley. Rare in summer (nonbreeding) in the Trans-Pecos. Thousands winter around El Paso.

Rusty Blackbird *(Euphagus carolinus)*—Rare winter visitor (December–February) to the eastern Edwards Plateau; casual elsewhere in the region.

Brewer's Blackbird *(Euphagus cyanocephalus)*—Fairly common to abundant migrant and winter resident (September–April) throughout, except only uncommon to occasional in the Lower Valley.

Common Grackle *(Quiscalus quiscula)*—Common resident, primarily in urban areas on the Edwards Plateau and locally in the Trans-Pecos west to Balmorhea. A rare, but increasing winter resident in El Paso. Accidental in the Lower Valley in winter and spring.

Boat-tailed Grackle *(Quiscalus major)*—Although a locally common resident on the central and upper Texas coasts, this species is strictly accidental south to Willacy County in the Lower Valley.

Great-tailed Grackle *(Quiscalus mexicanus)*—Abundant permanent resident to the Lower Valley and along the eastern Edwards Plateau. Abundant summer resident and fairly common and more localized winter resident to larger cities throughout the Trans-Pecos. Seldom found far from urban or agricultural areas in west Texas.

BRONZED COWBIRD *(Molothrus aeneus)*—Common summer resident in Lower Valley and Edwards Plateau; locally uncommon in migration and in winter. Uncommon and local summer resident in Trans-Pecos. Rare but increasing west to El Paso and Las Cruces. Most often found in disturbed areas and fragmented forest. Bronzed Cowbirds can often be located during winter amidst the large "blackbird" roosts in McAllen between the Best Western Hotel and the McAllen Medical Center.

Brown-headed Cowbird *(Molothrus ater)*—Fairly common to abundant resident throughout. Migration localizes, and seems to reduce, Trans-Pecos populations in winter.

Black-vented Oriole *(Icterus wagleri)*—Accidental; one record from Rio Grande Village, Big Bend National Park. A bird was found 27 February 1967 and returned for the next two summers.

Orchard Oriole *(Icterus spurius)*—Uncommon to fairly common migrant throughout, except extreme west Texas (El Paso County). Uncommon to locally common breeder in much of the region, but absent from much of the Lower Valley, and local in the Trans-Pecos, mostly along the Pecos and the Rio Grande west through Hudspeth County. The *fuertesi* race—a distinct subspecies breeding in northeastern Mexico—is accidental in the Lower Valley in spring and summer as a migratory overshoot.

Hooded Oriole *(Icterus cucullatus)*—Rare to locally common summer resident along the Rio Grande from the Lower Valley to El Paso, including the Davis and Guadalupe Mountains of the Trans-Pecos. Fairly common in the Brownsville area where it prefers to nest in palms. Locally common on southwestern Edwards Plateau, rare elsewhere on the Edwards Plateau.

ALTAMIRA ORIOLE *(Icterus gularis)*—Uncommon resident in the Lower Valley upriver to Zapata, occasionally to San Ygnacio. Best spots seem to be the trailer loop at Bentsen SP and along the river at Salineño. Also found at Santa Ana NWR and in wooded residential areas throughout the Lower Valley, where it is local.

AUDUBON'S ORIOLE *(Icterus graduacauda)*—Rare to uncommon resident in south Texas west to Del Rio, most common along the Rio Grande between Fronton and Falcon Dam. Vagrant to southern Edwards Plateau. Look for at the Salineño feeders (November–March) and nearby woodlands and along the river below Falcon Dam.

Baltimore Oriole *(Icterus galbula)*—Fairly common migrant over the Lower Valley northward to the Edwards Plateau. Casual to accidental migrant in the Trans-Pecos; rare to accidental in the Lower Valley in winter.

Bullock's Oriole *(Icterus bullockii)*—Fairly common to common migrant and localized breeder (April–September) in the Trans-Pecos and Edwards Plateau;

uncommon to rare in the western Lower Valley (Falcon Dam area). Occasional in winter throughout and in migration along the coast.

Scott's Oriole *(Icterus parisorum)*—Fairly common summer resident (April–October) of oak-juniper woodlands and yucca grasslands in the Trans-Pecos and the western and central Edwards Plateau. Accidental visitor to Lower Valley. Can usually be found along the Window Trail in Big Bend National Park, at Davis Mountains and Franklin Mountains State Parks, Aguirre Springs in the Organ Mountains, McKittrick Canyon, and in Lost Maples State Natural Area.

Purple Finch *(Carpodacus purpureus)*—Rare winter visitor (December–February) to the eastern Edwards Plateau. Accidental in the Davis Mountains and the El Paso area.

Cassin's Finch *(Carpodacus cassinii)*—Rare to uncommon, irregular, winter visitor (November–April) in the Trans-Pecos. Absent many years. Accidental on the western Edwards Plateau.

House Finch *(Carpodacus mexicanus)*—Common resident in the Trans-Pecos and Edwards Plateau south to Laredo. Accidental in the Lower Valley.

Red Crossbill *(Loxia curvirostra)*—Rare to common, highly irregular, winter visitor (October–May) in the Trans-Pecos, and, more rarely, the Edwards Plateau. Accidental in the Lower Valley. A rare to uncommon, irregular breeder in the Davis Mountains and in the Guadalupes. May breed in odd localities after major invasion winters, such as that of 1996–1997.

Pine Siskin *(Carduelis pinus)*—Uncommon to common, irregular migrant and winter visitor (October–May) throughout, rarer in the Lower Valley. One old breeding record each from the Davis and Guadalupe Mountains.

Lesser Goldfinch *(Carduelis psaltria)*—Fairly common to uncommon permanent resident throughout the Edwards Plateau and much of the Trans-Pecos. Decidedly less numerous in winter in most areas. Localized as a breeder in the Trans-Pecos. A scarce migrant, visitor, and possibly a local breeder to the Lower Valley.

Lawrence's Goldfinch *(Carduelis lawrencei)*—Accidental to casual, highly irregular, winter visitor (October–April) to the Trans-Pecos. Prior to October 1996 there were only two accepted Texas records, along with numerous undocumented reports from earlier invasions. A major incursion in the 1996–1997 winter brought hundreds of birds to the El Paso/Las Cruces area, as well as scattered records throughout the western Trans-Pecos. Absent the great majority of years.

American Goldfinch *(Carduelis tristis)*—Common winter resident (November–May) throughout most of the region. Fairly common, but irregular in parts of the Trans-Pecos, including El Paso. A few birds often remain into May when the males reach alternate plumage.

Evening Grosbeak *(Coccothraustes vespertinus)*—Rare to casual, highly irregular, winter visitor to the Trans-Pecos and Edwards Plateau. Not to be expected most years.

House Sparrow *(Passer domesticus)*—Common resident throughout the region, especially around cities, towns, and other human habitations.

BUTTERFLIES OF THE TEXAS RIO GRANDE

Jeffrey S. Pippen

Research Associate, Department of Botany, Duke University

More than ever before birders are noticing butterflies, especially during the hotter hours of the day when bird activity wanes and butterfly activity peaks. In general, butterflies tend to fly more on warm, sunny days and may be conspicuously absent on cool, overcast days. The intention of this list is to acquaint the butterfly watcher with the species which may be found along the Rio Grande in Texas. Nomenclature for this checklist follows the 1998 North American Butterfly Association (NABA) official checklist. Ranges given are relevant only to the scope of this book, not to the species as a whole. Note that a species which occurs "throughout" the region may be abundant in certain areas, uncommon in other areas, and absent elsewhere. Abundance and flight times may also fluctuate by year. Good butterflying!

This list was compiled July 1998. Primary resources used include:

Neck, R.W. 1996. *A Field Guide to Butterflies of Texas.* Gulf Publishing Co. Houston, TX.

Opler, Paul A., Harry Pavulaan, and Ray E. Stanford. 1995. *Butterflies of North America.* Jamestown, ND: Northern Prairie Wildlife Research Center Home Page. http://www.npwrc.usgs.gov/resource/distr/lepid/bflyusa/bflyusa.htm (Version 03JUN98).

SWALLOWTAILS—Family PAPILIONIDAE

Swallowtails—Subfamily Papilioninae

Pipevine Swallowtail (*Battus philenor*)—throughout • various habitats • most of year

Polydamas Swallowtail (*Battus polydamas*)—Eastern Edwards Plateau to lower valley • open or disturbed habitats • Apr–Nov

Zebra Swallowtail (*Eurytides marcellus*)—rare in Edwards Plateau • moist woodlands and nearby areas • Mar–Dec

Dark Kite-Swallowtail (*Eurytides philolaus*)—very rare summer stray to Lower Valley

Black Swallowtail (*Papilio polyxenes*)—throughout • various open areas • most of year

Thoas Swallowtail (*Papilio thoas*)—rare stray to Lower Valley • tropical forests and edges • Apr–July

Giant Swallowtail (*Papilio cresphontes*)—throughout • various habitats • most of year

Ornythion Swallowtail (*Papilio ornythion*)—possible throughout • citrus groves and gardens • probably rare or local • Apr–Sep

Broad-banded Swallowtail (*Papilio astyalus*)—rare stray to Lower Valley • Apr–Oct

240

Eastern Tiger Swallowtail (*Papilio glaucus*)—Edwards Plateau • various habitats • Feb–Nov
Western Tiger Swallowtail (*Papilio rutulus*)—NM to El Paso • various habitats • Jun–Jul
Two-tailed Swallowtail (*Papilio multicaudata*)—NM to Edwards Plateau • var. habitats • most of year
Three-tailed Swallowtail (*Papilio pilumnus*)—recorded once from Lower Valley
Spicebush Swallowtail (*Papilio troilus*)—Edwards Plateau • various habitats • Mar–Nov
Palamedes Swallowtail (*Papilio palamedes*)—Edwards Plateau to Lower Valley • wet woods and gardens near coast • not usually common
Victorine Swallowtail (*Papilio victorinus*)—recorded from near Del Rio • very rare stray
Pink-spotted Swallowtail (*Papilio pharnaces*)—recorded once from Lower Valley
Ruby-spotted Swallowtail (*Papilio anchisiades*)—recorded from Lower Valley, Edwards Plateau and Presidio Co. • very rare

WHITES AND SULPHURS—Family PIERIDAE

Whites—Subfamily Pierinae
Mexican Dartwhite (*Catasticta nimbice*)—Lower Valley and Chisos Mts • very rare stray
Pine White (*Neophasia menapia*)—Guadalupe Mts • in or near conifers • summer months
Florida White (*Appias drusilla*)—possible throughout • fairly rare stray; more common along coast
Spring White (*Pontia sisymbrii*)—El Paso to Guadalupe Mts • various dry habitats • Mar–Apr
Checkered White (*Pontia protodice*)—throughout • various open areas • Mar–Nov
Cabbage White (*Pieris rapae*)—throughout • open areas • most of year
Great Southern White (*Ascia monuste*)—Lower Valley to Big Bend and Edwards Plateau • open areas • all year in Lower Valley; migrates along coast; fairly rare inland
Giant White (*Ganyra josephina*)—Lower Valley (rare stray to Edwards Plateau) • open, dry subtropical forest • Sep–Dec
Pearly Marble (*Euchloe hyantis*)—El Paso and throughout NM • deserts, rocky canyons, ridges, woodlands • Mar–Jun
Olympia Marble (*Euchloe olympia*)—northern edge of Edwards Plateau? • open areas • May
Pima Orangetip (*Anthocharis pima*)—El Paso • dry habitats • Feb–Apr
Sara Orangetip (*Anthocharis sara*)—NM to Trans-Pecos • various habitats • Mar–Apr
Falcate Orangetip (*Anthocharis midea*)—Edwards Plateau to Lower Valley • moist wooded areas • Mar–Jun

Sulphurs—Subfamily Coliadinae
Clouded Sulphur (*Colias philodice*)—throughout • open habitats • most of year
Orange Sulphur (*Colias eurytheme*)—throughout • open habitats • most of year
Southern Dogface (*Colias cesonia*)—throughout • open habitats • most of year
White Angled-Sulphur (*Anteos clorinde*)—possible throughout • various habitats • rare(?) stray; more likely in Lower Valley
Yellow Angled-Sulphur (*Anteos maerula*)—possible throughout • various habitats • rare stray
Cloudless Sulphur (*Phoebis sennae*)—throughout • open habitats • all year
Orange-barred Sulphur (*Phoebis philea*)—possible throughout • open areas, edges • most of year • stray; more likely in Lower Valley
Apricot Sulphur (*Phoebis argante*)—very rare stray in Lower Valley
Large Orange Sulphur (*Phoebis agarithe*)—throughout • open habitats • all year
Tailed Sulphur (*Phoebis intermedia*)—very rare stray to Lower Valley
Statira Sulphur (*Phoebis statira*)—possible stray throughout; regular migrant to Lower Valley • open areas, edges • Jun–Sep; Nov–Feb
Lyside Sulphur (*Kricogonia lyside*)—throughout • subtropical open areas • all year
Barred Yellow (*Eurema daira*)—possible throughout but rare, more likely in Lower Valley • open areas, edges • Aug–Oct
Boisduval's Yellow (*Eurema boisduvaliana*)—strays throughout but rare outside of Lower Valley • open areas, edges • Jun–Nov
Mexican Yellow (*Eurema mexicana*)—throughout • open areas • Jul–Sep
Salome Yellow (*Eurema salome*)—very rare fall stray into Lower Valley

Tailed Orange (*Eurema proterpia*)—possible throughout (more common in Lower Valley) • open areas • Aug–Nov
Little Yellow (*Eurema lisa*)—possibly throughout; more common in s TX • open areas • all year
Mimosa Yellow (*Eurema nise*)—possible but rare outside of Lower Valley • brushy areas • Sep–Nov
Dina Yellow (*Eurema dina*)—occasional stray to Lower Valley • Nov
Sleepy Orange (*Eurema nicippe*)—throughout • various habitats • all year
Dainty Sulphur (*Nathalis iole*)—throughout • open areas • all year

Mimic-Whites—Subfamily Dismorphiinae
Costa-spotted Mimic-White (*Enantia albania*)—very rare stray to Lower Valley • Sep

GOSSAMER-WING BUTTERFLIES—Family LYCAENIDAE

Harvesters—Subfamily Miletinae
Harvester (*Feniseca tarquinius*)—Edwards Plateau to Lower Valley • moist wooded edges • Feb–Sep • uncommon

Hairstreaks—Subfamily Theclinae
Mexican Cycadian (*Eumaeus toxea*)—very rare stray to Lower Valley
Strophius Hairstreak (*Allosmaitia strophius*)—very rare stray to Lower Valley
Great Purple Hairstreak (*Atlides halesus*)—Big Bend to Edwards Plateau to Lower Valley • various edge habitats • Feb–Apr; Jul–Oct
Creamy Stripe-streak (*Arawacus jada*)—rare stray to Lower Valley
Gold-bordered Hairstreak (*Rekoa palegon*)—very rare stray to Lower Valley • Nov
Marius Hairstreak [*Rekoa marius* (=*spurina*)]—very rare stray to Lower Valley • Sep–Dec
Black Hairstreak (*Ocaria ocrisia*)—very rare stray to Lower Valley • Nov
Telea Hairstreak (*Chlorostrymon telea*)—rare stray to Lower Valley • Jun
Silver-banded Hairstreak (*Chlorostrymon simaethis*)—Lower Valley (stray to Edwards Plateau) • Apr–May; Aug–Sep
Soapberry Hairstreak (*Phaeostrymon alcestis*)—Trans-Pecos to Edwards Plateau • Apr–Jul
Coral Hairstreak (*Satyrium titus*)—Edwards Plateau • May–Aug • fairly rare
Banded Hairstreak (*Satryium calanus*)—Edwards Plateau • May-Jun
Southern Hairstreak (*Satyrium favonius*)—Guadalupe Mts; Edwards Plateau to Lower Valley • Apr–Jul • uncommon
Poling's Hairstreak (*Satyrium polingi*)—Chisos, Davis, and Franklin Mts • May–Jun; Aug–Sep
Clench's Greenstreak (*Cyanophrys miserabilis*)—Lower Valley; strays farther north • May–Dec
Goodson's Greenstreak (*Cyanophrys goodsoni*)—Lower Valley • Jun–Dec
Tropical Greenstreak (*Cyanophrys herodotus*)—rare stray to Lower Valley, Big Bend • May–Oct
Xami Hairstreak (*Callophrys xami*)—throughout east of Trans-Pecos • Jun–Dec • rare (extirpated?)
Sandia Hairstreak (*Callophrys mcfarlandi*)—NM to Big Bend • Apr–Jun • local and fairly rare
Henry's Elfin (*Callophrys henrici*)—NM to Big Bend to Edwards Plateau • Apr–May
Thicket Hairstreak (*Callophrys spinetorum*)—El Paso to n Trans-Pecos • coniferous forests • May–Jul • local and rare
Juniper Hairstreak (*Callophrys gryneus*)—Trans-Pecos to Edwards Plateau • Mar–Sep
'Siva' Juniper Hairstreak (*Callophrys gryneus siva*)—NM to Trans-Pecos • higher elevations • Jun–Jul
Aquamarine Hairstreak (*Oenomaus ortygnus*)—very rare stray to Lower Valley • Dec
White M Hairstreak (*Parrhasius m-album*)—Edwards Plateau • Feb–Oct
Gray Hairstreak (*Strymon melinus*)—throughout • Feb–Oct
Red-crescent Scrub-Hairstreak (*Strymon rufofusca*)—Lower Valley • Mar–Dec • fairly rare
Red-lined Scrub-Hairstreak (*Strymon bebrycia*)—Lower Valley (stray in Big Bend and El Paso) • most of year • fairly rare
Yojoa Scrub-Hairstreak (*Strymon yojoa*)—Lower Valley • most of year (more likely Oct–Dec) • fairly rare (stray?)
White Scrub-Hairstreak (*Strymon albata*)—Lower Valley • fairly rare stray • Jun–Dec
Lacey's Scrub-Hairstreak (*Strymon alea*)—Edwards Plateau to Lower Valley • thornscrub • Apr–Dec • fairly rare

Mallow Scrub-Hairstreak (*Strymon columella*)—Lower Valley (occasional stray north and west) • most of year • local and uncommon
Tailless Scrub-Hairstreak (*Strymon cestri*)—Lower Valley • Mar; Oct • fairly rare
Lantana Scrub-Hairstreak (*Strymon bazochii*)—Lower Valley • Feb–Dec • uncommon
Bromeliad Scrub-Hairstreak (*Strymon serapio*)—Big Bend • Apr • probably rare
Muted Hairstreak (*Electrostrymon canus*)—Lower Valley • Apr–Dec • fairly rare
Red-banded Hairstreak (*Calycopis cecrops*)—Edwards Plateau and Lower Valley • rare
Dusky blue Groundstreak (*Calycopis isobeon*)   Guadalupe Mts; Edwards Plateau to Lower Valley • Feb–Nov
Red-spotted Hairstreak (*Tmolus echion*)—rare stray to Lower Valley • May
Pearly-gray Hairstreak (*Siderus tephraeus*)—rare stray to Lower Valley • Nov
Leda Ministreak (*Ministrymon leda*)—NM to Big Bend; Lower Valley; stray to Edwards Plateau • May–Jul; Sep–Oct
Clytie Ministreak (*Ministrymon clytie*)—Edwards Plateau to Lower Valley • most of year • stray
Gray Ministreak (*Ministrymon azia*)—Lower Valley; stray to Edwards Plateau and west • Mar–Sep
Arizona Hairstreak (*Erora quaderna*)—Big Bend • higher elevations • most of year

Blues—Subfamily Polyommatinae
Western Pygmy-Blue (*Brephidium exile*)—throughout • most of year
Cassius Blue (*Leptotes cassius*)—Edwards Plateau to Lwr Valley (stray farther west) • most of year
Marine Blue (*Leptotes marina*)—throughout • most of year
Cyna Blue (*Zizula cyna*)—throughout • Mar–Oct
Ceraunus Blue (*Hemiargus ceraunus*)—throughout • most of year
Reakirt's Blue (*Hemiargus isola*)—throughout • most of year
Eastern Tailed-Blue (*Everes comyntas*)—throughout (rare in Lower Valley?) • Feb–Nov
Spring Azure complex (*Celastrina ladon*)—NM to Edwards Plateau • Jan–Oct
Rita Blue (*Euphilotes rita*)—Big Bend • Jun–Sep
Melissa Blue (*Lycaeides melissa*)—higher elevations of Trans-Pecos and Big Bend • Apr–Oct
Acmon Blue (*Plebejus acmon*)—NM to Big Bend • Feb–Oct

METALMARKS—Family RIODINIADAE
Fatal Metalmark (*Calephelis nemesis*)—throughout • most of year
Rounded Metalmark [*Calephelis nilus* (includes *perditulis*)]—Edwards Plateau to Lower Valley • most of year
Rawson's Metalmark (*Calephelis rawsoni*)—Big Bend to Edwards Plateau to Lower Valley • moist areas in arid regions • Feb–Nov
'Freeman's' Rawson's Metalmark (*Calephelis rawsoni freemani*)—Trans-Pecos
Red-bordered Metalmark (*Caria ino*)—Edwards Plateau to Lower Valley • Feb–Nov
Blue Metalmark (*Lasaia sula*)—Lower Valley • Apr–Dec
Red-bordered Pixie (*Melanis pixe*)—Lower Valley • Jan–Nov
Curve-winged Metalmark (*Emesis emesia*)—rare stray to Lower Valley • Oct–Nov
Falcate Metalmark (*Emesis tenedia*)—very rare in Lower Valley • Aug; Oct
Mormon Metalmark (*Apodemia mormo*)—NM to Big Bend (rare in Edwards Plateau) • Mar–Jun; Aug–Oct
Narrow-winged Metalmark (*Apodemia multiplaga*)—rare stray to Lower Valley • Nov
Hepburn's Metalmark (*Apodemia hepburni*)—Chisos Mts in Big Bend • Jul • rare
Palmer's Metalmark (*Apodemia palmeri*)—NM to west edge of Edwards Plateau • Apr–Nov
Walker's Metalmark (*Apodemia walkeri*)—Lower Valley • May–Jun; Oct–Dec • usually fairly rare
'Chisos' Nais Metalmark (*Apodemia nais chisosensis*)—Chisos Mts in Big Bend • May–Aug • rare

BRUSH-FOOTED BUTTERFLIES—Family NYMPHALIDAE
Snouts—Subfamily Libytheinae
American Snout (*Libytheana carinenta*)—throughout • most of year
Heliconians and Fritillaries—Subfamily Heliconiinae
Gulf Fritillary (*Agraulis vanillae*)—Edwards Plateau through Lower Valley (strays north and west) • most of year

Mexican Silverspot (*Dione moneta*)—fairly rare stray throughout • Apr–Dec
Banded Orange Heliconian (*Dryadula phaetusa*)—rare stray to Lower Valley • Jul; Dec
Julia (*Dryas iulia*)—Lower Valley (strays north) • most of year
Isabella's Heliconian (*Eueides isabella*)—Edwards Plat. to Lwr Valley • Apr–Jun • periodic immigrant
Zebra (*Heliconius charitonius*)—possible throughout (more common in Lwr Valley) • most of year
Erato Heliconian (*Heliconius erato*)—rare stray to Lower Valley • Jun; Aug–Sep
Variegated Fritillary (*Euptoieta claudia*)—throughout • Feb–Dec
Mexican Fritillary (*Euptoieta hegesia*)—Lower Valley (strays north and west) • Jul–Dec

True Brush-foots—Subfamily Nymphalinae
Dotted Checkerspot (*Polydryas minuta*)—Trans-Pecos to Edwards Plateau • May–Sep
Theona Checkerspot (*Thessalia theona*)—throughout • Apr–Oct
Chinati Checkerspot (*Thessalia chinatiensis*)—Chinati Mts in Trans-Pecos • Jun–Oct
Fulvia Checkerspot (*Thessalia fulvia*)—NM to Big Bend • Apr–Oct
Bordered Patch (*Chlosyne lacinia*)—throughout • most of year
Definite Patch (*Chlosyne definita*)—Trans-Pecos to Lower Valley • Apr–Oct • fairly rare and local
Banded Patch (*Chlosyne endeis*)—Lower Valley (rare stray to Edwards Plateau) • Mar–Nov
Crimson Patch (*Chlosyne janais*)—Edwards Plateau to Lower Valley • Jul–Nov
Rosita Patch (*Chlosyne rosita*)—Lower Valley • most of year
Red-spotted Patch (*Chlosyne marina melitaeoides*)—rare stray to Lower Valley • Oct
Gorgone Checkerspot (*Chlosyne gorgone*)—Edwards Plateau • Apr–Sep
Silvery Checkerspot (*Chlosyne nycteis*)—Edwards Plateau • Mar–Sep
Sagebrush Checkerspot (*Chlosyne acastus*)—El Paso • Jun–Aug
Elf (*Microtia elva*)—very rare stray to Lower Valley • Jul–Aug
Tiny Checkerspot (*Dymasia dymas*)—throughout • Feb–Nov
Elada Checkerspot (*Texola elada*)—throughout • Apr–Oct
Texan Crescent (*Phyciodes texana*)—throughout • Mar–Nov
'Tulcis' Cuban Crescent (*Phyciodes frisia tulcis*)—Lower Valley (strays north and west) • May–Nov
Black Crescent (*Phyciodes ptolyca*)—very rare stray to Lower Valley • Mar; Nov–Dec
Vesta Crescent (*Phyciodes vesta*)—throughout • Feb–Dec
Phaon Crescent (*Phyciodes phaon*)—Trans-Pecos to Lower Valley (strays to NM) • most of year
Pearl Crescent (*Phyciodes tharos*)—throughout • most of year
Painted Crescent (*Phyciodes picta*)—throughout (rare in Edwards Plateau) • Apr–Oct
Mylitta Crescent (*Phyciodes mylitta*)—El Paso • Feb–Nov • fairly rare
Question Mark (*Polygonia interrogationis*)—throughout • most of year
Mourning Cloak (*Nymphalis antiopa*)—throughout • most of year
American Lady (*Vanessa virginiensis*)—throughout • most of year
Painted Lady (*Vanessa cardui*)—throughout • most of year
West Coast Lady (*Vanessa annabella*)—NM to Big Bend • Jul–Oct
Red Admiral (*Vanessa atalanta*)—throughout • most of year
Orange Mapwing (*Hypanartia lethe*)—recorded once from Lower Valley
Common Buckeye (*Junonia coenia*)—throughout • most of year
Mangrove Buckeye (*Junonia evarete*)—Lower Valley (strays to Edwards Plateau and Trans-Pecos) • Mar–Oct
Tropical Buckeye (*Junonia genoveva*)—stray (possibly resident)—in Lower Valley • Mar–Oct
White Peacock (*Anartia jatrophae*)—Lower Valley (strays to Edwards Plateau) • moist habitats • most of year
Banded Peacock (*Anartia fatima*)—Lower Valley (strays to Edwards Plateau) • Mar–May; Oct–Dec
Malachite (*Siproeta stelenes*)—Lower Valley (strays to Edwards Plateau and Trans-Pecos) • most of year

Admirals and Relatives—Subfamily Limenitidinae
Red-spotted Purple (*Limenitis arthemis*)—Trans-Pecos; Edwards Plateau • Apr–Oct

Viceroy (*Limenitis archippus*)—throughout • usually near willows or poplars • most of year
Weidemeyer's Admiral (*Limenitis weidemeyerii*)—NM to El Paso • fairly rare
Band-celled Sister (*Adelpha fessonia*)—regular stray to Lower Valley • any time of year
California Sister (*Adelpha bredowii*)—NM to Big Bend (strays to Edwards Plateau and Lower Valley) • Apr–Oct
Spot-celled Sister (*Adelpha basiloides*)—recorded once in Lower Valley
Common Banner (*Epiphile adrasta*)—recorded once in Lower Valley • Oct
Mexican Bluewing (*Myscelia ethusa*)—Lower Valley • most of year
Blackened Bluewing (*Myscelia cyananthe*)—rare stray to Lower Valley
Dingy Purplewing (*Eunica monima*)—stray to Lower Valley • Jun–Sep
Florida Purplewing (*Eunica tatila*)—stray to Lower Valley • Aug–Sep
Blue-eyed Sailor (*Dynamine dyonis*)—Lower Valley (strays to Edwards Plateau) • May–Nov
Cramer's Eighty-eight (*Diaethria clymena*)—recorded once from Big Bend
Mexican Eighty-eight (*Diaethria asteria*)—rare stray to Lower Valley • Jul
Common Mestra (*Mestra amymone*)—Edwards Plateau to Lwr Valley (strays to NM) • most of year
Red Rim (*Biblis hyperia*)—Big Bend; Lower Valley (strays in between) • Feb; Jul–Nov
Red Cracker (*Hamadryas amphinome*)—stray to Lower Valley • Sep
Gray Cracker (*Hamadryas februa*)—Lower Valley • Aug–Oct • rare
Variable Cracker (*Hamadryas feronia*)—rare stray to Lower Valley • Jul–Dec
Guatemalan Cracker (*Hamadryas guatemalena*)—recorded once in Lower Valley • Aug
Brownish Cracker (*Hamadryas iphthime*)—very rare stray to Lwr Valley (Edwards Plateau?) • Aug
Orion (*Historis odius*)—rare stray to Lower Valley
Karwinski's Beauty (*Smyrna karwinskii*)—very rare stray to Lower Valley
Blomfild's Beauty (*Smyrna blomfildia*)—very rare stray possible throughout • Nov–Dec
Waiter Daggerwing (*Marpesia coresia*)—very rare stray to El Paso and Lower Valley • Jul; Oct
Many-banded Daggerwing (*Marpesia chiron*)—stray to Big Bend, Edwards Plateau and Lower Valley • Feb; Jul–Oct
Ruddy Daggerwing (*Marpesia petreus*)—rare to regular migrant to Big Bend, Edwards Plateau and Lower Valley • any time of year

Leafwings—Subfamily Charaxinae
Tropical Leafwing (*Anaea aidea*)—Big Bend to Edwards Plateau to Lower Valley • most of year • occasional wanderer
Goatweed Leafwing (*Anaea andria*)—throughout • all year (except Jun)
Angled Leafwing (*Anaea glycerium*)—rare stray to Lower Valley • Jul
Pale-spotted Leafwing (*Anaea pithyusa*)—Lower Valley • Mar; Jul; Sep; Nov

Emperors—Subfamily Apaturinae
Hackberry Emperor (*Asterocampa celtis*)—throughout • Mar–Oct
Empress Leilia (*Asterocampa leilia*)—throughout • most of year
Tawny Emperor (*Asterocampa clyton*)—throughout • most of year
Pavon Emperor (*Doxocopa pavon*)—regular stray to Lower Valley • May; Aug–Dec
Silver Emperor (*Doxocopa laure*)—regular stray to Lower Valley • Jul–Dec

Satyrs—Subfamily Satyrinae
Canyonland Satyr (*Cyllopsis pertepida*)—NM to Big Bend • May–Oct
Gemmed Satyr (*Cyllopsis gemma*)—Edwards Plateau to Lower Valley • Feb–Nov
Carolina Satyr (*Hermeuptychia sosybius*)—Edwards Plateau to Lower Valley • most of year
Little Wood-Satyr (*Megisto cymela*)—Edwards Plateau • Mar–Sep
Red Satyr (*Megisto rubricata*)—throughout (less common in Lower Valley) • Apr–Sep
Common Wood-Nymph (*Cercyonis pegala*)—Trans-Pecos to Edwards Plateau • May–Sep
Mead's Wood-Nymph (*Cercyonis meadii*)—NM to Big Bend • mountain areas • Jul–Sep
Red-bordered Satyr (*Gyrocheilus patrobas*)—NM to El Paso • mtn coniferous open forests • rare

Monarchs—Subfamily Danainae
Monarch (*Danaus plexippus*)—throughout • most of year

Queen (*Danaus gilippus*)—throughout • most of year
Soldier (*Danaus eresimus*)—Edwards Plateau to Lower Valley • Aug–Dec
Tiger Mimic-Queen (*Lycorea cleobaea*)—rare stray to Big Bend and Lower Valley
Klug's Clearwing (*Dircenna klugii*)—very rare stray to Lower Valley

SKIPPERS—Family HESPERIIDAE

Firetips—Subfamily Pyrrhopyginae
Dull Firetip (*Pyrrhopyge araxes*)—rare stray to Big Bend • Jun–Sep

Spread-wing Skippers—Subfamily Pyrginae
Guava Skipper [*Phocides palemon* (=*polybius*)]—Lower Valley • Feb–Apr; Jun–Sep
Mercurial Skipper (*Proteides mercurius*)—rare stray to Lower Valley and Edwards Plateau • Apr–Oct
Silver-spotted Skipper (*Epargyreus clarus*)—possible (but not common) throughout • most of year
Broken Silverdrop (*Epargyreus exadeus*)—rare stray to Lower Valley
Hammock Skipper (*Polygonus leo*)—rare stray to Big Bend, Edwards Plateau and Lower Valley
Manuel's Skipper (*Polygonus manueli*)—rare stray to Lower Valley • Aug–Sep
White-striped Longtail (*Chioides catillus*)—Lower Valley (strays throughout) • most of year
Zilpa Longtail (*Chioides zilpa*)—strays to Trans-Pecos, Edwards Plateau and Lower Valley • Sep–Nov
Gold-spotted Aguna (*Aguna asander*)—rare stray to Lower Valley • Apr–Nov
Emerald Aguna (*Aguna claxon*)—rare stray to Lower Valley • Oct
Tailed Aguna (*Aguna metophis*)—fairly rare stray to Lower Valley • Aug–Nov
Mottled Longtail (*Typhedanus undulatus*)—fairly rare stray to Lower Valley • Sep–Oct
Mexican Longtail (*Polythrix mexicana*)—fairly rare stray to Lower Valley • Jun–Oct
Eight-spotted Longtail (*Polythrix octomaculata*)—fairly rare stray to Lower Valley • Mar–Oct
Short-tailed Skipper (*Zestusa dorus*)—Guadalupe Mts to Trans-Pecos • Juniper-oak woodlands • Apr–Jul
White-crescent Longtail (*Codatractus alcaeus*)—rare stray to Big Bend and Lwr Valley • Jun; Oct
Arizona Skipper (*Codatractus arizonensis*)—Big Bend • desert mountains • Apr–Oct
Long-tailed Skipper (*Urbanus proteus*)—Lower Valley (but regularly disperses throughout) • Jul–Dec
Pronus Longtail (*Urbanus pronus*)—rare stray to Lower Valley • Oct
Esmeralda Longtail (*Urbanus esmeraldus*)—very rare stray to Lower Valley • Aug
Dorantes Longtail (*Urbanus dorantes*)—Edwards Plateau to Lower Valley • most of year
Teleus Longtail (*Urbanus teleus*)—Lower Valley • most of year
Tanna Longtail (*Urbanus tanna*)—rare stray to Lower Valley • Jun
Plain Longtail (*Urbanus simplicius*)—rare stray to Lower Valley • Apr
Brown Longtail (*Urbanus procne*)—Lower Valley (rarein Edwards Plateau) • most of year
White-tailed Longtail (*Urbanus doryssus*)—rare stray to Lower Valley • Mar; Nov
Two-barred Flasher (*Astraptes fulgerator*)—Lwr Valley (stray to Edwards Plateau) • most of year
Small-spotted Flasher (*Astraptes egregius*)—rare stray to Lower Valley • Oct
Frosted Flasher (*Astraptes alardus*)—rare stray to Lower Valley • Jun–Oct
Gilbert's Flasher (*Astraptes gilberti*)—rare stray to Lower Valley • Oct
Yellow-tipped Flasher (*Astraptes anaphus*)—fairly rare stray to Lower Valley • Apr–May; Sep–Oct
Golden-banded Skipper (*Autochton cellus*)—Big Bend • Feb–Sep
Chisos Banded-Skipper (*Autochton cincta*)—Big Bend • Mar–Sep
Hoary Edge (*Achalarus lyciades*)—Edwards Plateau • May–Oct
Desert Cloudywing (*Achalarus casica*)—Trans-Pecos to Big Bend (disperses to Edwards Plateau) • May–Oct
Skinner's Cloudywing (*Achalarus albociliatus*)—recorded once from Edwards Plateau
Coyote Cloudywing (*Achalarus toxeus*)—regular stray to Edwards Plateau and Lower Valley • most of year
Jalapus Cloudywing (*Achalarus jalapus*)—rare stray to Lower Valley • Jul–Oct
Southern Cloudywing (*Thorybes bathyllus*)—eastern Edwards Plateau • Mar–Dec

Northern Cloudywing (*Thorybes pylades*)—Trans-Pecos to Edwards Plateau • Mar–Dec
Confused Cloudywing (*Thorybes confusis*)—Edwards Plateau • Feb–Oct
Drusius Cloudywing (*Thorybes drusius*)—Trans-Pecos to Big Bend • open oak woodlands, desert grasslands • Apr–Jun
Potrillo Skipper (*Cabares potrillo*)—Lower Valley (strays to Edwards Plateau) • dependably observed at Santa Ana NWR • most of year
Fritzgaertner's Flat (*Celaenorrhinus fritzgaertneri*)—fairly rare stray to Lower Valley • Feb
Stallings' Flat (*Celaenorrhinus stallingsi*)—stray to Lower Valley • Jun, Nov
Falcate Skipper (*Spathilepia clonius*)—rare stray to Lower Valley • May–Jul; Oct–Nov
Mimosa Skipper (*Cogia calchas*)—Lower Valley • usually near water • Mar–Nov
Acacia Skipper (*Cogia hippalus*)—NM to Big Bend (strays to Lower Valley and Edwards Plateau) • Apr–Aug
Outis Skipper (*Cogia outis*)—Edwards Plateau to Lower Valley • Mar–Oct
Starred Skipper (*Arteurotia tractipennis*)—rare stray to Lower Valley
Purplish-black Skipper (*Nisoniades rubescens*)—rare stray to Lower Valley • Oct–Nov
Confused Pellicia (*Pellicia angra*)—rare stray to Lower Valley • Mar–Nov
Glazed Pellicia (*Pellicia arina*)—rare stray to Lower Valley • Mar–Apr; Jun–Dec
Morning Glory Pellicia (*Pellicia dimidiata*)—very rare stray to Lower Valley • Oct
Mottled Bolla (*Bolla clytius*)—periodic stray to Lower Valley • Jun–Nov
Obscure Bolla (*Bolla brennus*)—rare stray to Lower Valley • Oct
Golden-headed Scallopwing (*Staphylus ceos*)—throughout • Apr–Dec
Mazans Scallopwing (*Staphylus mazans*)—Edwards Plateau to Lower Valley • most of year
Hayhurst's Scallopwing (*Staphylus hayhurstii*)—Edwards Plateau • Mar–Nov
Variegated Skipper (*Gorgythion begga*)—recorded once in Lower Valley • Mar
Blue-studded Skipper (*Sostrata bifasciata*)—recorded once in Lower Valley • Oct
Hoary Skipper (*Carrhenes canescens*)—very rare stray to Lower Valley • Feb–May; Oct–Dec
Glassy-winged Skipper (*Xenophanes tryxus*)—periodic resident in Lower Valley • Feb–Nov
Texas Powdered-Skipper (*Systasea pulverulenta*)—throughout • Feb-Dec
Arizona Powdered-Skipper (*Systasea zampa*)—NM to Big Bend • arid desert canyons and arroyos • Apr–Oct
Sickle-winged Skipper (*Achlyodes thraso*)—Lwr Valley (strays to Edwards Plateau) • most of year
Hermit Skipper (*Grais stigmatica*)—Lower Valley (strays throughout) • Apr; Jul–Oct
Brown-banded Skipper (*Timochares ruptifasciatus*)—Lower Valley (strays to Edwards Plateau) • Mar–Sep
White-patched Skipper (*Chiomara asychis*)—Lower Valley (strays to Edwards Plateau and Big Bend) • Mar–Jun; Aug–Dec
False Duskywing (*Gesta gesta*)—Lower Valley (strays to Edwards Plateau) • Apr–Nov
Sleepy Duskywing (*Erynnis brizo*)—NM to Edwards Plateau • Feb–Apr
Juvenal's Duskywing (*Erynnis juvenalis*)—Trans-Pecos to Edwards Plateau • Apr–Jun
Rocky Mountain Duskywing (*Erynnis telemachus*)—Guadalupe Mts to Big Bend • Apr–Jun
Meridian Duskywing (*Erynnis meridianus*)—NM to Edwards Plateau • oak thickets • Jun–Sep
Scudder's Duskywing (*Erynnis scudderi*)—NM to Big Bend • mtn woodlands • May–Aug • rare
Horace's Duskywing (*Erynnis horatius*)—Edwards Plateau (rare in Lower Valley) • most of year
Mournful Duskywing (*Erynnis tristis*)—NM to Big Bend (strays to Edwards Plateau and Lower Valley) • Mar–Nov
Mottled Duskywing (*Erynnis martialis*)—NM to Edwards Plateau • Mar–Dec • fairly rare
Funereal Duskywing (*Erynnis funeralis*)—throughout • Mar–Dec
Wild Indigo Duskywing (*Erynnis baptisiae*)—fairly rare in Edwards Plateau • Apr–Aug
Small Checkered-Skipper (*Pyrgus scriptura*)—NM to Big Bend • Mar–Nov
Common Checkered-Skipper (*Pyrgus communis*)—throughout • most of year
Tropical Checkered-Skipper (*Pyrgus oileus*)—Lwr Valley (strays to Edwards Plateau) • most of year
Desert Checkered-Skipper (*Pyrgus philetas*)—Big Bend to Lower Valley • most of year
Erichson's White-Skipper (*Heliopetes domicella*)—Trans-Pecos to Lower Valley • near water in arid areas • Apr; Aug–Oct
Laviana White-Skipper (*Heliopetes laviana*)—Lower Valley (stray to Edwards Plateau) • most of year

Turk's-cap White-Skipper (*Heliopetes macaira*)—Lower Valley (stray to Edwards Plateau) • May–Nov
Veined White-Skipper (*Heliopetes arsalte*)—regular stray to Lower Valley • Oct
Common Streaky-Skipper (*Celotes nessus*)—throughout • Mar–Nov
Scarce Streaky-Skipper (*Celotes limpia*)—NM to Big Bend • Mar–Sep
Common Sootywing (*Pholisora catullus*)—throughout • Feb–Dec
Mexican Sootywing (*Pholisora mejicana*)—Trans-Pecos • May–Sep
Saltbush Sootywing (*Hesperopsis alpheus*)—throughout (scarce in Edwards Plateau) • Apr–Nov

Grass Skippers—Subfamily Hesperiinae
Russet Skipperling (*Piruna pirus*)—rare stray to Trans-Pecos
Small-spotted Skipperling (*Piruna microstictus*)—rare stray to Lower Valley • Oct
Chisos Skipperling (*Piruna haferniki*)—Big Bend • grassy streambanks • Mar–Aug
Malicious Skipper (*Synapte malitiosa*)—Lower Valley • Mar–Nov
Salenus Skipper (*Synapte salenus*)—rare stray to Lower Valley • Aug
Redundant Skipper (*Corticea corticea*)—rare stray to Lower Valley • Sep–Dec
Pale-rayed Skipper (*Vidius perigenes*)—Lower Valley • Mar–Oct • periodic stray, occasionally common
Violet-patched Skipper (*Monca telata*)—Lower Valley • Jan–May; Oct–Dec • more common in wet years
Swarthy Skipper (*Nastra lherminier*)—rare stray (from North) to Edwards Plateau and Lower Valley • summer
Julia's Skipper (*Nastra julia*)—Trans-Pecos to Edwards Plateau to Lower Valley • Apr–Oct
Fawn-spotted Skipper (*Cymaenes odilia*)—Lwr Valley • grassy areas in woodlands • Apr–Dec • rare
Clouded Skipper (*Lerema accius*)—throughou • Feb–Nov
Liris Skipper (*Lerema liris*)—rare stray to Lower Valley • Aug–Oct
Fantastic Skipper (*Vettius fantasos*)—recorded once from Lower Valley • Oct
Green-backed Ruby-eye (*Perichares philetes*)—rare stray to Lower Valley • flies at dusk! • Nov–Dec
Osca Skipper (*Rhinthon osca*)—rare stray to Lower Valley • wooded areas • Oct
Double-dotted Skipper (*Decinea percosius*)—Lower Valley • Apr–Nov
Hidden-ray Skipper (*Conga chydaea*)—rare stray to Lower Valley • Jul–Oct
Least Skipper (*Ancyloxypha numitor*)—Edwards Plateau (rare in Lower Valley) • near wet areas • most of year
Tropical Least Skipper (*Ancyloxypha arene*)—throughout • near water in arid regions • Mar–Sep
Edwards' Skipperling (*Oarisma edwardsii*)—Trans-Pecos • arid montane woodlands • Apr–Jul
Orange Skipperling (*Copaeodes aurantiacus*)—throughout • grasslands, lawns, arid woodlands • most of year
Southern Skipperling (*Copaeodes minimus*)—Edwards Plateau to Lower Valley • most of year
Sunrise Skipper (*Adopaeoides prittwitzi*)—Davis Mts in Trans-Pecos • May–Jun; Sep
Fiery Skipper (*Hylephila phyleus*)—throughout • most of year • common
Morrison's Skipper (*Stinga morrisoni*)—Trans-Pecos • mountain meadows • May; Sep
Uncas Skipper (*Hesperia uncas*)—Trans-Pecos • sagebrush, prairie, open woodlands • May–Sep
Common Branded Skipper (*Hesperia comma*)—Trans-Pecos • Jul–Sep
Apache Skipper (*Hesperia woodgatei*)—Trans-Pecos; Edwards Plateau • montane open grassy areas • Sep–Oct
Pahaska Skipper (*Hesperia pahaska*)—NM to Big Bend • Apr–Oct
Green Skipper (*Hesperia viridis*)—Trans-Pecos to Edwards Plateau • Apr–Jun;Aug–Oct
Rhesus Skipper (*Polites rhesus*)—Trans-Pecos • prairies • Jun
Carus Skipper (*Polites carus*)—Trans-Pecos • desert grassland; oak woodland • Apr–Sep
Whirlabout (*Polites vibex*)—Edwards Plateau to Lwr Valley (rare stray to Trans-Pecos) • all year
Southern Broken-Dash (*Wallengrenia otho*)—Edwards Plateau to Lower Valley • most of year
Little Glassywing (*Pompeius verna*)—Edwards Plateau to Lower Valley • Apr–Sep • rare
Sachem (*Atalopedes campestris*)—throughout • most of year
Arogos Skipper (*Atrytone arogos*)—Edwards Plateau • Mar–May; Aug–Sep • rare
Delaware Skipper (*Anatrytone logan*)—possible throughout • Feb–Sep

Taxiles Skipper (*Poanes taxiles*)—NM to Big Bend • clearings near water • Jun–Aug
Broad-winged Skipper (*Poanes viator*)—Edwards Plateau • May–Aug
Umber Skipper (*Poanes melane*)—Big Bend • May–Sep
Common Mellana (*Quasimellana eulogius*)—stray to Lower Valley • May; Sep
Dun Skipper (*Euphyes vestris*)—possible throughout • Apr–Sep
Viereck's Skipper (*Atrytonopsis vierecki*)—NM to Big Bend • arid grasslands, open woodlands • Apr–May
White-barred Skipper (*Atrytonopsis pittacus*)—NM to Big Bend • rocky slopes, dry streambeds • Mar–May (Sep?) • rare
Python Skipper (*Atrytonopsis python*)—NM to Big Bend • May–Jul • rare
Sheep Skipper (*Atrytonopsis edwardsii*)—Trans-Pecos • Apr–Jun
Simius Roadside-Skipper (*Amblyscirtes simius*)—Trans-Pecos • Apr–Aug
Cassus Roadside-Skipper (*Amblyscirtes cassus*)—Davis Mts in Trans-Pecos • Jun–Aug
Bronze Roadside-Skipper (*Amblyscirtes aenus*)—Trans-Pecos to Big Bend; Edwards Plateau • May–Sep
Oslar's Roadside-Skipper (*Amblyscirtes oslari*)—Trans-Pecos; Big Bend; Edwards Plateau • Apr–Aug
Texas Roadside-Skipper (*Amblyscirtes texanae*)—Trans-Pecos to Big Bend (rare farther east) • dry, rocky ravines • Apr–Sep
Slaty Roadside-Skipper (*Amblyscirtes nereus*)—s. Trans-Pecos to Big Bend • Mar–Sep • rare
Nysa Roadside-Skipper (*Amblyscirtes nysa*)—throughout • most of year
Dotted Roadside-Skipper (*Amblyscirtes eos*)—NM to Edwards Plateau (rare in Lower Valley) • Apr–Sep
Celia's Roadside-Skipper (*Amblyscirtes celia*)—Edwards Plateau to Lower Valley (strays to Trans-Pecos) • May–Sep (all year in Lower Valley)
Orange-headed Roadside-Skipper (*Amblyscirtes phylace*)—Trans-Pecos to Big Bend • Jun–Aug
Orange-edged Roadside-Skipper (*Amblyscirtes fimbriata*)—southern Trans-Pecos to Big Bend • Jun–Jul
Eufala Skipper (*Lerodea eufala*)—throughout (more common east of Big Bend) • open sunny areas; agricultural areas • most of year
Olive-clouded Skipper (*Lerodea dysaules*)—Lower Valley • Jun–Nov
Brazilian Skipper (*Calpodes ethlius*)—throughout (more common in Lower Valley) • most of year
Obscure Skipper (*Panoquina panoquinoides*)—Lower Valley • coastal marshes, dunes • Feb–Dec • uncommon
Ocola Skipper (*Panoquina ocola*)—Edwards Plateau to Lower Valley (strays to Trans-Pecos) • most of year
Hecebolus Skipper (*Panoquina hecebola*)—Lower Valley • Jul–Dec • stray (occasionally common)
Purple-washed Skipper (*Panoquina sylvicola*)—regular stray to Lower Valley (rare stray to Edwards Plateau) • usually near sugar cane • Aug–Dec
Evans' Skipper (*Panoquina fusina*)—stray to Lower Valley • Oct–Nov
Violet-banded Skipper (*Nyctelius nyctelius*)—stray to Lower Valley and Edwards Plateau • May–Dec
Chestnut-marked Skipper (*Thespieus macareus*)—stray to Lower Valley • Jul–Nov

Giant-Skippers—Subfamily Megathyminae
Orange Giant-Skipper (*Agathymus neumoegeni*)—NM to Big Bend • montane areas • Sep–Oct
Mary's Giant-Skipper (*Agathymus mariae*)—NM to western Edwards Plateau • Oct–Nov
Coahuila Giant-Skipper (*Agathymus remingtoni*)—western Edwards Plateau • Sep–Oct
Yucca Giant-Skipper (*Megathymus yuccae*)—throughout • Mar–Apr
Strecker's Giant-Skipper (*Megathymus streckeri*)—Edwards Plateau • Apr–Jul
Ursine Giant-Skipper (*Megathymus ursus*)—NM to just east of Big Bend • Apr–Jun
Manfreda Giant-Skipper (*Stallingsia maculosa*)—EP to Lower Valley • thorn forests; pine forests • Apr–May; Sep–Oct

OTHER VERTEBRATES
EXCLUSIVE OF FISH

Allan H. Chaney

ALLIGATORS

American Alligator—Ponds, resacas, streams; South Texas except coastal.

TURTLES

Common Snapping Turtle—Some permanent waters; Edwards Plateau.
Yellow Mud Turtle—Permanent waters with mud bottoms; throughout
Big Bend Mud Turtle—Rare, cattle tanks; Presidio County.
Desert and Ornate Box Turtle—Sandy plains, prairies, bottomlands; throughout.
Texas Map Turtle—Clear vegetated streams; central Colorado River basin only, Edwards Plateau.
Cagle's Map Turtle—Clear streams; Guadalupe River Basin only, Edwards Plateau.
Big Bend Slider Turtle—Muddy bottom ponds and streams; Brewster, Presidio, and Hudspeth counties.
Red-eared Slider Turtle—Muddy streams and ponds; throughout except Big Bend.
Zug's River Cooter—Clear streams and ponds; Pecos and Rio Grande drainages
Texas River Cooter—Clear streams; Guadalupe and Colorado river basins, Edwards Plateau.
Western Painted Turtle—Clear streams; Culberson and El Paso counties.
Texas Tortoise—Dry brushlands and sandy areas; South Texas to Val Verde County.
Spiny Softshells (2)—Rivers, lakes, ponds; throughout.
Stinkpot—Muddy bottom streams and ponds; eastern Edwards Plateau.

LIZARDS

Mediterranean Gecko—Introduced, commensal with man in buildings; South Texas, Val Verde, Brewster, and El Paso counties.
Texas Banded Gecko—Rocky areas; throughout except eastern Edwards Plateau and eastern South Texas.
Reticulated Gecko—Dry rocky areas; Presidio and Brewster counties.
Western Spiny-tailed Iguana—Escapees; Brownsville area.
Green Anole—Commensal with man, spreading; eastern and lower South Texas and Del Rio.
Collared Lizards (3)—Rocky areas; Balcones Escarpment to El Paso.
Reticulate Collared Lizard—Sandstone rock outcrops; Eagle Pass to McAllen.
Longnose Leopard Lizard—Desert flats; Big Bend to El Paso.
Texas and Southwestern Earless Lizard—Rocky areas; throughout to Cameron County.
Speckled Earless Lizard—Desert washes; Trans-Pecos.
Plateau and Southern Earless Lizard—Brushlands and road margins; Edwards Plateau to upper South Texas.
Keeled Earless Lizard—Sandy savannahs and dry brushlands; Laredo east to the Gulf.
Rosebelly Lizard—Brushlands and rocky areas; South Texas.
Mesquite Lizard—Commensal with man, in mesquite trees; South Texas.
Crevice Spiny Lizard—Rocky areas; Edwards Plateau to El Paso.

Blue Spiny Lizard—Rocky areas; Del Rio to McAllen.
Twin-spotted Spiny Lizard—Dry areas; Trans-Pecos.
Texas Spiny Lizard—Woodlands; throughout, Big Bend to Brownsville.
Prairie and Fence Lizards—Many habitats; throughout.
Canyon Lizards (3)—Rocky canyon walls; Del Rio through Big Bend.
Eastern and Big Bend Tree Lizards—Trees and rocky areas; Trans-Pecos, Edwards Plateau, and along Rio Grande to Brownsville.
Desert Side-blotched Lizard—Desert flats; Trans-Pecos.
Texas Horned Lizard—Open terrain; throughout.
Mountain Short-horned Lizard—Forests; Davis and Guadalupe mountains.
Round-tailed Horned Lizard—Dry, open, rocky terrain; Trans-Pecos, western Edwards Plateau, Zapata County.
Texas Spotted Whiptail—Rocky grasslands; throughout except Hudspeth and El Paso counties.
New Mexico Whiptail—Sandy washes; El Paso Valley.
Gray-checkered Whiptail—Dry rocky areas; Presidio County.
Chihuahuan Spotted Whiptail—Open area habitats; Big Bend to El Paso.
Desert Grassland Whiptail—Open grasslands; El Paso Valley.
Plateau Spotted Whiptail—Dry rocky flats; Big Bend.
Trans-Pecos Striped Whiptail—Dry rocky foothills; Trans-Pecos.
Prairie-lined and Yellow-headed Race Runners—Open sandy areas; South Texas to Del Rio.
Colorado Checkered Whiptail—Rocky flats; Trans Pecos.
Marbled Whiptail—Desert flats; Laredo to El Paso.
Laredo Striped Whiptail—Open dry areas; Rio Grande basin, Laredo to McAllen.
Ground Skink—Oak woodlands; Edwards Plateau and eastern South Texas to Willacy County.
Short-lined and Four-lined Skinks—Many variable habitats; throughout except Guadalupe Mountains.
Great Plains Skink—Sandy and loamy soils; throughout.
Variable Skink—Debris piles; Davis and Guadalupe mountains.
Western Slender Glass Lizard—Sandy coastal soils near water; coastal South Texas.
Texas Alligator Lizard—Rocky woodlands; Edwards Plateau and Brewster County.

SNAKES

New Mexico and Plains Blind Snakes—Variable moist habitats; throughout.
Trans-Pecos Blind Snake—Rocky areas near water; Del Rio to El Paso.
Diamondback Water Snake—Ponds, tanks, and streams; throughout from Big Bend east.
Blotched Water Snake—Ponds and streams; Davis Mountains, Big Bend, Edwards Plateau, Starr County, NE South Texas.
Texas Brown Snake—Variable habitats; South Texas.
New Mexico Garter Snake—Near water; El Paso.
Eastern Checkered Garter Snake—Near water; throughout.
Blackneck Garter Snakes (2)—Near water, Trans-Pecos and Edwards Plateau.
Ribbon Snakes (4)—Near water; throughout from Big Bend east.
Texas Lined Snake—Under debris; Edwards Plateau and Duval, McMullen, and LaSalle counties.
Eastern Hognose Snake—Variable habitats; eastern Edwards Plateau and northern South Texas.
Mexican and Dusky Hognose Snakes—Variable habitats; throughout.
Regal and Prairie Ringneck Snakes—Woodland; Trans-Pecos and Edwards Plateau.
Racers (3)—Variable habitats, open areas; Davis Mountains, eastern South Texas, and eastern Edwards Plateau.
Western Coachwhip—Open areas; throughout.
Whipsnakes (2)—Variable habitats; throughout
Western Rough Green Snake—River thickets; throughout except Big Bend to El Paso.
Speckled Racer—Resaca and river thickets; Cameron County.
Texas Indigo Snake—Variable habitats; South Texas from Del Rio east.
Big Bend Patchnose Snake—Rocky lowlands; Big Bend to El Paso.
Texas and Mountain Patchnose Snakes—Rocky areas; throughout.

Trans-Pecos Rat Snake—Rocky areas; El Paso to Uvalde.
Great Plains Rat Snake—Variable habitats; throughout.
Texas Rat Snake—Variable habitats; South Texas and eastern Edwards Plateau.
Baird's Rat Snake—Rocky outcrops; Big Bend and western Edwards Plateau.
Glossy Snakes (3)—Sandy and dry open habitats; throughout except Edwards Plateau.
Sonoran Gopher and Bull Snakes—Variable dry habitats; throughout.
Gray-banded Kingsnake—Dry rocky areas; Trans-Pecos east to Edwards County.
Prairie Kingsnake—Coastal brushland and open pasture; eastern South Texas to Willacy County.
Desert Kingsnake—Variable habitats; throughout.
Texas Longnose Snake—Friable and sandy soils; throughout except central Edwards Plateau.
Texas Scarlet Snake—Sandy areas of south Texas.
Milk Snakes (2)—Variable habitats; throughout.
Ground Snake—Open terrain under rocks and debris; throughout.
Black-striped Snake—Under debris; Lower Rio Grande Valley.
Western Hooknose Snake—Under debris in arid open regions; Trans-Pecos and Edwards Plateau.
Mexican Hooknose Snake—Under debris in arid open regions; South Texas.
Texas Night Snake—Under debris in various habitats; throughout.
Northern Cat-eyed Snake—Near water; coastal South Texas and Hidalgo County.
Big Bend Blackhead and Devils River Blackhead Snakes—variable habitats; Val Verde, Brewster, Presidio, Pecos, and Jeff Davis counties.
Flathead Snake—Under debris and rocks; Brewster County, Edwards Plateau south to McAllen.
Texas Blackhead Snake—Under debris and rocks, variable habitats; throughout.
Southwestern Blackhead Snake—Under rocks and debris in dry areas; Webb County, Trans-Pecos, Edwards Plateau.
Rough Earth Snake—Under rocks and debris; Coastal South Texas to Willacy County.
Trans-Pecos and Broad-banded Copperhead—Woodland and rocky habitat; absent from South Texas and west of Davis Mountains.
Western Cottonmouth—Near ponds and rivers; eastern Edwards Plateau.
Texas Coral Snake—Variable habitats; Pecos County east and south throughout.
Massasaugas (2)—dry and sandy grasslands; Trans-Pecos except Big Bend, South Texas.
Western Diamondback Rattlesnake—Various habitats; throughout.
Mojave Rattlesnake—Desert and foothills; Big Bend to El Paso.
Prairie Rattlesnake—Prairies and rocky areas; Trans-Pecos.
Blacktail Rattlesnake—Rocky desert areas; Edwards Plateau and Trans-Pecos.
Banded and Mottled Rock Rattlesnakes—Rocky cliffs of higher elevations; Edwards Plateau and Trans-Pecos.

SALAMANDERS

Lesser Sirens (2)—Isolated ponds and resacas; South Texas.
Barred Tiger Salamander—Isolated ponds; South Texas and Trans-Pecos.
Black-spotted Newt—Isolated ponds; coastal counties of South Texas.
Whitethroat Slimy Salamander—around springs and caves; Balcones Escarpment.
Texas Salamander—Helotes Creek Spring; Balcones Escarpment.
Texas Blind Salamander—Springs and caves; extreme eastern Balcones Escarpment.
Blanco Blind Salamander—Springs and caves; extreme eastern Balcones Escarpment.
Comal Blind Salamander—Springs and caves; extreme eastern Balcones Escarpment.
Barton Springs Salamander—Springs; Hays County, Balcones Escarpment.
San Marcos Salamander—Springs; Hays County, Balcones Escarpment.
Fern Bank Salamander—Springs; Hays County, Balcones Escarpment.
Cascade Cave Salamander—Cave; Kendall County, Balcones Escarpment.
Unnamed, several new species—Springs; Kerr, Bandera, Real, Medina, Gillespie, Uvalde, Val Verde counties.
Valdina Farms Salamander—Sinkhole; Medina County, Balcones Escarpment.
Unnamed, a new species—Springs; Bell, Travis, Williamson counties.

TOADS AND FROGS

Mexican Burrowing Toad—Rare around Falcon Lake; Starr and Zapata counties.
Hurter's Spadefoot—Temporary water on sandy plains; South Texas.
Couch's Spadefoot—Temporary water in variable habitat; throughout.
Plains Spadefoot—Temporary water in variable habitat; South Texas and Trans-Pecos except Big Bend.
New Mexico Spadefoot—Temporary water in grasslands; Trans-Pecos and western Edwards Plateau.
White-lipped Frog—Near water; Hidalgo and Starr counties, South Texas.
Eastern Barking Frog—In crevices and under limestone rocks; Edwards Plateau.
Cliff Chirping Frog—Cracks and crevices in limestone cliffs; Edwards Plateau.
Spotted Chirping Frog—Wet rocky areas; Big Bend.
Rio Grande Chirping Frog—Moist areas; Cameron and Hidalgo counties, South Texas.
Woodhouse's Toads (2)—Lowland ponds; Trans-Pecos and coastal Lower Rio Grande Valley.
Gulf Coast Toad—Various habitats near water; throughout from Brewster County, south and east.
Great Plains Toad—Temporary water; Brewster County north and west to border.
Texas Toad—Temporary water in lowlands; throughout.
Red-spotted Toad—Under stones near water; throughout except eastern South Texas.
Green Toads (2)—Under debris and rocks in various habitats; throughout.
Giant Toad—Ponds, lakes, resacas; Lower Rio Grande Valley.
Blanchard's Cricket Frog—Edges of streams and lakes; throughout except west of Big Bend.
Green Tree Frog—Pond and lake shores; coastal South Texas.
Canyon Tree Frog—Rocky canyons and streams; Big Bend and Davis Mountains.
Mexican Tree Frog—Cities and near woodland ponds; Cameron and Hidalgo counties.
Gray Tree Frog—Trees near temporary water; eastern Edwards Plateau.
Spotted Chorus Frog—Ditches and temporary pools in grasslands; eastern Edwards Plateau and South Texas.
Strecker's Chorus Frog—near water in various habitats; eastern Edwards Plateau and Kenedy, Brooks, and Willacy counties in South Texas.
Great Plains Narrowmouth Toad—Ditches and pools, grasslands; throughout except El Paso Valley.
Sheep Frog—Sandy brushlands and coastal plains; eastern South Texas.
Bullfrog—Permanent waters; throughout except Presidio and counties north.
Rio Grande Leopard Frog—near water in various habitats; throughout.

MARSUPIALS

Opossum—Woodlands, cities and farms; South Texas and Edwards Plateau.

SHREWS AND MOLES

Desert Shrew—Brushlands and deserts; throughout.
Least Shrew—Grasslands; South Texas.
Eastern Mole—Sandy soils; eastern South Texas.

BATS

Ghost-faced Bat—Caves; Big Bend, Edwards Plateau, South Texas.
Mexican Long-nosed Bat—Cave; Chisos Mountains.
Hairy-legged Vampire Bat—Caves; Val Verde County.
Little Brown Myotis—Rare, elevated areas; Hudspeth County.
Yuma Myotis—Caves and crevices; Trans-Pecos.
Cave Myotis—Caves; Trans-Pecos and Edwards Plateau.
Fringed Myotis—Caves and crevices; Trans-Pecos.
Long-legged Myotis—Caves, crevices, buildings; Trans-Pecos.
California Myotis—Wooded canyons, caves, buildings; Trans-Pecos.
Western Small-footed Myotis—Deserts, caves, buildings; Trans-Pecos.

Silver-haired Bat—Caves and buildings; Davis Mountains; Edwards Plateau.
Western Pipistrel—Caves and crevices; Trans-Pecos.
Eastern Pipistrel—Caves and crevices; Edwards Plateau, South Texas.
Big Brown Bat—Woodlands, caves, buildings; Trans-Pecos.
Eastern Red Bat—Woodlands; throughout.
Seminole Bat—Woodlands; Edward's Plateau, South Texas.
Hoary Bat—Woodlands; throughout.
Northern and Southern Yellow Bats—Palm trees; Lower Rio grande Valley.
Evening Bat—Woodlands; Edwards Plateau, South Texas.
Spotted Bat—Crevices; Big Bend, El Paso Valley.
Townsend's Big-eared Bat—Caves and crevices; Trans-Pecos.
Pallid Bat—Crevices and buildings; Trans-Pecos, Edwards Plateau.
Brazilian Free-tailed Bat—Caves and buildings; throughout.
Pocketed Free-tailed Bat—Caves and crevices; Trans-Pecos.
Big Free-tailed Bat—Caves and crevices; Trans-Pecos.
Western Mastiff Bat—Caves and buildings; Trans-Pecos.

CARNIVORES

Black Bear—Rare, forests; mountains of Trans-Pecos.
Raccoon—variable habitats except deserts; throughout.
White-nosed Coati—Rare, woodlands along Rio Grande; throughout.
Ringtail—Brushlands and rocky areas; throughout except South Texas.
Long-tailed Weasel—Rare, variable habitats; throughout.
American Badger—Grasslands and deserts; throughout.
Eastern and Western Spotted Skunks—Variable habitats; throughout.
Striped Skunk—Variable habitats; throughout.
Hooded Skunk—Rare, woodlands and rocky areas; Trans-Pecos.
Common Hog-nosed Skunk—Varied habitats; throughout.
Coyote—Varied habitats; throughout.
Kit Fox—Deserts; Trans-Pecos.
Common Gray Fox—Woodland, brushland, rocky areas; throughout.
Mountain Lion—Rare, canyons and brushlands; throughout.
Ocelot—Rare, thick brush; South Texas.
Jaguarundi—very rare, thick brush; South Texas.
Bobcat—Brushlands and rocky areas; throughout.

RODENTS

Rock Squirrel—Rocky areas; Trans-Pecos, Edwards Plateau.
Mexican Ground Squirrel—Sandy grasslands and brushlands; throughout.
Spotted Ground Squirrel—Sandy grasslands and deserts; throughout except Edwards Plateau.
Texas Antelope Squirrel—Rocky areas of deserts; Trans-Pecos.
Gray-footed Chipmunk—Forests; Guadalupe Mountains.
Eastern Fox Squirrel—Woodlands and cities; Edwards Plateau, South Texas.
Black-tailed Prairie Dog—Prairies; Trans-Pecos.
Desert Pocket Gopher—Friable and sandy soils; Trans-Pecos.
Plains Pocket Gopher—Grasslands; eastern Edwards Plateau.
Botta's Pocket Gopher—Varied soils desert to montane; Trans-Pecos and western Edwards Plateau.
Yellow-faced Pocket Gopher—Alluvial soils along streams; Trans-Pecos and Lower Rio Grande Valley.
Texas Pocket Gopher—Sandy soils; South Texas.
Mexican Spiny Pocket Mouse—Palm and brush thickets; Lower Rio Grande Valley.
Silky Pocket Mouse—Varied dry habitats; throughout.
Desert Pocket Mouse—Sandy deserts; Trans-Pecos.
Rock Pocket Mouse—Rocky areas; western Trans-Pecos.

Nelson's Pocket Mouse—Rocky slopes; Trans-Pecos.
Hispid Pocket Mouse—Varied habitats; throughout except western Trans-Pecos.
Banner-tailed Kangaroo Rat—Grasslands; northern and western Trans-Pecos.
Ord's Kangaroo Rat—Sandy deserts and grasslands; Trans-Pecos and western South Texas.
Padre Island Kangaroo Rat—Sandy grasslands; eastern South Texas.
Merriam's Kangaroo Rat—Deserts and grasslands; Trans-Pecos.
American Beaver—Wooded streams; throughout.
Plains Harvest Mouse Grasslands; Trans-Pecos, Edwards Plateau.
Western Harvest Mouse—Grasslands and deserts; Trans-Pecos.
Fulvous Harvest Mouse—Grasslands; throughout except western Trans-Pecos.
Cactus Mouse—Low rocky deserts; Del Rio to El Paso.
Deer Mouse Varied habitats; Trans-Pecos, eastern Edwards Plateau.
White-ankled Mouse—Rocky woodlands and brushlands; Trans-Pecos and Balcones Escarpment.
Northern Pygmy Mouse—Short grasslands, sandy soil; South Texas.
Brush Mouse Rocky montane slopes; Trans-Pecos.
Pinyon Mouse—Rocky pinyon-juniper slopes; Guadalupe Mountains.
Rock Mouse—Rocky peaks of mountains; Trans-Pecos.
Texas Mouse—Rocky juniper associations; eastern Edwards Plateau.
Northern Grasshopper Mouse—Grasslands; throughout except Big Bend.
Mearn's Grasshopper Mouse—Grasslands and deserts; Trans-Pecos.
Southern Plains Woodrat—Deserts and brushlands; throughout.
White-throated Woodrat—Desert brushlands; Trans-Pecos.
Mexican Woodrat—Rocky elevated areas; Trans-Pecos.
Marsh Rice Rat—marshlands; coastal northern South Texas.
Coues' Rice Rat—marshlands; Lower Rio Grande Valley.
Hispid Cotton Rat—Tall grasslands and fields; throughout.
Yellow-nosed Cotton Rat—Tall grasslands; Big Bend and Davis Mountains.
Tawny-bellied Cotton Rat—Tall grasslands; Davis Mountains.
Mexican Vole—Open forests; Guadalupe Mountains.
Muskrat—Drainage ditches; El Paso.
Roof Rat—Cities; Lower Rio Grande Valley.
Norway Rat—Cities; throughout.
House Mouse Cities and farms; throughout.
Porcupine—woodlands in rocky areas; Trans-Pecos, Edwards Plateau.
Nutria—Marshes, ponds and streams; South Texas, Edwards Plateau.

RABBITS

Black-tailed Jack Rabbit—Open areas in varied habitats; throughout.
Eastern Cottontail—Open brushlands and woodlands; throughout except western Trans-Pecos
Desert Cottontail—Open plains and deserts; throughout except coastal South Texas.

EVEN-TOED UNGULATES

Collared Peccary—Brushlands and desert; throughout.
Elk—Forests; Guadalupe Mountains.
Mule Deer—Deserts, brushlands, forests; Trans-Pecos.
White-tailed Deer—Varied wooded habitats; throughout.
Pronghorn—Prairies; Trans-Pecos.
Mountain Sheep—Rare, rocky terrain; Big Bend and adjacent areas.
Bison—Reintroduced to prairies; Trans-Pecos.

EDENTATES

Nine-banded Armadillo—Woodlands and brushlands; Edwards Plateau and South Texas.

Introduced Exotics That Have Escaped
and Established Wild Populations

Axis Deer
Fallow Deer
Sika Deer
Nilgai
Barbary Sheep
Blackbuck
Aoudad

References

Chaney, Allan H., 1982 revised 1996, **Keys to the Vertebrates of Texas Exclusive of Birds**. Biology Department, Texas A&I University.

Dixon, James R., 1987, **Amphibians and Reptiles of Texas**. Texas A&M University Press.

Schmidley, David J., 1977, **The Mammals of Trans-Pecos Texas**. Texas A&M University Press.

SELECTED REFERENCES

Ajilvsgi, G. 1984. **Wildflowers of Texas**. Shearer Publishing, Bryan, Texas.

American Ornithologists' Union. 1998. **The A.O.U. Check-list of North American Birds**. 7th edition. Allen Press, Kansas.

Benson, L. 1982. **Cacti of the United States and Canada**. Stanford University Press, Stanford, Calif.

Bomar, G.W. 1983. **Texas Weather**. University of Texas Press, Austin, Texas.

Bryan, K., T. Gallucci, G. Lasley, M. Lockwood, and D.H. Riskind. **A Checklist of Texas Birds**. Texas Parks and Wildlife Press, Austin, Texas.

Chaney, A.H. 1982, revised 1996. **Keys to the Vertebrates of Texas Exclusive of Birds**. Biology Department, Texas A&I University..

Cox, P., and P. Leslie. 1988. **Texas Trees: A Friendly Guide**. Corona Press, San Antonio, Texas.

Davis, W.B., and D.J. Schmidly. 1994. **The Mammals of Texas**. Texas Parks and Wildlife Press, Austin, Texas.

Dixon, J.R. 1987. **Amphibians and Reptiles of Texas**. Texas A&M University Press, College Station, Texas.

Enquist, M. 1987. **Wildflowers of the Texas Hill Country**. Lone Star Botanical, Austin, Texas.

Everitt, J.H., and D.L. Drawe. 1993. **Trees, Shrubs & Cacti of South Texas**. Texas Tech University Press, Lubbock, Texas.

Garrett, J.M., and D.G. Baker. 1987. **A Field Guide to Reptiles and Amphibians of Texas**. Texas Monthly Press, Austin, Texas.

Holt, Harold R. 1993. **A Birder's Guide to the Texas Coast**. American Birding Association, Colorado Springs, Colorado.

Howell, S.N.G., and S. Webb. 1995. **A Guide to the Birds of Mexico and Northern Central America**. Oxford University Press, New York.

Lasley, G. W., and C. Sexton. 1998. **Rare Birds of the Texas Master List of Review Species**. Photocopied report.

Lellinger, D.B. 1985. **Field Manual of the Ferns and Fern-allies of the United States and Canada**. Smithsonian Press, Washington, D.C.

Lonard, R.I., J.H. Everitt, and F.W. Judd. 1991. **Woody Plants of the Lower Rio Grande Valley, Texas**. Misc. Paper #7. Texas Memorial Museum, University of Texas at Austin, Texas.

Loughmiller, C., and L. Loughmiller. 1984. **Texas Wildflowers: A Field Guide**. University of Texas Press, Austin, Texas.

Kutac, E. A. 1998. **Birder's Guide to Texas**. Lone Star Books, Houston, Texas.

Kutac, E., and S.C. Caran. 1993. **Birds & Other Wildlife of South Central Texas**. University of Texas Press, Austin, Texas.

McKinney, B. 1997. **A Checklist of Lower Rio Grande Valley Birds**. Published by the author.

Neck, R.W. 1996. **A Field Guide to Butterflies of Texas**. Gulf Publishing Co., Houston, Texas.

Neihaus, T.F. 1984. **A Field Guide to the Southwestern and Texas Wildflowers**. Houghton Mifflin Company, Boston, Mass.

Oberholser, H.C. 1974. **The Bird Life of Texas**. University of Texas Press, Austin, Texas.

Opler, P.A., H. Pavulaan, and R.E. Stanford. 1995. **Butterflies of North America**. Northern Prairie Wildlife Research Center Home Page, Jamestown, North Dakota. http://www.npwrc.usgs.gov/resource/distr/lepid/bflyusa.htm (version 03JUN98).

Peterson, R.T. 1963. **A Field Guide to the Birds of Texas**. Houghton Mifflin Company, Boston, Mass.

Powell, A.M. 1998. **Trees and Shrubs of Trans-Pecos Texas, including Big Bend and Guadalupe Mountains National Park**. University of Texas Press, Austin, Texas.

Powell, A.M. 1994. **Grasses of the Trans-Pecos and Adjacent Areas**. University of Texas Press, Austin, Texas.

Richardson, A. 1990. **Plants of Southernmost Texas**. University of Texas at Brownsville, Brownsville, Texas.

Robertson, B. 1985. **Rio Grande Heritage, A Pictorial History**. Donning Company Publishers, Norfolk/Virginia Beach, Virginia.

Schmidley, D.J. 1977. **The Mammals of Trans-Pecos Texas**. Texas A&M University Press, College Station, Texas.

Schmidly, D.J. 1991. **The Bats of Texas**. Texas A&M University Press, College Station, Texas.

Scott, J.A. 1986. **Butterflies of North America, a natural history and field guide**. Stanford University Press, Stanford, Calif.

Spearing, D. 1991. **Roadside Geology of Texas**. Mountain Press Publishing Company, Missoula, Montana.

Taylor, R.B., J. Rutledge, and J.G. Herrera. 1994. **A Field Guide to Common South Texas Shrubs**. Texas Parks and Wildlife Press, Austin, Texas.

Tennant, A. 1984. **The Snakes of Texas**. Texas Monthly Press, Austin, Texas.

Texas Bird Records Committee. 1995. **Checklist of the Birds of Texas**. Texas Ornithological Society, Austin, Texas.

Vines, R. 1960. **Trees, Shrubs, and Woody Vines of the Southwest**. University of Texas Press, Austin, Texas.

Warnock, B.H. 1970. **Wildflowers of the Big Bend Country, Texas**. Sul Ross University Press, Alpine, Texas.

Warnock, B.H. 1974. **Wildflowers of the Guadalupe Mountains and the Sand Dune Country, Texas**. Sul Ross University Press, Alpine, Texas.

Warnock, B.H. 1977. **Wildflowers of the Davis Mountains and the Marathon Basin, Texas**. Sul Ross University Press, Alpine, Texas.

Wauer, R.H. 1980. **Naturalist's Big Bend**. Texas A&M University Press, College Station, Texas.

Wauer, R.H. 1996. **A Field Guide to the Birds of the Big Bend**. Gulf Publishing, Houston, Texas.

Woolridge, R. A., and R. B. Vezzetti. 1982. **Brownsville, a Pictorial History**. Donning Company Publishers, Norfolk/Virginia Beach, Virginia.

INDEX

ABBREVIATED TABLE OF CONTENTS

ABBREVIATED TABLE OF CONTENTS

TBRC MASTER LIST OF REVIEW SPECIES

The Texas Bird Records Committee of the Texas Ornithological Society requests details, including descriptions and photos if possible, of all records of the following species. Those species marked with an asterisk (*) are under special study by the TBRC. Records of these ten species will not be formally reviewed by the TBRC, but documentation is requested to assist in these studies.

Red-throated Loon
Pacific Loon
Yellow-billed Loon
Red-necked Grebe
Yellow-nosed Albatross
White-chinned Petrel
*Cory's Shearwater
Greater Shearwater
Sooty Shearwater
Manx Shearwater
Wilson's Storm-Petrel
Leach's Storm-Petrel
Red-billed Tropicbird
Blue-footed Booby
Brown Booby
Red-footed Booby
Jabiru
Greater Flamingo
Brant
Trumpeter Swan
*Muscovy Duck
(non-domesticated)
Eurasian Wigeon
American Black Duck
White-cheeked Pintail
Garganey
Harlequin Duck
Barrow's Goldeneye
Masked Duck
Snail Kite
Northern Goshawk
Crane Hawk
*Common Black-Hawk
Roadside Hawk
Short-tailed Hawk
Collared Forest-Falcon
* Aplomado Falcon
Paint-billed Crake
Spotted Rail
Double-striped Thick-knee
Collared Plover
Northern Jacana
Wandering Tattler
Eskimo Curlew
Surfbird
Red-necked Stint
Sharp-tailed Sandpiper
Purple Sandpiper
Curlew Sandpiper

Ruff
Red Phalarope
*Pomarine Jaeger
*Parasitic Jaeger
Long-tailed Jaeger
Little Gull
Black-headed Gull
Heermann's Gull
Mew Gull
California Gull
Thayer's Gull
Iceland Gull
Slaty-backed Gull
Western Gull
Kelp Gull
Great Black-backed Gull
Sabine's Gull
Black-legged Kittiwake
Elegant Tern
Brown Noddy
Black Noddy
White-crowned Pigeon
Ruddy Ground-Dove
Ruddy Quail-Dove
Dark-billed Cuckoo
Mangrove Cuckoo
Snowy Owl
Northern Pygmy-Owl
Mottled Owl
*Spotted Owl
Northern Saw-whet Owl
White-collared Swift
Green Violet-ear
Green-breasted Mango
Broad-billed Hummingbird
White-eared Hummingbird
Berylline Hummingbird
Violet-crowned Hummingbird
Costa's Hummingbird
Allen's Hummingbird
Elegant Trogon
Lewis's Woodpecker
*Williamson's Sapsucker
Red-breasted Sapsucker
Ivory-billed Woodpecker
Greenish Elaenia
Tufted Flycatcher
Greater Pewee
Dusky-capped Flycatcher

Sulphur-bellied Flycatcher
Social Flycatcher
Thick-billed Kingbird
Gray Kingbird
Fork-tailed Flycatcher
Rose-throated Becard
Masked Tityra
*Northern Shrike
Yellow-green Vireo
Black-whiskered Vireo
Yucatan Vireo
Clark's Nutcracker
Black-billed Magpie
Gray-breasted Martin
Black-capped Chickadee
American Dipper
Northern Wheatear
Orange-billed
   Nightingale-Thrush
White-throated Robin
Rufous-backed Robin
Varied Thrush
Aztec Thrush
Black Catbird
Bohemian Waxwing
Gray Silky-flycatcher
Olive Warbler
Crescent-chested Warbler
Connecticut Warbler
Gray-crowned Yellowthroat
Red-faced Warbler
Slate-throated Redstart
Golden-crowned Warbler
Rufous-capped Warbler
Flame-colored Tanager
Yellow-faced Grassquit
Baird's Sparrow
*Henslow's Sparrow
Golden-crowned Sparrow
Yellow-eyed Junco
Snow Bunting
Crimson-collared Grosbeak
Blue Bunting
Shiny Cowbird
Black-vented Oriole
Pine Grosbeak
White-winged Crossbill
Common Redpoll
Lawrence's Goldfinch

TOS Texas Bird Records Committee Report Form

The TRBC requests the following information from those submitting reports:

Common and scientific name

Number of individuals, sexes, ages, general plumage (e.g., two adults in breeding plumage)

Location (include county)

Date and time observed

Reporting observer and address

Other observers

Light conditions

Optical equipment

Distance to bird

Duration of observation

Specific habitat

Description (Include only what was actually seen, not what "should have been seen.") Include, if possible, body bulk, shape, bill, eye, plumage pattern, color, and other physical characteristics. Describe voice, behavior, and anything else that could help to identify the bird.)

How were similar species eliminated?

Was it photographed (by whom, is photo attached?)

Previous experience with species

List any books used in identification (a) at the time of observation and (b) after observation

Tell whether this description was written from (a) notes made during observation, (b) notes made after observation, or (c) memory.

Tell whether you are positive of your ID and if not, why not?

Sign the report with the date and time of writing it.

Send to Mark Lockwood, Secretary, Texas Bird Records Committee, 2001 Fort Davis Hwy #15, Alpine, TX 79830 *or* Dr. Keith Arnold, Dept. of Wildlife and Fisheries Sciences, Texas A&M University, College Station, TX 77843.

NEW MEXICO ORNITHOLOGICAL SOCIETY
BIRD RECORDS COMMITTEE REVIEW LIST

Details are requested for the following species for New Mexico sightings. You can follow the guidelines spelled out on page 275 in the TBRC report form. Send, with photos, videos, or recordings, to NMOS, PO Box 3068, Albuquerque, NM 87190.

Red-throated Loon
Pacific Loon
Yellow-billed Loon
Red-necked Grebe
Least Storm-Petrel
Anhinga
Magnificent Frigatebird
Reddish Egret
Yellow-crowned Night-Heron
White Ibis
Glossy Ibis
Roseate Spoonbill
Wood Stork
Black Vulture
Black-bellied Whistling-Duck
Fulvous Whistling-Duck
Brant
Trumpeter Swan
Garganey
Harlequin Duck
Surf Scoter
White-winged Scoter
Black Scoter
Barrow's Goldeneye (outside
  San Juan County)
Swallow-tailed Kite
Gray Hawk
Red-shouldered Hawk
Crested Caracara
Aplomado Falcon
Sage Grouse
Sharp-tailed Grouse
Yellow Rail
Purple Gallinule
American Golden-Plover
Piping Plover
Whimbrel
Hudsonian Godwit
Ruddy Turnstone
Red Knot
Semipalmated Sandpiper (west
  of Pecos Valley)
Sharp-tailed Sandpiper
Curlew Sandpiper
Buff-breasted Sandpiper
Ruff
Short-billed Dowitcher
American Woodcock
Red Phalarope

Pomarine Jaeger
Long-tailed Jaeger
Laughing Gull
Little Gull
Heermann's Gull
Mew Gull
Thayer's Gull
Western Gull
Glaucous-winged Gull
Glaucous Gull
Black-legged Kittiwake
Arctic Tern
Black Skimmer
Ancient Murrelet
Common Ground-Dove
Ruddy Ground-Dove
Black-billed Cuckoo
Groove-billed Ani
Whiskered Screech-Owl
  (outside Peloncillo Mtns)
Short-eared Owl
Chuck-will's-widow
Buff-collared Nightjar
White-eared Hummingbird
Berylline Hummingbird
Cinnamon Hummingbird
Blue-throated Hummingbird
  (outside Catron, Grant, and
  Hidlago Ctys)
Lucifer Hummingbird (outside
  Peloncillo Mtns)
Ruby-throated Hummingbird
Costa's Hummingbird (outside
  of Grant and Hildago Ctys)
Elegant Trogon (outside
  Peloncillo Mtns)
Red-bellied Woodpecker
Eastern Wood-Pewee
Yellow-bellied Flycatcher
Acadian Flycatcher
Pacific-slope Flycatcher
Buff-breasted Flycatcher
Great Crested Flycatcher
  (west of Pecos Valley)
Great Kiskadee
Sulphur-bellied Flycatcher
Piratic Flycatcher
Couch's Kingbird
White-eyed Vireo

Blue-headed Vireo
Philadelphia Vireo
Yellow-green Vireo
Carolina Wren
Sedge Wren
Veery (outside Peñasco area)
Gray-cheeked Thrush
Wood Thrush
Rufous-backed Robin
Varied Thrush
Long-billed Thrasher
Sprague's Pipit (west of Pecos
  Valley)
Bohemian Waxwing
Blue-winged Warbler
Golden-winged Warbler
Magnolia Warbler
Cape May Warbler
Black-thr. Green Warbler
Blackburnian Warbler
Yellow-throated Warbler
Pine Warbler
Prairie Warbler
Palm Warbler
Bay-breasted Warbler
Blackpoll Warbler
Cerulean Warbler
Worm-eating Warbler
Louisiana Waterthrush
Kentucky Warbler
Mourning Warbler
Canada Warbler
Slate-throated Redstart
Scarlet Tanager
Eastern Towhee
Botteri's Sparrow (outside
  Animas Valley)
Worthen's Sparrow
Baird's Sparrow
Le Conte's Sparrow
Snow Bunting
Bobolink (outside Los Ojos area)
Rusty Blackbird
Baltimore Oriole
Purple Finch
White-winged Crossbill
Lawrence's Goldfinch

AMERICAN BIRDING ASSOCIATION
PRINCIPLES OF BIRDING ETHICS

Everyone who enjoys birds and birding must always respect wildlife, its environment, and the rights of others. In any conflict of interest between birds and birders, the welfare of the birds and their environment comes first.

CODE OF BIRDING ETHICS

1. Promote the welfare of birds and their environment.

1(a) Support the protection of important bird habitat.

1(b) To avoid stressing birds or exposing them to danger, exercise restraint and caution during observation, photography, sound recording, or filming.

Limit the use of recordings and other methods of attracting birds, and never use such methods in heavily birded areas or for attracting any species that is Threatened, Endangered, or of Special Concern, or is rare in your local area.

Keep well back from nests and nesting colonies, roosts, display areas, and important feeding sites. In such sensitive areas, if there is a need for extended observation, photography, filming, or recording, try to use a blind or hide, and take advantage of natural cover.

Use artificial light sparingly for filming or photography, especially for close-ups.

1(c) Before advertising the presence of a rare bird, evaluate the potential for disturbance to the bird, its surroundings, and other people in the area, and proceed only if access can be controlled, disturbance can be minimized, and permission has been obtained from private land-owners. The sites of rare nesting birds should be divulged only to the proper conservation authorities.

1(d) Stay on roads, trails, and paths where they exist; otherwise keep habitat disturbance to a minimum.

2. Respect the law and the rights of others.

2(a) Do not enter private property without the owner's explicit permission.

2(b) Follow all laws, rules, and regulations governing use of roads and public areas, both at home and abroad.

2(c) Practice common courtesy in contacts with other people. Your exemplary behavior will generate goodwill with birders and non-birders alike.

3. Ensure that feeders, nest structures, and other artificial bird environments are safe.

3(a) Keep dispensers, water, and food clean and free of decay or disease. It is important to feed birds continually during harsh weather.

3(b) Maintain and clean nest structures regularly.

3(c) If you are attracting birds to an area, ensure the birds are not exposed to predation from cats and other domestic animals, or dangers posed by artificial hazards.

4. Group birding, whether organized or impromptu, requires special care.

Each individual in the group, in addition to the obligations spelled out in Items #1 and #2, has responsibilities as a Group Member.

4(a) Respect the interests, rights, and skills of fellow birders, as well as those of people participating in other legitimate outdoor activities. Freely share your knowledge and experience, except where code 1(c) applies. Be especially helpful to beginning birders.

4(b) If you witness unethical birding behavior, assess the situation and intervene if you think it prudent. When interceding, inform the person(s) of the inappropriate action and attempt, within reason, to have it stopped. If the behavior continues, document it and notify appropriate individuals or organizations.

Group Leader Responsibilities [amateur and professional trips and tours].

4(c) Be an exemplary ethical role model for the group. Teach through word and example.

4(d) Keep groups to a size that limits impact on the environment and does not interfere with others using the same area.

4(e) Ensure everyone in the group knows of and practices this code.

4(f) Learn and inform the group of any special circumstances applicable to the areas being visited (e.g., no tape recorders allowed).

4(g) Acknowledge that professional tour companies bear a special responsibility to place the welfare of birds and the benefits of public knowledge ahead of the company's commercial interests. Ideally, leaders should keep track of tour sightings, document unusual occurrences, and submit records to appropriate organizations.

PLEASE FOLLOW THIS CODE— DISTRIBUTE IT AND TEACH IT TO OTHERS.

Additional copies of the Code of Birding Ethics can be obtained from: ABA, PO Box 6599, Colorado Springs, CO 80934-6599, (800) 850-2473 or (719) 578-1614; fax: (800) 247-3329 or (719) 578-1480; e-mail: member@aba.org

This ABA Code of Birding Ethics may be reprinted, reproduced, and distributed without restriction. Please acknowledge the role of ABA in developing and promoting this code

7/1/96

OTHER GUIDES IN THE ABA SERIES

*A Birder's Guide to
Alaska*
George C. West

*A Birder's Guide to
Metropolitan Areas
of North America*
Paul Lehman

*A Birder's Guide to the
Bahamas*
Anthony R. White

*A Birder's Guide to
Virginia*
David Johnston

*A Birder's Guide to
Colorado*
Harold R. Holt

*A Birder's Guide to
Florida*
Bill Pranty

*A Birder's Guide to
New Hampshire*
Alan Delorey

*Birdfinder: A Birder's
Guide to Planning
North American Trips*
Jerry A. Cooper

*A Birder's Guide to
Southeastern Arizona*
Richard Cachor Taylor

A Birder's Guide to Arkansas
Mel White

*A Birder's Guide to
Eastern Massachusetts*
Bird Observer

*A Birder's Guide to the
Texas Coast*
Harold R. Holt

A Birder's Guide to Wyoming
Oliver K. Scott

*A Birder's Guide to the
Rio Grande Valley*
Mark W. Lockwood
William B. McKinney
James N. Paton
Barry R. Zimmer

*A Birder's Guide to
Southern California*
Brad Schram

American Birding Association Sales
PO Box 6599, Colorado Springs, Colorado 80934
Phone: 800/634-7736 or 719/578-0607
Fax: 800/590-2473 or 719/578-9705
www.americanbirding.org

278

American Birding
A S S O C I A T I O N

Join the American Birding Association

When you become a member of the American Birding Association, you join tens of thousands of birders who are eager to improve their knowledge and skills to get the most out of their birding experiences.

- ✔ Network with friends and share the passion of birding.

- ✔ Learn more about birds and birding.

- ✔ Sharpen and augment your birding skills.

- ✔ Participate in workshops, conferences, and tours.

- ✔ Receive our full-color magazine, *Birding*, and our monthly newsletter, *Winging It*.

- ✔ Use our directory and catalogs to expand your birding horizons.

You don't have to be an expert birder to be a member of the American Birding Association. You're qualified simply by having a desire to learn more about birds, their habitats, and how to protect them.

ABA membership offers you the opportunity to meet and learn from experts and to improve your skills through our internationally attended conferences and conventions, Institute for Field Ornithology workshops, specialized tours, and volunteer opportunities. It is great way to get to know others who share your passion.

Sign Up Today!

American Birding
A S S O C I A T I O N

Name _____

Address _____

_____

City _____ State _____ Zip _____

Country _____ Phone _____

Email _____

Each level entitles members to certain benefits.
Visit <www.americanbirding.org/memgen.htm> or call 800-850-2473 to find out more.

❑ Individual . . . . US$ 40

❑ Joint . . . . US$ 47

❑ Student[a] . . . . US$ 20

❑ International / Canada Individual[b]. . . US$ 50

❑ International / Canada Joint[b] . . . . . . US$ 50

❑ International / Canada Student[ab] . . . US$ 50

[a] Please include your birth date, school name, and graduation date
[b] Canadian dues include GST, which is paid to the Canadian government
All membership dues include $30 for **Birding** magazine and
    $10 for **Winging It** newsletter

Sent this form to:

ABA Membership
PO Box 6599
Colorado Springs, CO
80934-6599

You may also join by phone fax, or web:
Phone 800-850-2473
Fax 719-578-1480
www.americanbirding.org/memgen.htm

Membership: US$ _____

Additional Contribution: US$ _____ for: ❑ Unrestricted ❑ Conservation ❑ Education

Total: US$ _____

Check or money order payable to American Birding Association, or charge to:

❑ VISA   ❑ Mastercard   ❑ Discover

Card # _____ Exp Date _____

Signature _____